Harvard English Studies 13

Reconstructing American
Literary History

HARVARD ENGLISH STUDIES 13

Reconstructing American Literary History

Edited by
Sacvan Bercovitch

Harvard University Press
Cambridge, Massachusetts
and London, England
1986

Emily Dickinson's poetry is reprinted by permission
of the publishers and the Trustees of Amherst
College from *The Poems of Emily Dickinson,* edited
by Thomas H. Johnson, Cambridge, Mass.: The
Belknap Press of Harvard University Press,
Copyright 1951, © 1955, 1979, 1983 by the President
and Fellows of Harvard College; poem 102 from
Emily Dickinson Face to Face, Copyright 1932 by
Martha Dickinson Bianchi, © renewed 1960,
reprinted by permission of Houghton Mifflin Company.

This book is printed on acid-free paper, and
its binding materials have been chosen
for strength and durability.

Library of Congress Cataloging-in-Publication Data
Main entry under title:

Reconstructing American literary history.

(Harvard English studies ; 13)
Includes bibliographies.
Contents: "We hold these truths" / Robert A.
Ferguson—Popular fiction and critical values / Morris
Dickstein—Origin and authority / Barbara Packer—
[etc.]
1. American literature—History and criticism—
Addresses, essays, lectures. I. Bercovitch, Sacvan.
II. Series.
PS92.R4 1986 810'.9 85–21972
ISBN 0–674–75085–3 (alk. paper)
ISBN 0–674–75086–1 (alk. paper)

To the memory of
F. O. Matthiessen
and Perry Miller

Preface

The need for a new American literary history seems clear and unexceptionable. A lot has happened, critically and creatively, since Robert Spiller and his colleagues issued their monumental *Literary History of the United States* (1948). Besides, as Spiller then pointed out, every generation should produce its own literary history. That revisionist challenge has special resonance for Americanists. It recalls Jefferson's appeal for social renewal with every generation. It echoes the summons of Emerson's *American Scholar:* "Each age must write its own books; or rather, each generation for the next succeeding. The books of an older period will not fit this." There are new insights, new outlooks, new texts. Why should we grope among the monuments of the past?

An unexceptionable demand, in the American grain—and compounded in our time by certain un-American developments. I refer to the political-academic upheavals of the late sixties and to the recent impact of European critical theories. From both these perspectives, we have become increasingly aware of the shortcomings of traditional methods of analysis: on the one hand, the narrow textuality of the New Criticism; and on the other hand, the naiveté of the old historicism as "background" or "context." We have also become increasingly uncomfortable about the restrictions inherent in the consensus that shaped our concept of American literary history: specifically, the consensus on the meaning of the term *literary* that involved the legitimation of a certain canon, and the consensus on the term *history* that was legitimated by a certain vision of America. During the past two decades, consensus of all sorts has broken down—left and right, political and aesthetic—broken down, worn out, or at best opened up. It was the achievement of the Spiller *History* to consolidate a powerful literary-historical movement. It will be the task of the present generation to reconstruct American literary history by making a virtue of dissensus.

That is the burden of the essays in this volume. The contributors are Americanists trained in the sixties and early seventies. They represent no particular approach, school, or set of principles, except the principles of excellence and balance. They were chosen for the quality of their work and for their diversity of views and interests. Those views do not necessarily entail a rift between generations. Some of these young scholars may be seen as traditionalists; others are clearly building upon the work of teachers and predecessors. But all of them express a distinctive generational experience of discontinuity and disruption. In one form or another, that is, their essays convey the self-reflexiveness that characterizes this period of critical interregnum. And to some extent they share similar convictions about the *problematics* of literary history: for example, that race, class, and gender are formal principles of art and therefore integral to textual analysis; that language has the capacity to break free of social restrictions and through its own dynamics to undermine the power structures it seems to reflect; that political norms are inscribed in aesthetic judgment and therefore inherent in the process of interpretation; that aesthetic structures shape the way we understand history, so that tropes and narrative devices may be said to use historians to enforce certain views of the past; that the task of literary historians is not just to show how art transcends culture, but also to identify and explore the ideological limits of their time, and then to bring these to bear upon literary analysis in such a way as to make use of the categories of culture, rather than being used by them.

These convictions stem from contending approaches in contemporary critical discourse. But as they are applied or developed here they point to a certain coherence in the enterprise at large. In particular, these essays suggest two main directions, methodological and practical, in American literary scholarship. The methodological direction may be described as a return to history. For all their diversity, these essays find a common ground in their attempt, *through* the insights of recent theories, to ground textual analysis in history; and more than that, to make history a central category of aesthetic criticism. And they do so, let me add, not because the authors happen to be engaged in writing literary history, but because they are convinced (correctly, I believe) that the tendency of literary theory, in all its current varieties—from deconstruction and semiotics to feminism, ethnicity, and reader-response theory—lies in that direction. In practical terms, the common ground of these essays is their dialogic mode of analysis. I mean dialogic as distinct from eclectic, synthetic, or indeterminate. These essays are remarkably open and flexible because they engage the conflicts at issue, rather than seeking either to resolve them or to rest in irreconcilability. Characteristically, it is not the assumed relation between text and context but the problems raised by such assumptions which give substance and texture to the argument. All the contributors have a marked resistance to closure, including the forms of closure implicit in pluralism. All of them show an instinctive distrust of totalizing answers, especially those dictated by parochial themes of the past, such as the Americanness of American literature.

Methodologically, then, a shared concern with history and, practically, a dialogic open-endedness: the force of these essays lies in their capacity to make these directions mutually sustaining. They are flexible precisely because of their concern with the problematics of history; and their flexibility in exploring conflict enriches their engagement with the problematics of history. It amounts to an exemplary venture in revaluation. Considered as a whole, this volume is no less significant for the issues it raises than for the answers it suggests. The essays succeed in using literary techniques to illuminate the dynamics of culture, and historical analysis to open up literary interpretation. They provide fresh perspectives on the major points of current debate, concerning canon-formation, intentionality, evaluation, and influence, "popular" vis-à-vis "classic" literature, the import of modernism (and postmodernism), the connections between myth and ideology, American and European developments, rhetoric and social action. They offer persuasive new readings of particular texts, and wholesale reformulations of cultural continuities and disjunctions. To judge by this volume, the re-construction of American literary history is not only a project to be urged, but a process already well under way Dissensus may yield a rich harvest after all, in due time.

S. B.

Contents

Reconstructing American
Literary History

ROBERT A. FERGUSON

"We Hold These Truths": Strategies of Control in the Literature of the Founders

There are new and compelling reasons for studying the writings of the Founding Fathers as literature. We are in a better position than previous generations to understand how these texts actually work. The recent stress upon ideological perceptions in American historiography has encouraged the examination of ideas in context—a crucial advantage in approaching documents that have been given such timeless significance. The same history of ideas also has increased literary scholars' access to the debate about early American culture by making the text as text a more strategic consideration for all concerned. Critic and historian have come to share the enterprise of textual interpretation as never before. They do so because ideological concerns necessarily privilege the printed word as a source of investigation and confirmation. Bernard Bailyn, to take only the most obvious example, is an editor of texts when he announces "the 'interior' view" that guides a generation of historians in American studies. *The Ideological Origins of the American Revolution,* arguing that perceptions controlled realities in 1776, takes shape as an introduction to pamphlets from the period. It tells us not what those pamphlets mean now but what they meant then and why. We are halfway to the literary critic's own questions about how a text accomplishes its purposes.

1

The method is peculiarly valuable in dealing with the literature of the Founders. It counters what Quentin Skinner has
called "the mythology of doctrines." Texts, to use Bailyn's terms,
return a reader to "the unpredictable reality" of history, where
they are worth the confusion they reintroduce because they are
also "to an unusual degree, *explanatory.*" They represent the
irreducible artifacts that challenge received history. At issue
are "the assumptions, beliefs, and ideas—the articulated world
view—that lay behind the manifest events of the time."[1] Ideally,
the historian recognizes a heightened validity in the text while
the critic sacrifices the autonomy of interpretation, and the two
meet over the text as an intended act of communication for a
specific readership.

A textual approach to the Founders also recovers one of their
few forgotten virtues—their very conscious sense of themselves
as men of letters. No generation has looked more carefully to
the written word for identity. In eighteenth-century America,
the accomplished man demonstrates his worthiness for place
and influence by writing about the world around him. The young
Thomas Jefferson makes himself a prominent figure overnight
with one essay, *A Summary View of the Rights of British America*
in 1774. The same can be said of Thomas Paine two years later
with *Common Sense.* Alexander Hamilton and James Madison
also prosper in part through their works on government and the
Constitution. Compare the more limited success of those peers
who leave no comparable body of works, John Hancock and
Patrick Henry for example. Even George Washington looms
larger for his writings, his circular to the states on leaving the
army in 1783 and his presidential farewell address in 1796.
Benjamin Franklin, of course, makes his fortune as printer
and author. "[P]rose writing," he notes in something of an
understatement, "has been of great use to me in the course

1. Bernard Bailyn, *The Ideological Origins of the American Revolution* (Cambridge, Mass.: Harvard University Press, 1967), pp. v–vii. See also Bailyn, ed.,
Pamphlets of the American Revolution, 1750–1776, vol. I, *1750–1765* (Cambridge, Mass.: Harvard University Press, 1965). See also Quentin Skinner,
"Meaning and Understanding in the History of Ideas," *History and Theory,* 8
(1969), 3–53.

of my life, and was a principal means of my advancement."[2]
This regard for the text does not stop with reputation. Ultimately, the Founders lend themselves to textual study because
they expect so much from what they write. The eighteenth-
century American work invariably alludes to its own importance
as historical and intellectual event. Thomas Paine's *Common
Sense* begins not with tales of British oppression but with the
grave errors that other writers have foisted upon the world.
Correcting those errors, the task of the author, will in itself
change history. The careful reader of *Common Sense* becomes
another Noah in the process. "We have it in our power," Paine
contends, "to begin the world over again." This magniloquence
is intrinsic. *The Federalist* papers claim to be the best discussion
of the most important question of the age. Franklin's autobiography assumes the praise of posterity, the attention of all
future great men, and a niche somewhere above the writings of
Caesar and Tacitus. All three texts share an important premise
about writing: anything is possible with the proper word, which
is desperately needed for a crisis at hand. Always the same, that
crisis is best summarized in *Common Sense*. "The present state
of America," writes Paine, "is truly alarming to every man who
is capable of reflection . . . The instance is without a precedent,
the case never existed before, and who can tell what may be
the event?"[3]

The tensions here between assurance and uncertainty, plan
and chaos, imposition and effacement, gladness and gloom are
central to Revolutionary and early national writings. The point,
however, is not just to catalogue a juxtaposition of opposites
but rather to understand the way these manic-depressive tendencies come together in a unified aesthetic. The great statements
of the period set the dichotomy on edge. When Franklin delivers
his witticism over the Declaration of Independence ("we must,
indeed, all hang together, or most assuredly we shall all hang

2. Benjamin Franklin, *Memoirs*, parallel text edition, ed. Max Farrand
(Berkeley: University of California Press, 1949), p. 32.
3. Thomas Paine, *Common Sense* in *The Complete Writings of Thomas Paine*,
ed. Philip S. Foner, 2 vols. (New York: Citadel Press, 1945), I, 4, 8, 24, 45,
43, and Benjamin Franklin, *Memoirs*, pp. 2–4, 186–198.

separately"), a realistic fear balances the statement of policy.[4] The fear itself is not only realistic but enduring. In the 1770s the Founders are competing propagandists who trade in treason for an uncertain cause and a mixed audience. Confused and divided, they face enormous problems in deciding what to say to whom and when. Neither the British nor the French but factionalism is and remains their clearest enemy. Indeed, the possibility of collapse through internal dissension continues to haunt both political considerations and the literary imagination for generations. Royall Tyler's *The Contrast* (1787), Hugh Henry Brackenridge's *Modern Chivalry* (1792–1815), Charles Brockden Brown's *Wieland* (1798), and Washington Irving's *A History of New York* (1809) are all dominated by voices locked in ideological conflict and mutual misapprehension. Each plays off of an inveterate acrimony and a fear that have at least as much to do with eighteenth-century America as do the more familiar chronicles of heroism and statesmanship.[5]

The Founders use their faith in the text to stabilize the uncertain world in which they live. They either invest given anxieties, problems, and unknowns on the page, to be subsumed in the substances of print, proof, style, and form, or they rigorously exclude them from what still pretends to be "a comprehensive" treatment of the subject. Jefferson's debate with the rest of the Continental Congress over slavery in the Declaration of Independence offers a clear case in point. The alternatives are either to make the horror of slavery a major grievance and then to blame it on the King of England or to remove all mention of it from Jefferson's draft as the final document, in fact, does. Both strategies, investment and exclusion, effectively put the reality of the text above experience in the world. Neither Jefferson nor his opponents want to deal with

---

4. Jared Sparks, ed., *The Works of Benjamin Franklin*, 10 vols. (Boston: Tappan & Whittemore, 1840), I, 408. For a seminal study of "pronounced manic-depressive tendencies" in the literature of the period, see William Hedges, "Charles Brockden Brown and the Culture of Contradictions," *Early American Literature*, 9 (Fall 1974), 107–142.

5. For one of the best descriptions of this general acrimony, see John R. Howe, Jr., "Republican Thought and the Political Violence of the 1790s," *American Quarterly*, 19 (Summer 1969), 147–165.

the fact of slavery as such, and their glosses should give us pause. On the one hand, the way lies open for a more creative study of writers who have been treated more as scribes than as originators of language and thought. On the other, the accusation of an imposed history takes on new meaning. What standing should manipulated and manipulative texts have in a larger understanding of the period?

Imposing the text as a higher reality solves a number of problems for the Founders. On a basic level, it minimizes the dangers of an unknown world. These dangers, in ascending order, include the Indian threat compounded by European interventionism, the more general fear of a contaminating wildness or barbarism (best captured in Crevecoeur's "What is an American?"), and the anxiety that a vast and still mysterious continent will somehow swallow the promise of representative government in America. Typically, *Notes on the State of Virginia* presides over the extinction of the Indians while preserving a touch of their presence in conveniently static outline form. "I will reduce within the form of a Catalogue," Jefferson explains, "all those [tribes] within, and circumjacent to, the United States, whose names and numbers have come to my notice." The one Indian spokesman in Jefferson's treatment, Chief Logan, appears only to announce his own departure: "Who is there to mourn for Logan?—Not one."[6] Similar ploys assimilate Nature's unknowns into the evolving patterns of American civilization. "It has often given me pleasure to observe," writes Publius in "Federalist No. 2," "that independent America was not composed of detached and distant territories, but that one connected, fertile, wide-spreading country was the portion of our western sons of liberty. . . . A succession of navigable waters forms a kind of chain round its borders, as if to bind it together; while the most noble rivers in the world, running at convenient distances, present them with highways for the easy communication of friendly aids."

6. Thomas Jefferson, *Notes on the State of Virginia*, ed. William Peden (New York: W. W. Norton & Co., 1972), pp. 102, 63.

These devices are important because so obvious to all concerned; they are conscious fabrications in the writer's search for
a higher truth, and, as such, they betray a willingness, even an
eagerness, to reshape and gild the cruder facts with which they
contend. As devices, they are also the counterparts of far more
subtle stratagems in the literature of republican idealism, and
the homology points directly to the largest problem that writing
poses for the Founders. Demystifying a superficially compliant
natural world is one thing, forging artificial unities amidst active
competitors and a contentious, far-flung populace is quite another. The Founders lead a deeply divided people in the Revolution and after. Their assumed task is to extract consensus at
all costs, and they write with a paradoxical brand of creativity
in mind—a creativity of agreement. Thomas Jefferson's summary of the Declaration of Independence speaks for every major
work of the period:

Not to find out new principles, or new arguments, never before thought
of, not merely to say things which had never been said before; but to
place before mankind the common sense of the subject, in terms so
plain and firm as to command their assent . . . Neither aiming at originality of principle or sentiment, nor yet copied from any particular
and previous writing, it was intended to be an expression of the American mind.[7]

Here is the key to the greatest achievement in writing of the
age: namely, the literature of public documents in all of its
forgotten subtlety. These documents are routinely viewed as
distillations of what already had been said at the time, but the
many negatives in Jefferson's comment—"Not to find out new
principles . . . not merely to say things which had never been
said . . . Neither aiming at originality . . . nor yet copied"—
these negatives convey a lost distilling process and its frustra-
tions. The deft business of securing assent through language
must be understood against the Founders' frequent despair in
the attempt. Franklin, for one, comes to accept division as the
inescapable norm of human affairs. "Men . . . are generally

7. Jefferson to Henry Lee, 8 May 1825, in Adrienne Koch and William
Peden, eds., *The Life and Selected Writings of Thomas Jefferson* (New York:
Random House, 1944), p. 719.

more easily provok'd than reconcil'd," he writes near the end
of the Revolution, "more disposed to do Mischief to each other
than to make Reparation, much more easily deceiv'd than un-
deceiv'd, and having more Pride and even Pleasure in killing
than in begetting one another."[8] John Adams agrees. "[N]either
Philosophy, nor Religion, nor Morality, nor Wisdom, nor Interest," he warns Jefferson in 1787, "will ever govern nations
or Parties against their Vanity, their Pride, their Resentment
or Revenge, or their Avarice or Ambition."[9] Idealistic in their
assertions, the Founders put pen to paper with shabbier needs
in mind. The truth may indeed be self evident, but people must
be humored, duped, coaxed, and provoked into accepting it.

The fact of acrimony, the need to impose a truth upon it, and
the major strategies for so doing all come to life in a noted aside
between Jefferson and Franklin during congressional debate
over the Declaration of Independence. When Jefferson complains against the "depredations" and "mutilations" of his draft,
Franklin responds with an anecdote that catches the essence of
the writer's problem:

"I have made it a rule," said [Franklin], "whenever in my power, to
avoid becoming the draughtsmen [sic] of papers to be reviewed by a
public body. I took my lesson from an incident which I will relate to
you. When I was a journeyman printer, one of my companions, an
apprentice hatter, having served out his time, was about to open shop
for himself. His first concern was to have a handsome signboard, with
a proper inscription. He composed it in these words, 'John Thompson,
Hatter, makes and *sells hats* for ready money,' with a figure of a hat
subjoined; but he thought he would submit it to his friends for their
amendments. The first he showed it to thought the word '*Hatter*' tau-
tologous, because followed by the words 'makes hats,' which show he
was a hatter. It was struck out. The next observed that the word '*makes*'
might as well be omitted, because his customers would not care who
made the hats. . . . He struck it out. A third said he thought the words

8. Franklin to Joseph Priestly, 7 June 1782, in Frank Luther Mott and Chester
E. Jorgenson, eds., *Benjamin Franklin: Representative Selections* (New York:
American Book Company, 1936), p. 444.
9. Adams to Jefferson, 9 October, 1787, in Lester J. Cappon, ed., *The
Adams-Jefferson Letters: The Complete Correspondence between Thomas Jef-
ferson and Abigail and John Adams,* 2 vols. (Chapel Hill: University of North
Carolina Press, 1959), I, 202–203.

'for ready money' were useless, as it was not the custom of the place
to sell on credit . . . [The words] were parted with, and the inscription
now stood, 'John Thompson sells hats.' *'Sells hats!'* says his next friend.
Why nobody will expect you to give them away, what then is the use
of that word? It was stricken out, and *'hats'* followed it, the rather as
there was one painted on the board. So the inscription was reduced
ultimately to 'John Thompson' with the figure of a hat subjoined."[10]

The parallels to founding a nation are deliberate and amus-
ingly apt. The apprentice who opens his own shop is like the
colonies that declare their independence. Both have embarked
on a risky enterprise that may fail. The success of a step already
taken now depends upon how others respond to the signification
of that event. Accordingly, the written representation, whether
signboard or Declaration of Independence, appears as a symbol
of vulnerability; this is where others enter into the success or
failure of the enterprise, this is where opinions are crucial. The
hatter will lose his shop if friends do not act upon his advertisement. The Revolution will be for naught without a united
front behind the claim for independence. Humor flows from the
thankless role of the writer or sign-maker, who must stoop to
the lowest common denominator to find agreement. Unchecked
debate, Franklin is telling us, produces a negative result in matters large and small.

Of more immediate interest, however, is the actual making
of a text within a consensual setting. The anecdote leaves the
beleaguered writer four alternatives. Most obviously, from the
perspective of modern authorship, one can simply impose a
private writing on a public audience. The hatter can hang his
sign without consulting anyone, hoping that the fait accompli
will minimize conflict. This, in effect, is the strategy of Jefferson's *A Summary View of the Rights of British America* and
Paine's *Common Sense,* both of which captivate in their daring.
But the risk of discord from unilateral assertion is also great,
particularly for writers with a paramount sense of community.
Second, one can draw up a text in the marketplace of debate

10. "Anecdotes of Benjamin Franklin" in Thomas Jefferson to Robert Walsh,
4 December 1818, in *The Life and Selected Writings of Jefferson,* pp. 178–179.

as the Founders do with the Declaration of Independence and the Constitution. Here, in fact, is the creative norm of the times. In making a finished text, the eighteenth-century man of letters distributes private drafts to a large circle of friends for advice before publication—a practice that explains how the debates over language in the Continental Congress and the Constitutional Convention can be conducted with such skill and cooperation. The problem, of course, lies in the hatter's comic inability to please his friends. What happens when agreement proves impossible?

The answer, a third alternative, appears in Franklin's punch line. One reduces the public text into an article of faith or icon. The sign becomes an incontestable fact when just a name subjoined to the figure of a hat. Most of the important texts of the Revolution have this figural quality. They are composed to be seen and believed in without necessarily being read or mastered. Newspaper length, they are short enough to be taken in at a glance, and they seek substantiating form at every turn. The Declaration of Independence is couched within the frame and language of legal pleading, the *declaration* or *count* that initiates an action in English common law. *Notes on the State of Virginia* relies upon the extrinsic questionnaire of the French legation in Philadelphia for its chapter headings. *The Federalist,* cut into eighty-five parts, never violates its originating form in the occasional newspaper essay. Both here and in the Constitution, the numerology of articles, sections, and papers provides an apparent structure and sense of place that can be seen as well as read.

Each of these texts also carries the legitimizing name of Founding Father, the "John Thompson" on the sign. The signers of the Declaration of Independence and Constitution are themselves literalized on the signboards in question. James Madison understands the hieroglyphic significance of those signatures as early as 1788. "Had the Constitution been framed & recommended by an obscure individual, instead of a body possessing public respect & confidence," he writes during the fight for ratification, "there can not be a doubt, that altho' it would have stood in the identical words, it would have commanded little attention from most of those who now admire its wisdom."[11] Gaining agreement or commanding attention, as Madison puts it, means engraving the separate authority of the author on the text—a policy that easily carries beyond name, signature, and even verifiable fact. When John Dickinson writes *Letters from a Farmer in Pennsylvania* (1768), he is neither a farmer nor, strictly speaking, a Pennsylvanian but a wealthy lawyer and rising politician from tiny Delaware. The figure on the page, strategically sequestered on a small farm in a large middle colony, does a better job of convincing British Americans that Dickinson writes objectively and for all of them.[12] The ingenuity of the persona responds to a larger quest for entitlement, the Revolutionary writer's need for visible posting. The hatter can accept any change that leaves him on the sign.

Thus far the strategies of a consensual literature are easily traced in texts that have been imposed, negotiated, reduced, and concretized, but there is a fourth possibility in Franklin's anecdote, the implications of which are much harder to grasp. Franklin reserves that fourth alternative for himself in his imputed silence, his strategy of avoidance. "I have made it a rule," he tells us, "whenever in my power, to avoid becoming the draughtsmen of papers to be received by a public body." This comment frames the narrative, creating a strange inversion. As we listen, sound justifies silence, verbiage praises reticence, language explains its own absence. The writer himself thrives on such ironies; *"many Words won't fill a Bushel,"* says Poor Richard at the beginning of his long speech in "The Way to Wealth."[13] But Franklin is also extremely serious about his larger claim. Agreement often requires the second of his thirteen enumerated virtues: silence.

11. Madison to Edmund Randolph, 10 January 1788, in *The Papers of James Madison,* ed. Robert A. Rutland et al., 14 vols. (Chicago and Charlottesville: University of Chicago Press and University Press of Virginia, 1962–1984), X, 355. [The papers are now complete through 1792.]

12. Forrest Donald, ed., "Introduction," *Empire and Nation* (Englewood Cliffs, N.J.: Prentice-Hall, 1962), p. x, and John Dickinson, *Letters from a Farmer in Pennsylvania, to the Inhabitants of the British Colonies,* in Paul Leicester Ford, ed., *The Writings of John Dickinson,* vol. I, *Political Writings, 1764–1774* (Philadelphia: The Historical Society of Pennsylvania, 1895), p. 307.

13. *Benjamin Franklin: Representative Selections,* p. 281.

From beginning to end disputation is the major source of evil
in the autobiography. Since words breed only words, and then
anger, Franklin the boy must first learn to use them carefully
and with restraint. The writer's proper creed also comes early,
from Pope's *An Essay on Criticism:*

> Men must be taught as if you taught them not
> And things unknown propos'd as things forgot.

Each assumed character in turn, the printer's apprentice, the
town organizer, the philosopher, the leading politician, and the
renowned scientist, demonstrates these lessons.[14] Collectively,
and against the writing that contains them, they also prove that
silence is the best policy in a dispute. Silence Dogood, Franklin's
first pseudonym, literally proclaims the point, and so does the
worst moment in the political figure's long career. Hauled before
the Privy Council of Parliament as colonial agent in 1774, Franklin stands motionless and silent, enduring the wrath and invec-
tive of the king's ministers for more than an hour without change
of expression or reply.[15] Where agreement is the goal, refutation
feeds what it fights. This is Franklin's assumption and Jefferson's
as well when he contrasts the reserve of Franklin and Washington to "the morbid rage of debate" and "singular disposition
of men to quarrel" around them. "I never heard either of them
speak ten minutes at a time," notes Jefferson, explaining how
he, in emulation, "could sit in silence" during "wordy debate."
John Adams gives the best overall summary of the phenomenon:
"The Examples of Washington, Franklin and Jefferson are enough
to shew that Silence and reserve in public are more Efficacious
than Argumentation or Oratory."[16]

The purpose of silence is to control difference. In not writing
the Declaration of Independence, Franklin nonetheless secures

14. Franklin, *Memoirs,* pp. 40–44, 202–204, 282, 330, 384–386.

15. For standard descriptions of "The Privy Council Outrage," see James
Parton, *Life and Times of Benjamin Franklin,* 2 vols. (New York: Mason Broth-
ers, 1864), I, 582–598, and Carl Van Doren, *Benjamin Franklin* (New York:
Viking Press, 1938), pp. 467–478.

16. "Autobiography," *The Life and Selected Writings of Jefferson,* pp. 57–
60, and L. H. Butterfield, ed., *Diary and Autobiography of John Adams,* 4
vols. (1961; rpt. New York: Atheneum, 1964), III, 335–336.

a place on the relevant committee and quietly makes alterations in Jefferson's draft. Those who remain uncommitted in debate define common ground; they may even hope to do so on their own terms. The published word that follows inevitably claims for itself the realms of simplicity, clarity, moderation, and, thereby, universality. Simplicity and clarity, to paraphrase the Pennsylvania Farmer in his fourth letter, give certainty to expression and safety to conduct; moderation avoids the "torrent of angry and malignant passions" that Publius fears in "Federalist No. 1"; universality guarantees appeal. We must not overlook the conscious fabrication in these tactics. The whole thrust of such writing is to mask an uglier actuality and to keep dangerous passions below the combustion level. *Un*self-evident truths, the realities of difference, belong to private writings long after the fact. Half of the pleasure in reading the autobiographies of Franklin, Jefferson, and Adams comes from the writers' own eagerness to correct a public record.

Silence is the vital interstice in a consensual literature; what is written is peculiarly a function of what *cannot* be written *there*. The Constitution and the men who make it demonstrate the idea perfectly. The Federal Convention can succeed in spite of radical innovation because it maintains a strict public silence. The fifty-five delegates agree "that nothing spoken in the House be printed, or otherwise published or communicated without leave." Enormous pressures notwithstanding, they stick to their "rule of secrecy" from the middle of May to the middle of September.[17] What similar group could hope to so protect its deliberations today? More than mass communications intervenes between question and answer.

As for the Convention itself, the Founders decide that "a member shall not speak oftener than twice, without special leave, upon the same question; and not the second time, before every other, who had been silent, shall have been heard." Only the speaker of the moment may talk or, just as important, read during deliberations. And this reserve and care in speech carry naturally into the writing process. In creating a national federal

---

17. See James Madison, *Notes of Debates in the Federal Convention of 1787* (New York: W.W. Norton & Co., 1966), pp. 26, 27–28, 220, 299.

republic, the Founders never mention the words "national," "federal," or "republic" in their document. Slavery is guaranteed, but the term is banished. Other words, "president," "congress," and "union" survive only after scrupulous interrogation. Just five thousand words within a one-sentence preamble and seven brief articles, the Constitution condenses four months of often florid and bitter debate into a concise document of the simplest prose. And yet to read the prose alone is not to master the text.

The words of the Constitution celebrate the possible at a time when most Americans manifestly object to the notion of a strong federal union. A great deal has been left out; too much, in fact, for political expediency to explain. For if the gift of leaving things unsaid has been traced to the vaunted political pragmatism of the Founders—something that they insist upon themselves—this reserve actually has more to do with questions of underlying belief. Formal agreement has a special meaning for the writers of the Constitution. They believe that knowledge expressed in the language of reason leads to virtue and then harmony. These abstractions have very practical implications for both the literal word on the page and the space around it.

As figures of the Enlightenment, the Founders assume that reason and feeling participate in a higher truth or design; that an appreciation of truth is a matter of cumulative knowledge (finding the design in diverse components); and that order and virtue depend upon striking a balance between available components. These are the ideals that encourage a good society in the midst of endless antagonism and human depravity—ideals that have been traced in politics (the mixed constitution and checks and balances), philosophy (natural rights and contract theory), and history (the English common law and the Whig theory of history). Much less, however, has been written about the Enlightenment as part of a specific literary aesthetic in Revolutionary writings. The appeal to reason, of course, is always noticed as the most obvious part of that aesthetic, but the Founders already have solved more important problems before this act of recognition can take place. Basic issues of style and form dominate the literary task of subsuming difference within a unified text.

To return to the Constitution for a moment, we now see how that document can be comprehensive and remain as short as it is. The Founders do not need to enumerate every difference as long as all major antagonisms have been poised against each other.[18] Big state balances small, central government matches local, executive branch answers legislative answers judicial, and so on. The counterpoise of opposites in an appropriate design assures harmony. Significantly, the greater danger lies in the removal of central antagonisms, not in new ones. Publius describes the first situation in "Federalist No. 15," where the withdrawal of vested interests weakens structure to the point of collapse, and the second in "Federalist No. 51," where "the multiplicity of interests" strengthens a design whose vital parts have remained "the means of keeping each other in their proper places." Good government, like knowledge itself, grows through accumulation and the awareness of design.

Awareness of design is what every Revolutionary writer seeks to convey, and it consists in the knowledge of connection between social harmony and the natural order in things. John Adams summarizes the need for dispensing such knowledge in the first salvo of protests against British tyranny. "[W]herever a general knowledge and sensibility have prevailed among the people," he urges in *A Dissertation on the Canon and the Feudal Law* (1765), "arbitrary government and every kind of oppression have lessened and disappeared in proportion." A citizenry can hope for so much because of "*Rights,* that cannot be repealed or restrained by human laws—*Rights,* derived from the great Legislator of the universe."[19] Adams' ally, James Otis, makes the parallels involved more explicit in *The Rights of the British Colonies Asserted and Proved* (1764), the most widely read American pamphlet of its day. "The analogy between the

18. See, for example, Arthur O. Lovejoy, "The Theory of Human Nature in the American Constitution and the Method of Counterpoise," *Reflections on Human Nature* (Baltimore: Johns Hopkins Press, 1961), pp. 40–46.

19. *A Dissertation on the Canon and the Feudal Law,* in Charles Francis Adams, ed., *The Life and Works of John Adams,* 10 vols. (Boston: Little, Brown and Co., 1856), III, 448–449.

natural, or material, as it is called, and the moral world is very obvious," writes Otis, comparing "the intervention or combination of a *number* of simple principles" in astronomy and political science. Gravitation and attraction are to the revolving planets as equality and the power of the whole are to government. The ultimate controls in such discourse, as Jonathan Mayhew sees even in 1750, have less to do with specific acts of Parliament than they do with "the eternal *laws* of truth, wisdom and equity, and the everlasting *tables* of right reason—tables that cannot be *repealed*, or *thrown down* and *broken* like those of *Moses*."[20] Adams, Otis, and Mayhew are able to pass from a troubling political context to the comforts of fixed universal law and back again because, like other Enlightenment thinkers, they see government as a function of human nature, and this allows them to make humanity itself the bridge between Nature and Society.

Several things can be said about the language within the thought. It conflates the vocabulary of science, law, and religion. It invariably seeks to encompass the particularity of difference within framing personae, formal presentation, and an abstract consensus. It works from above or from an assumed perspective of greater knowledge, and, where possible, it enlists constitutive metaphors of unity from human relations. Typically, the "we" that holds self-evident truths and that forms a more perfect union in the Declaration of Independence and the Constitution dominates preamble and terminus so as to envelop a long list of interposed particulars, which are cast in the objective third person. This "we" appears within the most abstract assertions of general belief and, in both cases, seizes upon a symbol of overriding social cohesion, "the people." Everything about the language employed—"the course of human events," "to assume among the powers of the earth," "the laws of nature and of nature's God," "to form a more perfect Union," "and secure the Blessings of Liberty to ourselves and our posterity"—reaches beyond immediate context toward an extrinsic permanence. Safely

20. James Otis, *The Rights of the British Colonies Asserted and Proved,* and Jonathan Mayhew, *A Discourse Concerning Unlimited Submission and Nonresistance to the Higher Powers,* in Bailyn, ed., *Pamphlets of the American Revolution,* I, 428, 242.

enclosed are the specific conflicts that make the writing itself necessary.

The same tendencies inform a work like Dickinson's *Letters from a Farmer in Pennsylvania.* Here the established persona appears detached between Nature and Society and claims to write objectively with "a contented grateful mind" and "greater knowledge . . . than is generally attained by men of my class." From this vantage point, the farmer hopes to end confusion and discord through a clarification of general principles. "Small things grow great by concord" is his initial motto, and everything is written with that goal in mind. His solution to problems is the conventional balance of opposites, though so complicated in this instance as to defy exact expression. The true patriot must make it "impossible to determine whether an *American's* character is most distinguishable, for his loyalty to his Sovereign, his duty to his mother country, his love of freedom, or his affection for his native soil."

Forced eventually to choose between loyalty and resistance, Dickinson insists instead upon a simile that reconciles contradiction. "The *legal authority* of *Great-Britain* may indeed lay hard restrictions upon us," admits the farmer in his last letter, "but, like the spear of *Telephus,* it will cure as well as wound." The craft of the image lies in its accommodation of twin qualms; Dickinson fears anarchy in America as much as tyranny from England. Reason alone stands between justified anger and the combustion point of "an incurable rage." When that happens, warns the farmer, "a blind fury governs, or rather confounds all things." Meanwhile, language must also serve to warn every American of "the most imminent dangers" from parliamentary usurpation. The writer's intricate duty is to engender "a sedate, yet fervent spirit" that will encourage "prudence, justice, modesty, bravery, humanity, and magnanimity" all at once.[21] Only a figure of the Enlightenment could believe in so much balance.

Appropriately, the master of accommodation and counterpoise is Benjamin Franklin—the writer who fears discord most.

---

21. Dickinson, *Letters from a Farmer in Pennsylvania,* pp. 307–308, 312, 324–327, 401.

Franklin, however, substitutes humor for Dickinson's tortured "language of affliction and veneration." He turns exacting parallels into comic congruities. The odd thing about this humor is that it is taken for granted when even a glance beyond Franklin reveals a staggering aberration. No other Founder employs humor, and for most—Washington, Adams, Hamilton, Madison—laughter implies a contradiction in terms. Franklin's "stories," as they were called, are partial exceptions in a literature of solemn rule; they subvert the solemn in the name of rule. Even so, this humor is rarely understood for what it is in context. The oldest Founder has won just enough detachment from the world and just enough esteem within it to parody the devices that every Revolutionary writer must use.

In "The Ephemera: An Emblem of Human Life" (1778), Franklin listens carefully to "a kind of little fly, called an ephemera" whose generations breed and expire within the minutes of an hour. Comprehending perfectly, he understands little because so many speak at once, "disputing warmly" in "their national vivacity." Petty conflicts fill these little lives. Even the wisest fly speculates falsely from its narrow perspective. The tale or "emblem" depends upon the narrator's placement both above and within the frame, and that tension literally explodes when Franklin bids farewell as the oldest ephemera. His game of levels spoofs the whole notion of a detached objectivity. The Olympian voice that announces self-evident truths cannot sustain itself here.[22] In "An Edict by the King of Prussia" (1773), Franklin ridicules British policies in America by couching them, twice removed, in the newspaper account of an official document. Hoax and irony dominate, and the double frame mimics the penchant for proclamation among pamphleteers on both sides of the Atlantic. The whole distinction between "principles of equity" and *"Jeux d'Esprit"* disappears in Franklin's gloss.[23]

Swiftian in form, these satires are Addisonian in tone. They prefer the smile of recognition to the sneer in exposure, the amiable correction in the Spectator Club to the sardonic censure

22. *Benjamin Franklin: Representative Selections,* pp. 402–404.
23. Ibid., pp. 358–363.

of Lilliput. More than anything, Franklin seeks agreement. He wants disputants to concur, and the humorist arranges his mock battles accordingly. "The Handsome and Deformed Leg" (1780), "Dialogue between Franklin and the Gout" (1780), and "A Petition of the Left Hand" all present extremes in debate that implicitly yield to the symmetry of the human form under the control of reason.[24] Physicality, instead of marking difference, as in Swift, underlines the prospect in unity.

Notably, it is Franklin who urges the Constitutional Convention of 1787 to face the world as one body in either "our real or apparent unanimity." He enters the Convention believing "an assembly of great men is the greatest fool upon earth," and, after five weeks of debate, he fears "we shall succeed in this political Building no better than the Builders of Babel"— such is the "Melancholy Proof of the Imperfection of the Human Understanding." His final plea for unanimity comes with an explicit recognition of hopeless divergence: "when you assemble a number of men . . . you inevitably assemble with those men all their prejudices, their passions, their errors of opinion, their local interests, and their selfish views." Nevertheless, the only opinion to be expressed by the body so constituted must be "a sacrifice to the public good" through "joint wisdom" or the voice of reason. To refuse would be to trivialize oneself back into individuality, or, in Franklin's humorous vein, it would make one like "a certain French Lady, who, in a little dispute with her sister, said: 'But I meet with nobody but myself that is *always* in the right.' "[25]

The difficulty with Franklin's measured solutions is that they encourage understanding rather than belief. We see as much in a last essay of presumed balances, Thomas Jefferson's famous dialogue of the Head and the Heart on parting with Maria

24. Ibid., pp. 430–432, 424–430, 520–521. The date of composition for "A Petition of the Left Hand" is unknown.

25. Benjamin Franklin to Benjamin Vaughan, 26 July 1784, "Motion for Prayers in the Convention, June 28, 1787," "A Speech in the Convention at the Conclusion of its Deliberations, September 17, 1787," in *Benjamin Franklin: Representative Selections*, pp. 473, 489–493.

Cosway in 1786.[26] The conceit begins with all of the parts in place for a conventional agreement. Jefferson, having said farewell, peoples his loneliness with a debate between the Head and the Heart as the representatives of reason and feeling. The anatomical designations already imply an organic whole that might be lacking in comparable designations like mind and body, and the disputants speak as friends in mutual distress. But the debate soon dislodges these bonds and wheels out of control in a fight over the human condition. "Everything in this world is a matter of calculation," advises the Head. "Advance then with caution, the balance is in your hand." The Heart responds by spurning this "mathematical balance" and by arguing against "a miserable arithmetic" in human relations. In what proves to be the last word, it also rejects the Head's "sovereign control" over conduct, insisting instead upon "a divided empire." "I do forever, then," warns the Heart, "disclaim your interference in my province."

The division signifies that certain human events transcend intellection—an important admission for a child of the Enlightenment. Jefferson may or may not be choosing here between Lockean rationalism and Scottish moral sense theory.[27] But philosophical consistencies aside, he is certainly claiming that qualities like courage, endurance, and enthusiasm resist calculation; they involve a whole different way of seeing and being. The Heart, be it noted, takes credit for the American Revolution. The risk in rebellion requires a faith beyond reason, and this conviction must come from beyond mere knowledge. The Head may indeed "ride serene and sublime above the concerns of this mortal world, contemplating truth and nature, matter and motion." The Heart cannot.

Jefferson, perhaps without meaning to, demonstrates that Enlightenment norms carry Revolutionary thought and writing

26. Thomas Jefferson to Maria Cosway, 12 October 1786, *The Life and Selected Writings of Jefferson*, pp. 395–407.

27. An answer in either direction probably exaggerates the philosophical import of a love letter *about* feeling, but see Garry Wills, *Inventing America: Jefferson's Declaration of Independence* (New York: Doubleday and Co., 1978), pp. 200, 275–280, and Morton White, *The Philosophy of the American Revolution* (New York: Oxford University Press, 1978), pp. 118–122.

only so far. Moreover, the texts bear him out. Beyond nature
and truth, beyond reason and balance, a biblical faith is what
makes Americans the chosen of God in Revolutionary rhetoric.
That rhetoric clarifies, in Jonathan Mayhew's words, "the side
of Liberty, the BIBLE, and Common Sense, in opposition to
Tyranny, PRIEST-CRAFT, and Nonsense."[28] The importance
of the combinations lies in their *joint* contribution to identity.
Epistemologically, a chosen people have no choice. Both knowledge and belief must take the form of scripture.

The result is a strange medley of religious and secular voices
in the eighteenth-century American text, and the ensuing tangle
remains the single greatest puzzle in interpretations of the period. It is not as if one voice begins where the other ends in
these texts, or that one responds where the other falters, or that
believers and skeptics divide easily on the page. The consensual
nature of the literature of the Founders forces a genuine mix
of antithetical tendencies—a mix that, once achieved, seems
peculiarly American. Certainly the combination itself is not an
easy one. The thought of the Enlightenment, by definition,
dwells upon the human context. Psychologically, it presumes
an understanding of the world through apparent faculties. Politically, it expresses itself in the rule of law. American religious
thought, in contrast, turns upon revelation and divine sanction.
Psychologically, it waits upon a supernatural grace that transforms. Politically, it takes the millennial aspects of Puritanism
to project a special American destiny upon the history of the
world.

But these differences are also instructive. The signers of the
Declaration of Independence clearly want both forms of expression in their document, and they extend the language of Jefferson's draft to get the right combination. Accepting his words
about the search for a "separate and equal station" through
"the laws of nature and of nature's God," they then add a final
appeal "to the supreme judge of the world for the rectitude of
our intentions." As the first phrase assigns a sure place within
design, so the second elevates a colonial struggle to the level

28. Mayhew, *A Discourse Concerning Unlimited Submission*, in Bailyn, ed.,
Pamphlets, p. 213.

of cosmic event. Taken together, they strike the beginnings of what will soon be called a *manifest* destiny.

An obvious shift in language supports the combination of secular and religious impulses. No one would confuse the Founders' "supreme judge of the world" with the biblical counterpart sitting in awful judgment. Time and again, the inflated terminology of the Founders avoids denominational affiliation and doctrinal difference. Less obvious, however, is the actual basis of this secularization in language. There is a startling discrepancy here. To be sure, denominational groupings begin to splinter, the clergy starts to lose its status, and materialism increases in this period, but in 1776 these tendencies beg a harder question. How do the Founders secularize language amidst the continuing and explosive vitality of eighteenth-century religious discourse? The most zealous of Calvinist divines, the evangelical followers of Jonathan Edwards, do more than any other grouping to trigger the Revolution. Then, too, a whole new burst of revivalism, the Second Great Awakening, begins in the 1790s. Many of the democratic tendencies, some of the vocabulary of freedom, the greater part of early aspirations toward union, and much of the antiauthoritarianism in colonial rhetoric originate in theological debate. And these ingredients translate into political power. Adams always believes that Jefferson wins the election of 1800 because Aaron Burr, the grandson of Jonathan Edwards, is his running mate. "Burr," Adams writes Jefferson, "had 100,000 votes from the single Circumstance of his descent."[29]

The Founders never underestimate the power of the cloth. Instead they assume it, disenfranchising the clergy in the process. Not a single divine appears in the first rank of the Found-

---

29. Adams to Jefferson, 15 November 1813, *The Adams-Jefferson Letters,* II, 399. More generally, see Alan Heimert, *Religion and the American Mind from the Great Awakening to the Revolution* (Cambridge, Mass.: Harvard University Press, 1966); Jack P. Greene, ed., *The Reinterpretation of the American Revolution, 1763–1789* (New York: Harper and Row, 1968), pp. 42–45; Robert Middlekauf, "The Ritualization of the American Revolution," in Stanley Coben and Lorman Ratner, eds., *The Development of American Culture* (Englewood Cliffs, N.J.: Prentice-Hall, 1970), pp. 31–44; and Donald G. Mathews, "The Second Great Awakening as an Organizing Process, 1780–1830: An Hypothesis," *American Quarterly,* 21 (Spring 1969), 23–43.

ers. Not one major text in the act of creation comes from a
clergyman—a deliberate maneuver on the part of those who do
write. Adams, Jefferson, Madison, and Franklin fill their correspondence and private papers with warnings about priest-
hoods and dogma. Never more than here are they cognizant of
the need to exclude through literary manipulation—of the power
of the text to preempt and co-opt. Their tools are the doctrine
of separation of church and state in conjunction with their own
clear willingness to mix religion and politics on their own terms.
The first relegates the clergy to limbo in all discussions of civic
matters, and the second transfers all of the emotional power of
religious reference to secular hands.

Two examples should suffice. Madison can explain the correct
language for "Executive Proclamations of fasts & festivals" in
"consecrating [a day] to religious purposes" in the same letter
where he announces the importance of "every new & successful
example . . . of a perfect separation between ecclesiastical and
civil matters." Franklin can just as easily interrupt the Constitutional Convention to urge morning prayer upon its wrangling
members. "[H]ow has it happened, Sir," Franklin asks Washington, "that we have not hitherto once thought of humbly
applying to the Father of Lights to illuminate our Understandings?" Neither the language of science nor archness of delivery
should disguise the priestly function of such language. The
Founders understand the vital business of managing the sacred
and guiding belief. After detailing the "artificial structure and
regular symmetry" of his own creation in "Federalist No. 37,"
Madison finds the ultimate unities of the Constitution in "a
finger of that Almighty hand which has been so frequently and
signally extended to our relief in the critical stages of the revolution." Franklin interrupts his colleagues on the floor of the
Convention for the same purpose, to record "instances of a
superintending Providence in our Favour."[30] Both reminders,
for so they must be taken amongst the faithful, make unanimity
an expression of divine will. Artifice thus merges into ritual. To

30. James Madison to Edward Livingston, 10 July 1822, in Gaillard Hunt,
ed., *The Writings of James Madison*, 9 vols. (New York: G.P. Putnam's Sons,
1900–1910), IX, 100–101; and Franklin, "Motion for Prayers in the Convention,
June 28, 1787," in *Benjamin Franklin: Representative Selections*, pp. 490–491.

believe is to accept the necessary fabrication and oversimplification of a crafted unity. The power and the method of the appeal are unmistakable. Thomas Paine makes *Common Sense* the most influential text of the age by initiating just such an exercise in belief. He is the first to realize that presumptions of unity and oversimplification are the essential correlatives of national identity. Independence becomes "a single simple line"; reconciliation with England, "*a matter exceedingly perplexed and complicated.*" In a fusion of secular and millennialist impulses, *Common Sense* reduces a complex intellectual continuum to vivid moral contrasts that require immediate choice—patriotism or treason, union or disintegration, history or chaos. In spite of their clarity, these choices demand an act of faith. Although they come from "the simple voice of nature and reason," they still require "a new method of thinking" as part of the next stage of history, the impending millennium of republican culture.[31]

Patriotism and salvation are the same things in Paine's version of America, and all who disagree are condemned. Even those who equivocate, literally a majority of the country in 1776, find themselves with the damned. "[T]here is," writes Paine in one of a hundred biblical allusions, "no punishment which that man doth not deserve." On the positive side, Nature reveals, reason explains, and God ordains that "the birthday of a new world is at hand." Because this event partakes of "the glorious union of all things," it marks the beginning of "a continental form of government" that will make America "the glory of the earth." God reigns above this creation as "the king of America." On earth, "the Word of God" appears as the rule of law in the emerging republic. Thus, "in America the law is king," and the division between religious and secular thought disappears in entwining imagery.[32]

These passages score both the remarkable prescience of Paine's vision and the intricate conflation of religious and political images that makes it possible. *Common Sense* actually outlines every vital aspect of the unfolding experiment beforehand, in-

---

31. Paine, *Common Sense,* in *Complete Writings,* I, 43, 6, 17.
32. Ibid., I, 21–29, 45, 31.

cluding its continental scope, its republican nature, its representative form, and even its denouement in a federal convention and a written constitution. But Paine can suggest so much only because he possesses a set of religious ideas about what *should* happen. The spontaneous creation of a continental union simply cannot be conceived of in strictly secular terms in 1776. The language of political reference then in use will not justify the extrapolation. Meanwhile, the notion of God's New Israel proves exceedingly useful in this regard. "The Reformation was preceded by the discovery of America," we learn in *Common Sense*, "as if the Almighty graciously meant to open a sanctuary to the persecuted in future years."[33] Paine's notorious religious skepticism only underlines his compelling intellectual need for such rhetoric. Irrespective of belief, the frame of mind within which the Founders operate has a vital religious component, and that component is richly connotative. "In God we trust" is more than just the motto of American republicanism; it points back in time to a central premise in the language of national creation.[34]

How best to explain this language of national creation remains problematic. Works like *Common Sense* are thematically simple but rhetorically complex, and the combination is what counts. Many have traced the basic themes of liberty and union. Recently almost as many have wrestled with the more bewildering combinations of rhetoric—the interplay of the "country" style of Whig oratory with the dissenting tradition of radical protestantism, the philosophical and legal base of eighteenth-century British and continental thought, and the ethical standards of the Scottish moral sense school. We now know more about why these writings take the form that they do. But neither the discovery of proto-American characteristics in the first approach nor the search for philosophical consistencies in the second explains the vitality of the works in question.

33. Ibid., I, 26–29, 21.
34. The actual motto is produced during the Civil War under the direction of Salmon P. Chase, then Secretary of the Treasury.

Again, it is the combination that counts. Thematic simplicity and rhetorical complexity seem a peculiar blend, but they always connect in a language of political statement. We have seen that the Founders are political writers who create a consensual literature for a diverse and divided citizenry. They write to reconcile. A language of many levels naturally helps to make this possible—a language, to use J. G. A. Pocock's terms, in which "the same utterance will simultaneously perform a diversity of linguistic functions."[35] The mix of intellectual modes is the point of such discourse. A choice in the forms of expression (and, hence, in the options of response) facilitates agreement. The rationale of political statement, of course, is the prospect of power. The disinterested mien and the inclusive tone of the Founders' rhetoric should not obscure this truth. Implicit in the denial of British rule is the self-conscious awareness of a new ruler.

Virtually every characteristic that we have traced in the literature of the Founders fits within an essential hegemonic function.[36] The writers who displace the ministry while appropriating its language illustrate the classic formula of a dominant hegemony over its residual precursor. They borrow actively residual meanings in millennialist prophecy to verify the political claims of the present. Their metaphors of balance and counterpoise can be read in the same way—as part of a mediation between selective traditions and as part of the alertness that every hegemonic process must exercise over alternatives that question or threaten its dominance. The related language of science supplies its own justification of hegemony by tying a new political superstructure to a determining base. Think, for example, of Paine's claim in *Common Sense* that the island of Britain can no more rule the continent of America than a planet can circle a satellite.[37]

35. J. G. A. Pocock, *Politics, Language and Time: Essays on Political Thought and History* (New York: Atheneum, 1973), p. 17.

36. The ensuing discussion relies upon two essential sources for vocabulary. Antonio Gramsci, *Selections from the Prison Notebooks*, ed. Quintin Hoare and Geoffrey Nowell Smith (New York: International Publishers, 1971), pp. 12, 105–106, 181, 241, 333, 404; and Raymond Williams, *Marxism and Literature* (Oxford: Oxford University Press, 1977), pp. 106–123.

37. Paine, *Common Sense*, in *Complete Writings*, I, 24.

Here as elsewhere, political rhetoric contains a basic act in mutual recognition on the part of leaders and led. It instills the consciousness of belonging to a particular hegemonic force. The language of 1776 helps a governing group to realize that it is, in fact, governing. Ending in physical unity as they do, Franklin's anatomical balances typify an intense search for collectivity. The same search necessarily excludes and discriminates. *E Pluribus Unum* does not call upon the people anywhere near as much as it confirms an agenda in the separate language of a self-conscious elite. Franklin, Adams, and Jefferson suggest the slogan for the Continental Congress or, in social terms, for the American gentleman as revolutionary leader.

The hegemonic also discards whole areas of significance in the exercise of power. We see this in the way the Founders quickly remove an entrenched loyalism and antifederalism from acceptable intellectual exchange. In 1783, when Franklin's fable of the Revolution sets the English lion against his American dogs, those dogs who side with the lion are not really dogs at all but "a mongrel race, derived from a mixture with wolves and foxes." Unnatural and inherently false, they deserve and receive no consideration from either side.[38] The same strategy serves Publius four years later. In "Federalist No. 2" supporters are "our best and wisest citizens." Their unnamed counterparts appear only as "certain characters" who oppose the "safety and happiness of union."

More frequently and subtly, the hegemonic controls by incorporation. *E Pluribus Unum* does not divide and conquer, an exercise in outright domination. It combines and subsumes. The number of American voices that are silenced or that are hidden in silence in this process remains a matter of vital archeological investigation. The statement "all men are created equal" is a synecdoche for humanity in only a special sense. The Civil War takes place over that special sense, though Abigail Adams articulates the problem at its inception. "I cannot say, that I think you are very generous to the ladies," writes Abigail to John in 1776, "for, whilst you are proclaiming peace and good-will to men, emancipating all nations, you insist upon retaining an

---

38. "Apologue," *Benjamin Franklin: Representative Selections*, pp. 458–459.

absolute power over wives.''[39] For the deaf ear of the Founders
as fathers, we need only recall Franklin's belittling aside on the
French sisters who cannot agree. Jefferson, as usual, summarizes the thought of the times: "the tender breasts of ladies were
not formed for political convulsions . . . ladies miscalculate much
their own happiness when they wander from the true field of
their influence into that of politicks.''[40]

The joint venture of historian and critic cannot create voices
where they do not exist, but it can reconstruct the restrictive
hegemonic code that determines the circumstances and the form
that speech must take then and later. Abigail Adams, alone in
1776, must restrict herself to private or domestic communication, a letter to her husband. We can, however, sense the in-
directions that public speech must assume when she responds
to an outsider's complaint about learned ladies. Casting her
antagonist, Judge F. A. Vanderkemp, into the third person,
Mrs. Adams heaps ironies upon him: "And in the first place,
to put him perfectly at his ease, I assure him that I make not
any pretensions to the character of a learned lady, and therefore,
according to his creed, I am entitled to his benevolence." A
pathos within irony follows. "There are so few women who may
be really called learned," she concludes, "that I do not wonder
they are considered as black swans.''[41] This language resists what
it must admit. Pressing against hegemonic assumptions, it clarifies otherwise obscure ideological boundaries.

Theories of hegemony are useful because they stimulate descriptions on a different level. They resist the surface appeal of
political rhetoric to concentrate on its pressures and limits. A
study of ideological assertions replaces a narrative of ideological
confirmations. The ensuing exposure of ideological functions
demythologizes belief, but it also reveals the driving edge of a

39. Abigail Adams to John Adams, 7 May 1776, in Charles Francis Adams,
ed., *Letters of Mrs. Adams, The Wife of John Adams*, 2 vols. (Boston: Charles
C. Little and James Brown, 1841), I, 100.
40. Thomas Jefferson to Angelica Schuyler Church, 21 September 1788, in
Julian P. Boyd, ed., *The Papers of Thomas Jefferson*, 21 vols. (Princeton:
Princeton University Press, 1950–), XIII, 623.
41. Abigail Adams to F. A. Vanderkemp, 3 February 1814, in *Letters of
Mrs. Adams*, II, 277–279.

leadership's assurance. We see how belief becomes language. The Founders can employ a rubric of "advice and consent" because their writings, in their own minds, articulate the truth of an apparent design. Their language, like history itself, cooperates with and is bolstered by an unfolding order in things. Words, agreement, and objective reality can cohere in such a world. "In disquisitions of every kind," Hamilton explains in "Federalist No. 31," "there are certain primary truths or first principles, upon which all subsequent reasonings must depend." Properly articulated, these truths command assent. Where they do not, the fault proceeds "from some defect or disorder in the organs of perception, or from the influence of some strong interest, or passion, or prejudice." The authority that is thus bestowed upon the written word is enormous; so is the corresponding advantage of a leader who would dismiss a lesser opponent.

The complete interpenetration of language, belief, and power in the Revolutionary American text informs even the simplest and most famous of statements. "We hold these truths to be self evident," announce the Founders in 1776. There can be, in other words, no legitimate challenge to the claims that follow. But we understand those claims fully only when we realize that the statement in question secures two kinds of protection in a dual assertion. We must pay attention to the mechanics of political implication. The same words that describe permanent truths everywhere in the world also introduce and impose an explicit political group, the new holders of truth in North America. Truth and its holders share self-evidence and, hence, a common security from challenge. Acceptance of the former means acquiescence to the latter in a ceremony of silence that ratifies both. Wrapped in the same invulnerable mantle, they appear as one: truth invested in a national leadership. Nothing could be more American. This is as close as we come to the act of national creation.

Popular Fiction and Critical Values: The Novel as a Challenge to Literary History

The growth of academic criticism in the twentieth century has come partly at the expense of other kinds of writing about literature, including literary journalism, belles lettres, and literary history. Great changes have occurred, for example, in biographical writing. In the nineteenth century a grandiose "life and letters" was often entrusted as a pious duty to either a family member—Scott's son-in-law, Macaulay's nephew, Hawthorne's son—or trusted protégé like Forster or Froude. (Later Thomas Hardy would exploit this moribund tradition by writing his own biography under the name of his second wife.) The mockery and brevity of Lytton Strachey put an end to these family affairs; in the hands of a new breed of glib popular writers, biography became a branch of narrative history, as smooth and digestible as a novel—or as a novel used to be. But the coming of an Age of Criticism, along with the general decline of popular interest in writers' lives, made this kind of confection anomalous. Literary biography passed from the professional biographers, innocent of all critical insight, to the verbose academic scholars, innocent of the ability to shape dramatic scenes, select vivid details, and tell a gripping story. With some significant exceptions like Ellmann's *Joyce*, literary biographies became overlong critical studies bulked out with a mass of chronological information about writers' day-by-day lives, or guided by some pet psychological theory about the writer's development. Criticism and psychoanalysis have given biographers new tools toward a deeper understanding of their subjects, but they have bloated the biographies themselves, which turn static or break down under the pressure of so much analytical argument and organized evidence.

The spirit of criticism has also altered the nature of literary history. As omnivorous antiquarian scholars like Saintsbury gave way to severely judgmental critics like Leavis, a hierarchical canon of great writers came to dominate the landscape of literary history, giving enormous priority to imaginative writing over discursive writing and leaving most writers as mere footnotes to a small band of acknowledged geniuses in each age. In C. H. Herford's once-standard handbook *The Age of Wordsworth* (first edition, 1897), the staggering range of writers who appear in less than 300 pages marks the book as a product of its time. Herford includes French and German Romantics, political philosophers like Godwin and Bentham, religious thinkers and historical writers, essayists, novelists, and dramatists, to say nothing of minor poets like Bowles, Crabbe, Hogg, and Landor, all in addition to the major writers. A typical work of our own period, Harold Bloom's *The Visionary Company* (1961), devotes more than 400 pages to poem-by-poem readings of the six major Romantic poets, followed by brief chapters on three minor poets. Informed by a revisionist view of the place of the Romantics in English literature, it treats literary history of the old kind as an irrelevance. It tells us that literary history inheres in the poems themselves and in their imaginative dialogue with other great poems from the Renaissance to the modern period, not in the circumstances of their composition, or in biographical relationships, or political and intellectual "backgrounds." Though Bloom sets out to overturn nearly all the judgments of the New Critics, he implicitly ratifies their emphasis on close reading and canon-formation. Behind his approach, like theirs, is an almost religious affinity for great poetry as secular scripture, and a sense of minor poetry and discursive writing as spiritually deficient, faulty in their worldliness. For Herford literary history is a branch of history; for Bloom it is a branch of criticism, or of the spiritual history to which critical reading gives us access.

An even more drastic reshaping of literary history along critical lines has taken place within American literature. When I was in high school in the 1950s, the line of American poetry still enshrined in our textbooks ran from Bryant, Longfellow, Whittier, and Lowell in the nineteenth century to Stephen Vincent Benet, Carl Sandburg, Robert Frost, and Edna Millay. Of these figures not even Frost can be said to survive today: the Frost who now bestrides the canon like a latter-day Wordsworth is quite different from the harmless, avuncular gaffer we were forced to read. In those textbooks, Whitman and Dickinson were treated like quirky, eccentric individualists, outside the main line, like Hopkins in England. Eliot and Pound were a distant rumor, Stevens and Hart Crane not even a rumor. For new figures like Robert Lowell you had to read *Partisan Review,* no staple in my high school.

In prose the upheaval has probably been less great, except for the rediscovery of Melville in the 1920s, but Emerson and Thoreau were renovated almost as sweepingly as Robert Frost. As the influence of modernism spread with the critical techniques which it spawned, nearly every older writer's work took on a new coloring, and methods of interpretation were soon translated into canons of taste, judgment, and critical discrimination. Fresh from a study of T. S. Eliot, F. O. Matthiessen helped create the canon of the American Renaissance, and this was inevitably reflected in Spiller's *Literary History of the United States,* to which Matthiessen contributed. The first edition of this work came out in 1948, the same year as Leavis's rigorously selective study of the English novel, *The Great Tradition.* As a collective work of scholarship the Spiller volume was hardly a book in the same class as the Leavis, but in its own terms it was in every way a work more discriminating and less catholic than *its* predecessor, *The Cambridge History of American Literature* (1917–1921). The Cambridge volumes, relatively speaking, are precanonical, premodern history as C. H. Herford might have written it. The Cambridge scholars deal with every kind of writing from discursive and religious tracts to imaginative writing, from dialect writers to newspaper and magazine writers to children's authors. The last chapters include studies of economists, scholars, patriotic songs and hymns, oral literature, popular bibles (like *The Book of Mormon* and *Science and Health*), book publishers, the English language itself, writings in German, French, and Yiddish, as well as native American myths and folktales ("Aboriginal").

From a later point of view, no doubt, there was something slightly monstrous—or at least deplorably miscellaneous—about the inclusion of all these matters in a literary history: a blinding nationalism and a default of critical judgment, if not some kind of obtuse ignorance about the very word "literature" enshrined in the title. Or so it must have seemed to the more advanced authors of the *Literary History of the United States,* who included some of these items, along with a good deal of political and intellectual history, as background or interchapters in a work that centers on major authors from Jonathan Edwards and Benjamin Franklin to Edwin Arlington Robinson, Theodore Dreiser, and Eugene O'Neill. In the closing section of this work, "A World Literature," the cosmopolitan modernism of Eliot and his school gets its due; it jostles for primacy with the remnants of the left-wing literary culture of the 1930s. But although the contributors include leading leftist critics like Malcolm Cowley, Matthiessen, and Maxwell Geismar, the accounts of individual authors tend to float free of any cultural context. Thanks to the new spirit of criticism, literary history is reduced to a succession of the great and near-great. Background chapters which begin each section are frequently entrusted directly to historians like Allan Nevins and Henry Steele Commager, as if to acknowledge that critics no longer feel equipped to write literary history.

In the second edition of 1953 this split is formally recognized, as the new preface indicates: "In the listing of chapters, the titles of those which were designed to supply information about the history of thought and the instruments of culture have now been distinguished from those which deal more directly with literature by being set in italics. The master plan of the work may thus be seen more clearly, it is hoped, as a literary history of the United States rather than as a history of American literature."[1] But the goal of seeing literature in relation to culture is seriously undercut by such an arbitrary mechanical division. Since the individual critics seem unable to develop an intrinsic cultural perspective, the enlightened sentences that follow seem like an attempt to disarm objections and compensate for felt deficiencies: "The view of literature as the aesthetic expression of the general culture of a people in a given time and place was, from the start, an axiom in the thinking of the editors and their associates. Rejecting the theory that history of any kind is merely a chronological record of objective facts, they adopted an organic view of literature as the record of human experience." Discarding the fact-bound positivism of the old history, the editors appeal implicitly to a new "organic" history that descends from Hegel and Coleridge to Croce and the New Criticism. Unfortunately, there is a deep contradiction between the historicism of Hegel and the ahistorical organicism of the New Critics. In Hegel, culture and history are part of the foreground, crystallized in the work itself; but to the New Critic the "well wrought urn" is a unique artifact, detached from history, the "foster child of silence and slow time," occupying its own imaginative space and pursuing its own formal and rhetorical strategies.

The conflict helps account for the slippery use of words like "literature" and "aesthetic expression" in this interesting preface. Is literature seen as "the aesthetic expression of the general culture" and a "record of human experience," or is it to be confined to the critic's choice of the best poems, plays, novels, and autobiographies, as in the actual body of this work? Interpretive insight and critical discrimination are things to be valued in any consideration of the arts, including literary history. Evaluation is as instinctive and inevitable as breathing. But the more vigorous the discrimination, the more limited the canon of accepted works is likely to be, and the more skewed the literary history may become. Critics in recent years have re-

1. Robert E. Spiller et al., eds., *Literary History of the United States,* 2nd ed. (New York: Macmillan, 1953), p. ix.

peatedly drawn attention to exclusions based on ethnocentrism
or on gender and class. "In the twenties," writes Paul Lauter,
"processes were set in motion that virtually eliminated black,
white female, and all working-class writers from the canon."[2]
Less attention has been paid to the exclusion of popular culture
and of borderline works on the margin between high and popular art. By resolutely refusing to fit, these works bring into
question the hierarchical basis of the canon itself. When scholars
venture into film history, there is no question that whatever has
been made is potentially part of the subject, not just the accepted masterpieces. There is no workable definition of "film"
that ignores the mass of existing movies, as there *are* definitions
of "literature"—and histories of literature—that exclude most
of the novels, poems, and plays ever written.

A great many of them, of course, are of little interest to
anyone. My concern here is not with what is ignored, rightly or
wrongly, but with what is categorically excluded or devalued
because of critical preconceptions. Here judgments of quality,
themselves very variable, are never the sole determinant.[3] Continuous innovation is a key feature of artistic activity since the
middle of the eighteenth century. This is partly the result of the
commodification process, the shift from a conservative patronage system to the needs of the marketplace, where artists are
forced to differentiate their products from those of other artists,
and even from the things they themselves have already produced. But innovation can also arise from a rejection of the
marketplace by a Wordsworth or Coleridge who is revolted by
the popular taste and following his own star. In either case, the
marketplace creates a demand for criticism that can mediate
between the growing number of artists and the expanding
middle-class audience, uncertain of its bearings in the brave new
world of culture.

2. Paul Lauter, "Race and Gender in the Shaping of the American Literary Canon: A Case Study from the Twenties," *Feminist Studies* 9 (Fall 1983),
435.

3. See Frank Kermode, "Institutional Control of Interpretation," in *The Art
of Telling: Essays on Fiction* (Cambridge, Mass.: Harvard University Press,
1983), pp. 168–184.

This system works better in theory than in practice. At times a whole new body of criticism may arise to serve and interpret a new movement in the arts, as it did during the modernist period. At other times the artists themselves will move to create the criticism they are not receiving from their contemporaries, as Wordsworth and Coleridge did, as Poe and James did after them, as Eliot and Pound did in the twentieth century. Art as we know it is inherently dynamic and unstable, while criticism seems intrinsically synthetic and retrospective. Like the French general staff, criticism is always fighting the previous battle, the last war; its standards are inevitably drawn from an earlier phase of creative activity, from which it codifies the rules that artists feel almost obliged to violate.

Sometimes this balance of innovation is reversed. For reasons that also relate to the marketplace, popular art is often more conservative than vanguard art, wary of drastic innovation, given to repeating formulas which have worked in the past. Faced by the crowd-pleasing formulas of mass culture, sometimes combined with advances in technology that seem to threaten the existing arts, the critic falls back on originality and high seriousness as the sine qua non of all genuine art. He relegates popular culture to the history of taste and turns it over willingly to the sociologist and the historian. A work like the *Literary History of the United States* resembles a topographical map with all peaks and no valleys, not even the most lush and verdant ones. For example, nearly a quarter of all the new novels published in the 1930s were detective stories, rising from 12 in 1914 to 97 in 1925 to 217 by the last year of the thirties.[4] Dashiell Hammett was certainly one of the best writers who worked in this form, and he was at the height of his fame by 1948, after a series of films and radio programs based on his characters; yet we search the *Literary History of the United States* in vain for any substantive discussion of what he wrote. Instead, in a

4. James D. Hart, *The Popular Book: A History of America's Literary Taste* (Berkeley: University of California Press, 1950), p. 259. See also Warren I. Susman, "The Thirties," in *The Development of an American Culture,* ed. Stanley Cohen and Lorman Ratner, 2nd ed. (New York: St. Martin's Press, 1983), pp. 239–240.

chapter on fiction, we find a parenthetical reference to "the talented mystery writer Dashiell Hammett"[5] (though the context actually refers to his politics), along with three more references in a concluding chapter on American books abroad, where Hammett's literary quality was better recognized than at home. Popular culture in general gets short shrift in Spiller's capacious volume, though it does include literary discussions of major writers like Cooper and Poe who happened at some point to be popular. (We never learn how they accomplished this paradoxical feat.)

Some of the serious gaps in the *Literary History of the United States* are filled when we turn to indispensable works like James D. Hart's *The Popular Book: A History of America's Literary Taste* (1950) and Russel Nye's *The Unembarrassed Muse: The Popular Arts in America* (1970). Each contains materials that would never belong in any literary history. Hart includes both foreign books that were popular here and nonliterary works like Bruce Barton's biography of Jesus as an American-style huckster, *The Man Nobody Knows*, and Dale Carnegie's manual on *How To Win Friends and Influence People*. Nye aptly brings in everything from dime novels and popular music to film and television. Yet these books are also mirror images of academic literary histories. They offer essential missing links and highlight all that is shadowy or absent in the official literary canon. Just as Tom Stoppard cleverly looked at Hamlet from the point of view of Rosencrantz and Guildenstern, Hart and Nye see Hawthorne and Melville from the tilted angle of the "mob of scribbling women" who—so they felt—stood between them and their rightful readership.[6] No history of our literary culture is complete without some account of these writings.

Hart and Nye are not simply drawing attention to the popular or forgotten works. For them the whole social history of reading, writing, and publishing are an intrinsic part of any history of literature. Thus Nye writes about changes in the marketplace, the growth of the reading public, the vast increase in the number of newspapers and magazines in the early nineteenth century,

5. Spiller, *Literary History of the United States*, p. 1313.
6. Hart, *The Popular Book*, p. 93.

and the "succession of technological innovations in the mechanics of printing" that enabled publishers to produce "the
acres of print demanded by this huge audience."[7] For the
Spiller group, however, such matters are peripheral at best.
Literary history is a record of the imaginative heights scaled by
talent and genius, with little regard for the conditions under
which they worked, the cultural factors that helped determine
how their work was conceived and received, and the different
kinds of talent and intensity that could operate in the popular
arts.

The artificial separation of the "literary" and the "popular,"
and the parallel split between the "critical" approach and the
"cultural" one, is especially vexing when we are dealing with
fiction. Most modern critical techniques were developed to deal
with the more self-contained artifacts of lyric poetry. The novel,
with its looser weave, was the child of the marketplace. It was
born only after the old patronage system gave way before the
spread of literacy and leisure within the new middle-class audience.[8] No form better illustrates the time lag between creative practice and critical acceptance. As Leslie Fiedler has
written,

> From any traditional point of view, then, from the standpoint of
> those still pledged in the eighteenth century to writing epics in verse,
> the novel already seemed anti-literature, even post-literature . . . In
> the jargon of our own day, the novel represents the beginning
> of popular culture, of that machine-made, mass-produced, mass-
> distributed *ersatz* which, unlike either traditional high art or folk art,
> *does not know its place;* since, while pretending to meet the formal
> standards of literature, it is actually engaged in smuggling into the
> republic of letters extra-literary satisfactions.[9]

7. Russel Nye, *The Unembarrassed Muse: The Popular Arts in America* (New
York: Dial Press, 1970), p. 24.
8. The classic account of this process is still Ian Watt, *The Rise of the Novel*
(Berkeley: University of California Press, 1957), esp. chap. 2.
9. Leslie Fiedler, "The End of the Novel," in *Perspectives on Fiction,* ed.
James L. Calderwood and Harold E. Toliver (New York: Oxford University
Press, 1968), p. 193.

While Fiedler is certainly accurate about the resistance to the
novel among the upholders of high culture in the eighteenth
century, the way he poses the issue ratifies the presumed gap
between the literary and the popular by defending popular culture against its detractors, then and now. In what sense was the
novel "*pretending* to meet the formal standards of literature"?
It invented new formal standards that were also literary, besides
being instantly understood by nearly all readers. In what sense
did the novel illicitly provide "extra-literary satisfactions"? That
can only be so if we limit our definition of the literary as strictly
as any elitist critic might wish. Fiedler's wild-man stance is his
way of thumbing his nose at the critic he once was.

Even in the heyday of modernism, the novel never entirely
lost its roots in popular storytelling. Publishers today may find
it convenient to distinguish between popular and literary fiction,
but this refers to the size of the audience, not to any absolute
formal differences. Most fiction continues to occupy the large
middle ground between self-conscious experimentation and the
predictable formulas of the best-seller list. The formal qualities
of the novel were established early on by Defoe, Richardson,
and Fielding, who each felt in different ways that he was creating
"a new species of writing," quite distinct from epic and romance.[10] The narrative devices they used were so quickly understood and accepted that they could be manipulated with impunity
by Fielding, wildly parodied by Sterne, and turned into self-
conscious play by Sterne's French follower, Diderot. Despite
these formal elements, a grey area blurs the line between fiction
and romance and between fiction and nonfiction. A good measure of looseness and ambiguity distinguishes all fiction from
the beginnings of the eighteenth century to the present. As John
J. Richetti writes of the forgotten books he surveys in *Popular
Fiction Before Richardson*, "many narratives of the period, presented as fact and accepted as such by many, were sheer fabrications. Many 'novels' were only thinly disguised romans à
clef, gross mixtures of slander and scandal. It is, in short, extremely difficult to separate fact from fiction in a great many of

10. Quoted by Lennard J. Davis, *Factual Fictions: The Origins of the English
Novel* (New York: Columbia University Press, 1983), pp. 182–183.

the prose narratives of the period that are customarily called fiction."[11]

It would be wrong to attribute this ambiguity solely to the immaturity of pre-Richardsonian fiction. Even the major writers hid behind a screen of truthfulness, posing as the mere editors of their material. In other words, they used a blatantly fictive device to ward off charges of lying and creative invention. But even after this fiction was discarded, the course of the novel right up to the present has continued to rely on some confusion between art and life. In his notes for an autobiographical lecture, Lionel Trilling described the novel as "the genre which was traditionally the least devoted to the ideals of *form* and to the consciousness of formal consideration . . . of all genres the most indifferent to manifest shapeliness and decorum, and the most devoted to substance, which it presumes to say is actuality itself."[12] The novel as a genre "presumes to say" this, Trilling hints, though we ourselves, with our heightened formal awareness, are confident that we know better. Trilling is as conscious as we are of the fictive character of all human constructions. Yet he continues to stand with the great apologists for the novel, D. H. Lawrence and Henry James, when he describes it as "the literary form which most directly reveals to us the complexity, the difficulty, and the interest of life in society, and which best instructs us in our human variety and contradiction."[13]

In a famous passage in his essay "Why the Novel Matters," Lawrence had boasted that "being a novelist, I consider myself superior to the saint, the scientist, the philosopher, and the poet, who are all great masters of different bits of man alive, but never get the whole hog."

The novel is the one bright book of life. Books are not life. They are only tremulations on the ether. But the novel as a tremulation can make the whole man alive tremble. Which is more than poetry, philosophy, science, and any other book-tremulation can do.

11. John J. Richetti, *Popular Fiction Before Richardson: Narrative Patterns, 1700–1739* (Oxford: Clarendon Press, 1969), p. 7.

12. Lionel Trilling, "Some Notes for an Autobiographical Lecture," in *The Last Decade: Essays and Reviews, 1965–75* (New York and London: Harcourt Brace Jovanovich, 1979), p. 228.

13. Trilling, "Art, Will, and Necessity," *The Last Decade,* p. 140.

The novel is the book of life. In this sense, the Bible is a great
confused novel.[14]

From Aristotle to Wordsworth and Matthew Arnold, critics and
poets had used this argument to defend poetry and to proclaim
its universality against the more factual claims of history and
science. Lawrence directs the same argument against poetry
itself, in the name of a form whose dignity and truth were still
in question as he was writing. "The crown of literature is poetry," wrote Matthew Arnold in 1887, after taking due note of
the creative ferment in French, English, and Russian fiction.
Here, at the end of his life, Arnold ruefully acknowledged that
fiction was "the form of imaginative literature which in our day
is the most popular and the most possible,"[15] but this was further
evidence to him that literature had fallen on hard times. Arnold's conservatism exemplifies the time lag between creative
achievement and critical recognition. The popular character of
fiction, for him, was an argument against it.

     This was the very period when Flaubert and Henry James
were bidding to elevate fiction from popular culture into art by
holding it to an unheard-of standard of formal control. This can
be observed in the exacting craftsmanship of their novels and
stories, but also in Flaubert's letters and James's reviews, essays,
and prefaces—documents in their struggle to achieve a precision
of language and a consistency of narrative viewpoint that were
alien to the early novelists. Yet the novels of both men, like
later "serious" fiction, include generous helpings of romance
and melodrama, those indispensable staples of popular fiction.
Henry James's legacy to later criticism and fiction was especially
ambiguous. In the hands of Percy Lubbock and the academic
critics who came after him, James's critical prefaces were turned
into rules of craft that made "creative writing" less creative and
more teachable, rules that the best novelists had usually felt
free to ignore. Lawrence, one of the writers who broke those

14. D. H. Lawrence, "Why the Novel Matters," in *Phoenix: The Posthumous
Papers of D. H. Lawrence,* ed. Edward D. McDonald (1936; rpt. London:
William Heinemann, 1961), p. 535.
     15. Matthew Arnold, "Count Leo Tolstoi," *Essays in Criticism: Second Se-
ries,* ed. S.R. Littlewood (London: Macmillan, 1938), p. 150.

rules most flagrantly, wrote that "a character in a novel has got to live, or it is nothing."[16] James's general view of the novel is really not very different from Lawrence's.

The revival of Henry James in the 1940s and 1950s coincided with a certain academic deadness and tame respectability that invaded the novel. Yet the key terms in Henry James's essays on the novel, such as "The Art of Fiction," are not "form" or "point of view" but "experience" and "freedom." Like Lawrence he stresses "life" rather than "art," sincerity, vitality, accuracy, and variety rather than mere consistency of design. The novel, says James in his preface to *The Portrait of a Lady*, has not only the power to deal with an immense range of individual experience, but also "positively to appear more true to its character in proportion as it strains, or tends to burst, with a latent extravagance, its mould."

The house of fiction has in short not one window, but a million—a number of possible windows not be reckoned, rather; every one of which has been pierced, or is still pierceable, in its vast front, by the need of the individual vision and by the pressure of the individual will.[17]

James feared the moral censorship of his age more than any deficiency of craft; he saw how preconceived ideas could blind a writer to the variety of life and to his own wealth of experience. In a letter to the students at the Deerfield summer school, he wrote:

There are no tendencies worth anything but to see the actual or the imaginative, which is just as visible, and to paint it. I have only two little words for the matter remotely approaching to rule or doctrine; one is life and the other freedom. Tell the ladies and gentlemen, the ingenious inquirers, to consider life directly and closely, and not to be put off with mean and puerile falsities, and to be conscientious about it. It is infinitely large, various, and comprehensive. Every sort of mind will find what it looks for in it, whereby the novel becomes truly multifarious and illustrative. That is what I mean by liberty; give it its

16. Lawrence, "Why the Novel Matters," p. 537.
17. Henry James, preface to *The Portrait of a Lady*, in *Literary Criticism: French Writers, Other European Writers, The Prefaces to the New York Edition*, ed. Leon Edel, with Mark Wilson (New York: Library of America, 1984), p. 1075.

head, and let it range. If it is in a bad way, and the English novel is, I think, nothing but absolute freedom can refresh it and restore its self-respect.[18]

This is the real significance of point of view in James: not a limiting rule of craft, as it is applied mechanically in writing courses, but an individual aperture from the house of fiction onto the plenitude of life. There is almost a Paterian emphasis in James's insistence that "a novel is in its broadest definition a personal, a direct impression of life: that, to begin with, constitutes its value, which is greater or less according to the intensity of the impression . . . The form, it seems to me, is to be appreciated after the fact."[19] Later on in this essay, "The Art of Fiction," James tries to define the impressions and intuitions that constitute novelistic "experience":

The power to guess the unseen from the seen, to trace the implications of things, to judge the whole piece by the pattern, the condition of feeling life in general so completely that you are well on your way to knowing any particular corner of it—this cluster of gifts may almost be said to constitute experience . . . Therefore, if I should certainly say to a novice, "Write from experience and experience only," I should feel that this was rather a tantalising monition if I were not careful immediately to add, "Try to be one of the people on whom nothing is lost!"   (p. 53)

Far from laying down a set of rules for the novel, "The Art of Fiction" is directed against the mechanical prescriptions of another writer, Walter Besant, who, in a misguided way, was trying to have fiction recognized belatedly as one of the fine arts. When Besant advises the aspiring writer to carry a notebook and jot down what he observes, James comments that "his case would be easier, and the rule would be more exact, if Mr. Besant had been able to tell him what notes to take. But this, I fear, he can never learn in any manual; it is the business of his life" (p. 54). Henry James would dearly love to have the

18. Henry James, letter to the Deerfield Summer School, in *Literary Criticism: Essays on Literature, American Writers, English Writers,* ed. Leon Edel, with Mark Wilson (New York: Library of America, 1984), pp. 93–94.

19. James, "The Art of Fiction," ibid., p. 50. Further references, identified by page numbers in the text, are to this edition.

imaginative potential of the novel acknowledged and to have
its cultural status secured. But he refuses to do so by codifying
its techniques into a practical routine, which was just what some
later critics would extract from his own novels and essays. The
seemingly modest shift from James's *art* of fiction to Percy Lubbock's *craft* of fiction is really an ominous devolution toward
an academic model.

Trilling once described this questionable process as a way of
bolstering the superego of the novel. Lawrence and James see
the dead hand of formal rigor as a contrivance of classifying
critics and cultural watchdogs, not as a true understanding of
what fiction is. "The only classification of the novel that I can
understand," writes James,

> is into that which has life and that which has it not. The novel and the
> romance, the novel of incident and that of character—these clumsy
> separations appear to me to have been made by critics and readers for
> their own convenience, and to help them out of their occasional queer
> predicaments, but to have little reality or interest for the producer,
> from whose point of view it is of course that we are attempting to
> consider the art of fiction. (p. 55)

I have gone into James's view in such detail because he is usually
taken as the leading defender of the novel as an art form, and
as the point of origin of the formal and academic study of fiction
and its techniques. Yet James himself is eager to deter such
pedantry, which has increased immeasurably since his time. But
since reality itself is unstable, the language of fiction, so long
as it was to remain responsive to the real world, could hardly
remain unchanged. This was the wrinkle that complicated the
realist program of later James and other modern writers. According to Frank Kermode, the split between advanced and
traditional fiction became critical during the Edwardian period, with James, Conrad, and Ford Madox Ford leagued
against Wells, Galsworthy, and Arnold Bennett. "Much of the
history of the novel in the present century," Kermode writes,
"is dominated by the notion that technical changes of a radical
kind are necessary to preserve a living relation between the
book and the world."[20] Kermode views the split entirely from

20. Kermode, *The Art of Telling,* p. 40.

the vantage point of the incipient modernism, yet he justifies technical innovation in terms of fidelity to life, as James does, not simply as experiments in language. From this point of view, Molly Bloom's stream-of-consciousness monologue in *Ulysses* is the last word in fictional realism, however much it may have widened the new chasm between vanguard fiction and the popular audience. This was a separation that James himself regretted and deplored, unlike the critics who followed his wake.

Even in its many experimental adventures and deformations, the novel remained the wild child of literature, the natural son that could never be fully legitimated. While making the case for realism, craftsmanship, and imagination in fiction, James confirms its essential character as an open and indeterminate form, oriented toward life rather than self-referential. "Many people speak of it as a factitious, artificial form, a product of ingenuity," James writes, only to insist that the contrary is true: "Catching the very note and trick, the strange irregular rhythm of life, that is the attempt whose strenuous force keeps Fiction upon her feet" (p. 58).

This openness toward life is one of the key features of Mikhail Bakhtin's theory of the novel, the only modern theory that does full justice to the novel as a mixed and indeterminate genre, an uncompleted genre constantly in process of formation. Bakhtin's view helps account for the fierce resistance to fiction by the upholders of culture, for he sees the novel not as a genre like epic and tragedy but as a parodic, destabilizing force which renovates older genres but also "infects them with its spirit of process and inconclusiveness."[21] Even in ancient times, he argues, the spirit of the novel was one of contemporaneity, a spirit which undermined the classical vision of "a world projected into the past, on to the distanced plane of memory, but not into a real, relative past tied to the present by uninterrupted temporal transitions; it was projected rather into a valorized past of beginnings and peak times."[22] In Bakhtin's theory, epic and tragedy are completed genres in which the "past is distanced, finished

21. M. M. Bakhtin, *The Dialogic Imagination*, ed. Michael Holquist (Austin: University of Texas Press, 1981), p. 7.
22. Ibid., p. 19.

and closed like a circle." The novel, on the other hand, with its deflationary immediacy, its self-consciousness about genre, and its awe before the mystery of individual behavior, embodies the spirit of modernity that resists the closure of genre and recreates the open weave of life itself.

This carefully created illusion that fiction gives us life "*without rearrangement*," without artifice, is deeply ingrained in the early history of the novel. It helps explain why the novel was so long ignored or viewed with suspicion by critics and aestheticians. In its transparency and popularity it remained a challenge to literary history, and it violated classical decorum in both its style and subject. Arguing against those who hoped to see fiction *elevated* into art, purified of its gross realism (especially the French kind), James wrote that "art is essentially selection, but it is a selection whose main care is to be typical, to be inclusive" (p. 58). If Defoe was our first novelist, it was partly because he seemed so artless and unselective, so rooted in matter-of-fact. In *Factual Fictions* Lennard J. Davis has written a convincing study of the origins of fiction in the journalism of the eighteenth century. Davis's starting points are the many assertions of documentary veracity that distinguished early novelists from writers of romance, who trafficked in the marvelous, the exotic, and the improbable. Thus Lord Chesterfield described a romance as "twelve volumes, all filled with insipid love, nonsense, and the most incredible adventures." According to Dr. Johnson, "Why this wild strain of imagination found reception so long, in polite and learned ages, it is not easy to conceive." The novel, on the other hand, in the words of Clara Reeve, "gives us a familiar relation of such things, as pass everyday before our eyes, such as may happen to our friend, or to ourselves and we are affected by the joys or distresses of the person in the story, as if they were our own."[23] If the novelists of the period, says Davis, "refused to concede that they were writing fiction, perhaps it was because fiction was too limiting a concept for them; they were in their own sense of themselves still writing news—only,

23. Quoted by Davis, *Factual Fictions*, pp. 103–104.

in this case, news stripped of its reference to immediate public events."[24]

Daniel Defoe is the crucial case, the prototype of the journalist-turned-novelist who did not even take up fiction until he was nearly sixty. In his own time he was known almost exclusively as a prolific journalist and political pamphleteer. "Defoe the great novelist is an invention of the nineteenth century," says Pat Rogers. "In his own day . . . he was thought of as a controversialist."[25] After his death he was forgotten for decades. Yet *Robinson Crusoe* stood apart from his other work to become perhaps the most famous book of the eighteenth century, as widely read and frequently imitated on the continent as in England and America. *Robinson Crusoe*'s position in the history of the novel is likely never to be fully pinned down, for some of the very qualities that make Defoe a novelist also separate him from most of his successors. The flatness of his prose is part of his remarkable realism of circumstantial detail, yet it carries over into a flatness of emotional tone that limits the subjective element so important to fictional realism. Though Defoe's novels are cast as autobiographical narratives, his protagonists are too engrossed in the struggle for existence to waste much time on feeling or sensibility. The psychological novel begins with Richardson rather than Defoe or Fielding.

Robinson Crusoe creates special difficulties for the historian of fiction. Though it is often described as the first English novel, its isolated setting and lonely hero belong more to the exotic realm of travel writing, adventure, and romance than to the social world of the novel. Davis is only the most recent of many critics who express uneasiness with the accepted place of Defoe's novel at the head of the fictional line: "*Robinson Crusoe*, in many ways, seems like the wrong locus—the exquisitely wrong place—to begin a consideration of the origins of the novel. *Crusoe* is such an atypical work, so devoid of society, of human interaction, so full of lists and micro-observations."[26]

He goes on to suggest that perhaps it is precisely their art-

24. Davis, *Factual Fictions*, p. 192.
25. Pat Rogers, ed., *Defoe: The Critical Heritage* (London and Boston: Routledge & Kegan Paul, 1972), p. 4.
26. Davis, *Factual Fictions*, p. 154.

lessness, their intermediate status between fact and fiction, that accounts for the paradoxical centrality of Defoe's novels within the fictional tradition. If it is true that his novels have "no dazzling plots, not much in the way of form—just a kind of dogged attention to the cumulative details, to getting the story down on record,"[27] then this is peculiarly consistent with James's remark that "the air of reality (solidity of specification) seems to me to be the supreme virtue of the novel—the merit on which all its other merits . . . helplessly and submissively depend" (p. 53). This is a good explanation of Defoe's importance, as well as his ambiguous status, but it doesn't account for the special fame of *Robinson Crusoe,* which was universally known and read long before Defoe's other novels began to be rediscovered. The oddity of *Crusoe's* position dissolves when we see it as a landmark in popular culture, not just as the first English novel.

Though fiction itself, as we have argued, is prototypical of the popular arts, there are fictional genres and individual novels that have achieved a special hold on the popular imagination. Often these works compensate for their literary deficiencies— clumsiness of plot, shallow characterization, merely workman-like style—by their strength as parables or archetypes, their mythic force, or their psychological reverberations. Typically, the characters and their stories transcend the works themselves; they go into orbit as proverbial lore and get translated repeatedly into other media—into puppet shows, plays, comic books, and films, where they become known to many who have not read the originals, to many who can not even read. One of the marks of popular art, as Leslie Fiedler has argued, is that it depends so little on its original form, as if its author has accidentally tapped into a psyche much larger than his own, and made himself irrelevant in the process. The power of such works seems capable of surviving an infinite range of adaptation, simplification, even betrayal. Many critics and literary historians see these novels as merely crude and deficient, or worse still, pandering to mass taste, even when they themselves have helped create that taste. In the standard histories of literature these

27. Ibid., p. 155.

works are often peripheral or missing entirely, but when included they are consigned to a twilight zone, a no-man's land
between art and the popular imagination. If they come from
the pen of major authors—I'm thinking of *Crusoe* here, or
Cooper's Leatherstocking Tales, Poe's detective and horror stories, and Hawthorne's and H. G. Wells's prototypes of science
fiction—they slip in under the *auteur* theory, or as significant
items for cultural history or the study of genres. Other enduring
works like Bram Stoker's *Dracula* or Owen Wister's *The Vir-
ginian* are rarely admitted, despite their importance to the popular myths and genres that flow from them like irresistible
undercurrents in literary history.

   Though not strictly original themselves, these books initiate
vigorous, almost unkillable popular traditions. The mutations
of Gothic can be traced from Walpole's *Castle of Otranto* to the
most recent horror films. *Robinson Crusoe* gave rise to hundreds
of adventure novels, though Paul Zweig has argued that its hero,
cautious, calculating, and methodical, is anything but an adventurer himself.[28] Its influence is most obvious in boys' novels
and children's literature, but it can be found more subtly in
every variety of masculine action story, with its emphasis on
plot, its paucity of inwardness and complex emotion, and its
concentration on risk, physical action, individual fortitude, and
survival. I have already mentioned other genres and their pro-
genitors—Poe and the detective story, Cooper and the Western,
Wells and science fiction. There are also works which engendered indestructible myths—*Frankenstein, Dracula, Tarzan of
the Apes*. These and other novels could be discussed as anomalous popular fiction that tests the boundaries of the canon,
confounds traditional criticism, and stymies literary history. For
the remainder of this essay, however, I'll confine myself to the
strand of action and adventure that descends from *Crusoe* and
the strain of lurid sentiment and sensuality that is an important
element of Gothic. As a prototype for Gothic I'll use not the
frigid, cerebral *Castle of Otranto* but Matthew G. Lewis's genuinely terrifying and lubricious novel *The Monk* (1796), one of

28. Paul Zweig, *The Adventurer* (New York: Basic Books, 1974), pp. 113–
123.

the wildest excesses of Gothic fiction—an immensely popular
and scandalous work in its period. Between these two dialectical
poles I hope to cover a broad spectrum of popular fiction: masculine and feminine, natural and supernatural, behavioral and
psychological, asexual and hypersexual, action-oriented and
feeling-bound.

In one sense these popular novels seem to violate the prescriptions of Lawrence and James: they are elaborately formal, highly
patterned works. Lawrence writes that "in the novel, the characters can do nothing but *live*. If they keep on being good,
according to pattern, or bad, according to pattern, or even
volatile, according to pattern, they cease to live, and the novel
falls dead."[29] But when Lawrence set out to confront the classics
of American literature, he was quick to grasp the mythic and
psychological patterns in Cooper, Poe, Hawthorne, and Melville. Though many of their books were far from popular when
they first came out, the quasi-mythic patterns of American
romance are closer to popular fiction than to the European novel
of social realism. This didn't mean that the romance writer was
free of the need to be concrete and credible, within the limits
of his *donnée* or objective. "I can think of no obligation to
which the 'romancer' would not be held equally with the novelist," wrote Henry James. "The standard of execution is equally
high for each" (p. 56). In his famous comparison of *Treasure
Island*—one of *Robinson Crusoe*'s best-known descendants—
with a novel by Edmond de Goncourt about "a little French
girl," James wrote that "one of these productions strikes me as
exactly as much of a novel as the other, and as having a 'story'
quite as much. The moral consciousness of a child is as much
a part of life as the islands of the Spanish Main" (pp. 61–62).
James here is insisting on the eventfulness of his own fiction of
"moral consciousness" but his point is broader and cuts both
ways.
   Popular fiction generally combines a realism of detail with a
premise that is mythical, exotic, or formulaic. As Robert War-

29. Lawrence, "Why the Novel Matters," p. 537.

show says of popular film genres like the gangster film and the Western, "one goes to any individual example of the type with very definite expectations." In another essay he writes, "the proper function of realism in a Western movie can only be to deepen the lines of that pattern."[30] This may put too strict an emphasis on formula, not enough on the realism that makes the formula fresh and credible. The closer a piece of writing comes to the fantastic and the surreal, the more it depends on vivid details to make the fantasy believable. This was one of the lessons of Kafka's style that was lost on most of his imitators.

All fiction requires a degree of projection and identification on the reader's part, but popular works appeal more directly to the reader's (or viewer's) fantasy life and less to his sense of verisimilitude, his recognition of lived reality. Soap operas and pornographic works are extreme examples of stories that obey their own laws, with only occasional resemblances to the real world. They appeal to their audience's fantasy lives directly, within a self-enclosed setting. In a work like *Robinson Crusoe,* the enclosed setting is minutely realized, just as Kafka methodically constructs Gregor Samsa's life as an insect (in a story in which only the first sentence, the premise, stretches the laws of nature: everything else flows naturally from it). Thus Robinson Crusoe makes himself and his own life the object of almost scientific observation. This is Defoe's conception of the novelist's craft as well as Crusoe's character. After describing some of his own reactions to things, Crusoe writes: "Let the naturalists explain these things, and the reason and manner of them; all I can say to them is to describe the fact, which was even surprising to me when I found it."[31]

Within the popular novel, as in the traditions of the American romance, the relationship to nature is often more important than social relationships. *Robinson Crusoe* is a prototypical story of isolated man and the quest for survival apart from the props of social life. Crusoe is presented at the outset as an unskilled man who must learn all the crafts and skills on which human

30. Robert Warshow, *The Immediate Experience* (Garden City, N.Y.: Doubleday, 1962), pp. 130, 146.
31. Daniel Defoe, *Robinson Crusoe* (New York and Toronto: New American Library, 1961), p. 185.

survival was founded, from making clothes and hunting to boat-
building, agriculture, and the raising of domestic animals. (John
J. Richetti has written of "Crusoe's informal recapitulation of
the history of civilization."[32]) The book has been imitated in
other stories about survival influenced by Freud's account of
the conflict between biological man and social man, such as
William Golding's *Lord of the Flies* and Bernard Malamud's
recent *Crusoe* imitation, *God's Grace*. The latter work, like
other recent social fables, portrays a postnuclear devastation in
which the social structure has disappeared, leaving unaccom-
modated man to act out the logic of his own nature.

In the eighteenth century, this Freudian questioning of the
imperatives of civilization—or of a particular social order—was
a major theme of travel literature and its fictional imitations,
such as *Crusoe*, *Gulliver's Travels*, Montesquieu's *Persian Letters*, Voltaire's *Candide*, and Diderot's *Supplement to Bougain-
ville's "Voyage"*. The descendants of these works in the nineteenth
century were in the literature of adventure and the novel of
imperialism, such as Conrad's *Heart of Darkness*, where a jungle
of inner and outer horror takes the place of the seraglio of
Montesquieu and the island paradise of Diderot. This is a kind
of test-tube literature, a set of controlled experiments on human
nature, and its findings have darkened with the passage of time.
In the twentieth century this fundamental moral probing gives
a serious dimension to popular culture; each genre in its own
way tries to define the fringes and limits of civilization. Science
fiction is one obvious example, but Westerns and hard-boiled
detective novels also pursue this theme.

In the frontier setting of the Western, the rule of law and the
norms of society have either been suspended or are scarcely in
place. Like Crusoe on his island, the Western hero is an isolated
man who imposes his own kind of order in a world of moral
chaos and physical danger. But Crusoe is less a hero than a
survivor, a cunning and resourceful man. He is like the ordinary
Englishman raised to the highest power, nursing his fears, building barriers against the unknown, accumulating, defending, and

32. John J. Richetti, *Defoe's Narratives: Situations and Structures* (Oxford:
Clarendon Press, 1975), p. 50.

domesticating everything around him. Yet for all his homely virtues, his wanderlust was his original sin; his hankering for adventure and fortune made it impossible for him to follow the tepid, prudent advice of his father. Quiet times are anathema to him and lead him into spectacular errors of judgment; only danger brings out his skill, fortitude, and practical sharpness.

The hero of the Western is a transitional figure for a transitional stage of culture. When he creates at least a minimum of order out of a situation of lawless violence he renders himself irrelevant. Once evil has been expelled, as at the end of *High Noon*, he can remove his badge and fade away into the peaceful sunset of love and marriage, or, like John Wayne at the end of *Stagecoach*, to a ranch in Mexico where he will be "saved from the blessings of civilization." But in the detective novels of Dashiell Hammett, James M. Cain, Raymond Chandler, and Ross Macdonald, evil is not something that can simply be expelled by solving a crime or closing a case. The desert island and the wild frontier give way to the urban jungle whose mean streets reflect a corruption that seems implacable and ineradicable. Though these stories are set in populated towns and cities, the men charged with bringing order are as solitary as Crusoe and his man Friday, and as terse as the tight-lipped Man of the West.

Very few serious modern novels allow their characters to claim any real mastery over the world they live in, or even over their own inner lives. Only in popular culture do we find a remnant of the old heroes of epic, imperfect men who are now often implicated in the corruption of their environment. "Down these mean streets a man must go who is not himself mean, who is neither tarnished nor afraid," wrote Raymond Chandler in his famous tribute to the hard-boiled detective created by Dashiell Hammett and the *Black Mask* writers of the 1920s. Yet in the same essay in which he romanticizes this hero, he praises Hammett and the genre he created for their realism, at least in comparison to the cerebral and abstract puzzle-mysteries that preceded them: "Hammett gave murder back to the kind of people that commit it for reasons, not just to provide a corpse; and with the means at hand, not with hand-wrought dueling pistols, curare and tropical fish. He put these people down on paper as they were, and he made them talk and think in the language they customarily used for these purposes."[33]

Though Hammett's plots could be baroque and his style a little purple, in some ways he did to the murder mystery what Defoe had done to the literature of travel and adventure: he brought to it a new realism of detail and simplicity of style. At the same time he personalized it around the experiences of memorable and authentic characters. Perhaps under the influence of Hemingway as well as his own laconic personality, Hammett was a great believer in clean, simple, and direct writing. His biographer, Diane Johnson, has unearthed a miniature essay on style which he wrote for an advertising magazine in 1926. It attacks florid and gaudy writing not for being too literary but as "not sufficiently literary." The plain style, with the shortest sentences, he argues, is the hardest thing in the world for literature to achieve, and the last place we would find it is in a transcription of actual conversation:

There are writers who do try it, but they seldom see print. Even such a specialist in the vernacular as Ring Lardner gets his effect of naturalness by skillfully editing, distorting, simplifying, coloring the national tongue, and not by reporting it verbatim.

Simplicity and clarity are not to be got from the man in the street. They are the most elusive and difficult of literary accomplishments, and a high degree of skill is necessary to any writer who would win them.[34]

But Hammett not only knew his craft—he described himself in a letter, in a rare spasm of immodesty, as one of the few people interested in making "literature" of the detective story— he also knew his subject. How much Hammett had learned from

33. Raymond Chandler, *The Simple Art of Murder* (New York: Pocket Books, 1952), pp. 193, 190. The introduction and title essay of this volume are among the best statements ever made on the relation of genre fiction to serious art. Chandler writes, for example: "To exceed the limits of a formula without destroying it is the dream of every magazine writer who is not a hopeless hack" (p. ix).

34. Diane Johnson, *Dashiell Hammett: A Life* (New York: Random House, 1983), pp. 54–55.

observation, and from his experience as a Pinkerton agent, is clear enough from his fiction but also from another essay dug up by Johnson, this one on being a private detective, from the *Saturday Review*. With his usual brevity and understatement, Hammett itemizes twenty-four nuts-and-bolts details about weapons, wounds, corpses, fingerprints, and even criminal argot— all things that ignorant or indifferent detective-story writers usually get wrong. (These sometimes remind me of Blake's "Proverbs of Hell.")

6. When you are knocked unconscious you do not feel the blow that does it.

Others emerge jokingly from the trained ear of a writer who listens:

18. "Youse" is the plural of "you."

Still others have the patient, pedantic simplicity of a manual:

19. A trained detective shadowing a subject does not ordinarily leap from doorway to doorway and does not hide behind trees and poles. He knows no harm is done if his subject sees him now and then.

21. Fingerprints are fragile affairs. Wrapping a pistol or other small object up in a handkerchief is much more likely to obliterate than to preserve any prints it may have.[35]

Despite this emphasis on realistic detail, Hammett's wildly complicated plots are as far-fetched as his slangy dialogue is dated. Just as the brisk, busy action of *Robinson Crusoe* is framed by a religious allegory that resembles *Pilgrim's Progress,* the gang wars and innumerable murders in *Red Harvest,* Hammett's first novel, form a parable of corruption that touches even the detective himself. The Bunyanesque name of the town, Personville, has become "Poisonville"—toxic to all who pass through it, including the detective, who says: "I've arranged a killing or two in my time, when they were necessary. But this is the first time I've ever got the fever. It's this damned burg. You can't go straight here." Later he adds: "Poisonville is right. It's poisoned me." At one point he suspects himself of having

35. Ibid., pp. 88–89.

murdered the one person there who means anything to him—
a woman who is also the all-purpose traitor in a town in which
anyone will sell anything and betrayal is a way of life. The
detective cleans up the town in an unorthodox way, by setting
the rival gangs up against each other. But he's upset to find he's
begun to enjoy it: "I've got hard skin all over what's left of my
soul, and after twenty years of messing around with crime I can
look at any sort of a murder without seeing anything in it but
my bread and butter, the day's work. But this getting a rear
out of planning deaths is not natural to me. It's what this place
has done to me."[36]

The tough skin of the hard-boiled hero is like the defensive
shell Crusoe develops to survive on his desert island. He too
rarely lets moral qualms stand in his way. There are few moments in the book when Crusoe's motivation doesn't seem entirely secular, expedient, and self-interested. This leaves room
for many readers to ignore or doubt the importance of the
religious framework of the novel. Martin Green does not even
bother to argue that "the spiritual autobiography aspect of the
book is unimportant," because "everything that is vivid and
exciting in the book is independent of that framework."[37] The
best evidence for Green's position is that very few readers even
noticed this framework until scholars like G. A. Starr and
J. Paul Hunter made an issue of it in the 1960s.[38] Crusoe has
neither the depth nor the vocation for a protagonist of spiritual

36. Dashiell Hammett, *Red Harvest* (1929; New York: Vintage Books, 1972),
pp. 142–143, 145. There are good accounts of Hammett's work, and Chandler's,
by Julian Symons in his *Critical Observations* (New Haven and New York:
Ticknor & Fields, 1981), pp. 166–177, 156–165. See also his history of the
detective story, *Bloody Murder* (London: Faber and Faber, 1972) and Robin
W. Winks's anthology *Detective Fiction: A Collection of Critical Essays* (Englewood Cliffs, N.J.: Prentice-Hall, 1980). The best recent book is Stephen
Knight, *Form and Ideology in Crime Fiction* (London: Macmillan, 1980), which
deals with Chandler rather than Hammett, but is excellent on the early history
of crime fiction.

37. Martin Green, *Dreams of Adventure, Deeds of Empire* (New York: Basic
Books, 1979), p. 76.

38. G. A. Starr, *Defoe and Spiritual Autobiography* (Princeton: Princeton
University Press, 1965); J. Paul Hunter, *The Reluctant Pilgrim* (Baltimore:
Johns Hopkins University Press, 1966).

autobiography. Yet this motif recurs frequently enough in the
novel to dispel any hint of insincerity on Defoe's part. Still,
Crusoe's recurring bouts of self-accusation have so little connection to his practical skills and worldly motives that they call
to mind the rhetoric of sin, damnation, and redemption that
sometimes frames works of pornography. There too we sometimes find puritanical authors deeply immersed in all they condemn; there too it can be said that "everything that is vivid and
exciting is independent of that framework." There too, as in a
great deal of popular culture, there may be unresolved conflicts
of values rather than a deliberate cynicism. Or else a moral
framework may be a defense mechanism against the kind of
social censorship that is quick to condemn popular fantasies and
to insist on strict poetic justice.

Crime and detective stories are among the last outposts of
the kind of individualism that enters fiction with *Robinson Crusoe:* the belief in the power of the individual to solve problems,
to correct wrongs, and to control his own destiny. The classic
detectives like Dupin and Holmes express a nineteenth-century
faith in the power of mind to create order out of a welter of
mean motives and jealous passions. In the twentieth century
this kind of mastery survives *only* in popular culture, as a fantasy
which compensates for the widespread feeling that larger, more
impersonal forces now dominate the destiny of individuals. Heroism becomes a beleaguered and questionable idea. The hard-
boiled detective is very close to the moral chaos of his opponents, skirting the edge of the law in a world where law itself
has been bought and corrupted. His individualism has been
reduced from a belief in an ordered, rational society only temporarily out of balance to a mere personal code, a stubborn,
irrational insistence on some kind of individual honor among
grasping people in an insane and arbitrary world. "You'll never
understand me, but I'll try once more and then we'll give it up,"
says Sam Spade to Brigid O'Shaughnessy at the end of *The
Maltese Falcon,* as he's about to send her up. "Listen. When a
man's partner is killed he's supposed to do something about it.
It doesn't make any difference what you thought of him. He
was your partner and you're supposed to do something about
it." But he also has other, less honorable motives. Though he

loves the treacherous Brigid, again and again he says, "I'm not
going to play the sap for you." Later he adds, "Don't be too
sure I'm as crooked as I'm supposed to be."[39] Even some of the
killers in Hammett's world have the same stoical virtues. Of
one of them at the end of *Red Harvest* we're told, "He meant
to die as he had lived, inside the same tough shell."[40] This was
the way Hammett himself died, some thirty years later.

The moral chaos we find in hard-boiled fiction can also be found
in the Gothic novel going back to the eighteenth century. If
Robinson Crusoe comes at the beginning of a whole line of
masculine adventure stories, full of laconic, purposeful, un-
emotional heroes, the Gothic novel sets in motion a feminine
line of popular fiction—elusive, lubricious, impassioned, and
centered around female vulnerability rather than male mastery.
This is the most Freudian of all literary modes, built on dreams,
fears, and sexual fantasies to an amazing degree, and often
hedged about by a teasing moralistic framework. These episodic
works resemble modern serials and soap operas. J. M. S. Tompkins sums up the usual plot of an Ann Radcliffe romance in the
following way:

> They play, for the most part, in glamorous southern lands and belong
> to a past which, although it is sometimes dated, would not be recognized
> by an historian. In all of them a beautiful and solitary girl is persecuted
> in picturesque surroundings, and, after many fluctuations of fortune,
> during which she seems again and again on the point of reaching safety,
> only to be thrust back into the midst of perils, is restored to her friends
> and marries the man of her choice.[41]

In M. G. Lewis's *The Monk* there are no neat resolutions and
happy endings. Instead of picturesque surroundings we find grim

---

39. Dashiell Hammett, *The Maltese Falcon* (1930; New York: Vintage Books,
1972), pp. 226, 225, 227.
40. Hammett, *Red Harvest*, p. 197.
41. J. M. S. Tompkins, *The Popular Novel in England, 1770–1800* (1932;
London: Methuen, 1969), pp. 251–252. For a more detailed history of Gothic
fiction, see Devendra P. Varma, *The Gothic Flame* (1957; New York: Russell
& Russell, 1966).

convents and monasteries which sit atop secret passages and charnel-like catacombs where women are sadistically tormented and sexually abused under the guise of religious severity. The lawless isolation of the Gothic convent or castle is like a nocturnal phantasmagoria of Crusoe's solitude on his desert island. Both are northern, Protestant visions, one of industry, sublimation, and salvation through good works, the other of Mediterranean Catholic decadence, self-indulgence, and immorality.

The violent settings of Gothic novels go back to the Spanish and Italian locale of Elizabethan revenge tragedies and gory Jacobean dramas of lust, incest, fratricide, and religious hypocrisy. To this the writers add touches of the Restoration rake, Clarissa Harlowe's interminable, operatic defense of her innocence, and the new taste for medieval ballads, supernatural tales, German romances, graveyard poetry, and sublunar Romantic melancholy. The claptrap of Gothic exists on two levels, a mumbo-jumbo of trite superstition and cumbersome machinery and a deeper psychological penetration of the kind we meet in Ambrosio, the diabolical, depraved monk of Lewis's scabrous novel. When we first meet Ambrosio he is like Shakespeare's Angelo in *Measure for Measure,* a man so repressed and severe that he "scarce confesses / That his blood flows."[42] We hear it said that "too great severity" may be his "only fault" (p. 48), making him as harsh on others as he is on himself. But these rigid spirits are the first to fall, especially in a world so repressed, yet so saturated with desire, that even a glimpse of skin can evoke murderous, all-consuming passions. The core of *The Monk* is the same sex and violence that have been the mainstays of popular culture ever since. The moral and religious framework is a mere container for garish fantasies of sin and violation, sex and damnation. We are meant to identify with both the seducer Ambrosio and the virgins he despoils; the book plays on our fantasies of both omnipotence and vulnerability, violence and violation.

---

42. From the epigraph to chapter 1 of Matthew G. Lewis, *The Monk,* ed. Louis F. Peck (1952; New York: Grove Press, 1959), p. 35. Further references, identified by page numbers in the text, are to this edition.

Significantly, Ambrosio's own tutor in evil is an androgynous woman—really an agent of the devil—who has disguised herself as a boy to get close to him. In male action stories men flee from women, ignore them, or use and discard them. Robinson Crusoe does not even seem to be sublimating, as Gulliver does, for sex and women mean little or nothing to him. He lives in a daylight world of doing rather than feeling, surviving and accumulating rather than desiring. But the equally self-enclosed world of the Gothic novel belongs to the night-side of consciousness, full of irrational needs and sexual symptoms. Women are demonic goddesses in this world, figures of irresistible innocence or unfathomable deviousness setting up a fatal field of attraction in a secret world cut off from our norms of law and morality. The most lucid and consistent exponent of Gothic is the Marquis de Sade, who performs experiments on the parts of human nature Defoe leaves out.

One striking feature of *The Monk* that is still with us in recent horror films is the association of sex with terror, putrescence, and decay. The novel's two heroines, the innocent virgin, Antonia, and the pure but fallen woman, Agnes, end up imprisoned in dungeons beneath the holy convent. There Antonia is finally ravished and later stabbed by the lustful monk (actually her long-lost brother), who has been coveting her tender flesh through most of the novel, and Agnes actually gives birth to a baby, who eventually dies and decays under her very eyes. ("It soon became a mass of putridity, and to every eye was a loathsome and disgusting object, to every eye but a mother's" [p. 393].) Most of the novel is not quite this ghoulish, but when Agnes, who survives, tells her story, this is the kind of thing we hear:

My slumbers were constantly interrupted by some obnoxious insect crawling over me. Sometimes I felt the bloated toad, hideous and pampered with the poisonous vapour of the dungeon, dragging his loathsome length along my bosom. Sometimes the quick cold lizard roused me, leaving his slimy track upon my face, and entangling itself in the tresses of my wild and matted hair. Often have I at waking found my fingers ringed with the long worms which bred in the corrupted flesh of my infant. At such times I shrieked with terror and disgust;

and, while I shook off the reptile, trembled with all a woman's weakness. (pp. 395–396)

This reads like an unintentional parody of Edmund Burke's recent definition of the sublime as a form to beauty founded on terror, a catharsis of pain and fear. It could only have been written when religious ideas of heaven and hell had begun to lose their following and to migrate into pop mythology. Like some of the work of the Marquis de Sade, *The Monk* is a genuine product of that revolutionary decade, the 1790s, when the Enlightenment both came to fulfillment and turned into the Terror, with its dreams of reason transformed into the nightmares of unreason.[43]

Gothic novels, like detective stories and tales of adventure, are among the bastard children of literature, naked and artless in their emotional appeal yet artificial and formulaic in their literary strategies. They are stories in which the machinery of plot and atmosphere overshadows individual characters, yet this machinery and the people caught in it can reach us with surprising power, as they do in the last pages of *The Monk,* where the gruesome fate of Ambrosio takes on some of the fierce coloring of the downfall of Milton's Satan, and becomes a link to the Byronic criminal-heroes of the nineteenth century. Donald Fanger has shown how a significant strain of the Gothic and the grotesque runs through the great European realists like Balzac, Dickens, and Dostoevsky, and helps account for the heightened and intense effects they achieve.[44] The importance of the Gothic line in American fiction, from Brockden Brown, Poe, and George Lippard to Faulkner, Carson McCullers, and other Southern writers, has been discussed too frequently to need further comment here. Richard Chase explains this by arguing that

melodrama is suitable to writers who do not have a firm sense of living in a culture. The American novelists tend to ideology and psychology; they are adept at depicting the largest public abstractions and the smallest and most elusive turn of the inner mind. But they do not have

43. See Paul Zweig, *The Adventurer,* pp. 177–184.
44. See Donald Fanger, *Dostoevsky and Romantic Realism* (1965; Chicago: University of Chicago Press, 1967).

a firm sense of a social arena where ideology and psychology find a concrete representation and are seen in their fullest human significance.[45]

This is well formulated but also very much of its time, the 1950s, for it implies an aesthetic hierarchy in which social realism is the norm and melodrama the mutation, the despised variant, not fully formed, unevenly developed. This becomes clear when he remarks wittily that melodrama is "tragedy in a vacuum," or that "the American novel abounds in striking but rather flatly conceived *figures*" but "has been poor in notable and fully rounded *characters*."[46] But tragedy, canonical as it is, has been available to writers at only a few periods of Western cultural history, and "fully rounded characters" may not be what an author most needs to express the world as he imagines it.

Chase's remarks may help explain why Gothic has played such an important part in another branch of literary history: in women's writing. Ellen Moers devotes two important chapters in *Literary Women* to what she calls Female Gothic. This includes her famous interpretation of Mary Shelley's *Frankenstein* as a birth fantasy, built around "the revulsion against newborn life, and the drama of guilt, dread, and flight surrounding birth and its consequences." But comments like this may be too literal-minded to be of much use, as when Moers adds that "most of the novel, roughly two of its three volumes, can be said to deal with the retribution visited upon monster and creator for deficient infant care."[47] Perhaps a broader view of Female Gothic may be adapted from Chase's assertion that "melodrama is suitable to writers who do not have a firm sense of living in a culture." This is more true of women writers, deprived of any role in public life, barred from most economic activity outside

45. Richard Chase, *The American Novel and Its Tradition* (Garden City, N.Y.: Doubleday Anchor Books, 1957), p. 41.

46. Ibid., p. 40.

47. Ellen Moers, *Literary Women* (Garden City, N.Y.: Doubleday, 1976), p. 93. But Moers somewhat impoverishes the Gothic when she says it has only "one definite auctorial intent: to scare . . . to get to the body itself, its glands, muscles, epidermis, and circulatory system, quickly arousing and quickly allaying the physiological reactions to fear" (p. 90). This is like those who persist in seeing Hitchcock only as "the master of suspense."

the home, than it is for American writers in general. The themes
of enclosure, imprisonment, and victimization which are central
to Gothic have a quite realistic relation to women's lives in the
eighteenth and nineteenth centuries, however exotically they
appear in the novels. Melodrama abstracts women from a social
space where their behavior is constricted, into a realm of exaggerated feeling which is all the more intense for reflecting an
essential powerlessness. Male critics in turn have marked down
Gothic as second-rate literature or subliterature, having helped
create the social vacuum and psychological maelstrom which
defines the limits of the genre.

The surprising thing about the dismissal of Gothic from the
domain of literature is that, because of its hothouse atmosphere,
its artificiality, the form is intensely literary. We have a ster-
eotype of popular fiction as something transparent, artless, and
essentially unwritten. This is far from true of most Gothic writing, which tends often to be literary in the wrong sense: as
decorated or ornate as the architectural style to which it is
distantly indebted. The temptation for Gothic writers—or for
neo-Gothic filmmakers like Brian De Palma—is to turn their
work into exercises in style, leaving a good deal of human reality
behind. But the Gothic novel is also literary in a more serious
sense, in its elaborate structural complexities. The interminable
subplot of *The Monk* is a negative example, interestingly parallel
to the main plot but only tenuously and clumsily interwoven
with it. Important characters, including the protagonist Ambrosio, disappear for more than a hundred pages at a time,
suspended in mid-gesture while the reader seems to have fallen
into a different novel. But this eccentric architecture reflects
the labyrinthine vision of the novels.

Works like Mary Shelley's *Frankenstein* and Bram Stoker's
Dracula, which have come down to us in simplified film versions,
are prodigies of internal complexity; their stories, told in an
arch and elevated style, reach us by way of a hall of mirrors of
multiple narrators: fragments, confessions, letters, diaries, with
third-person accounts alternating with first-person accounts, as
if the essential reality were far too terrible to be approached
directly, as if the heart of the novel were a conundrum rather

than explanation. The morbid and shadowy mysteries of Gothic make the simpler mysteries of most detective stories seem like child's play rather than a truly problematic vision of the nature of things. "This secret is nothing at all," Edmund Wilson complained.[48] "A good writer," adds Geoffrey Hartman, "will make us feel the gap between a mystery and its laying to rest . . . Most popular mysteries are devoted to solving rather than examining the problem. Their reasonings put reason to sleep, abolish darkness by elucidation, and bury the corpse for good."[49] But all the creaky conventions of Gothic cannot conceal a more truly frightening depiction of human irrationality and vulnerability.

When these conventions are refreshed by a first-rate writer, like Melville and Hawthorne, or like Emily Brontë in *Wuthering Heights,* the wheels-within-wheels of Gothic narrative take on exceptional and mysterious power. *Moby-Dick,* with its heightened, claustral environment and baroque language, with Queequeeg's coffin and the deformed Ahab's obsessive pursuit of revenge, can be seen as a specimen of shipboard Gothic—a weird cross between Gothic and adventure.[50] Reading *Wuthering Heights,* like reading *Frankenstein* and *Dracula,* is like peeling away the layers of the onion or opening a series of Chinese boxes. The various narrators refract the tales through their own partial perceptions, giving us fragments of the past while amplifying what is terrible and strange about it. Realistic fiction, by contrast, aims at transparency, a world in which the social surface is continuous with the human reality. Thus Erich Auerbach in *Mimesis* stresses "the complementary relation between persons and milieu" in Balzac, as in Madame Vauquer's

48. Edmund Wilson, "Who Cares Who Killed Roger Ackroyd?" in Winks, *Detective Fiction,* p. 39.

49. Geoffrey H. Hartman, "Literature High and Low: The Case of the Mystery Story," in *The Fate of Reading and Other Essays* (Chicago: University of Chicago Press, 1975), pp. 210, 212.

50. For a suggestive study of Hawthorne's and Melville's relation to the novel as a "mixed medium" constantly exploring its own premises, see Richard H. Brodhead, *Hawthorne, Melville, and the Novel* (Chicago: University of Chicago Press, 1976). This book takes a quite Bakhtinian view of fiction, though it appeared before his essays on the novel were translated.

boarding house in *Le père Goriot,* where "sa personne explique
la pension, comme la pension implique sa personne."[51] But
Gothic novels, like many mystery stories, insist on the difference between surface and substance, between the clarity of
outward forms and the shadowy reality of inner motives and
intentions.

Why have Gothic and other forms of genre fiction been ignored or rejected by critics and literary historians, just as the
novel in general was long excluded from serious literature, just
as movies were consistently belittled as commercial entertainment when the greatest directors in film history had already
done their best work? There's probably no higher a proportion
of pure trash in popular culture than of mediocre, derivative
works in high culture, yet we judge poetry and drama by their
deepest reaches, not by their mean product. In the case of
Gothic, there's probably something in the outlook of the genre
that specially offends the critical mind, a lurid, garish vision of
life that sets our orderly procedures and rational assumptions
at nought. (Classical British detective stories may be the only
kind of genre fiction that doesn't do outrage to the academic
mind; that must be why so many dons dashed them off on the
side.)

Classically trained critics in the eighteenth and nineteenth
centuries condescended to fiction because, like its middle-class
audience, it lacked pedigree, decorum, and elevation of manner.
Its cast of characters was neither tragic nor dignified; its realist
aesthetic was antiformal; it blurred the lines between art and
life and broke sharply with the respected genres of ancient writing. But with the triumph of literary realism and the arrival of
a new breed of middle-class critic, the same animus was directed
against genre fiction—for being *too* formal, *too* generic. Now
its audience became the rabble who trampled on standards and
knew nothing about art, who abused their newly gained literacy
with trashy, mass-produced fantasies. The coming of modernism
sharpened the split between high and popular fiction by em-

51. Erich Auerbach, *Mimesis: The Representation of Reality in Western Literature,* trans. Willard Trask (1953; Garden City, N.Y.: Doubleday Anchor
Books, n.d.), pp. 413–415.

phasizing originality, difficulty, and experimentation and devaluing the formulaic, stereotypical elements which modern mass culture shares with the folk cultures of the past. It also led to a distrust of storytelling—the vital core of all narrative, from folklore and epic through nineteenth-century fiction. But the writers themselves rarely heeded this split, and always borrowed freely from every part of the cultural spectrum. Only the critics, sociologists, and literary historians drew sharp boundaries, routinizing the imaginative.

Well, we live in an age of Affirmative Action, even in cultural history. The academic establishment has grown so large that it's always hungry for new subjects, and since the 1960s a new generation has done much to enlarge the canon and to recuperate excluded works for critical study. We forget that in its own time even *The Great Tradition* was a work of recuperation, designed not to limit the English novel to five writers but to gain a more respectful hearing, within a slack and genteel literary culture, for the novel of controlled moral realism. In more recent years, the excluded traditions of blacks and women have been given rooms of their own in the academic structure—in critical studies, anthologies, and course assignments. We can see the beginnings of the same redress in popular culture as well, as the eclectic, antihierarchical spirit of the 1960s inspires a reshaping of the literary canon. Books like Paul Zweig's *The Adventurer*, John G. Cawelti's *Adventure, Mystery, and Romance*, Martin Green's *Dreams of Adventure, Deeds of Empire*, and Leslie Fiedler's *What Was Literature?* apply the same kind of critical attention to popular genres that has already been directed at such excluded categories as the bourgeois novel, the classic film genres, and the writings of blacks and women.

Some of these books on popular writers, like Green's and Fiedler's, have a distinct autobiographical tinge; they read like specimens of conversion literature by critics once committed exclusively to high culture. This gives their writings, especially Fiedler's, a proselytizing edge: a misplaced zeal for popular forms and a polemical bias against something called the "art novel," which evidently includes some of the best fiction ever written. The effect is to confirm the split between high and popular art by inverting it, and to keep popular culture in a gilded ghetto instead of integrating it into a broader, more pluralistic version of literary history. Like fiction as a whole, popular fiction since *Robinson Crusoe* has been created by new kinds of artists for audiences which had never existed before. Not all popular culture is art, but no conception of how art and culture have interacted over the last two and a half centuries can be complete without understanding the role it has played, the needs it satisfies, and the antipathies it arouses among conservative and nostalgic guardians of the old order.[52]

52. I am grateful to The Research Foundation of the City University of New York for its support toward the preparation of this essay.

BARBARA PACKER

Origin and Authority:
Emerson and the Higher Criticism

For, with each new study of the printed page, further
and further behind it, deeper and deeper into regions
where no man so much as undertakes to follow it,
retreats the power, which is for us all already, as
truly as if we had confessed it to ourselves, the
unknown, the unnamed.

> Delia Bacon, "William Shakespeare and His
> Plays"

In a distraught letter written from Waterford on 24 February
1832, Emerson's aunt, Mary Moody Emerson, tries to persuade
her nephew to reconsider his decision to abandon the ministry,
a decision she calls "parrisidical." She taxes him with aban-
doning the faith of his ancestors and the ministerial tradition of
his family; she contemptuously dares him to explain the pos-
tulates of his new, "intuitive" religion:

And may I ask what you mean by speaking of a great truth whose
authority you feel is its own? In the letter of Dec. 25 you ask "whether
the heart were not the Creator." Now if this withering Lucifer doctrine
of pantheism be true, what moral truth can you preach or by what
authority should you feel it?[1]

Mary's attack was shrewdly calculated to strike Emerson at his
weakest point, since the question of authority made him acutely
uncomfortable. The strange little catalogue of physical "ax-

1. Houghton Library. In an earlier letter on the subject of miracles (13 June
1826), Mary made a similar point: "If prophecy & miracles are none, what
proof of a revelation that would come with authority to the multitude?" Mary
Moody Emerson's letters are quoted by permission of the Houghton Library,
Harvard University, Cambridge, Mass.

67

ioms" translatable into moral truths in the "Discipline" section of *Nature* can be read as one of Emerson's many attempts to answer objections to his "withering Lucifer doctrine of pantheism." Moral truth depends on discrimination, rejection; if everything in nature is equally good, or emanates from the same divine heart, upon what principle can any action be recommended or forbidden? Emerson's need to find a principle of difference within natural law itself led him to pounce with glee upon Euler's Law of Arches: "This will be found contrary to all experience, yet it is true."[2] Euler here becomes a scientific counterpart of Jesus himself, whose Sermon on the Mount Emerson once described as "the utterances of the Mind contemning the phenomenal world."[3]

Natural law can corroborate moral intuition, but Emerson's real envy was reserved for the teacher whose axioms persuade without corroboration. In an early journal passage he observes: "It was said of Jesus that 'he taught as one having authority'—a distinction most palpable. There are a few in every age I suppose who teach thus" (*JMN*, III, 185). How do the others teach? The Gospel of Matthew identifies them: "For he taught them as one having authority, and not as the scribes."[4]

Scribes are the preservers and transmitters of a culture. They guard and pass on a text by whose authority they presume to

2. Euler's "sublime remark" is quoted in the "Idealism" chapter of *Nature*, in *The Collected Works of Ralph Waldo Emerson*, ed. Robert Spiller, Alfred R. Ferguson, et al. (Cambridge, Mass.: Harvard University Press, 1971–), I, 34; hereafter cited as *CW*.

3. *The Journals and Miscellaneous Notebooks of Ralph Waldo Emerson*, ed. William H. Gilman, et al., 16 vols. (Cambridge, Mass.: Harvard University Press, 1960–1982), V, 273; hereafter cited as *JMN*.

4. Matthew 7:28–29. Emerson preached several sermons on this text. The two complete versions in the Houghton Library are dated 30 May 1830 and 31 March 1832. In the first of them he writes: "A tone of authority cannot be taken without the truths of authority . . . Jesus hath it, but he has not monopolized it." In the second he repeats the assertion. Authority belongs to truth and is "not confined to the pure & benevolent Founder of Christianity but may & must belong to all disciples in that measure in which they possess themselves of the truth which was in him. Jesus has not monopolized it." Houghton Library; quoted by permission of the Houghton Library.

speak.[5] Yet their very fidelity to its language keeps them from sharing in its power. Can the canon ever be opened to new prophecy, and the truth liberated from the condition of mere reference? In an early journal Emerson sounds confident enough; he declares: "I will no longer confer, differ, refer, prefer, or suffer. I renounce the whole family of *Fero*. I embrace absolute life" (*JMN*, V, 53).

He had before him, of course, the example of Jesus, whose war with the Scribes of his own day had opened the canon to a whole new Testament. "Jesus Christ belonged to the true race of prophets," Emerson said in the Divinity School *Address*. "Alone in all history he estimated the greatness of man." In his "jubilee of sublime emotion" he speaks those truths heard by the bystanders with astonishment: "I am divine. Through me, God acts; through me, speaks" (*CW*, I, 81).

Yet the absolute authority of Jesus could not protect his message from undergoing a radical distortion at the hands of a new generation of scribes—scribes now of his own religion. In the Divinity School *Address* Emerson suggests that the real crucifixion was inflicted on Jesus not by the Romans but by his own followers, by the Christians who take the "high chant" from the prophet's lips and render it into squalid and murderous dogma: " 'This was Jehovah come down out of heaven. I will kill you, if you say he was a man' " (*CW*, I, 81).

Yet if scribes and prophets are perpetually at war, they are also perpetually dependent upon one another. The scribe gives us the text from which the prophet offers to liberate us; the prophet's message of liberation, if it is successful, is transmitted as dogma by the next generation of scribes. Then what does it mean to speak with authority? And what kind of authority can the record of that speaking possess? Can a text *ever* possess authority? Or is authority always out of reach behind the text it generates, an instant of pure power whose "sepulchre" is the scripture we mistakenly revere? These questions began as re-

5. On the relationship among priests, scribes, and prophets in Jewish culture, see Robert Gordis, *Koheleth—the Man and His Work: A Study of Ecclesiastes*, 3d augmented ed. (New York: Schocken Books, 1968).

ligious ones for Emerson, but since he thought of religion itself
as a kind of codified poetry, they quickly came to dominate his
poetic theories as well. These theories grow, in part, from the
circumstances under which he first encountered the authority
of texts.

The German biblical scholars whom Eichhorn called "the higher
critics" evolved their hypotheses about Ur-manuscripts, oral
traditions, manuscript derivation, and the like, to explain vexed
questions like the harmonies and variations among the synoptic
Gospels or the meaning of miracle stories. Their researches were
naturally of interest to a young man seeking to enter the ministry, and even more to a young man seeking to leave. Emerson's
interest in the technical side of the higher criticism did not
outlive the decade of struggle that ends with the Divinity School
Address. Eichhorn and Michaelis and Gieseler were scholars,
not visionaries; they never become permanent residents in
Emerson's mind, as Plotinus and Coleridge and even Sweden-
borg did. But if the complicated models of manuscript origin
and transmission the higher critics invented lost their primary
fascination for Emerson as his belief in "historical Christianity"
waned, they retained a powerful interest for him as models for
explaining a different kind of inspired text.

    When secular critics speak of the "authority" of a manu-
script, they are referring to its closeness to the author's original
manuscript or to the author's probable intentions, not its closeness to absolute truth. Even in secular criticism, attacks on
traditional datings or ascriptions could be felt to be deeply dis-
turbing, as the "Phalaris" controversy of the 1690s in England
shows.[6] But when the texts in question are the Old and New
Testaments, textual and moral authority tend to blend together:
whoever questions the first may subvert the second. Even the
great Richard Bentley, the "slashing Bentley" who demolished
the Epistles of Phalaris and rewrote Milton, was careful to assure

----

    6. On the "Phalaris" controversy, see R. C. Jebb, *Bentley* (New York: Harper
and Brothers, [1887]), chaps. 4 and 5; Hugh Kenner, *The Counterfeiters: An
Historical Comedy* (New York: Anchor Books, 1973), chap. 1.

subscribers to his proposed edition of the Greek New Testament in 1720 that "the author is very sensible, that in the Sacred Writings there's no place for conjectures or emendations."[7] But Bentley never published his edition. His biographer guesses that he gradually became troubled by "a growing sense of complexity in the problem of the text."[8] Unwilling either to betray his scholarly principles or to question the authority of his chief manuscripts, he left the vast project unfinished when he died.

Later scholars were less deferential. Throughout the eighteenth century biblical critics showed an increasing willingness to turn on the biblical texts the same principles of critical analysis that had been employed in the study of classical authors. E. A. Shaffer has argued that the premise that the Bible is to be approached like any other literary text, while apparently innocuous, had radical implications: it "entailed the freedom to amend the 'Holy Spirit' by establishing an accurate text, sifting the historical sources, questioning the traditional ascription of authorship and date, scrutinizing the formation of the canon, and comparing the Scriptures coolly with the sacred and secular writings of other nations."[9] Whatever the motives of the individual critics—and many were pious—the net effect of their procedures was to undermine substantially the "orthodox belief in the uniqueness of the Scriptures and their 'inspiration' by God."[10]

These practices were widely felt to be distressing, yet few serious theologians could afford to ignore the higher critical researches. Their evidence was too persuasive. In the early decades of the nineteenth century a number of American theologians studied the Germans assiduously, attempting to profit from their researches without being compromised by their skepticism.

7. Jebb, *Bentley*, p. 158.
8. Ibid., p. 161.
9. E. A. Shaffer, *Coleridge, "Kubla Khan," and the Fall of Jerusalem: The Mythological School in Biblical Criticism and Secular Literature, 1770–1880* (Cambridge: Cambridge University Press, 1975), p. 62.
10. Ibid., p. 21. Ralph L. Rusk points out that Waldo Emerson once asked William "to mark, in the works of Eichhorn or others, the passages that would tend to destroy a candid inquirer's belief in the divine authority of the New Testament." *The Life of Ralph Waldo Emerson* (New York: Columbia University Press, 1949), p. 152.

In *The Rise of Biblical Criticism in America,* Jerry Wayne Brown
has traced the various routes by which German biblical studies
reached New England. Joseph Buckminster, a young minister
who was to have been Harvard's first Dexter lecturer in sacred
literature (he died before he could assume the post) tried to
explain the significance of the new criticism to his countrymen
in a series of articles for the *Monthly Anthology;* he collected
a large library abroad, including many theological works, and
persuaded Harvard to sponsor a printing of Griesbach's definitive text of the New Testament. Andrews Norton, also a Dexter
lecturer (later professor), studied Eichhorn and Michaelis, though
he expressed anxiety about the skeptical habit of mind such
writers seemed to engender. Theodore Parker was a frank enthusiast who published translations from a variety of German
biblical scholars in a journal called *The Scriptural Interpreter,*
while George Bancroft and Edward Everett, both of Harvard,
actually studied in Göttingen with Eichhorn himself.[11]

Emerson's chances of coming into contact with the new ideas,
then, would have been great even if his older brother William
had not chosen to emulate Bancroft and Everett by traveling
to Göttingen in 1823 to study theology. But William's experiences there—his excited embracing of the new critical methods,
and the spiritual crisis they helped to precipitate—gave Waldo
Emerson an unusually vivid sense both of the importance and
the dangers of the new scholarship.

William Emerson arrived in Göttingen on 5 March 1824. He
found the difficulties of spoken German appalling, and for a
time was confined to conversing solely with his servant. But by
the time the spring semester began in May he was fluent enough
to begin attending Eichhorn's lectures on the first three evangelists. He soon came to revere Eichhorn as his "idol," and
credited Eichhorn's teaching and writings with effecting a surprising revolution in his mind. At first the excitement of this
revolution seemed wholly beneficial. In a letter to Waldo on 15

11. *The Rise of Biblical Criticism in America, 1800–1870: The New England
Scholars* (Middletown: Wesleyan University Press, 1969), chaps. 1 and 2.

August 1824, he wrote: "The effect of even these few months
of study I feel in every nerve of the moral frame. My moral
horizon seems incredibly widened . . . But do not think that I
am gloomy—I was never so happy before. My profession I love
better every day . . . And I ardently look foward to the time
when I shall enter upon the duties of a Christian minister in my
native land."[12] Twelve days later he sent another letter urging
Waldo to "read all of Herder you can get, and Eichhorn's critical, but not his historical works. If you have a taste for Hebrew,
cherish it—if not, borrow it from Herder."[13]

To one accustomed to the prevailingly rationalist tone of Unitarian scriptural commentary, with its careful weighing of prob-
abilities and marshalling of sensory evidences, the works of
Herder and Eichhorn must indeed have seemed revolutionary.
Herder's *Spirit of Hebrew Poetry* proposes "to set in their true
light, the obscure and misinterpreted histories of Paradise, of
the fall, of the tower of Babel, of the wrestling with the Elohim,
& c.,"[14] by treating the Bible as Oriental poetry, rather than as
theology or natural history. Its opening dialogue focuses on the
particular genius of the Hebrew language, and later dialogues
go on to explain things like Genesis and Job as typical forms
of Oriental moral fable. Throughout, Herder communicates a
passionate sense of the beauty of Hebrew poetry, its power and
freshness. Herder and Eichhorn were friends and correspon-
dents, and Eichhorn—who was actually a professor of Oriental
languages—also treated the Bible as Oriental myth, though he
went beyond Herder in extending this principle to the New
Testament as well as the Old.

Looked at in one way, Herder and Eichhorn seemed to offer
a way of rescuing the Scriptures from decades of Enlightenment
scorn. "Rational" Christianity had tried to fight the enemy with
its own weapons, and had ended up by ceding to it ever larger
amounts of territory. This new method offered a new hope. The

12. Karen Lynn Kalinevitch, "Ralph Waldo Emerson's Older Brother: The
Letters and Journal of William Emerson" (Ph.D. diss., University of Tennessee,
1982), p. 129.
13. Ibid., p. 136.
14. J[ohann]. G[ottfried]. Herder, *The Spirit of Hebrew Poetry*, trans. James
Marsh, 2 vols. (Burlington, Vt., 1833), I, 18.

higher criticism made it possible to see Genesis not as inept science but as Oriental fable; the miracles of Jesus not as tricks played by a charlatan but as natural events transformed both by the intense emotions of the viewers and by the hyperbolic style of Oriental poetry.

But such explanations clearly cut both ways. If the Bible resembles other Semitic literatures and can be explained by comparison with them, does it not lose in authority what it gains in comprehensibility? The scholar may feel he has solved the problem of miracles by identifying them as a common *topos* of Oriental religious narrative, but the average Christian is likely to find the explanation more distressing than the problem itself. William's letters home betrayed no hint of the spiritual crisis that had been gradually overtaking him, but he found his faith in the tenets of revealed religion deeply shaken by the critical questions he had been learning to ask. He made a pilgrimage to the aged Goethe in Weimar to confess his doubts and ask for advice. Goethe urged him not to abandon the ministry just because he could no longer in good faith claim to share all of his parishioners' beliefs; he thought that William could preach to the people what they wanted while keeping his private opinions to himself. William's problem must have been a common enough one among religious young men of that era, and Goethe's advice was doubtless not as cynical as it sounds: a learned clergyman might deviate widely from his parishioners' interpretation of particular dogmas and still share with them the essential elements of faith.[15]

But a violent storm during the homeward voyage forced William to confront his conscience with particular honesty, and when he returned home he announced his plans to abandon the ministry altogether. And a letter Aunt Mary wrote to Waldo several years after William's return indicates that the latter's skepticism was even more radical than his family had then supposed. She is apparently recording a conversation she had with William on theological subjects, including the one that was to involve Waldo himself in so much controversy after the Divinity

---

15. On William's visit with Goethe, see Kalinevitch, "Emerson's Older Brother," pp. 20–26, and Rusk, *Life,* p. 112.

School *Address.* "Wm has obliged me by his frankness—he attaches no infamy to his situation—thinks Hume's arguments against miracles never answered." She marvels at the "strange apathy of the sceptics of this period . . . who have been born under so terrible an influence as to enjoy existence without a God." And she angrily rejects the higher critics' attempt to treat the Bible as fable. "It may have a truth of infinite weight like other fables. But it is not a fable I know. It answers to the living conscience of God's impress on the soul. It develops the divinity within. Not the poetic gospelless divinity of German idealism."[16]

Mary's response to the new ideas William brought home from Germany had not always been so hostile. "German" material figures prominently in a letter she wrote to Waldo in 1826 as part of their ongoing theological debate. She discusses with casual confidence the opinions of Gesenius, Eichhorn, and Michaelis, noting with approval the latter's proof of the genuineness of the Gospels but rejecting as unnecessarily complicated his theories of manuscript transmission.[17]

Her real command of the subject was probably not very great, any more than Waldo's was. Where they were not dependent upon William's accounts, they relied on a handful of secondary sources and English translations. But if these latter were no substitute for German philological and theological training, they at least could give an interested reader a summary of the chief ideas in the movement and a history of their development. Emerson cribbed shamelessly from two such sources for a lecture he gave on the origin of the three first Gospels in the spring of 1831: the "Dissertation on the Origin of our Three First Canonical Gospels" affixed by Bishop Herbert Marsh to the final volume of his translation of Michaelis' *Introduction to the New Testament,* and Bishop Connop Thirlwall's long "Introduction" to his translation of Schleiermacher's *Critical Essay upon the Gospel of St. Luke.* Marsh's translation was published in 1803; Thirlwall's, in 1825. Both men attempted to give a history of the various theories on the subject up to their own day, so that Emerson was able to give a sense of historical sweep

16. Letter to Ralph Waldo Emerson, August 1829, Houghton Library.
17. Letter to Ralph Waldo Emerson, 27 April 1826, Houghton Library.

simply by splicing pieces of their writings together—though the resultant text is uneven in style and tone, since Marsh's scholarly convolutions differ markedly from Thirlwall's urbane ironies.[18]

But Emerson, like a desperate undergraduate, was in no condition to care much about the consistency of the manuscript he confected. The lecture on the three Gospels was part of a series of "vestry lectures" on scriptural subjects given for young people during the closing months of his ministerial career. They came at a time of great personal stress. His young wife Ellen had died only a month before the first lecture began; by the time the series was over he had reached his decision to resign from the ministry.[19] Still, if he cannot really be said to have *composed* the lecture on the three first Gospels, the manuscript at least demonstrates his interest in details of the scholarly controversy.

The controversy about the origin of the synoptic Gospels was one of the chief concerns of biblical criticism in the later eighteenth century; in 1793 the University of Göttingen proposed it

18. Marsh's translation of Michaelis' augmented fourth German edition of the *Introduction to the New Testament*, 2d. ed., 4 vols. (London, 1802), was one of the works checked out of the Harvard College Library by Charles or Edward Emerson for Waldo's use, according to library records. Marsh's translation was checked out on 28 February 1831. See Kenneth Cameron, *Ralph Waldo Emerson's Reading* (Raleigh, N.C.: Thistle Press, 1941), p. 46. Thirlwall's translation of Schleiermacher's *Critical Essay* (London, 1825) was in Emerson's own library (hereafter cited as *CE,* with page number, in the text). See Walter Harding, *Emerson's Library* (Charlottesville, Va.: University of Virginia Press, 1967).

19. Ellen died on 8 February 1831; the volumes of Michaelis were checked out of the Harvard Library only twenty days later for a series of lectures that began on 8 March. The lecture labeled "Origin of Three First Gospels" was no. 4 in the series; it was delivered on 29 March. The series was supposed to contain thirty-six lectures (only six of which are extant); by October of 1831 Emerson had given twenty-two of them and was already troubled both by growing religious doubts and by a "positive dislike of the church." Rusk, *Life,* p. 159. The six extant lectures, with notes on sources, have recently been edited by Kenneth Walter Cameron and published under the title *The Vestry Lectures and a Rare Sermon* (Hartford, Conn.: Transcendental Books, 1984).

as the topic for a prize dissertation.[20] The perplexing combination of harmony and variation among the first three Gospels led an increasing number of scholars to attempt an explanation of their origin and derivation. Some supposed that the later evangelists copied from the first written Gospel (whichever that was); others supposed that all three drew from a common source— either a document or an oral tradition—supposed to contain an outline of the teachings of Jesus and the principal events of his life.

The mere fact of variations among the Gospels had always been recognized, of course. In the prologue to his *Tale of Melibee* Chaucer says:

> . . . ye woot that every Evaungelist,
> That telleth us the peyne of Jhesu Crist,
> Ne saith nat alle thynge as his felawe dooth;
> But natheless hir sentence is all sooth,
> And alle acorden as in hire sentence,
> Al be ther in hir tellyng difference.[21]

But once biblical critics left behind Chaucer's tolerant concentration on the "sentence," their attempts to explain how and why the "tellyng" differed threatened essential Christian beliefs. Connop Thirlwall remarks how frequently it is asserted "that the hypotheses which have been invented to explain the relation of our three first Gospels to each other tend to destroy the reverence with which Christians are accustomed to regard these works as Holy Writ and containing the word of God." He locates the reason for this hostility in "the alleged inconsistency of these hypotheses with the inspiration of the gospels" (*Critical Essay*, p. x).

Thirlwall admits that all the various hypotheses he describes are indeed "equally and decidedly irreconcilable" with a notion of inspiration that sees the evangelists as "merely passive organs or instruments of the Holy Spirit." But a more liberal under-

20. Marsh, "Dissertation on the Origin of our Three First Canonical Gospels," in Michaelis, *Introduction*, vol. III, pt. 2, p. 24.

21. *The Works of Geoffrey Chaucer*, ed. F. N. Robinson (Boston: Houghton Mifflin, 1961), p. 167.

standing of "inspiration" need not find anything unsettling in
the idea that the evangelists depended upon *human* sources for
their material. He argues that critical study of the Gospels is
neither degrading to their authors nor fatal to their credibility
(*CE,* p. xi).

What are the hypotheses Thirlwall surveys? He gives a highly
condensed account of the preceding century's debate, which
began when a critical study of the three first evangelists had
discovered in their texts a complicated pattern of harmony and
variations that could not be explained by traditional accounts
of their composition. Two chief modes of explanation for these
phenomena were devised, and divided learned opinion between
them:

> The first was the hypothesis that the later evangelists borrowed from
> the writings of the earlier. This theory of course admitted of a great
> variety of modifications. Any one of the three might be supposed the
> original, and either of the other two might be supposed to have drawn
> from him, and the third from either or both of the two former. The
> precedence was accordingly assigned in a different order by different
> critics, and almost every possible shape of the hypothesis found an
> advocate. The second mode of explanation which suggested itself was
> the hypothesis that all the three evangelists, or at least two of them,
> drew from some common source. This hypothesis is likewise susceptible
> of many forms. For not only might there be several sources or one,
> but, if only one, this one might be either oral tradition or a written
> document; and if the latter, that might either be imagined so copious
> as to occasion different selections, or so scanty as to occasion different
> enlargements.   (*CE,* p. vii)

With hypotheses of the first class neither Marsh nor Thirlwall
is really concerned. Marsh gives a rather laborious summary of
their chief permutations, but he regards them as superseded by
theories that conjecture a single original *document* from which
all Evangelists drew. Michaelis (1782) argued for the existence
of a common Greek document; Lessing (1784) thought the language of the original must have been Aramaic. Eichhorn (1794)
tried by a complicated scheme of analysis actually to recover,
or reconstruct, the original document: it contained "a short but
well connected representation of the principal transactions of
Christ, from his baptism to his death." Marsh's own hypothesis

is a variant of Eichhorn's; he conjectures various redactions in various languages intervening between the Ur-Gospel (which Marsh designates by the Hebrew letter aleph) and the received Gospels; he publishes a complicated stemma showing the derivation of each Gospel from these redactions.[22]

Thirlwall regards Eichhorn and Marsh with amused disbelief. His arguments against the existence of an Ur-Gospel are various; the chief of them concerns the nature of the supposed document, as Eichhorn reconstructs it, which is in places so laconic as to be unintelligible to all save its author, in others is full of "superfluous details" (*CE,* p. xxviii). Thirlwall's grotesque metaphor for the document reminds one of Pope's comparison of textual critics to Medeas offering "new Editions" of old Aeson:

Its peculiarity is, that it is neither a full body nor a dry anatomy; it rather presents the appearance of a disjointed skeleton, in which some of the bones are missing, others out of their place, and the interstices are here and there covered with a fragment of skin or flesh. (*CE,* p. xxx)

Nor is Eichhorn's complicated method of accounting for the generation of our present Gospels from this repellent cadaver very convincing. Emerson does not appear to have read far into the text of the *Critical Essay* itself, but Schleiermacher's "Introduction" contains a passage of gentle mockery that Emerson liked well enough to incorporate in his own lecture.

For my part, I find it quite enough to prevent me from conceiving the origin of our three Gospels according to Eichhorn's theory, that I am to figure to myself our good evangelists surrounded by five or six open books, and that too in different languages, looking by turns from one into another, and writing a compilation from them. I fancy myself in a German study of the eighteenth or nineteenth century, rather than in the primitive age of Christianity; and if this resemblance diminishes perhaps my surprise at the well-known image having suggested itself to the critic in the construction of the hypothesis, it renders it the less possible for me to believe that such was the actual state of the case. (*CE,* pp. 6–7)

22. Marsh, "Dissertation," pp. 18–43, 194–202.

But if Eichhorn's methods of analysis and reduction cannot recover the origin of the Gospels, where is it to be found? Thirlwall considers toward the end of his long account of the controversy the hypothesis of Gieseler, who argued that the source of the Gospels must have been not a document but an oral tradition. Like all critics, Gieseler argues partly from internal evidences. Verbal agreement among the Gospels is greatest in passages of importance, or in recordings of the sayings of Jesus, and least in transitions and connecting passages—a fact that suggests that the most significant traditions were committed to memory, while the method of arranging them was left to the discretion of the individual evangelist. But many of Gieseler's arguments grow out of a concern for the social and religious circumstances of primitive Christianity. Literacy was rare among the lower classes in Palestine; Jewish tradition favored oral rather than written transmission of doctrine; the language of the apostles suggests that oral communication was the chief mode of public instruction in their day; the earliest Christians could have had no wish to replace the books of the Old Testament, which it was "the great object of their ministry to expound," with a new scripture of their own. The apostles, who lived together for a time in Jerusalem after Christ's death, by repeating among themselves and to their converts the chief sayings of Christ and the major events of his ministry, gradually evolved "an historical cyclus," and this Aramaic epic was eventually translated into Greek. (Gieseler cites historical parallels for such oral collections in the rabbinical and Druidical traditions, which both attest that complicated material can be handed down intact through many generations. And he also refers to the well known passage in Plato's *Phaedrus* concerning the superiority of oral tradition to written documents; *CE,* pp. cxvi–cxxvi.)

From this cyclus individual Christians may indeed have made written transcriptions, but these were individual selections made for private use. Then how and why were four Gospels alone accepted as canonical, and hence divinely inspired? The most unsettling—and potentially intoxicating—of Gieseler's revelations concerns this matter of canonicity. He points out that for over one hundred years following the death of Christ, no *writ-*

ings at all had acquired canonical rank in the Church. The evangelical citations of the apostolic fathers are never to written documents but rather to "the words of Christ" or "the words of the Lord." The need for written Gospels arose only when false teachers and Heresiarchs like Marcion began making misleading selections from the original cyclus and leading the faithful astray. At this point the primitive Church found it necessary to adopt the "most authentic works" of the apostolic age "as a rule and badge" for Christians; "and thus our Canonical Gospels, about the middle of the second century, were introduced into general and public use, and thenceforth became the objects of constantly increasing veneration" (*CE,* pp. cxxxii–cxxxix).

Emerson's collection of extracts from Marsh and Thirlwall traces what is apparently a simple progression in the history of higher critical theory. From three sacred and authoritative texts, to one primary text and two others derived from it, to a document (the Ur-Gospel) prior to all three canonical Gospels, to an oral cyclus from which all written accounts derive—with each step the source grows more numinous and less accessible, with an authority that is absolute at the source and perpetually dwindling in transmission. The Ur-Gospel is more "original" than the three synoptic Gospels we possess, and the oral cyclus is more original still. But at every step the number of editors and redactors between the original Gospel and its final textual incarnations grows, and with this distance arise the possibilities for error and distortion. Perhaps more significant, believers in the oral hypothesis treat the decision to canonize only four of the redactions as a human one, prompted by historical necessity. Is "inspiration" then the power that engenders the text, or merely the honorific title it receives, like a posthumous decoration, from the community that has decided to declare it canonical?

Emerson had reason to be attracted to the oral hypothesis: attracted equally by the power and mystery of the spoken source it imagined and by the impotence of that source to limit the number or content of its derivatives. In the Divinity School *Address* he complains bitterly of the resentment felt by the young man who is "defrauded of his manly right in coming into nature, and finding not names and places, not land and professions, but even virtue and truth foreclosed and monopolized" (*CW*, I, 82). The oral hypothesis suggested instead a Gospel infinitely generous, infinitely generative, like the "one central fire" of *The American Scholar* that flames first "out of the lips of Etna," then "out of the throat of Vesuvius" (*CW*, I, 66). The notion that the Gospels had once been a poetic cyclus of orally transmitted legends and apothegms from which each believer was free to make his own selection, the notion that the canon of Scripture was a product of human choice and hence open to human revision—both appealed strongly to a young prophet alternately resentful of tradition and ambitious to be included in it.

So strong was the appeal of the oral hypothesis to Emerson, in fact, that he was willing to distort his sources considerably to make his brief history end with Gieseler's triumph. For in truth both Schleiermacher and Thirlwall reject the oral hypothesis. Both are sure that *written* documents must lie at the origin of our canonical Gospels—not a single document, as Eichhorn believed, but a collection of them. The final pages of Thirlwall's introduction, in fact, consist of a point-by-point refutation of Gieseler. We know that Emerson read these pages, since he lifts whole paragraphs from them. But he quotes only Thirlwall's summaries of Gieseler's doctrines, never the refutations that follow them (*CE*, pp. cxxix–cliv). Julie Ellison has recently written of Emerson's attraction to tendencies in his intellectual culture that enhance "the critic's power over the text he interprets and the scholar's power to shape myth and history retroactively."[23] The lessons Emerson learned from the higher criticism he turned immediately on the higher critics themselves, shaping their own histories to suit his needs.

Most of the obvious effects of Emerson's crash course in the higher criticism are short-lived and relatively nugatory. The only full-scale exercise in higher critical interpretation he ever attempted is the sermon he preached to his congregation outlining

---

23. *Emerson's Romantic Style* (Princeton, N.J.: Princeton University Press, 1984), p. 5.

his reasons for wishing to abolish or radically alter the communion ritual. "The Lord's Supper" is an odd pastiche of Unitarian rationalism and higher critical attempts to reinterpret Jesus's words at the Last Supper by imaginatively reconstructing the cultural context out of which they arose.[24] But the seriousness of Emerson's need for the new scholarship is called into question by the cosmic insouciance of the final "argument" he advances against the rite: "That is the end of my opposition to it, that I am not interested in it."[25] The higher criticism offered reassurance to anyone seeking to locate authority within the self rather than outside it, but the man who dismisses a sacrament because it bores him could probably have reached his conclusions without scholarly help.

Traces of higher critical jargon are present in the Divinity School *Address* too, of course, but they are used in ways that are provocative rather than systematic. Like most young intellectuals, Emerson enjoyed baiting his elders with offensive terminology. *Nature* had annoyed the Harvard Lockeans with terms taken from the post-Kantian Idealists; the Divinity School *Address* flaunts the jargon of the higher critics with similar intent to annoy. "Oriental" is one code word: by referring to the Bible as "the Oriental scriptures" Emerson invokes one of the movement's central strategies—interpreting the Bible as Oriental poetry, poetry with obvious parallels in other Near Eastern literatures.[26] Another identifying badge is the use of Latin words like "cultus" and "cyclus" and even the mock-Latin "mythus." German scholars used Latin words as technical terms, and in imitating them Emerson hopes both to suggest their attitude and share in their prestige. When he finishes the innocent exordium of his address and asks his hearers to consider "the Christian Church," his sudden display of learned detachment is more provocative than frank blasphemy: "As the Cultus, or established worship of the civilized world, it has great historical

24. I am indebted to the Rev. Gary Hall for this observation.
25. *The Complete Works of Ralph Waldo Emerson*, ed. Edward Waldo Emerson, Centenary Edition, 12 vols. (Boston and New York: Houghton Mifflin, 1903–04), XII, 24; hereafter cited as *W*.
26. On the strategy of comparing Biblical texts with other Oriental literatures, see Shaffer, *Coleridge*, pp. 20–21.

interest for us." (A sentence like this makes one understand why Andrews Norton eventually grew to distrust German scholarship so much that he refused to allow his son even to study the language. As Renan observed later in the century: "In Germany, Voltaire would have been a professor in the faculty of theology."[27])

The names and technical vocabulary of the higher critics largely vanish from Emerson's journals and published writings after the Divinity School *Address;* but their sophisticated models for imagining the relationship between inspiration and text continued to fascinate him long after his brief interest in the origin of the Gospel texts had flickered out. They offered a way out of the impasse Emerson could not help creating for himself whenever he tried to explain the relationship between *poetic* inspiration and the text it eventuated in.[28]

His attitude toward poetry was from the beginning complex and frequently self-contradictory. In one mood, he could rebel against the authority of texts revered as canonical (hence all those fierce denunciations of influence in "The American Scholar"), but in another mood he could deplore the triviality of modern literature and long for the rigors of a sacred poetry whose inspiration was as unquestionable as its vision was unswerving. Writing of the poet in *Representative Men,* he said: "There have been times when he was a sacred person: he wrote Bibles, the first hymns, the codes, the epics, tragic songs, Sybilline verses, Chaldean oracles, Laconian sentences, inscribed on temple walls. Every word was true, and woke the nations to new life. He wrote without levity and without choice" (*W,*

27. On Andrews Norton's distrust of German scholarship, see, Conrad Wright, *The Beginnings of Unitarianism in America* (Boston: Starr King Press, 1955), p. 76. Renan's remark is quoted by Shaffer, *Coleridge,* p. 201.

28. As Shaffer remarks, "the men who were prepared to apply the methods of secular literary criticism to the Bible were naturally quick to carry the results of their Biblical criticism back into secular literature." And she adds: "The intricate relationship between *critica sacra* and *critica profana* in this period has never been traced." *Coleridge,* p. 63.

IV, 269). From the severe heights of this ethical absolutism, even the greatest of aesthetic poets can receive a stinging rebuke. Emerson freely concedes that Shakespeare was the greatest poet in the world. But what did his genius produce? "He converted the elements which waited on his command, into entertainments. He was master of the revels to mankind" (W, IV, 217). Emerson sees the plays as a tragic—maybe even a sinful—perversion of genius: "One remembers again the trumpet-text in the Koran,—'The heavens and earth and all that is between them, think ye we have created them in jest?' " (W, IV, 217–18).

Yet in one of those sudden retreats into sanity that make him endearing, Emerson draws himself back from the brink of this militant intellectual terrorism. Would he really have *wanted* a Shakespeare who wrote "without levity and without choice"? Of course not. Look at what happened to the sacred writers. Like Shakespeare, they penetrated the secrets of nature and of man; all the elements waited on their commands: "And to what purpose? The beauty straightway vanished; they read commandments, all-excluding mountainous duty; an obligation, a sadness, as of piled mountains, fell on them, and life became ghastly, joyless, a pilgrim's progress, a probation" (W, IV, 219). A similar observation lies behind the poem "The Problem." In lines that even Yvor Winters conceded he would have admired had they been written by someone else, Emerson envies the creative genius of the artist whose miraculous and unconscious art is wholly subservient to God:

> The hand that rounded Peter's dome
> And groined the aisles of Christian Rome
> Wrought in a sad sincerity;
> Himself from God he could not free;
> He builded better than he knew;—
> The conscious stone to beauty grew. (W, IX, 7)

What constitutes the "problem" for Emerson is the distaste he feels at considering such a life and such an art for himself: "Why should the cowl on him allure / Which I could not on me endure?" (W, IX, 6). The poem begins and ends as a gently self-mocking meditation on the bad faith of the nineteenth-century medievalist, but the lament for lost power that forms the body of the poem is perfectly serious.

But *was* the conflict between the ethical and aesthetic uses of poetry really the source of our dissatisfaction with it? In darker moments Emerson suspected that something more fundamental lay beneath our persistent sense that all poetry is failed poetry. In "The Poet" he offers a fable about the origin of poetry that is as distressing as it is rhapsodic:

> For all poetry was written before time was, and whenever we are so finely organized that we can penetrate into that region where the air is music, we hear those primal warblings, and attempt to write them down, but we lose ever and anon a word, or a verse, and substitute something of our own, and thus miswrite the poem. The men of more delicate ear write down these cadences more faithfully, and these transcripts, though imperfect, become the songs of the nations.   (*CW*, III, 5–6)

This pre-existent Poem—like Gieseler's oral cyclus in the early days of Christianity—is potentially transcribable by everyone, but even the most determined of transcribers cannot capture it without error. It is a pretty fable to assert that "the sea, the mountain-ridge, Niagara, and every flower-bed, pre-exist, or super-exist, in pre-cantations, which sail like odors in the air, and when any man goes by with an ear sufficiently fine, he overhears them, and endeavors to write down the notes, without diluting or depraving them" (*CW*, III, 15), but the fiction begins to look demonic when one remembers the flat assertions of *Nature:* "Words cannot cover the dimensions of what is in truth. They break, chop, and impoverish it" (*CW*, I, 28). Whether the corrupting force is the personality of the writer or the inherent poverty of language, the poet is as doomed to distort his inspiration as the evangelist is to mutilate the integrity of that "oral cyclus" whose message of redemption he is only trying to transmit. First the precantation, then the poet, then the scholar, then the bookworm—each step in the decay of inspiration corresponds to one in the history of religion: first the Words of the Lord, then the evangelists, then the scribes, and finally the systematic theologians, who hear the good news and say: " 'This was Jehovah come down out of heaven. I will kill you, if you say he was a man' " (*CW*, I, 81).

Was there any alternative to this gloomy pattern of decline? Emerson experiments in places with a different model, one in which poetry could fight its own tendency to petrifaction by a sort of perpetual rhetorical motion. The long essay "Poetry and Imagination" begins with a discussion of natural metamorphosis as a perfect analogy for the imaginative act. Just as everything in nature "is on wheels, in transit, always passing into something else, streaming into something higher," so poetry must manifest a similar lability:

As the bird alights on the bough, then plunges into the air again, so the thoughts of God pause for but a moment in any form. All thinking is analogizing, and it is the business of life to learn metonymy. The endless passing of one element into new forms, the incessant metamorphosis, explains the rank which imagination holds in the catalogue of mental powers.   (*W*, VIII, 15)

By reproducing the play of forms through a play of tropes, imagination can shock the mind out of its lethargy and revivify language itself, which daily use is perpetually wearing down into cliché. Hence Emerson's insistence that the poet needs to acquire above all "the habit of saliency, of not pausing but going on," which he defines as "a sort of importation or domestication of the Divine effort in a man" (*W*, VIII, 72). But God rested on the seventh day, and pronounced his works good. Emerson's poet can never rest, because his works are never quite good enough. Like the sun in Stevens' "Esthetique du Mal," who fills space with his "rejected years" in his doomed quest for the perfect lunar transformation, Emerson's poet is trying to suggest metamorphosis in a medium necessarily fixed, and can never hope to capture in language the "flying Perfect" that is at once "the inspirer and the condemner of every success" (*CW*, II, 179).

With the notion of a poetry consisting of a perpetual play of tropes, which aims to represent infinity not analogically but successively (like Kant's mathematical sublime), Emerson is

finally weaning himself from the concept of origins that had
tantalized him for so long. An absolute origin has numinous
prestige, but since it is different in essence from the texts which
derive from it, its radiance mocks them even as they try faithfully
to transmit it. By giving up the search for an origin, by finding
radiance in the electricity generated by the differences between
tropes rather than in the tropes themselves, Emerson appears
to have solved the problem of inspiration—it is not something
in the text, but something that is generated in its interstices,
which is to say, in the reader. Yet the text itself, in this account,
still seems full of pathos, an inert heap of tropes. Like one of
the shades given voice by Odysseus's trench of blood, it lives
only for a moment in the imagination of the reader before
slipping back to the underworld that constitutes literary history.

But Emerson's poetic theory did not end in this sad skepticism. In *Representative Men* (1850) and in the brilliant, quirky
lecture "Quotation and Originality" (1859; published 1875),
Emerson circles back to a theory of literary origins curiously
like the one he had rejected when compiling his lecture on the
three first Gospels. There he had refused to follow Thirlwall
and Schleiermacher into a theory that saw written *documents*
as the source; he was instead attracted to the numinous prestige
of an oral cyclus that lay behind and outside the written texts.
Now he slowly begins to be intrigued by the idea that texts
might give rise to inspiration, and not inspiration to texts, that
the poet is the scribe's successful brother, that the best poet is
a "huge borrower" (*W*, IV, 197), and that the term "originality"
is simply the compliment we pay to the skill of his compilations
or the daring of his thefts.

Signs of the change in theory appear in the differences between the metaphors used to describe the relationship between
language and usage at different stages of his career. In "The
Poet" he says: "The etymologist finds the deadest word to have
been once a brilliant picture. Language is fossil poetry. As the
limestone of the continent consists of infinite masses of the shells
of animalcules, so language is made up of images, or tropes,
which now, in their secondary use, have long ceased to remind
us of their poetic origin" (*CW*, III, 13). Here the metaphor is
one of decay, loss of power. Language, like poetry itself, is

lamented as "the effluvia and residue or eternal force of a presence no longer present."[29]

But when a similar metaphor appears sixteen years later in "Quotation and Originality" it has undergone a subtle but important shift in emphasis. "Language is a city to the building of which every human being brought a stone; yet he is no more to be credited with the grand result than the acelaph which adds a cell to the coral reef which is the basis of the continent" (*W*, VIII, 199). Language is still fossil poetry, but the emphasis is now on its gradual accretion, not its decay; and the users of language—who in *Nature* and "The Poet" were the debasers of meaning—now are credited with its slow but massive accumulation.

As with individual words, so with the larger materials out of which the poet constructs his edifice. The "Shakespeare" essay of *Representative Men* begins with a determined attack upon the notion that the highest praise of genius is original invention.

> Great men are more distinguished by range and extent than by originality. If we require the originality which consists in weaving, like a spider, their web from their own bowels; in finding clay and making bricks and building the house; no great men are original. (*W*, IV, 189)

Shakespeare's dazzling originality consisted not in invention, but in assimilation and recasting of the materials accumulated by the culture around him: proverbs, old poems, the mass of old plays, "waste stock" (*W*, IV, 193) generated by the popular theater of the preceding generation. "Great genial power, one would almost say, consists in not being original at all; in being altogether receptive; in letting the world do all, and suffering the spirit of the hour to pass unobstructed through the mind" (*W*, IV, 191).

As the essay progresses these metaphors of passive yielding to the *Zeitgeist* give way to ones that suggest a connection between originality and larceny. Both "Shakespeare" and "Quotation and Originality" contain passages of bravura sourcehunting:

29. Joseph Riddel, "Reading America / American Readers," *MLN*, 99 (1984), 905.

Chaucer, it seems, drew continually, through Lydgate and Caxton,
from Guido da Colonna, whose Latin romance of the Trojan war was
in turn a compilation from Dares Phyrgius, Ovid and Statius. Then
Petrarch, Boccaccio, and the Provencal poets are his benefactors: the
Romaunt of the Rose is only judicious translation from William of
Lorris and John of Meung: Troilus and Creseide, from Lollius of Ur-
bino: the Cock and the Fox, from the *Lais* of Marie: the House of
Fame, from the French or Italian: and poor Gower he uses as if he
were only a brick-kiln or stone-quarry out of which to build his
house. (*W*, IV, 197–98)

*   *   *

Goethe's favorite phrase, "the open secret," translates Aristotle's an-
swer to Alexander, "These books are published and not published."
Madame de Stael's "Architecture is frozen music" is borrowed from
Goethe's "dumb music," which is Vitruvius's rule, that "the architect
must not only understand drawing, but music." Wordsworth's hero
acting "on the plan which pleased his childish thought" is Schiller's
"Tell him to reverence the dreams of his youth," and earlier, Bacon's
Consilia juventutis plus divinitatis habent." (*W*, VIII, 185)

This manic display of scholarship is not meant to locate an origin
but to explode the idea of its possibility. "The originals are not
original. There is imitation, model, and suggestion to the very
archangels, if we knew their history." The same delight in the
fragmentation of the text lies behind Emerson's admiration for
that more radical form of source study that ends by exploding
the identity of the author. His interest in the higher critical
disintegration of the evangelists has already been discussed, but
the same process attracted him in the study of secular texts as
well. He once wrote: "From Wolf's attack upon the authenticity
of the Homeric poems dates a new epoch of learning."[30] He
was even moved to admiration by the "bold theory" of Delia
Bacon that Shakespeare's plays were written "by a society of
wits" (*W*, VIII, 197), though he gently but firmly indicated his
disbelief in its literal truth.[31]

30. Quoted in Moncure Conway, *Emerson at Home and Abroad* (Boston:
James R. Osgood and Co., 1882), p. 106.
31. On the life and theories of Delia Bacon, see Vivian Hopkins, *Prodigal
Puritan: A Life of Delia Bacon* (Cambridge, Mass.: Harvard University Press,
1959).

To remove the origin from the Beginning and place it in that "instant eternity" which is the present moment opens the canon again to new sacred books; hence Whitman's delighted embracing of the doctrine. "There was never any more inception than there is now,"[32] he says exultantly in *Song of Myself.* To dissolve the author into a welter of quotations is only to reveal his kinship with us: "Every book is a quotation; and every house is a quotation out of all forests and mines and stone-quarries; and every man is a quotation from all his ancestors" (*W,* VIII, 176).

But in demystifying the notion of origins, what has happened to the notion of authority? The higher critics, after all, had not been out to destroy the authority of the Gospels, but to place them on a firmer foundation by locating the true origin from which they derive. If the very notion of origin is exploded, and the text dissolved into a heap of fragments, by what right does the poet speak? Emerson's answer is half psychological, half pragmatic. "Did the bard speak with authority?" he asks. "The appeal is to the consciousness of the writer . . . All the debts which such a man could contract to other wit would never disturb his consciousness of originality; for the ministrations of books and of other minds are a whiff of smoke to that most private reality with which he has conversed" (*W,* IV, 199). Less transcendental is his justification of Chaucer: "He steals by this apology,—that what he takes has no worth where he finds it and the greatest where he leaves it" (*W,* IV, 198). This blend of larceny and self-confidence is most happily exemplified by Wordsworth, who steals and then with sublime complacency represses the very consciousness of the theft. "Wordsworth, as soon as he heard a good thing, caught it up, meditated upon it, and very soon reproduced it in his writing. If De Quincey said, 'That is what I told you,' he replied, 'No: that is mine,—mine, and not yours.' On the whole, we like the valor of it" (*W,* VII, 192). And he quotes with approval Landor's reply to the critics who charged Shakespeare with debts to his sources: "Yet he

---

32. *Song of Myself,* line 40, in *The Collected Writings of Walt Whitman,* Comprehensive Reader's Edition, ed. Harold Blodgett and Sculley Bradley (New York: W. W. Norton and Co., 1965), p. 30.

was more original than his originals. He breathed upon dead bodies and brought them to life" (*W*, VII, 191).

Landor's metaphors of resurrection return us at last to the figure of Jesus, with whom Emerson's excursions into the higher criticism began. In the vestry lectures on the origin of the first three Gospels, Jesus is the numinous source whose words and deeds the oral cyclus strives to preserve; in "The Lord's Supper" he is the authority Emerson first attacks and then tries to enlist; in the Divinity School *Address* he is the archetype of the doomed poet, whose words of truth are betrayed into dogma by the treachery of language. He makes one final, brief appearance in the essay on "Shakespeare," where he has now joined the company of those artists whose work is "original" because it crowns the "wide social labor" of thousands (*W*, IV, 199). Emerson notes with interest Grotius' observation that the "single clauses" of which the Lord's Prayer is composed "were already in use in the time of Christ, in the Rabbinical forms." Like Shakespeare, like Homer, like Chaucer, Jesus is a poet who originates by appropriating. "He picked out the grains of gold" (*W*, IV, 200).

ERIC J. SUNDQUIST

Benito Cereno and New World Slavery

In the climactic scene of *Benito Cereno,* after the terrified Spanish captain has flung himself threateningly into Captain Delano's boat, followed by his servant Babo, dagger in hand, Melville writes: "All this, with what preceded, and what followed, occurred with such involutions of rapidity, that past, present, and future seemed one." The revelation of Babo's true design, as his disguise of dutiful slave falls away to reveal a "countenance lividly vindictive, expressing the centered purpose of his soul," is mirrored in the countenance of Delano himself, who, as if "scales dropped from his eyes," sees the whole host of slaves "with mask torn away, flourishing hatchets, and knives, in ferocious piratical revolt."[1] The masquerade staged by Babo and Benito Cereno to beguile the benevolent Delano probes the limits of the American's innocence at the same time it eloquently enacts the haltingly realized potential for slave rebellion in the New World and, in larger configuration, the final drama of one stage in New World history.

The American, the European, and the African, yoked together in the last crisis as they are throughout the pantomime

1. *Benito Cereno, Great Short Works of Herman Melville,* ed. Warner Berthoff (New York: Harper and Row, 1969), pp. 294–295.

of interrupted revolution that constitutes Melville's story, play parts defined by the climactic phase slavery in the Americas had entered when Melville composed his politically volatile tale during the winter and spring of 1854–55. The American Civil War reduced New World slavery to Cuba and Brazil; it brought to an end the threatened extension of slavery throughout new territories of the United States and Caribbean and Latin American countries coveted by the South. In the 1850s, however, the fever for such expansion was at a pitch, and Melville's tale brings into view the convulsive history of the entire region and epoch— from the Columbian discovery of the Americas, through the democratic revolutions in the United States, Haiti, and Latin America, to the contemporary crisis over the expansion of the "Slave Power" in the United States. "In 1860 pressures, past, present, and future, blasted the Union apart," writes Frederick Merk in his study of manifest destiny.[2] Unable to see the future but nonetheless intimating its revolutionary shape, Melville adds to these recent national pressures an international structure of exceptional scope and power, such that past, present, and future do indeed seem one aboard the *San Dominick*.

Benito Cereno's general significance in the debates over slavery in the 1850s is readily apparent; moreover, Melville's exploitation of the theme of balked revolution through an elaborate pattern of suppressed mystery and ironic revelation has helped draw attention to the wealth of symbolic meanings the slave revolt in San Domingo in the 1790s would have for an alert contemporary audience. Even so, the full implications of Melville's invocation of Caribbean revolution have not been appreciated, nor the historical dimensions of his masquerade of rebellion completely recognized.

In changing the name of Benito Cereno's ship from the *Tryal* to the *San Dominick,* Melville gave to the slave revolt a specific character that has often been identified. Haiti, known as San

2. Leon Howard, *Herman Melville: A Biography* (Berkeley: University of California Press, 1951), pp. 218–222; Frederick Merk, *Manifest Destiny and American Mission in American History* (1963; rpt New York: Vintage-Random, 1966), p. 214.

Domingo (Saint-Domingue) before declaring its final independence from France in 1804 and adopting a native name,[3] remained a strategic point of reference in debates over slavery in the United States. Abolitionists claimed that Haitian slaves, exploiting the upheaval of the French Revolution, had successfully seized the same Rights of Man as Americans two decades earlier; whereas proslavery forces claimed that the black revolution led to wholesale carnage, moral and economic degradation, and a political system that was (in the words of the British minister to Haiti in the 1860s) "but a series of plots and revolutions, followed by barbarous military executions." The outbreak of revolution in 1790 produced a flood of white planter refugees to the United States, some 10,000 in 1793 alone, most of them carrying both slaves and tales of terror to the South. Thereafter, especially in the wake of Nat Turner's bloody uprising in 1831 and the emancipation of slaves in British Jamaica in the same year, Haiti came to seem the fearful precursor of black rebellion throughout the New World. When Melville altered the date of Amasa Delano's encounter with Benito Cereno from 1805 to 1799, he accentuated the fact that his tale belonged to the age of democratic revolution, in particular the period of violent struggle leading to Haitian independence presided over by the heroic black general Toussaint L'Ouverture.[4]

After Napoleon's plans to retake San Domingo (in order to retrieve in the Gulf of Mexico glory he had lost in the Medi-

3. In English and American usage of the nineteenth century, the entire island at times and even after the revolution the western half (a French possession since the seventeenth century) was often designated San Domingo or St. Domingo. The Spanish, eastern half (the Dominican Republic after 1844) was usually designated Santo Domingo, as was the principal city founded by the Columbian expeditions and named in memory of Columbus's father, Dominick.

4. Spenser St. John, *Hayti, or the Black Republic* (London: Smith, Elder, 1884), p. x; C. L. R. James, *The Black Jacobins: Toussaint L'Ouverture and the San Domingo Revolution,* rev. ed. (New York: Vintage Books, Random House, 1963), p. 127; Clement Eaton, *The Freedom-of-Thought Struggle in the Old South,* rev. ed. (New York: Harper and Row, 1964), pp. 89–90; Eugene D. Genovese, *From Rebellion to Revolution: Afro-American Slave Revolts in the Making of the New World* (1979; rpt. New York: Vintage Books, Random House, 1981), pp. 35–37, 94–96; Winthrop D. Jordan, *White over Black: American Attitudes toward the Negro, 1550–1812* (1968; rpt. New York: Norton, 1977), pp. 375–402.

terranean) were undercut by the demise of Leclerc's army in 1802, he lost the main reason to retain and occupy Louisiana. "Without that island," Henry Adams wrote, the colonial system "had hands, feet, and even a head, but no body. Of what use was Louisiana, when France had clearly lost the main colony which Louisiana was meant to feed and fortify?" The ruin and seeming barbarism of the island, and the excessive expense and loss of lives it would require to retrieve and rebuild, made San Domingo a lost cause of large dimensions to France and at the same time the key to the most important territorial expansion of the United States—an expansion that would soon make the Caribbean appear as vital to American slave interests as it had to France and prepare the way for the crisis question of slavery's expansion into new territories. In making their country "the graveyard of Napoleon's magnificent army as well as his imperial ambitions in the New World," Eugene Genovese has written, the slaves of San Domingo thus cleared the way for a different expression of New World colonial power destined to have more decisive and lasting effect on the stage of world history.[5]

Were the noble and humane Toussaint the only representative figure of the Haitian revolution, fears of slave insurrection in the United States might not have taken on such a vicious coloring. The black activist William Wells Brown compared him in an 1854 lecture not only to Nat Turner ("the Spartacus of the Southampton revolt") but also to Napoleon and Washington—though with the withering irony that whereas Washington's government "enacted laws by which chains were fastened upon the limbs of millions of people," Toussaint's "made liberty its watchword, incorporated it in its constitution, abolished the slave trade, and made freedom universal amongst the people." Brown's lecture on San Domingo, subtitled "Its Revolutions and Its Patriots," adopted the familiar antislavery strategy of declaring the San Domingo uprising the model for an American

5. Ludwell Lee Montague, *Haiti and the United States, 1714–1938* (Durham: Duke University Press, 1940), pp. 35–46; Rayford W. Logan, *The Diplomatic Relations of the United States with Haiti, 1776–1891* (Chapel Hill: University of North Carolina Press, 1941), pp. 112–151; Henry Adams, *History of the United States during the Administrations of Jefferson and Madison*, quoted in Logan, *Diplomatic Relations*, p. 142; Genovese, *From Rebellion to Revolution*, p. 85.

slave rebellion that would bring to completion the stymied revolution of 1776. When Americans contemplated what would happen if the San Domingo revolt were "reenacted in South Carolina and Louisiana" and American slaves wiped out "their wrongs in the blood of their oppressors," however, not Toussaint but his successor as general-in-chief, Dessalines, sprang to mind. Whatever ambivalent gratitude might have existed toward Haiti for its mediating role in the United States' acquisition of Louisiana was diluted by the nightmarish achievement of independence under Dessalines, whose tactics of deceitful assurance of safety to white landowners, followed by outright butchery, enhanced his own claim that his rule would be initiated by vengeance against the French "cannibals" who have "taken pleasure in bathing their hands in the blood of the sons of Haiti." When he made himself emperor in 1804 Dessalines wore a crown presented by Philadelphia merchants and coronation robes from British Jamaica; but in the histories of San Domingo available in the early nineteenth century, both these ironies and unofficial economic ties to the island tended to be forgotten amid condescending accounts of his pompous reign and the frightful bloodshed that accompanied it. Although a sympathetic writer could claim in 1869 that the independence of Haiti constituted "the first great shock to this gigantic evil [slavery] in modern times," what Southerners in particular remembered were accounts of drownings, burnings, rapes, limbs chopped off, eyes gouged out, disembowelments—the sort of Gothic violence typified by an episode in Mary Hassal's so-called *Secret History; or, The Horrors of St. Domingo* (1808), in which a young white woman refuses the proposal of one of Dessalines' chiefs: "The monster gave her to his guard, who hung her by the throat on an iron hook in the market place, where the lovely, innocent, unfortunate victim slowly expired."[6]

6. William Wells Brown, *St. Domingo: Its Revolutions and Its Patriots* (Boston: Bela Marsh, 1855), pp. 23, 36–38, 32–33; James, *Black Jacobins*, pp. 370–374; Charles MacKenzie, *Notes on Haiti, Made During a Residence in that Republic*, 2 vols. (London: Colburn and Bentley, 1830), II, 61; Jonathan Brown, *The History and Present Condition of St. Domingo*, 2 vols. (Philadelphia: William Marshall, 1836), II, 152–154, 147–148; Mark B. Bird, *The Black Man; Or, Haytian Independence* (New York: American News Co., 1869), pp. 60–

While Hassal's "history" both in form and substance more
resembles such epistolary novels as *Wieland*, its account of the
Haitian trauma is hardly more sensational than the standard
histories and polemics of the day. Antislavery forces for good
reason hesitated to invoke Haiti as a model of black rule; even
those sympathetic with its revolution considered its subsequent
history violent and ruinous. Until the 1850s, moreover, most
Americans agreed with assessments holding "that specious and
intriguing body, the society of the *Amis des Noirs*," responsible
for the rebellion and subsequent descent of the island "into the
lowest state of poverty and degradation." What Bryan Edwards
asserted of the British West Indies in 1801 remained persuasive
in the United States for decades: if encouragement is given to
those "hot-brained fanaticks and detestable incendiaries, who,
under the vile pretense of philanthropy and zeal for the interests
of suffering humanity, preach up rebellion and murder to the
contented and orderly negroes," the same "carnage and destruction" now found in San Domingo will be renewed throughout the colonial world. Precisely the same fears permeated the
South, even in exaggerated form after Jamaica itself was added
to the list of revolutionized colonies in 1831. Lasting paranoia
among slaveholders about abolitionist responsibility for slave
unrest thus continually referred back to San Domingo and became, according to David Brion Davis, "an entrenched part of
master class ideology, in Latin America as well as the United
States." Implicit in the assumption of abolitionist conspiracy,
of course, is a doubt of the slaves' own ability to organize and
carry out a revolt, a doubt contradicted by any of the slave
revolutionaries Melville might have had in mind—by Toussaint,
by Dessalines, by Nat Turner, by Cinque (the notorious leader
of the revolt aboard the slave ship *Amistad*), and by Mure, the
original of his own Babo.[7]

*   *   *

_____

61; Mary Hassal, *Secret History; or, The Horrors of St. Domingo* (Philadelphia:
Bradford and Inskeep, 1808), pp. 151–153.

7. James Franklin, *The Present State of Hayti* (London: John Murray, 1828),
pp. 90–96, 409–410; Bryan Edwards, *An Historical Survey of the Island of Saint
Domingo* (London: John Stockdale, 1801), p. 226; David Brion Davis, *The*

When the sixty-three slaves aboard Benito Cereno's ship revolted, killing twenty-five men, some out of simple vengeance,
they especially determined to murder their master, Don Al-
exandro Aranda, "because they said they could not otherwise
obtain their liberty." To this Melville's version adds that the
death would serve as a warning to the other seamen; not only
that, but a warning that takes the form of deliberate terror.
Aranda's body, instead of being thrown overboard, as in reality
it was, is apparently cannibalized and the skeleton then *"substituted for the ship's proper figure-head—the image of Cristobal
Colon, the discoverer of the New World,"* from whose first contact with the New World in Hispaniola—that is, San Domingo—
flowed untold prosperity and human slavery on an extraordinary
scale. The thirty-nine men from the *Santa Maria* Columbus left
at the north coast base of Navidad on Hispaniola in 1492 were
massacred by the natives after quarreling over gold and Indian
women; on his second voyage in 1494 Columbus himself took
command, suppressed an Indian uprising, and authorized an
enslavement of Indians to work in the gold fields that was destined to destroy—by some estimates—close to one million natives within fifteen years.[8]

Responding to pleas of the Dominican priests, led by Bar-
tholomew de Las Casas, that the Indian population would not
survive slavery, Charles V, Holy Roman Emperor, in 1517 authorized the first official transport of African slaves to San Domingo: the New World slave trade, destined to carry some 15
million slaves across the Atlantic by 1865, had begun. The substitution of Negroes for Indians was justified by Las Casas on

---

Slave Power Conspiracy and the Paranoid Style (Baton Rouge: Louisiana State
University Press, 1969), p. 35.

8. Amasa Delano, *Narrative of Voyages and Travels in the Northern and
Southern Hemispheres* (Boston: E. G. House, 1817), p. 336; see also Harold
H. Scudder, "Melville's *Benito Cereno* and Captain Delano's Voyages," *PMLA*,
43 (1928), 502–532; Melville, *Benito Cereno*, p. 310; John Edwin Fagg, *Cuba,
Haiti, and the Dominican Republic* (Englewood Cliffs, N.J., Prentice-Hall, 1965),
pp. 114–115; Brown, *History and Present Condition of St. Domingo*, I, 22–33;
Edwards, *Historical Survey of the Island of Saint Domingo*, p. 208; Samuel Eliot
Morison, *Admiral of the Ocean: A Life of Christopher Columbus* (Boston: Little,
Brown, 1942), pp. 297–313, 423–438.

the humanitarian grounds that the blacks, unlike the Indians, were hardy and suited to such labors in a tropical climate. "Like oranges," wrote Antonio de Herrera in 1601, "they found their proper soil in Hispaniola, and it seemed even more natural than Guinea." Just so, added the American author who quoted Herrera in 1836: "The one race was annihilated by slavery, while the other has ever since continued to thrive and fatten upon it." Only the master class or their sympathizers made such an argument. Their antagonists, such as black abolitionist Henry Highland Garnett, especially stigmatized Charles V and his "evil genius," Las Casas; "clouds of infamy will thicken around them as the world moves on toward God."[9]

Alongside the paradoxical outcome of the Columbian discovery and settlements, the forms of debate in the antebellum period over the Christian justification of slavery are compressed by Melville into a structure of monastic symbolism meant to evoke the role of the Catholic Church, the Dominicans in particular, in the initiation of New World slavery. The comparison of Benito Cereno to Charles V, who became a virtual tool of the Dominicans in the end of his reign, and Delano's momentary vision of the *San Dominick* as "a whitewashed monastery" or a shipload of Dominican "Black Friars pacing the cloisters," are only the most central of the ecclesiastical scenes and metaphors that animate the tale. The aura of ruin and decay that links Benito Cereno and his ship to Charles V and his empire point forward in addition to the contemporary demise of Spanish power in the New World and the role of slave unrest in its revolutionary decline. The less apparent Islamic symbolism in *Benito Cereno* indicates Melville borrowed from several contemporary sources—Irving's portrait of Las Casas in his *Life* of Columbus, Bancroft's *History of the United States,* and Charles Sumner's *White Slavery in the Barbary States*—in order to invoke an Islamic-Christian conflict predating by some seven hundred

9. Daniel P. Mannix and Malcolm Cowley, *Black Cargoes: A History of the Atlantic Slave Trade, 1518–1865* (1962; rpt. New York: Viking/Compass, 1965), pp. viii, 1–5; Brown, *History and Present Condition of St. Domingo,* I, 36–37; Henry Highland Garnett, *The Past and Present Condition and Destiny of the Colored Race* (1848; rpt. Miami: Mnemosyne Publishing, 1969), pp. 12–13.

years the introduction of African slaves into America. Bancroft
in particular remarked the hypocritical coincidence of Charles
V's military liberation of white Christian slaves in Tunis and his
enslavement of Africans bound for the Americas, and emphasized the further coincidence, its irony commonplace by Melville's day, that "Hayti, the first spot in America that received
African slaves, was the first to set the example of African liberty."[10]
It is this coincidence and its ironic origins that are illuminated
by Babo's symbolic display of the skeleton of a modern slaveholder in place of the image of Columbus. Along with the chalked
admonition, *"Follow your leader,"* it too appears to Delano at
the climactic moment when Benito Cereno and Babo plunge
into his boat and the piratical revolt is unveiled; but the benevolent American, self-satisfied and of good conscience, remains oblivious to the end to the meaning of Babo's terror and
to the murderous irony summoned up in Melville's symbolic
gesture. Like those of Aranda, the sacred bones of Columbus,
rumored still in 1830 to have been lodged in the cathedral of
Santo Domingo before being transferred to Havana upon the
Treaty of Basle in 1795, might well join those of the millions
of slaves bound for death in the New World. Of them is built
Benito Cereno's decaying ship as it drifts into the harbor of the
Chilean island of Santa Maria: "Her keel seem laid, her ribs
put together, and she launched, from Ezekiel's Valley of Dry
Bones."[11]

Delano, as Jean Fagan Yellin suggests, may portray the stock
Yankee traveler in plantation fiction, delighted by the warm

10. Melville, *Benito Cereno*, pp. 246, 240; H. Bruce Franklin, *The Wake of the Gods: Melville's Mythology* (Stanford: Stanford University Press, 1963), pp. 136–150; Gloria Horsley-Meacham, "The Monastic Slaver: Images and Mean-ing in *Benito Cereno*," *New England Quarterly*, 55, no. 2 (June 1983), 261–266; George Bancroft, *History of the United States of America*, 10 vols. (New York: Appleton and Co., 1885), I, 121–125.

11. MacKenzie, *Notes on Haiti*, pp. 263–266; Melville, *Benito Cereno*, pp. 296, 241.

patriarchal bond between the loyal, minstrel-like slave and his languid master; he may even, like Thomas Gray, who recorded and published Nat Turner's *Confessions,* penetrate the violent center of that relationship and yet prefer to ignore its meaning. Recognizing that "slavery breeds ugly passions in man" but banishing from mind the significance of that realization, Delano is a virtual embodiment of repression, not simply in the sense that he puts down the revolt aboard the *San Dominick* and thereby restores authority that has been overturned, but also in the sense that his refusal to understand the "shadow" of the Negro that has descended upon Benito Cereno is itself a psychologically and politically repressive act.[12]

Melville borrows Amasa Delano's trusting disposition and generosity directly from the captain's own account, which records that the *"generous captain Amasa Delano"* much aided Benito Cereno (and was poorly treated in return when he tried to claim his just salvage rights), and was saved from certain slaughter by his own "kindness," "sympathy," and "unusually pleasant" temperament. A passage earlier in Delano's *Narrative* might also have caught Melville's eye: "A man, who finds it hard to conceive of real benevolence in the motives of his fellow creatures, gives no very favourable testimony to the public in regard to the state of his own heart, or the elevation of his moral sentiments." The self-serving nature of Delano's remarks aside, what is notable is the manner in which Melville may be said to have rendered perversely ironic the entire virtue of "benevolence," the central sentiment of abolitionist rhetoric and action since the mid-eighteenth century. Delano's response is not "philanthropic" but "genial," it is true—but genial in the way one responds to Newfoundland dogs, natural valets and hairdressers, and minstrels set "to some pleasant tune." Delano's "old weakness for negroes," surging forth precisely at Melville's greatest moment of terrifying invention, the shaving scene, is the revolutionary mind at odds with itself, energized by the ideals of fatherly humanitarianism but, confounded by racialism, blind

12. Jean Fagan Yellin, *The Intricate Knot: Black Figures in American Literature, 1776–1863* (New York: New York University Press, 1972), pp. 215–227; Melville, *Benito Cereno,* pp. 283, 314.

to the recriminating violence they hold tenuously in check. Like that most eloquent advocate of benevolence, Harriet Beecher Stowe, for whom "the San Domingo hour" would be ushered in only by slaves with "Anglo Saxon blood . . . burning in their veins," Delano himself is emblematic of the paralyzed American revolution, at once idealistic and paternalistic, impassioned for freedom but fearful of continuing revolution.[13]

The brutal course of the San Domingo revolution led Jefferson, himself a reputed father of slave children, to remark in 1797 that "the revolutionary storm, now sweeping the globe," would soon be upon us; we shall be, if nothing prevents it, "the murderers of our own children." The fear of allowing the spread of revolutionary violence defines both Melville's tale and the course of slavery after the age of Revolution. The character of Delano speaks both for the founding fathers, who sanctioned slavery even as they recognized its contradiction to the Rights of Man, and the contemporary northern accommodationists, who too much feared sectional strife and economic turmoil to bring to the surface of consciousness a full recognition of slavery's ugliness in fact and in principle. The repressing "bright sun" and "blue sky" that have "forgotten it all," which Delano invokes at the tale's conclusion, echo Daniel Webster's praise of the Union and the founding fathers in the wake of the nearly insurrectionary struggle over the Compromise of 1850: "A long and violent convulsion of the elements has just passed away," Webster remarked, "and the heavens, the skies, smile upon us." Benito Cereno's reply?—"Because they have no memory . . . because they are not human."[14]

13. Delano, *Narrative of Voyages,* pp. 337, 323, 73; David Brion Davis, *The Problem of Slavery in Western Culture* (Ithaca: Cornell University Press, 1966), pp. 333–390; Melville, *Benito Cereno,* pp. 278–279; Harriet Beecher Stowe, *Uncle Tom's Cabin* (New York: Penguin, 1981), p. 392; cf. George Fredrickson, *The Black Image in the White Mind: The Debate on Afro-American Character and Destiny, 1817–1914* (New York: Harper and Row, 1971), pp. 97–129.

14. Jefferson, letter of 1797, quoted in Jordan, *White over Black,* p. 387; Melville, *Benito Cereno,* p. 314; Daniel Webster, *The Writings and Speeches of Daniel Webster,* 18 vols. (Boston: Little, Brown, 1903), XIII, 405–407; cf. Michael Paul Rogin, *Subversive Genealogy: The Politics and Art of Herman Melville* (New York: Alfred A. Knopf, 1983), pp. 142–146.

Webster's memory, longer and more fraught with complications than Delano's, repressed the true meanings of the revolutionary traditions his own career had celebrated, but not so much or so easily as his opponents thought. In the 1843 case of the American slave ship *Creole,* whose cargo mutinied off the coast of Virginia and sailed to Nassau, where they were freed by British authorities, Webster's seemingly hypocritical protest was spurred by his suspicions about British intentions in the Caribbean, coupled with a more specific concern that would reach a new height by the time Melville was writing *Benito Cereno.* To the American consul in Havana Webster wrote in 1843 to beware a British plot to invade Cuba and put in power "a *black Military Republic* under British *protection.*" With 600,000 blacks in Cuba and 800,000 in her West Indian islands, Britain could "strike a death blow at the existence of slavery in the United States" and seize control of the Gulf of Mexico.[15] Webster's concern anticipated by ten years the climate of opinion about the Caribbean to which Melville's tale responds, but it throws into relief the split between revolutionary ideals and revolutionary sentiment that perenially compromised and postponed the question of slavery in the United States until it exploded in civil war—the "war of the rebellion." Although contention over the Gulf did not ultimately play a large role in the Civil War, it seemed a vital issue throughout the 1850s—all the more so because, like Melville's tale, it represented the shadow play, one might say, of America's own balked Revolution and its ensuing domestic turmoil.

As it happened, American hegemony in the New World was increased rather than retarded by the Civil War. From Melville's perspective, however, the nature and extent of future American power remained a function of the unfolding pattern of anticolonial and slave revolutions in the Americas. Even though slaves fought at different times on opposing sides, the national revolutions of South and Central America in the early part of the century helped undermine slavery throughout the region (in

15. Webster quoted in Mary Cable, *Black Odyssey: The Case of the Slave Ship Amistad* (1971; rpt. New York: Penguin, 1977), p. 152.

most cases, slaves were not freed immediately upon independence but legislation abolishing slavery was at least initiated—
in Mexico, Uruguay, Chile, Argentina, and Bolivia in the 1820s;
in Venezuela and Peru in the 1850s). The end of slavery in the
British West Indies in 1833 and in the Dutch and French Islands
in 1848 left the United States more and more an anomaly, its
own revolutionary drama absurdly immobilized. Thus, when
extremists of Southern slavery later sought to tie an extension
of the peculiar institution to new revolutions in a policy of
manifest destiny in Latin America, they ignored the decline of
colonial rule on the one hand and on the other the trepida-
tions expressed by one of the best known of South American
revolutionaries, Francisco Miranda, who wrote as early as
1798:

as much as I desire the liberty and independence of the New World,
I fear the anarchy of a revolutionary system. God forbid that these
beautiful countries become, as did St. Domingue, a theatre of blood
and of crime under the pretext of establishing liberty. Let them rather
remain if necessary one century more under the barbarous and imbecile
oppression of Spain.

Miranda's plea expresses well the paradox of New World liberation and of the United States' continued, expanding enslavement of Africans between 1776 and 1860. Drawn by the territorial
dreams opened by Louisiana, the post-Revolutionary generation advocated expansion through a conscious policy of America's manifest destiny to revolutionize the continent—eventually
the entire hemisphere—spreading Anglo-Saxon free institutions, as one writer put it, from the Atlantic to the Pacific and
"from the icy wilderness of the North to . . . the smiling and
prolific South." That dreams of a global millennium ever ex-
ceeded reality is less relevant here than the fact that the harsh
conflict between dream and reality was anchored in the wrench-
ing paradox that had come to define New World revolution
itself: would it advance freedom or increase slavery? At the
time of *Benito Cereno*'s publication, the question was concentrated in the Caribbean, where the energy of manifest destiny
had been redirected after its initial efforts had failed to bring

"All Mexico" into the United States orbit.[16] The region offered
in miniature an emblem of the hemisphere in its historical revolutionary moment, with the remnants of Spain's great empire,
free blacks who had revolutionized their own nation, and American expansionist interests all in contention. Melville's tale does
not prophecy a civil war but rather anticipates, as at the time
it might well have, an explosive resolution of the conflict between American democracy, Old World despotism, and Caribbean New World revolution.

Readers of *Benito Cereno* who take any account at all of Melville's use of the San Domingo revolution focus for the most
part on its extension of the French Revolution and the heroism
of Toussaint. Yet the island's continuing turmoil in subsequent
years not only kept it alive in the Southern imagination of racial
violence but also made it of strategic significance in counter-
arguments to Caribbean filibustering. For example, an 1850
pamphlet by Benjamin C. Clark, though sympathetic to Haitian
freedom, condemned the "condition worse than that of slavery"
into which he thought the island had been plunged by Great
Britain's political maneuvering in the Caribbean; Haiti's failure
to develop its resources and its continued threat of revolution
to Cuba and the Dominican Republic thus made it a barrier
both to the United States interests in the region and to the
emancipation of American slaves. On a different note, an essay
"About Niggers," appearing in one of the same 1855 issues of
Putnam's Monthly that carried the serialization of *Benito Cereno,* argued that Haiti, unlike the United States, demonstrated
that liberty and slavery cannot coexist and that the "terrible
capacity for revenge" unleashed in the San Domingo revolution
proves that the "nigger" is "a man, not a baboon." The sarcastic
article, in line with the general antislavery tone of *Putnam's,*

16. Genovese, *From Rebellion to Revolution,* pp. 119–121; C. Duncan Rice,
The Rise and Fall of Black Slavery (1975; rpt. Baton Rouge: Louisiana State
University Press, 1976), pp. 262–263; Miranda quoted in Salvador de Madar-
iaga, *The Fall of the Spanish American Empire* (London: Hollis, Carter, 1947),
pp. 322–323; James Bennett, quoted in Merk, *Manifest Destiny and Mission,*
p. 46; Merk, pp. 180–214.

anticipated black colonialists in voicing the novel hope that the black West Indies would one day develop "a rich sensuous civilization which will bring a new force into thin-blooded intellectualism, and save our noble animal nature from extreme emasculation and contempt."[17] Melville's tale, antislavery though it may be, contains no invocation of noble savagery and no such hope about the fruitful merging of cultures.

While Haiti had its defenders, the common opinion among those who studied it was that its record, like that of emancipated Jamaica, was largely one of economic sloth and political barbarism. *De Bow's Review,* the influential organ of Southern interests, carried an essay in 1854 typical in its critique of Haitian commerce and government. For over thirty years, the essay claims, the "march of civilization" has been dead in Haiti, its social condition one of sustained indolence and immorality:

From its discovery by Columbus to the present reign of Solouque, the olive branch has withered under its pestilential breath; and when the atheistical philosophy of revolutionary France added fuel to the volcano of hellish passions which raged in its bosom, the horrors of the island became a narrative which frightened our childhood, and still curdles our blood to read. The triumphant negroes refined upon the tortures of the Inquisition in their treatment of prisoners taken in battle. They tore them with red-hot pincers—sawed them asunder between planks—roasted them by a slow fire—or tore out their eyes with red-hot corkscrews.

Here, then, are the central ingredients that Melville's tale adds to Delano's own *Narrative.* The conflation of Spanish and French rule, coupled with the allusion to the Inquisition, yokes anti-Catholic and anti-Jacobin sentiment; indeed, the rhetoric of manifest destiny in the Caribbean was often a mix of the two, though with the submerged irony—one Melville treats with complex care—that Northern critics of Slave Power expansion liked as well to employ the analogies of European despotism and Catholic subversion in attacking the South. For the North, National expansion would morally entail the eradication of slav-

17. Benjamin C. Clark, *A Geographical Sketch of St. Domingo, Cuba, and Nicaragua* (Boston: Eastburn's Press, 1850), p. 7; "About Niggers," *Putnam's Monthly,* 6 (December 1855), 608–612.

ery, not its extension. It would illuminate the world in such a
way, Lyman Beecher had already argued in *A Plea for the West*
(1835), that "nation after nation, cheered by our example, will
follow in our footsteps till the whole earth is free . . . delivered
from feudal ignorance and servitude." The only danger, according to Beecher's anti-Catholic tract, lay in the Roman
Church's attempt to salvage its dying power by subversion of
liberty in the New World, notably in South America, Canada,
and San Domingo, which were "destined to feel the quickening
powers of Europe, as the only means remaining to them of
combating the march of liberal institutions . . . and perpetu-
ating for a season her political and ecclesiastical dominion."
The slave power of the South, said the generation of Beecher's
children, would behave in precisely the same way in order to
rescue and extend their dying institution.[18]

The antislavery imagination, no less than the proslavery, tended
to collapse history into timeless images of terror and damnation.
Theodore Parker, for instance, comparing the strength of Anglo-
Saxon free institutions to the decay of Spain and her colonies
in "The Nebraska Question" (1854), had no trouble linking
together the early butchery and plunder of Indians in Hispaniola
and greater Latin America in the name of the Virgin Mary, and
the contemporary confluence of Slave Power and Catholicism.
Spain "rolled the Inquisition as a sweet morsel under her
tongue . . . butchered the Moors and banished the plundered
Jews," Parker wrote; in San Domingo she "reinvented Negro
Slavery" six thousand years after it had vanished in Egypt and
"therewith stained the soil of America." With what legacy?
Spain's two resulting American empires, Haiti and Brazil, so
Parker saw it, were "despotism throned on bayonets"; over
Cuba, France and England "still hold up the feeble hands of
Spain"; most of South and Central America takes the form of
a republic "whose only permanent constitution is a Cartridge-
box"; and Mexico goes swiftly back to despotism, a rotting
carcass about which "every raven in the hungry flock of Amer-

18. "Hayti and the Haytiens," *De Bow's Review*, 16, no. 1 (January 1854),
35; Davis, *The Slave Power Conspiracy*, pp. 72–78; Lyman Beecher, *A Plea
for the West* (Cincinnati: Truman and Smith, 1835), pp. 37, 109, 144.

ican politicians . . . wipes his greedy beak, prunes his wings, and screams 'Manifest Destiny.' " Parker attacked the North for conciliating slave interests time after time (most recently in the Compromise of 1850) and predicted the Slave Power's attempted acquisition of Cuba, the Mesilla Valley, Nebraska, Mexico, Puerto Rico, Haiti, Jamaica and other Caribbean islands, the Sandwich Islands, and so on. Despotic, Catholic tyranny was at work, which so far the Puritan, Anglo-Saxon spirit of liberty and religious freedom had been unable to contain. "I never knew a Catholic Priest who favored freedom in America," Parker admonished; "a Slave himself, the medieval theocracy eats the heart out from the celibate Monk."[19]

Benito Cereno, as he delivers his halting, incoherent narrative to Delano, seems to be "eating of his own words, even as he ever seemed eating his own heart." This coincidence in phrasing need do no more than remind us that Don Benito, who resembles a monk or a "hypochondriac abbott" and in the end retires to a monastery to die, is made by Melville a symbol of American paranoia about Spanish, Catholic, slaveholding despotism. To the extent that he also represents the Southern planter, the dissipated cavalier spiritually wasted by his own terrifying enslavement, Benito Cereno requires the reader to see the tale in Parker's terms: North and South, like Delano and Cereno, play the parts of Anglo-Saxon and Roman-European currently working out the destiny of colonial territories in the New World. Benito Cereno, at once a genteel courtier ("a sort of Castilian Rothschild") and an impotent, sick master painfully supported by the constant "half embrace of his servant," virtually *is* the Spanish New World, undermined by slave and nationalist revolutions and adrift aboard a deteriorated ghost ship on the revolutionary waters of history, which are now "like waved lead that has cooled and set in the smelter's mold." For his part, Delano, like the nation he represents, vacillates between dark suspicion and paternalistic disdain of the Spaniard. What the tale cannily keeps hidden, of course, is that it is Babo who stages

19. Theodore Parker, "The Nebraska Question," *Additional Speeches, Addresses, and Occasional Sermons,* 2 vols. (Boston: Little, Brown, 1855), I, 301–303, 352, 367, 378.

the events Delano witnesses aboard the *San Dominick,* artistically fashioning his former master like "a Nubian sculptor finishing off a white statue-head."[20] Melville's scenario—driving between the example of *De Bow's Review,* which saw Haiti as a volcano of Jacobin horrors, and that of Theodore Parker, who saw the Slave Power itself as a manifestation of Old World despotism and popish insurgency—makes the Negro slave the subversive, the terrorist, and, in the tale's central imaginary scene, the inquisitor.

Melville's portrayal of Babo would have aroused memories of notorious American slave rebels like Gabriel Prosser, Denmark Vesey, and Nat Turner, all of them in one faction of the public mind artful and vicious men prompted to their deeds by madness, dreams of San Domingo, or—what was much the same thing—abolitionist propaganda. Turner in particular was perceived to be deranged, the victim of apocalyptic hallucinations. In contrast, Babo is a heroic figure—though full of that "art and cunning" the real Delano attributed to all African slaves. Melville's depiction of his ferocity and cruelty, his comparison of Babo to a snake and his followers to wolves, and most of all his attribution to him of great powers of deception—these characteristics make Babo fearsome and commanding at the same time. His masquerade of devotion to Benito Cereno concisely portrays the complexly layered qualities of rebellion and submission—of "Nat" and "Sambo" roles—that historians have detected among the accounts of slave behavior, and it is a virtual parody of Thomas Wentworth Higginson's observation in an 1861 essay on Turner: "In all insurrections, the standing wonder seems to be that the slaves most trusted and best used should be the most deeply involved." Higginson goes on to quote James McDowell, member of the Virginia House of Delegates, who remarked in the historic 1832 debates over emancipation and colonization that Southern paranoia was prompted by the "sus-

20. Melville, *Benito Cereno,* pp. 276, 245, 250–251, 258, 241, 239, 283; cf. Carolyn Karcher, *Shadow over the Promised Land: Slavery, Race, and Violence in Melville's America* (Baton Rouge: Louisiana State University Press, 1980), pp. 136–139.

picion that a Nat Turner might be in every family; that the same bloody deed might be acted over at any time and in any place; that the materials for it were spread through the land, and were always ready for a like explosion."[21]

The same debates produced Thomas Dew's famous "Abolition of Negro Slavery" (expanded as *Review of the Debate in the Virginia Legislature of 1831–2*), which characteristically called the Haitian revolution a failure, productive only of disorder and poverty; which predicted that emancipation would lead to the South's "relapse into darkness, thick and full of horrors"; and which asserted that black rebels, unlike contemporary revolutionaries in Poland and France, were "unfit for freedom" and should be considered *"parricides* instead of *patriots."* Dew's mixing of the rhetoric of slave paternalism with that of revolution is entirely to the point. Insurrection destroyed the cherished southern fiction of the tranquil plantation "family," revealed it as a charade. This, as Michael Rogin argues, is what Melville himself does in *Benito Cereno:* "By overthrowing slavery and then staging it as a play, Babo has conventionalized the supposedly natural relations of master and slave." Melville's tale "recontains a slave revolt inside a masquerade," just as it contains the American Revolution itself inside its own masquerade and the paternalistic fiction inside a fiction that Delano himself continues in his naivete to empower and authorize.[22]

No one saw the irony of slaveholding paternalism more clearly

21. Seymour L. Gross and Eileen Bender, "History, Politics, and Literature: The Myth of Nat Turner," *American Quarterly,* 23, no. 4 (October 1971), 487–518; Delano, *Narrative of Voyages,* p. 550; Melville, *Benito Cereno,* pp. 295, 299; John W. Blassingame, *The Slave Community: Plantation Life in the Antebellum South,* rev. ed. (New York: Oxford University Press, 1979), pp. 192–248; Thomas Wentworth Higginson, "Nat Turner's Insurrection," *Travellers and Outlaws: Episodes in American History* (Boston: Lee and Shepard, 1889), pp. 322–325; cf. Genovese, *From Rebellion to Revolution,* pp. 116–117, and Herbert Aptheker, *American Negro Slave Revolts* (New York: International Publishers, 1952), pp. 293–324.

22. Thomas R. Dew, "Abolition of Negro Slavery," in Drew Gilpin Faust, ed., *The Ideology of Slavery: Proslavery Thought in the Antebellum South, 1830–1860* (Baton Rouge: Louisiana State University Press, 1981), pp. 56–59; Rogin, *Subversive Genealogy,* pp. 215, 210.

than Frederick Douglass, whose revised autobiography, *My Bondage and My Freedom*, appearing the same year as *Benito Cereno*, advised that "a person of some consequence here in the north, sometimes designated *father*, is literally abolished in slave law and practice." This is all the more true when the slaveholder has the arrogance to invoke the "inalienable rights of man": "He never lisps a syllable in condemnation of the fathers of this republic, nor denounces any attempted oppression of himself, without inviting the knife to his own throat, and asserting the rights of rebellion for his own slaves." Or, as Higginson said in an 1858 address to the American Anti-Slavery Society: "I have wondered in times past, when I have been so weak-minded as to submit my chin to the razor of a coloured brother, as his sharp steel grazed my skin, at the patience of the negro shaving the white man for many years, yet [keeping] the razor outside of the throat." The American slave might soon act on his own, Higginson warned. "We forget the heroes of San Domingo."[23]

Melville's most significant moment of invention in *Benito Cereno*, the shaving scene, brings to a climax of terror the "juggling play" that Babo and Benito Cereno have been "acting out, both in word and deed," before him. The "play of the barber" compresses Delano's blind innocence, Cereno's spiritual fright, and Babo's extraordinary mastery of the scene's props and actors into a nightmare pantomime symbolic of the revenge of New World slaves upon their debilitated masters. The cuddy, with its "meagre crucifix" and "thumbed missal," its settees like an "inquisitor's rack" and its barbering chair that seems "some grotesque engine of torment," is a scene defined by symbols of Spain's violent Catholic history. Babo's use of the Spanish flag as a barber's apron, which through his agitation unfolds "curtain-like" about his master, heightens Delano's playful affection for "the negro" and coordinates the personal and historical dramas of vengeance that are acted out—dramas that

---

23. Frederick Douglass, *My Bondage and My Freedom*, ed. Philip S. Foner, (New York: Dover, 1969), pp. 35, 269–270; Higginson quoted in Tilden G. Edelstein, *Strange Enthusiasm: A Life of Thomas Wentworth Higginson* (New Haven: Yale University Press, 1968), p. 211.

Delano, as he often does, unwittingly or unconsciously glimpses but fails fully to comprehend:

Setting down his basin, the negro searched among the razors, as for the sharpest, and having found it, gave it an additional edge by expertly stropping it on the firm, smooth, oily skin of his open palm; he then made a gesture as if to begin, but midway stood suspended for an instant, one hand elevating the razor, the other professionally dabbling among the bubbling suds on the Spaniard's lank neck. Not unaffected by the close sight of the gleaming steel, Don Benito nervously shuddered; his usual ghastliness was heightened by the lather, which lather, again, was intensified in its hue by the contrasting sootiness of the negro's body. Altogether the scene was somewhat peculiar, at least to Captain Delano, nor, as he saw the two thus postured, could he resist the vagary, that in the black he saw a headsman, and in the white a man at the block. But this was one of those antic conceits, appearing and vanishing in a breath, from which, perhaps, the best regulated mind is not always free.

The conceit of decapitation—uniting Jacobin terror, the Inquisition, and slave vengeance—has here more actuality than the literal barbering that is taking place. It epitomizes Melville's masterful employment throughout the tale of metaphors whose submerged meaning momentarily exceeds in truth their literal contexts, only to be forced—repressed—once again beneath the conscious surface of Delano's mind and the story's narrative.[24] The entire tale, most of all its revolutionary import, is similarly repressed by the legalistic documents and the executions of the slave rebels that codify Delano's putting down of the piratical revolt. Yet in that very act the fullest rebellious power, like the energy of the unconscious, is released in Melville's questioning of the moral authority of such documents and tribunals.

Melville's fascination with revolt and mutiny, as the cases of *White Jacket* and *Billy Budd* remind us, was tempered always by his equal fascination with the mechanics of repression. Cap-

---

24. Melville, *Benito Cereno*, pp. 277–283; cf. Eric J. Sundquist, "Suspense and Tautology in *Benito Cereno*," *Glyph 8: Johns Hopkins Textual Studies* (Baltimore: Johns Hopkins University Press, 1981), pp. 103–126.

tain Vere's combined paternalism and rigid justice refine qualities found in both the fictional and the actual Captain Delano.
Even for the good captain, like the good master, benevolence
may be no barrier either to rebellion or to its consequences. "I
have a great horror of the crime of mutiny," wrote Delano in
a discussion of the case of the *Bounty* in his *Narrative*, for it
leads only to greater abuses against the mutineers. "Vengeance
will not always sleep, but wakes to pursue and overtake them."
A virtual "reign of terror" against blacks followed Turner's
insurrection; likewise, Delano had to prevent the Spanish crew
and Benito Cereno himself from "cutting to pieces and killing"
the Negroes after the *Tryal* had been retaken. But as Joshua
Leslie and Sterling Stuckey have shown, legal retribution followed the same instinct. At Conception, as graphically as in
Melville's tale, five of the rebels are sentenced to hanging and
decapitation, their heads then "fixed on a pole, in the square
of the port of Talcahuano, and the corpses of all . . . burnt to
ashes." Justice here echoes revolution: among more gruesome
brutalities, both sides in the San Domingo revolution displayed
the severed heads of their opponents; the heads of defeated
black insurrectionists in New Orleans in 1811 and Tennessee in
1856 were fixed on poles or carried in parades. Babo's head,
"that hive of subtlety," gazes across the Plaza towards St. Bar-
tholomew's Church, where the recovered bones of Aranda lie,
and beyond that the monastery where Benito Cereno lies dying,
soon to "follow his leader."[25]

The repressive mechanisms of justice—legal or not—worked
swiftly to contain slave insurrection in the United States when
it occurred. And aside from the revolt of Turner, the instances
that most drew public attention in the late antebellum period
took place aboard ships and involved international rights en-
tailing long court disputes. The case of the *Creole*, which prompted
Webster's warning about black military rule in Cuba, was the

25. Delano, *Narrative of Voyages*, pp. 146–147, 347; Aptheker, *American Negro Slave Revolts*, pp. 300–310; C. L. R. James, *Black Jacobins*, pp. 95–96; Genovese, *From Rebellion to Revolution*, pp. 43, 106; Melville, *Benito Cereno*, p. 315; Joshua Leslie and Sterling Stuckey, "Avoiding the Tragedy of Benito Cereno: The Official Response to Babo's Revolt," *Criminal Justice History*, vol. 3 (1982), 125–132.

subject of Frederick Douglass's short story, "The Heroic Slave," which appeared in Julia Griffiths' 1853 collection *Autographs for Freedom* and played ironically on the name of the revolt's leader, Madison Washington, to highlight the shadowed vision of the founding fathers. But the more famous case of the *Amistad*, whose slaves revolted in 1839 and eventually came ashore on Long Island after an abortive attempt to sail to Africa, is even more likely to have been on Melville's mind, not least because the enactment of the revolt resembled that aboard the *Tryal–San Dominick* and because the slave leader, Cinque, was viewed as an intriguing combination of guile and humanity whose "moral sentiments and intellectual faculties predominate considerably over his animal propensities," but who "killed the Captain and crew with his own hand, cutting their throats." Garnett and other abolitionists celebrated Cinque's heroism, even considered him an American patriot; and when John Quincy Adams won freedom for the slaves before the Supreme Court (much to the embarrassment of President Van Buren and the outrage of the Spanish authorities who had demanded their return to Cuba), he appealed to "the law of Nature and Nature's God on which our fathers placed our own national existence."[26]

What, though, was the "law of Nature" and what evidence was there that it was synonymous with the law of the fathers? Webster celebrated the *Amistad* decision but refused to recognize the same rights in American slaves aboard the *Creole:* the perceived threat of the spread of black rebellion was one difference, enduring contention with England another. Although Babo acts according to the laws both of Nature and of the Revolutionary fathers, Delano cannot conceive of such action in black slaves. Like the "naked nature" of the slave mothers aboard the *San Dominick,* which turns out to conceal in them a rage for torture and brutality surpassing that of the men (a

26. *New London Gazette,* August 26, 1839, quoted in John W. Barber, *A History of the Amistad Captives* (New Haven: E. L. and J. W. Barber, 1840), p. 4; Henry Highland Garnett, *Present Condition and Destiny,* p. 16; Adams, *Argument in the Case of the United States vs. Cinque* (1841; rpt. New York: Arno Press, 1969), p. 9; cf. Mary Cable, *Black Odyssey,* pp. 76–108, and Sidney Kaplan, "Herman Melville and the American National Sin," *Journal of Negro History,* 41 (October 1956), 311–338.

feminine brutality corroborated, it might be added, by accounts of the San Domingo rebellion), the "natural" relationship of master and slave defined by the fathers, despite their inclusive dream of freedom, remained a disguise and a delusion.[27]

Webster's warning about Cuba, a symptom of his own ambivalence about the tortured relationship between union and slavery, sheds a different light as well on Babo's symbolic role. Not only might Babo evoke Toussaint, Dessalines, Nat Turner, or Cinque, he surely brought to mind in Melville's audience the current ruler of Haiti, Faustin Soulouque, who came to power in 1847 and had himself made emperor on the model of Dessalines in 1849. His empire was renowned for its gaudy displays of pomp and feared for its brutality. He employed voodoo, priests, assassination, torture, and massacre to put down any threat of revolt; in 1849 he mounted the first of several attacks on Santo Domingo (that is, the Dominican Republic, independent since 1844) that were perceived as a campaign to exterminate the white race. An article in the *Democratic Review* in 1853 declared Soulouque "the dark image of Louis Napoleon" and ridiculed the reluctance of the United States, France, and England to join together in putting down this "despot of a horde of black savages, whose grandfathers murdered their masters, and whose fathers murdered their brothers . . . and [who] would as readily exterminate every white man, as would their ancestors in the jungle of Africa."[28] The fear that a black empire would spread throughout the Caribbean was in turn countered by (or acted as a cover for) Southern calls for American intervention that were spurred on by the arrival of Pierce's expansionist administration.

27. Melville, *Benito Cereno*, pp. 268, 310; Delano, *Narrative of Voyages*, p. 341; James, *Black Jacobins*, p. 117; Franklin, *Present State of Hayti*, p. 62.

28. Robert I. Rotberg, *The Politics of Squalor* (Boston: Houghton Mifflin, 1971), pp. 76–90; Bird, *The Black Man*, pp. 288–306; St. John, *Hayti, or the Black Republic*, pp. 90–99; "On the Rumored Occupation of San Domingo by the Emperor of France," *United States Democratic Review*, 32, no. 2 (February 1853), 181–183.

Among the constellation of historical and contemporary issues Melville invoked in the drama of the *San Dominick,* present
concern over the sporadic war between Haiti and the Dominican
Republic is central for several reasons. From the mid-1840s on,
claims had been made by Frederick Douglass and others that
Haiti would be annexed to protect American (slave) interests.
Now threats to the Dominican Republic—another Texas—seemed
to offer a suitable excuse. The significance of the whole island
was heightened by the simultaneous crisis over the Kansas-
Nebraska Act and the "Africanization of Cuba," a purported
plot by Spain and Britain to free slaves and put blacks in power.
In retrospect, the fact that the South spent energy on the battle
for Kansas that it might otherwise have directed toward Cuba,
a territory of greater value to it, does not contradict the fact
that at the time *both* seemed possible. Franklin Pierce's May
1854 interdiction against filibustering in Cuba was based on his
reports that Cuba was too well protected and on the great Northern pressure brought to bear on him as a result of his conciliation
of Slave Power in signing the Kansas-Nebraska Act the day
before. Cuba, in addition, would have been too much. If the
South, in David Potter's words, "sacrificed the Cuban substance
for the Kansas shadow," it did not do so intentionally. Besides,
the fears of endless slave expansion that Theodore Parker voiced
in "The Nebraska Question" were still echoed a year later in
an essay on "The Kansas Question" appearing in the October
1855 issue of *Putnam's* in which *Benito Cereno's* serialization
began. Kansas, the essay maintained, was still but the next step
in the spread of slavery to Mexico, the Amazon, and eventually
back to Africa. In the long run, the conjunction of Kansas and
Cuba devastated both the Democratic Party and the idea of
popular sovereignty; crushed the South's dream of a Caribbean
empire; lost a territory destined to be of strategic importance
to the United States in later years; rekindled fears about the
spread of Haitian terror and counterbalancing proslavery plots
against that republic; and at the same time sparked premonitions
of the greater domestic convulsion to come. "The storm clouds
of [war over] slavery were gathering so fast in the South," wrote
John Bigelow to Charles Sumner after an 1854 visit to Haiti,

"that writing letters about Hayti seemed like fiddling while the country was burning."[29]

Melville's tale circles continually around a plot against himself that Delano vaguely suspects Benito Cereno to be meditating, perhaps with the aid of Babo and the slaves. But Delano's own blindness and its psychological significance should not overshadow the secondary effects Melville surely counted on. Purported plots of slaves against their masters were outstripped at the time by fears of the two other "plots" we have touched on—that of the South to expand its power and that of Cuba to be Africanized. The supposed conspiracy of 1853 between Spain and Britain to end slavery and the slave trade in Cuba and promote armed black rule produced calls from Cuban and American slaveholders for American intervention. New Spanish policies liberalizing slave laws, combined with the seizure in February 1854 of the American steamer *Black Warrior* on a violation of port regulations, accelerated both legal and extralegal maneuvering to obtain Cuba before it became, as a State Department agent, Charles W. Davis, wrote in March 1854, another "Black Empire" like Haiti, "whose example they would be proud to imitate" in destroying the wealth of the island and launching "a disastrous bloody war of the races." The height of imperialistic rhetoric came after the crisis had passed and attempts to force a purchase of Cuba had failed, in the notorious Ostend Manifesto of October 1854, which declared that Cuba belonged "naturally to that great family of States of which the Union is the providential nursery" and that the United States would be justified "in wresting it from Spain . . . upon the very same principle that would justify an individual in tearing down

29. Dexter Perkins, *The Monroe Doctrine, 1826–1867* (Baltimore: Johns Hopkins University Press, 1933), pp. 253–317; Charles Callan Tansill, *The United States and Santo Domingo, 1798–1873: A Chapter in Caribbean Diplomacy* (Baltimore: Johns Hopkins University Press, 1938), pp. 137–212; Logan, *Diplomatic Relations,* pp. 238–292; Basil Rauch, *American Interest in Cuba, 1848–1855* (New York: Columbia University Press, 1948), pp. 280–294; David M. Potter, *The Impending Crisis, 1848–1861* (New York: Harper and Row, 1976), pp. 177–198, quote at p. 198; Robert E. May, *The Southern Dream of a Caribbean Empire, 1854–1861* (Baton Rouge: Louisiana State University Press, 1973), pp. 21–75; "The Kansas Question," *Putnam's Monthly,* 6 (October 1855), 425–433; John Bigelow, quoted in Logan, *Diplomatic Relations,* p. 281.

the burning house of his neighbor if there were no other means
of preventing the flames from destroying his own home." The
issue of Cuba, that is to say, was couched in the familiar rhetoric
that Lincoln would exploit, combining the domestic language
of the revolutionary fathers and that of slaveholding paternalism. And it brought together just those threats Delano perceives
aboard the *San Dominick:* Spanish misrule and deterioration,
and threatened black insurrection and liberation.[30]

The South's—and the Pierce administration's—plan to "rescue" Cuba from black rule presupposed the decay of the Spanish
empire and its replacement by an Anglo-Saxon empire in the
western hemisphere. Peculiar to the South's version of manifest
destiny, of course, was the extension of slavery and the shift of
national power geographically to the south. This, perhaps, more
than any single point of reference such as Haiti or Cuba, alerts
us to the complex dimensions of the actions dramatized in *Benito
Cereno.* The Southern dream of a Caribbean empire reached
its most extreme formulations in somewhat later documents such
as Henry Timrod's "Ethnogenesis," William Walker's *The War
in Nicaragua,* and Edward Pollard's *Black Diamonds Gathered
in the Darkey Homes of the South,* published in 1861, 1860, and
1859, respectively, but based on sentiments common throughout
the decade. Pollard, for example, claimed southern expansion
was not a sectional issue but one involving "the world's progress,
and who shall be the founders of its greatest empire of industry."
Eventually, he maintained, the seat of the Southern Empire
would be in Central America; control of the West Indies, the
isthmuses of Central America, and the production of the world's
cotton and sugar would complete America's destiny:

What a splendid vision of empire! How sublime in its associations!
How noble and inspiriting the idea, that upon the strange theater of

30. Rauch, *American Interest in Cuba,* pp. 275–277; Philip S. Foner, *A
History of Cuba and Its Relations with the United States,* 2 vols. (New York:
International, 1963), II, 75–85; Charles W. Davis quoted in Foner, II, 81–82;
"Ostend Manifesto," *Documents of American History,* 2 vols. in 1, ed. Henry
Steele Commager (New York: F.S. Croft, 1934), I, 333–335.

tropical America, once, if we may believe the dimmer facts of history, crowned with magnificent empires and flashing cities and great temples, now covered with mute ruins, and trampled over by half-savages, the destiny of Southern civilization is to be consummated in a glory brighter even than that of old, the glory of an empire, controlling the commerce of the world, impregnable in its position, and representing in its internal structure the most harmonious of all systems of modern civilization.

Walker, too, in one chapter of the account of his filibustering career in Sonora and Nicaragua, celebrated the destined rejuvenation of Central and South America. The effort the South wasted on the "shadow" of Kansas, Walker wrote, could have brought her the "substance" of Central America, a territory necessary to protect slavery, to raise the African from darkness and teach him the "arts of life," and to forestall the spread of degeneracy that has occurred in Haiti and Jamaica.[31]

Walker among others adopted in his rhetoric a new ideology of progress that paternalized the remnants of Spain's American empire. He believed too that popular sovereignty could be applied as effectively to the Caribbean and Central America as to Kansas, and that expansion was necessary to complete the republican defeat of dying European monarchism. (So extreme did this idea become in the early 1850s that at one point Louis Kossuth, the enthusiastically courted hero of the 1848 Hungarian revolution, became embroiled in a southern plot to invade Haiti on the pretext that Soulouque was a czarist agent.) "Empire" became a common word in discourse about the region— not only among such slave interests as the Knights of the Golden Circle, which promoted a Gulf circle of power drawing together New Orleans, Havana, Yucatan, and Central America, but remarkably also among black American colonizationists such as J. Dennis Harris, who proposed to build an "Anglo-African Empire" in Haiti, a mulatto utopia, and James T. Holly, who

31. A. Curtis Wilgus, "Official Expression of Manifest Destiny Sentiment Concerning Hispanic America, 1848–1871," *Louisiana Historical Quarterly,* 15, no. 3 (July 1932), 486–506; Edward A. Pollard, *Black Diamonds Gathered in the Darkey Homes of the South* (New York: Pudney and Russell, 1859), pp. 106–115; William Walker, *The War in Nicaragua* (Mobile: S.H. Goetzel, 1860), pp. 251–280.

imagined a similar regeneration originating in Haiti, "the Eden
of America," and overspreading the whole world.[32]
Although such visions counted for little against the South's
need to stabilize its economic and political power, they accentuate from a different angle the paradisial dream that the Americas continued to represent. California gold, the dream's great
symbol in this period, would soon so enrich the nation, claimed
De Bow's Review in 1854, that no possible investment would
be equal to it but the cultivation of the entire western hemisphere. Lying between two of the great valleys of the world,
the Mississippi and the Amazon, the Gulf would link the most
productive regions of the earth, and by unlocking trading access
to the wealth of the Pacific Basin (China, Australia, California)
make the Atlantic in the modern world what the Mediterranean
was "under the reign of the Antonics in Rome." Given the
continued dissolution of European political power and possession of Cuba, Santo Domingo, and Haiti, the United States
might control the Gulf and through it the world: "Guided by
our genius and enterprise, a new world would rise there, as it
did before under the genius of Columbus." This new Columbian
vision had a price, however, one which the circular argument
of the writer for *De Bow's* did little to hide:

Heretofore, the great difficulty in civilizing the barbarian races of the
world has been to procure cheap and abundant clothing for them. A
naked race must necessarily be a wild one. To Christianize or civilize
a man, you must first clothe his nakedness. In the three millions of
bags of cotton the slave labor annually throws upon the world for the
poor and the naked, we are doing more to advance civilization and the

32. C. Stanley Urban, "The Ideology of Southern Imperialism: New Orleans
and the Caribbean, 1845–1860," *Louisiana Historical Quarterly*, 39, no. 1 (January 1956), 48–73; Donald S. Spencer, *Louis Kossuth and Young America: A
Study of Sectionalism and Foreign Policy, 1848–1852* (Columbia: University of
Missouri Press, 1977), pp. 166–169; May, *Southern Dream*, pp. 148–150; Mannix and Cowley, *Black Cargoes*, pp. 266–274; J. Dennis Harris, "A Summer
on the Borders of the Caribbean Sea," (1860) in Howard H. Bell, *Black Separatism and the Caribbean, 1860* (Ann Arbor: University of Michigan Press,
1970), p. 172; James T. Holly, "A Vindication of the Capacity of the Negro
Race Demonstrated by Historical Events of the Haytian Revolution," in Bell,
Black Separatism, p. 64.

refinement of life than all the canting philanthropists of New and Old England will do in centuries.

As the author noted, "slavery and war have [always] been the two great forerunners of civilization."[33]

Of course the utopian schemes of the South now seem precisely that; but as the possibilities of renewed Caribbean revolution and civil conflict in the United States unfolded in the 1850s, they too served to focus with critical symbolic significance the historical and contemporary role of San Domingo in the question of slavery. Lincoln's diplomatic recognition of Haiti in 1862 ensured the island's harassment of Confederate privateers, and black rule was hardly an issue between the two governments once the South seceded; moreover, the Caribbean and Latin America ceased for the time being to be of pressing national interest once the issue of slavery was resolved and a transcontinental railroad completed later in the decade.[34] The disappearance from view of the region until conflicts fifty and a hundred years later brought it back into the public mind has contributed to the general disregard of its critical role in *Benito Cereno*. Still, there can be little doubt as to Melville's richness of allusion and dramatic enactment, his masterful exploitation of the revolutionary spirit locked in the heart of the American New World, in this most troubled and explosive tale of America's antebellum destiny.

33. "Destiny of the Slave States," *De Bow's Review*, 17, no. 3 (September 1854), 280–284; cf. Eugene Genovese, *The Political Economy of Slavery: Studies in the Economy and Society of the Slave South* (New York: Vintage Books, Random House, 1967), pp. 243–274.

34. Logan, *Diplomatic Relations*, pp. 293–314; Montague, *Haiti and the United States*, pp. 85–88.

SANDRA M. GILBERT

The American Sexual Poetics
of Walt Whitman
and Emily Dickinson

It is I, you women, I make my way,
I am stern, acrid, large, undissuadable, but I love you,
I do not hurt you anymore than is necessary for you,
I pour the stuff to start sons and daughters fit for these
  States, I press with slow rude muscle,
I brace myself effectually, I listen to no entreaties,
I dare not withdraw till I deposit what has so long
  accumulated within me.

  Walt Whitman, "A Woman Waits for Me"

Great Caesar! Condescend
The Daisy, to receive,
Gathered by Cato's Daughter,
With your majestic leave!

  Emily Dickinson

On the surface, Walt Whitman and Emily Dickinson would
seem to be almost exaggeratedly male and female in their
personal and poetic self-presentations, as if each had set
out to prove, through parodying the stereotypical sex roles of
nineteenth-century America, that there were two different,
distinctively male and female poetic traditions. Open-shirted,
broad-chested, muscular, hairy, Whitman's poetic persona is
of course that of the archetypal American rough. "Walt Whitman, a Kosmos, of Manhattan the son, / Turbulent, fleshy, sen-
sual, eating, drinking and breeding, / No sentimentalist . . .":
the famous self-definition appears at the heart of "Song of
Myself," and, indeed, in the 1855 *Leaves of Grass* this passage,

123

together with the equally famous daguerreotype of a bearded, insolently casual loafer, functioned not only as a sardonically authoritative auto-analysis but also as the book's sole authorial signature.

As a brawling rough, moreover, Whitman claims a special and specially masculine relationship to women. Frankly "singing the phallus," he becomes the only begetter of these States, the supreme patriarch, proclaiming, in the passage from "A Woman Waits for Me" which I have used as an epigraph here, that even rude sexual coercion may be necessary for real spiritual regeneration: "I press with slow rude muscle, / I brace myself effectually, I listen to no entreaties, / I dare not withdraw till I deposit what has so long accumulated within me."[1] Significantly, too, his name, in "Song of Myself" the signifier of his authorial presence, soon becomes a signature of his virtually apocalyptic male sexuality: "Be composed—be at ease with me—I am Walt Whitman, liberal and lusty as nature," he tells "a common prostitute" in 1860, assuring the "fallen" woman that "Not till the sun excludes you do I exclude you," and then appointing a redemptive rendezvous (p. 376). As early as 1856, moreover, in the strikingly titled "Bunch Poem" (later to be renamed "Spontaneous Me"), he actually defines the male genitals as "real poems," with "what we call poems being merely pictures" (p. 103). Here, indeed, even more frankly than such descendants as D. H. Lawrence and Henry Miller were to do, he celebrates not just himself but specifically "This poem drooping shy and unseen that I always carry, and that all men carry," noting that "wherever are men like me, are our lusty lurking masculine poems." Finally, as late as 1890, he reacts with a combination of bewilderment and rage to John Addington Symonds' imputation of homoeroticism to *Calamus's* poems of male "adhesiveness," implying that he is merely an acolyte of healthful masculine blood-brotherhood, and indignantly explaining that "Tho' always unmarried I have had six children—

---

1. *Leaves of Grass: A Norton Critical Edition*, ed. Sculley Bradley and Harold W. Blodgett (New York: Norton, 1973), p. 102; all references to Whitman's poetry will be to this edition and, where necessary, page numbers will be given parenthetically in the text.

two are dead—one living southern grandchild, fine boy, who writes to me occasionally."[2]

Furthermore, in "real life," despite the worrisome devotion of problematically sexed British disciples like Symonds, Swinburne, and Edward Carpenter, Whitman's American apostles generally take his claims of exaggeratedly perfect masculinity at face value. From Abraham Lincoln (who "commended the new poet's words for their virility") to Fanny Fern (who exclaimed "Walt Whitman the effeminate world needed thee"), a number of readers unquestioningly accept the poet's own apparent estimate of himself. But his closest friends are even more hyperbolical about his virtually ontological maleness, with William Douglas O'Connor describing his "manly majesty . . . and his form, regnant and masculine," John Burroughs exclaiming that "He reminds one of the first men—the beginners," and the renowned streetcar conductor Peter Doyle confiding to Richard Maurice Bucke and Horace Trauble that "Walt . . . was an athlete—great, great."[3]

If Whitman is parodically male, Emily Dickinson is certainly parodically female, trying on every possible feminine role for size as if it were a differently styled white dress—yet always, of course, a white dress. The "slightest in the house," inhabitant of "the smallest room," a dainty "Daisy," she is a virginal maiden, a lily of a lady, exemplar of a cult of purity incarnated in such different fictional characters as Hawthorne's Priscilla and Charlotte Bronte's Jane Eyre.[4] A tired little girl seeking refuge in "Midnight" (J. 425) or an unregenerate imp—"Old

2. Quoted in Stephen A. Black, *Whitman's Journeys into Chaos: A Psychoanalytic Study of the Poetic Process* (Princeton: Princeton University Press, 1975), p. 180. But see also Richard Maurice Bucke, ed., *Calamus: A Series of Letters Written During the Years 1868–1880 by Walt Whitman to a Young Friend* (Boston: Laurens Maynard, 1897).

3. The comments of Lincoln and Fern are quoted in Gay Wilson Allen, *The Solitary Singer* (New York: Grove Press, 1955), pp. 175 and 177; the remarks of O'Connor, Burroughs, and Doyle appear in *Calamus,* pp. 15 and 23.

4. For a discussion of the various Dickinsonian personae associated with this poet's fictionalization of herself as "A Woman—White," see Sandra M. Gilbert and Susan Gubar, *The Madwoman in the Attic: The Woman Writer and the Nineteenth-Century Literary Imagination* (New Haven: Yale University Press, 1979), pp. 581–650.

fashioned—naughty" (J. 70)—she is a professional daughter, refusing to grow up so as to escape not only the tedious cares of wifely housekeeping but also the brutish claims of (male) sexuality.[5] Worshipper of a "Madonna dim" (J. 918), keeper of a shadowy shrine, she is a secret sufferer, a wounded bird or deer whose pain makes her into a prophetess, a sibyl of fainting female sexuality.[6] Unselfish and benevolent—"I bring an unaccustomed wine / To lips long parching" (J. 132)—she is an Angel in the House, a devotee of female renunciation. Scared by "Ourself behind ourself, concealed" (J. 670), she is a Gothic heroine, courted by that Byronically "supple Suitor" death (J. 1445), whose "stealthy wooing" may sweep her away, like so many other nineteenth-century heroines, in the chariot of the "white plague." Triumphantly but secretly betrothed to an enthralling "Master," she is "the Wife—without the Sign! . . . Empress of Calvary"—not only victim but also covert victress in a theatrical adultery plot whose permutations as much as her poems make her the "Myth of Amherst" even during her lifetime.

And, like Whitman, myth she is, protagonist of a public legend as sexually charged as his. In fact, like Whitman's, Dickinson's contemporaries hasten to attest to her intensely sexualized genius, her perfect, exaggeratedly feminine idiosyncracies. Her niece, Mrs. Helen Knight Bullard Wyman, remembers her "soft, 'tawny' hair (somewhat like the soft ears of an Irish setter dog) . . . dressed similarly to that of Mrs. Browning." Mrs. Emily Fowler Ford recalls her "demure manner which brightened easily into fun, where she felt at home." "Miss Marian," an aged seamstress, testifies that she ate "like a bird." Bishop F. D. Huntington thinks her "hardly more terrestrial than ce-

5. All Dickinson references given parenthetically in the text are to poem numbers from *The Poems of Emily Dickinson*, ed. Thomas H. Johnson (Cambridge, Mass.: The Belknap Press of Harvard University Press, 1955). For an analysis of Dickinson's role as paradigmatic nineteenth-century daughter, see Barbara Antonina Clarke Mossberg, *Emily Dickinson: When a Writer Is a Daughter* (Bloomington: Indiana University Press, 1982).

6. For a discussion of Dickinson's use of the nineteenth-century trope of female sacrifice, see Cheryl Walker, *The Nightingale's Burden: Women Poets and American Culture before 1900* (Bloomington: Indiana University Press, 1982), pp. 87–116.

lestial,—a spirit with only as much of the mortal investiture as served to maintain her relations with this present world." Thomas Wentworth Higginson, besides wondering whether she is mad ("I saw my eccentric poetess Miss Emily Dickinson . . . I'm afraid Mary's . . . remark 'Oh why do the insane so cling to you?' still holds"), considers her comparable to a wayward heroine in one of Elizabeth Drew Stoddard's novels, the victim of "an excess of tension, and of an abnormal life."[7]

Whitman, then, is paradigmatically male; Dickinson, paradigmatically female, and if we look at the verse the two produced, won't we see these stereotypes reflected in their art? Can't we decide that Whitman's long lines, his expansive public oratorical declamations, must inevitably be set against Dickinson's short lines, her intensely compressed shy private religious musings? Can't we define the phallic Walt as a (parodic but also serious) male devil in the House of Poetry and the virginal Emily as its (sardonic but also sincere) angel? Five years ago I think this is the conclusion to which I would have come, but now I am not quite so certain.

For one thing, Whitman and Dickinson are alike in their production of verse that is shockingly unlike the verse of their contemporaries. For another, Whitman and Dickinson are alike in their experimentation with a kind of equivocal sexuality which one would not have expected to find in people who seem, on the surface, to have adopted such settled and stereotypical roles. Perhaps for this reason, moreover, Whitman and Dickinson are alike in representing themselves as having fragmented personalities, with Dickinson's self-defining "Ourself behind ourself, concealed" interestingly foreshadowed by Whitman's division of himself into an "I," an "electric self," and a "real Me." In addition, both are alike, or at least quite comparable, in their radical disaffection from most of the poetry written by their American contemporaries and thus in their apparently deliberate construction of "anti-careers." And finally, no doubt because of this last phenomenon, both are alike in their dependence on strange sources of thought, odd modes of literary skill, pe-

---

7. All quoted in Jay Leyda, *The Years and Hours of Emily Dickinson*, 2 vols. (New Haven: Yale University Press, 1960), II, 479, 478, 480, 152.

culiar wellsprings of aesthetic inspiration. In fact, I will argue here that Whitman and Dickinson became the father and mother of American poetry not because their poetry was the culmination of an ongoing American tradition but because they did not, in the terms of their time, write poetry at all, or, to be more precise, they wrote something that I shall be calling "not poetry."

It was, of course, the fact that Whitman and Dickinson did not compose "poetry," instead they wrote "not poetry," that alarmed and alienated so many of their earliest readers. To be sure, many of the reviewers of the 1855 *Leaves of Grass* seem at first to have been most shocked by the volume's frankly revolutionary sensuality, denouncing the book as a "gathering of muck," "a mass of stupid filth," "the rotten garbage of licentious thoughts."[8] Increasingly, however, as Whitman's reputation grew, critics emphasized the shockingly nonpoetic quality of Whitman's style: an 1897 *Introduction to American Literature* tells us that by many readers Whitman was "scarcely regarded as a poet at all,"[9] and even such early defenders as Saintsbury and Howells conceded that "A page of his work has little or no look of poetry about it" because "he produced a new kind in literature, which we may or may not allow to be poetry."[10]

Since Emily Dickinson barely published in her own lifetime, and—apart from her sister-in-law Susan Gilbert Dickinson and Helen Hunt Jackson, the friend and correspondent of her later

8. Quoted in Paul Zweig, *Walt Whitman: The Making of the Poet* (New York: Basic Books, 1984), p. 266.

9. Quoted in Charles B. Willard, *Whitman's American Fame: The Growth of His Reputation in America After 1892,* Brown University Studies, vol. 12, Americana Series no. 3, (Providence, 1950), p. 131; several other turn-of-the-century academic texts cited by Willard describe *Leaves of Grass* as "the very drybones of prose" and as "a strange volume of what cannot be called poetry" (p. 132), and in 1895, a German scholar, identifying Whitman's methods of versification with "degenerate insanity as well as sexual perversion," decided that the American writer's poetry was really "prose gone mad" (p. 159).

10. George Saintsbury, *"Leaves of Grass,"* in the Norton Critical Edition of *Leaves of Grass,* p. 788; William Dean Howells "[Whitman in Retrospect]," p. 790; in the same essay, Howells also declared that "the prose passages [in *November Boughs*] are, some of them, more poetic than the most poetic of the rhythmical passages" (p. 791).

years—she had, in her own words, "no Tribunal," her case was even more egregious than that of Walt Whitman. Not surprisingly, her benevolent but generally incomprehending "mentor," Thomas Wentworth Higginson, assumed from the start that she did not write what *he* would call "poetry." The man who asserted "It is no discredit to Walt Whitman that he wrote 'Leaves of Grass,' only that he did not burn it afterwards" inevitably thought his strange Amherst "scholar" wrote verses whose "gait" was "spasmodic," and inexorably urged her to relinquish "the Bells whose jingling cooled [her] Tramp."[11] Even the enthusiastic Mabel Loomis Todd had confessed herself "exasperated" by Dickinson's "carelessness of form," complaining that "the simplest laws of verse-making she ignored, and what she called rhymes grated on me."[12] As for Dickinson's other friends, those notable *literati* Samuel Bowles and Josiah Holland were clearly unimpressed by her literary efforts. In this they were similar to many readers of Dickinson's first volumes: over and over again, critics insisted that hers was "bad poetry . . . divorced from meaning, from music, from grammar, from rhyme," that "her style is clumsy, her language is poor; her technique is appalling," and that she wrote what Higginson called "poetry torn up by the roots"—or what Holland pronounced "not poetry."[13]

Can we speculate that Dickinson and Whitman produced a species of poetic composition that many of their contemporaries

11. Higginson's view of Whitman is quoted in Leyda, II, 127; Dickinson discusses her "Bells" and Higginson's opinion of them in letter 265, Thomas Johnson, ed., *The Letters of Emily Dickinson*, vol. 2 (Cambridge, Mass.: The Belknap Press of Harvard University Press, 1965), pp. 408–409 (hereafter, *Letters*).

12. Mabel Loomis Todd's remark is quoted in Ruth Miller, *The Poetry of Emily Dickinson* (Middletown: Wesleyan University Press, 1968), pp. 8–9.

13. Miller discusses Samuel Bowles's attitude toward Dickinson's verse (as well as his fondness for the "little poetic gems" offered him by the sentimental poetess Collette Loomis), on pp. 122–123; Hyatt Waggoner recounts Josiah Holland's refusal to publish Dickinson's verse in his 1873 *Illustrated Library of Favorite Song* and notes that "privately he thought [Dickinson's poems] 'not poetry' " in Hyatt H. Waggoner, *American Poets: From the Puritans to the Present* (Boston: Houghton Mifflin, 1968), p. 225. The reactions of other early critics are reviewed in Caesar Blake and Carlton Wells, *The Recognition of Emily Dickinson* (Ann Arbor: University of Michigan Press, 1964), pp. 27, 119, 121.

defined as "not poetry" because, despite their apparent adoption of stereotypical sex roles, their personalities were fragmented and, specifically, sexually ambiguous? Is it possible, in other words, that both experienced a covert alienation from social conventions which led to an overt alienation from literary conventions? At first, this seems likely even if we put aside the vexed questions of their alleged homosexuality or lesbianism. Certainly Dickinson presents herself as either literally or figuratively male in a number of poems. "We learned to like the Fire / By playing Glaciers—when a Boy—" (J. 689), she says, for instance, in one of several poems in which she defines herself, or, rather, her multiple selves ("We," "Ourself") as male. In "Her sweet weight on my Heart a Night" (J. 518), she composes an enigmatic lament—not, evidently, a dramatic monologue— about a lost "Bride." And in "My Life had stood—a Loaded Gun" she reincarnates herself as a suspiciously phallic weapon, dedicated to hunting the "Doe."

Similarly, in "The Sleepers" (perhaps more forcefully than anywhere else), the usually magisterial Whitman "becomes" an erotic woman: "I am she who adorn'd herself and folded her hair expectantly, / My truant lover has come, and it is dark." Even what is usually seen as the sensitive, delicate, and "audacious" parable of the twenty-ninth bather in "Song of Myself" can be read as an encoded fantasy of transsexualism, with Whitman himself, yearning and thoughtful, the "lonesome" lady who hides "aft the blinds of the window," dreaming that her/his hand might descend "tremblingly" from the "temples and ribs" of twenty-eight young men who "float on their backs, their white bellies bulg[ing] to the sun." Besides being stylistically unconventional, then, both poets would appear to have been psychologically unconventional; experimenting with odd forms and meters, both also appeared to record experiments with atypical sex roles.

We cannot, however, ignore the fact that both poets assimilated experimental passages such as those I have just cited into extended sequences whose sexual modalities appear continually to reiterate and reinforce traditional definitions of masculinity and femininity: lapses of gender, indeed, seem to occur because of lapses of genre rather than the other way around. In fact, it is likely that the subversions of stereotypical sexuality which do mark Whitman's and Dickinson's writings are consequences, rather than causes, of these poets' mutual disaffection from stereotypical "poetry," specifically from its coherent "voice," its cohesive "form," and its conventional language, rhyme, and meter. It is arguable, in other words, that for both poets the wellspring of all alienation was a profound literary alienation.

Certainly both Whitman and Dickinson were given to making sardonic, even scathing, statements in which they sharply differentiated their own aesthetic aims from those of their contemporaries; both, moreover, associated what they considered poetry with an intensity, even a quasi-sexual violence, conspicuously absent from most contemporary verse. Declaring in the letter to Emerson which functioned as a preface to the 1856 *Leaves of Grass* "that the body is to be expressed, and sex is," Whitman raged against genteel art, specifically against "this empty dish, gallantry . . . this diluted deferential love . . . in songs, fictions, and so forth [which] is enough to make a man vomit." But in one of his anonymous reviews of the 1855 *Leaves of Grass* he had already clarified the assumptions out of which he was writing here: attacking the "dandified forms" produced by "Tennyson, and his British and American élèves," Whitman had explained that "Americans . . . must cast around for men essentially different from the old poets, and from the modern successions of jinglers and snivellers and fops," representatives of an age in which "Everybody writes poetry, and yet there is not a single poet."[14] Years later, in a manuscript verse fragment entitled "Scantlings" (p. 654), he was still fulminating against the "White, shaved, foreign, soft-fleshed, shrinking" beings, "scant of muscle, scant of love-power," who made up what he had in 1856 called "the ranks of rhymesters, melancholy and swallow-tailed . . . the confectioners and upholsterers of verse."

If Dickinson did not so openly and fiercely defend the eccentric "Bells whose jingling cooled [her] Tramp," some of her confidences to Higginson suggest that, despite her fear that

14. Unsigned review, *American Phrenological Journal* (1856), in Milton Hindus, ed., *Walt Whitman: The Critical Heritage* (London: Routledge and Kegan Paul, 1971), p. 43.

Whitman was "disgraceful," she might well have shared his views. Her famous definition of poetry, for instance—"If I read a book and it makes my whole body so cold no fire ever can warm me I know *that* is poetry. If I feel physically as if the top of my head were taken off, I know *that* is poetry"—followed by the disingenuous disclaimers "These are the only ways I know of. Is there any other way," are curiously fierce and interestingly comparable to Whitman's claim that in true poetry "the body is to be expressed." In the same interview, Dickinson dismissed most writing with Whitmanesque hauteur: "When I lost the use of my eyes it was a comfort to think there were so few real *books* that I could easily find some one to read me all of them."[15]

Finally, though many of her references to established writers—Shakespeare, Keats, and the Brownings, for instance—were far more reverential than Whitman's, Dickinson was capable of elliptical expressions of literary scorn. The first two stanzas of poem 131 may be seen not just as a miniature, antipoetic ode to autumn but also as a small, sly essay in criticism:

> Besides the Autumn poets sing
> A few prosaic days
> A little this side of the Snow
> And that side of the Haze—
>
> A few incisive Mornings—
> A few Ascetic Eves—
> Gone—Mr. Bryant's "Golden Rod"
> And Mr. Thomson's "Sheaves."

Thus, even though Dickinson at one point glorifies "Poets" as the incarnation of "the Sun— / Then summer—Then the heaven of God—" (J. 569), her definition of aesthetic power is one that implies Emersonian prophetic authority, the poet as an incarnation of nature's genius rather than the sort of literary skill to "mend / The strain with rapture that with fire was penned" which Bryant advocated in his 1863 "The Poet." True poetic language, she observes, comes "unsummoned in," since "not unto nomination / The cherubim reveal" (J. 1126).

15. All these remarks were reported by Higginson, after his first meeting with Dickinson in August 1870, in several letters to his wife; see *Letters*, pp. 473–476.

It is not surprising, then, that besides depending heavily on Emerson's radically antiliterary essay "The Poet," with its insistence that "not metres, but a metre-making argument . . . makes a poem," both Whitman and Dickinson relied on strangely un-"poetic" sources to inspire their art. Whitman was influenced not only by his years of journalistic writing but also by the conventions of American oratory, by the grammatical parallelisms that characterize biblical rhetoric, and even by popular domestic and melodramatic fiction. Dickinson was influenced not only by hymnals, epitaphs, and religious rhymes for children but also by the conventions of female letter-writing and by themes and images deployed in a subcultural tradition of women's fiction. Ultimately, in both Whitman and Dickinson we see a self-conscious resistance to—and an almost exaggerated straining away from—the hegemonic "ranks of rhymesters."

What would account for such resistances to "poetry" in the careers of these ambitious poets? Let me begin by pointing out another similarity: both Walt Whitman and Emily Dickinson entered upon their lives as poets in just the position of alienation and anxiety that Emerson describes in "The Poet." As Americans, consciously (Whitman) or half-consciously (Dickinson) committed to a Myth of the New, they obviously found themselves drastically belated in relation to European tradition. With deceptive calm, Whitman opens the 1855 Preface by implicitly characterizing that tradition as a "corpse . . . slowly borne from the eating and sleeping rooms of the house," and he concedes, in a moment of willed (if supercilious) generosity, that "It was fittest for its days" before adding, grandly, "that its action has descended to the stalwart and wellshaped heir who approaches . . . and that he shall be fittest for his days." Clearly he, Whitman, the stalwart heir, is going to be the poet for whom Emerson has looked "in vain," the one who will sing the America that "is a poem in our eyes."

Yet in private notes and critical fragments, Whitman's posture is not so confident: struggling to assimilate the dates and details of Western cultural history, he produces elaborate chronologies of the careers of Shakespeare, Spenser, Rousseau, Keats, Corneille, Dante, and others, even while admonishing himself to "Make no quotations and no reference to any other writers."

Like Emerson, moreover, who explains in "The Poet" that
Americans require a greater poet than even Europe offers—
"Milton is too literary and Homer too literal and historical"—
Whitman resists, even as he transcribes, the daunting achievements of his European forebears: "Many little things are too
much over-colored in Shakespeare—*far too much,*" he insists;
Spenser's words are often "affected and strained"; "the Paradise
Lost is . . . nonsense"; "Wordsworth lacks sympathy with men
and women"; toward Goethe "the American glance descends
with indifference"; "Keats' poetry is . . . imbued with the sentiment, at secondhand, of the gods and goddesses of twentyfive
hundred years ago."[16]

Dickinson does not surface her distinctively American anxieties so specifically, but she too was a reader of "The Poet,"
and her worries about her American belatedness become clearer
if one conflates the claims she makes in a number of her more
self-consciously literary verses. Certainly there is something
problematic about the "precious—*mouldering*—pleasure" (italics mine, J. 371) she associates with "an Antique Book," and
there is something sinister in the devastation she connects with
the death of her beloved Elizabeth Barrett Browning ("Her—
'last Poems'— / Poets—ended— / Silver—perished—with her
Tongue—," J. 312).[17] The apparent oddity of her notorious "Nor
would I be a Poet— / It's finer—own the Ear— / Enamored—
impotent—content," may, then, be explained by her sense that
poetry, associated with European tradition, makes impotent the
American interlocutor. Like Whitman's, her defense seems to
be a determined nativism: the "Robin's my Criterion for Tune,"
she declares—not the traditional but foreign nightingale or sky-
lark—"Because I see—New Englandly" (J. 285).

But for Whitman and Dickinson to cut themselves off from
European poetic tradition did not mean assimilating themselves

16. Whitman's notes and comments here are all quoted from Richard Bucke,
ed., *The Complete Prose Works of Walt Whitman,* vol. VI, *Notes and Fragments
Left by Walt Whitman* (New York: G. P. Putnam's Sons, The Knickerbocker
Press, 1902), pp. 4, 76, 79, 97, 98, 114, 120.

17. See Vivian Pollak's fine discussion of the anxiety, even submerged hostility, implicit in this poem, in Vivian R. Pollak, *Dickinson: The Anxiety of
Gender* (Ithaca: Cornell University Press, 1984), pp. 241–243.

into an established tradition of American verse. On the contrary, as we have seen, both scorned America's "ranks of
rhymesters," precisely because, in Emerson's words, most were
timid acolytes of "the courtly muses of Europe," "meek young
men . . . in libraries, believing it their duty to accept the views
which Cicero, which Locke, which Bacon have given"—or, one
might add, meek young ladies in parlors accepting the roles
assigned them by sententious British bards. More specifically,
both Whitman and Dickinson would have had to come to terms
with an American poetry dominated by, on the one hand,
schoolroom sages—cultivated, Europeanized gentlemen like
William Cullen Bryant, Henry Wadsworth Longfellow, John
Greenleaf Whittier, Oliver Wendell Holmes, and James Russell
Lowell—and, on the other hand, by such sweetly Victorian
"singers" as Lydia Sigourney, Fanny Osgood, and Samuel
Bowles's favorite, Collette Loomis. No wonder, then, that both
might well have been awed by Emerson's advice: "Thou shalt
leave the world, and know the Muse only. Thou shalt not know
any longer the times, customs, graces, politics, or opinions of
men, but shalt take all from the Muse." More particularly, both
may have quite consciously begun to write "not poetry" in order
to act on his most painful injunction: *"The world is full of
renunciations and apprenticeships, and this is thine: thou must
pass for a fool and a churl for a long season"* (italics mine).

To be sure, both Whitman and Dickinson would have noticed
that America's literary marketplace was really dominated not
so much by the productions of second-rate poets as by the prose
works of novelists and essayists, many of whom were women.
These two aspiring poets found themselves enmeshed in a history in which, as Leslie Fiedler has observed, the invention of
America itself was both paralleled by and blended with the
invention of the novel in America.[18] For both writers, however,
such prose—by definition liberated from the daunting constraints of epic and lyric tradition—was a source of strength.
Whitman, for instance, began his career by writing domestic
and melodramatic fiction—indeed, no volume of his poetry ever

18. Leslie Fiedler, *Love and Death in the American Novel* (New York: Stein
and Day, 1975), p. 31.

sold as well as his temperance novel, *Franklin Evans*—and he famously stole the cover design for the 1855 *Leaves of Grass* from the best-selling collection *Fern Leaves from Fanny's Portfolio* (Second Series, 1854).

More to the point, the kinds of catalogues that Fanny Fern offered in some of her meditative essays and sketches of city and country life may well have functioned as models to be reworked in Whitman's own catalogues. Despite its tendentiousness and mechanical juxtapositions, for example, Fern's "Hour-Glass Thoughts" strikingly prefigures section 15 of "Song of Myself." Here are excerpts from Fern:

> The bride stands waiting at the altar; the corpse lies waiting for burial. . . .
>
> The starving wretch, who purloins a crust, trembles in the hall of Justice; liveried Sin, unpunished, riots in high places.
>
> Brothers, clad 'in purple and fine linen, fare sumptuously every day;' Sisters, in linsey-woolsey, toil in garrets. . . .
>
> The Village Squire sows, reaps, and garners golden harvests; the Parish Clergyman sighs as his casting vote cuts down his already meager salary.
>
> The unpaid sempstress begems with tears the fairy festal robe; proud beauty floats in it through the ball-room like a thing of air."[19]

And here is Whitman, in a brilliant transmutation:

> The pedlar sweats with his pack on his back, (the purchaser
>   higgling about the odd cent;)
> The bride unrumples her white dress, the minute-hand of the
>   clock moves slowly,
> The opium-eater reclines with rigid head and just-open'd lips,
> The prostitute draggles her shawl . . .

Elsewhere, moreover, Fern's rhetorical questions to her reader ("Do you suppose a *man's* opinions are in the market—to be bought and sold to the highest bidder?" or "Do you suppose he would laud a vapid book . . . ?"[20]) sound like comic preversions of characteristically Whitmanesque questions: "Have

19. Fanny Fern, *Fern Leaves from Fanny's Portfolio: Second Series* (1854; rpt. in *American Fiction Reprint Series* [Freeport, N.Y.: Books for Libraries Press, 1971]), p. 43.

20. Fern, p. 87.

you practis'd so long to learn to read? / Have you felt so proud
to get at the meaning of poems?" or "Has anyone supposed it
lucky to be born?" Moreoever, the great vignettes incorporated
into poems like "Song of Myself" and "The Sleepers"—for
instance, the vision of the "old-time sea fight" or the parable
of the twenty-ninth bather—are fundamentally fictional, calm
or calamitous tableaux of lives as they are lived in quasi-realistic
new stories and real news stories, "These so, these irretriev-
able."

   Dickinson's reliance on fictional styles and structures is harder
to document than Whitman's. Yet just as all her self-presenting
poses derive in one way or another from fictional models, so
the essentially narrative lines of many of her poems, together
with the epistolary or dialogical quality of many, support her
own assertion in poem 669 ("No Romance sold unto / Could
so enthrall a Man / As the perusal of / His Individual One")
that her life, as textualized in her poems, was a kind of episodic
novel—indeed, to recall Higginson's phrase, a novel "torn up
by its roots." From "There came a Day at Summer's Full" (J.
322) to "One need not be a Chamber—to be haunted" (J. 670),
she hints at romantic and Gothic plots as she inscribes herself
into a fictive world that is part a revision of *Jane Eyre*, in its
ambivalent allegiance to a powerful "Sir" or "Master," and part
a revision of *Aurora Leigh*, in its prideful devotion to the solemn
literary mysteries of "a woman—white." At the same time, in
colloquial outbursts like "Of course—I prayed— / And did God
care?" (J. 376) and telegraphic messages like "I send two Sun-
sets— / Day and I—in competition ran—" (J. 308) and "Just
lost, when I was saved!" (J. 160), she frankly writes a letter to
the world not unlike either the sentimental letters of Fanny Fern
or Whitman's grandiose oratorical letters.

   Having stationed herself so obliquely in relation to both
American and European poetry, Dickinson could well have said
of her own work, as Whitman actually did of his own in one of
his early self-reviews, *"If this is poetry, where must its foregoers
stand?"* (italics mine).[21] And indeed, even while she self-
deprecatingly defined herself as "the only Kangaroo among the

---

21. Hindus, ed., *Walt Whitman*, p. 44.

Beauty,"[22] she did imply a similar arrogance toward poetic tradition, conceding that "My Splendors are Menagerie" but then
boasting that "Their Competeless Show / Will entertain the
Centuries / When I am long ago" (J. 290). Like Whitman, she
acknowledges that what she has produced may be seen as problematic, even grotesque or subhuman ("menagerie"); but for
that very reason, liberated from the cage of verse convention,
her work is "competeless": because, like Whitman, she has
drawn upon alternative wells of energy, "foregoers" will have
nowhere to stand.

   Why was it Walt Whitman (not William Cullen Bryant, Thomas
Wentworth Higginson, or even Ralph Waldo Emerson) and
Emily Dickinson (not Lydia Sigourney, Maria Lowell, or even
Helen Hunt Jackson) who cleared such authoritative and uniquely
American spaces for themselves that they and their readers had
to ask "If this is poetry where must its foregoers stand?" Here
an explanation of the strangely comparable antipoetic courses
chosen by these two artists must rely on the differences that
paradoxically made Whitman and Dickinson similar even while
ultimately engendering what we will see are notable distinctions
between them. From the start, of course, Whitman and Dickinson were outsiders in literary culture but the reasons for their
alienation were antithetical: Whitman was an outsider because
he did not come from the "right" class, Dickinson because she
did.

   Not insignificantly, Whitman's dislike of Keats's "ornamen-
tal" poetry was closely associated with his sense that "Its feeling
is the feeling of a gentlemanly person lately at college . . . who
moves and would only move in elegant society, reading classical
books in libraries."[23] Because he was a rough self-made man
from an essentially working-class family—a family which was,
to say the least, problematic—Whitman experienced himself as
so marginalized in high culture that he *had* to make a new
literary self.[24] Dickinson, however, came from just the sort of
cultivated New England family which fostered the careers of

---

22. *Letters*, p. 412.
23. *Complete Prose Works*, p. 120.
24. On Whitman's family, see Zweig, *Walt Whitman*, passim.

men like Bryant, Lowell, and Emerson, a family, incidentally, very different from the working-class family whose exigencies obliged Lydia Sigourney to seek the patronage of Daniel Wadsworth.[25] But as numerous critics have observed, Dickinson's status as a privileged daughter, a sort of Yankee princess, meant that she had to guard her "snow"—her literary virginity, as it were—with special care. She may have been speaking sardonically in "Publication is the Auction / Of the Mind of Man" and in the famous letter where she told Higginson that the idea of publication was as "foreign to my thought as Firmament to Fin," but her irony seems to have masked a real ambivalence: her reported statement that "I would as soon undress in public as give my poems to the world" reflects exactly the genteel reticence that would have been inculcated in the ladylike daughter of a gentlemanly father who "buys me many books—but begs me not to read them—because he fears they joggle the mind."[26]

Yet although such reticence inevitably shaped the poet's mendacious claim to Higginson that "I made no verse, but one or two—until this winter—Sir," as well as her perhaps not so mendacious assertion that "My size felt small to me,"[27] it also left Dickinson in a position of privileged marginality not unlike Whitman's. But if, in dealing with that marginality and its aesthetic consequences, both poets began aggressively to write "not poetry," and specifically "not poetry" in which (as if anticipating the prescriptions of some recent feminist critics)[28] they overturned such traditional hierarchies as verse/prose or soul/body, they also increasingly differed from each other in what Harold Bloom would call their "swerves" from poetic convention— that is, in the revisionary gestures through which they con-

25. On Lydia Sigourney's relationship to Daniel Wadsworth, see Walker, p. 80, and Gordon Haight, *Lydia Sigourney: The Sweet Singer of Hartford* (New Haven: Yale University Press, 1930), pp. 7–11.

26. *Letters*, pp. 408 ("Firmament to Fin"), 404 ("joggle the mind"); Leyda, II, 482 ("undress in public").

27. *Letters*, pp. 404–405.

28. See Elaine Marks and Isabelle de Courtivron, ed., *New French Feminisms* (Amherst: University of Massachusetts Press, 1980), especially Hélène Cixous, "Sorties" and "The Laugh of the Medusa," and Luce Irigaray, "When the Goods Get Together."

structed their careers.[29] Such differences, in fact, seem to me
to help account for the formation of two different (male and
female) traditions in modern American poetry, even while they
reflect, and reflect back upon, a history of sexual difference in
poetry.

A marked difference between Whitman and Dickinson begins
to emerge when we examine two of the few verses by these
artists that were *not* "not poetry" but, rather, conventional
nineteenth-century poesy, and it is a difference that would at
first seem simply to mirror the stereotypically male and female
figures whom, as I noted earlier, Whitman's and Dickinson's
admirers consistently portrayed. Described by his editors as "the
most widely known and least characteristic poem that Walt
Whitman ever published," "O Captain! My Captain!" might be
called—in an appropriate oxymoron—a rousing elegy for the
fallen Lincoln. Speaking both as a fellow voyager on the Ship
of State and as an heir of his lost leader and "dear Father,"
Whitman also speaks for "the swaying mass" on the shore await-
ing the inward bound, victorious vessel. Alternating quatrains
of long iambic lines with balladlike stanzas that incorporate a
ritualized refrain ("Fallen cold and dead"), the poet becomes
a public orator, certifying his own institutionalization as representative man with, as it were, the insignia of regular rhyme
and meter. Momentarily transcending the alienation from audience and tradition implicit in his irregular "not poetry," he
also allays the anxieties inspired by the formlessness of the dark
death mother ("always gliding near with soft feet") who dominates "When Lilacs Last in the Dooryard Bloom'd," the more
radically innovative (and thus more characteristically Whitmanesque) companion poem to "O Captain!" And significantly,
Whitman's almost involuntary reliance on generic convention
is associated with an act of male bonding—with, in fact, a quasi-
Freudian bonding of putative son and dead father—that enables
him to confront (if not master) the mystery of mortality.

29. Bloom discusses "revisionary ratios" in *The Anxiety of Influence* (New
York: Oxford, 1973), and *A Map of Misreading* (New York: Oxford, 1975).

Dickinson's "If I can stop one Heart from breaking" (J. 919)
is just as conventional in style and substance as "O Captain!
My Captain!"—and just as stereotypically female as the Whitman verse is almost parodically male. Sweetly renunciatory,
privatized, incrementally lowering the shrunken sites of her ambition as she progresses, the speaker of this piece utters words
that generations of dutiful daughters might have stitched into
samplers:

> If I can stop one Heart from breaking
> I shall not live in vain
> If I can ease one Life the Aching
> Or cool one Pain
>
> Or help one fainting Robin
> Unto his nest again
> I shall not live in Vain.

As "*one* heart" modulates into "*one* Pain" and then, rather
ludicrously, into "*one* fainting Robin," the poet truncates her
verse, following a "normal" quatrain with a three-line stanza
whose abbreviation suggests her fatigue with the verse form
itself. And she herself, as speaker, seems also to diminish, exiled
not just from the ground of public triumph and defeat—the
burning deck on which Whitman so superbly stands, mourning
the dead father while exulting in victorious bells—but also,
potentially, from even the point of her own life. For what if no
fainting robin chirps for help, what if no small personal occasion
for self-justification presents itself? Qualified and indeterminate
in her self-assertion where Whitman constructs for himself an
authority that is determined and almost overdetermined, Dickinson withdraws from the certitudes of high cultural genre—the
defenses against death, the setting of form against chaos—even
as she ambivalently acquiesces in a stereotypically female mode
and in what is for her an unusually conventional sequence of
rhymes (breaking/aching, pain/vain).

Because "O Captain! My Captain!" and "If I can stop one
Heart from breaking" are both so uncharacteristically "poetic,"
they may seem mere lapses, trifling condescensions toward cer-
tification by readers (Bryant, Higginson) whose approval both
authors really believed they should reject. Yet I would argue

that in their flirtations with convention the two poems are telling, for they suggest relationships between genre and gender
that are, paradoxically enough, deeply embedded in the "not
poetry" for which their authors became famous. On the one
hand, "O Captain! My Captain!" tells us that Whitman, immersed in the antiform he himself "invented," needed to fortify
himself through the overt (or elsewhere, as we shall see, covert)
identification of his individual talent with tradition. On the other
hand, "If I can stop one Heart from breaking" tells us that
Dickinson, listening most of the time to her own "bells," could
find no outer chimes to hear except tinklings that would have
further alienated her from conventional paradigms of poetic
potency.

What I am claiming here may at first seem obvious: that
despite his own intense efforts at differentiation, Whitman was
an heir of male-dominated culture, and that Dickinson was
not an heiress, despite her own intense (if ambivalent) efforts
at assimilation. But I suspect that, beyond this obvious point,
the case histories of these poets—both striking up for a supposedly new world from positions of ostensible innocence—
significantly illuminate the sexual dialectic that long informed
literary tradition and that has shaped poetic modernism in
America.

Where might we locate a historical difference that would have
fostered differences between Whitman's and Dickinson's revisionary swerves from "poetry"? If we review the history of verse
upon which both these artists so frequently meditated, it becomes clear that such difference is most prominently manifested
not primarily at the level of language—as some theorists have
lately suggested[30]—but rather at the level of poetic *genre*, for
when we attempt to categorize women's use of poetic genres in
terms of the conventional modes that mark male-authored verse,
we find extraordinary gaps and absences. With the possible
exception of Barrett Browning's *Aurora Leigh* (which is itself

30. See, for example, *New French Feminisms* for discussions of women's
alienation from patriarchal language, a point made not only by Cixous and
Irigaray but also, in a somewhat different way, by Julia Kristeva; all are responding to Jacques Lacan's claim that woman is marginalized and subordi-
nated by language.

formally equivocal, judging by the writer's own definition of the work as a "verse-novel"), there are in the Anglo-American canon no successful pre-twentieth-century epics, book-length allegorical romances, or long satires composed by women: no *Beowulf, Faerie Queen, Paradise Lost,* or *Rape of the Lock.* Moreover, perhaps even more strikingly, such other traditional verse genres as the pastoral elegy, the philosophical epistle, and the high Romantic ode seem hardly to have been approached by women poets in England and America: there is no woman's "Lycidas," "Adonais," "Essay on Man," or "Ode: Intimations of Immortality."[31]

On the whole, the most ambitious female-authored poems tend to have an implicitly narrative core, or else, what is closely associated with such a core, an "occasional" purpose; in other words, the woman poet who is attempting a highly elaborated work appears to need to suggest that she is either "just" telling a story or "just" writing a kind of specialized "thank you" note to a patron, patroness, or friend—both attitudes which might on the surface appear to be functioning to justify (or even disguise) the author's stereotypically "unfeminine" literary aspirations. Yet what might seem to be comparatively circumscribed verse forms—the ode, the pastoral elegy—genres which in a sense constitute the foundation of the lyric traditon in English, also appear (with the exception of the sonnet sequence) to have been historically alien to the female imagination, and, again, on the surface such alienation might seem to reflect women's exclusion from the education in the classics which no doubt inspired male artists to resurrect and revise these Greek and Latin forms.

But can such literary differences be explained entirely in sociocultural terms—male access to authority and education, female deprivation of both—or might there be (as, say, Cixous

31. Exceptions to this "rule" could possibly be found in the works of such poets as Mary Tighe and Charlotte Smith, or even, indeed, among some of the writings of Elizabeth Barrett Browning (e.g., the early "Essay on Mind"); nevertheless, it became clear to Susan Gubar and me, as we assembled materials for the *Norton Anthology of Literature by Women: The Tradition in English* (New York: Norton, 1985), that women's most *successful* and powerful writings tended to evade a number of conventional generic definitions.

and Irigaray imply in their discussions of "male" and "female" language) differing male and female psychosexual imperatives? Might we, in fact, speculate that male poets have a deep, familially constructed need to inscribe the "masculine" through the deployment of aesthetically certifying forms while women simply have no need to inscribe the "feminine" in such a way? As Emerson's "The Poet" suggests, and as I hope my discussions of Whitman and Dickinson have implied, both male and female poets in nineteenth-century America appear to have suffered from extraordinarily intense feelings of anxiety about, and even hostility toward, the literally distant fathers of their literary art. I would argue, however, that for Whitman, despite all his disclaimers of dependence on tradition, these anxieties had to be resolved through a covert "positional" identification with the poetic modes that constitute verse tradition in English, while for Dickinson they did not. In fact, I would claim that, for Dickinson, distinctively American anxiety about belatedness was increasingly supplanted by a half-conscious acquiescence in a uniquely female alienation, an alienation which inspired skepticism, first, toward traditional verse structures, with their re-iteration of traditional (male) defenses against fear, and, secondarily, toward the very language which the poet must use to flesh out such structures. Thus, in works from "Out of the Cradle" to "Crossing Brooklyn Ferry" to "When Lilacs Last in the Dooryard Bloom'd," Whitman bridges the gulf between himself and "poetry" by covert allusions to genres that imply his potency, his authority, his resurrection—his masculinity. At the same time, in texts from "I want—it pleaded—All its life" and "I heard a Fly Buzz," to "My Life had stood—a Loaded Gun" to "This Chasm, Sweet, upon my life," Dickinson increasingly distances herself from the conventions of "poetry" by enacting her alienation from genre and emphasizing the fluidity, even the indefinability, of her selfhood—her femininity.[32]

32. Here I am relying heavily on a conflation of the accounts of asymmetrical male and female psychosexual development offered by Sigmund Freud and by the revisionary feminist theorist Nancy Chodorow with the critic Walter Ong's hypothesis that, until the late nineteenth century, the study of the classics functioned as a male "initiation ritual." Chodorow, in particular, argues in *The Reproduction of Mothering: Psychoanalysis and the Sociology of Gender* (Berke-

Finally, I would propose that, after Whitman and Dickinson, the exuberantly defiant, distinctively American imagining of "not poetry" facilitates composition for both men and women, all equally caught in the net of their belatedness toward England. But I would add that, even as it defies "paternal" authority, "not poetry" threatens a loss of literary masculinity— a lapse into the (implicitly maternal) undifferentiation of prose— so that American male poets, following Whitman's footsteps, soon begin to integrate the complex outlines of traditional generic "poetry" into their apparently innovative verse; while women's "not poetry" continues, as Dickinson's did, by and large to move away from traditional poetic genre toward quasi-narrative, quasi-journalistic, and quasi-epistolary modes, as though, for women poets, narrative and confession, with their mediation of experience through plot and their evasion of powerful ego assertion, reiterate the effect of "affect," of persistent familial ties, that seems to be characteristic of female psychosexual development.

It is no accident, after all, that, next to the schoolroom favorite "O Captain! My Captain!," Whitman's most frequently taught and read poem is "When Lilacs Last in the Dooryard

ley: University of California Press, 1978) that, given Western child-rearing arrangements, the father is a more distant figure than the mother, and therefore one whose image requires from a boy a "positional" identification which fosters "abstract or categorical role learning rather than . . . personal identification (p. 177). In addition, she observes that, for the growing boy, "Masculinity becomes an issue in a way that femininity does not" for the developing girl because, in order to overcome his pre-Oedipal dependence on, and his Oedipal enthrallment to, his mother, the boy must "repress those qualities he takes to be feminine inside himself" (p. 181). Thus "masculine identification processes stress differentiation from others, the denial of affective relation, and categorical universalistic components of the masculine role," while for girls, enmeshed in ongoing relationships with familiarly present mothers, "femininity and the feminine role remain . . . all too real and concrete" (pp. 176–177). Her hypotheses usefully supplement and illuminate both Freud's "Female Sexuality" (1931) and Ong's *Fighting for Life* (Ithaca: Cornell University Press, 1981). For different perspectives on Dickinson's relationship to romanticism and to poetic genre, see Joanne Feit Diehl, *Dickinson and the Romantic Imagination* (Princeton: Princeton University Press, 1981), and Sharon Cameron, *Lyric Time: Dickinson and the Limits of Genre* (Baltimore: Johns Hopkins University Press, 1979).

Bloom'd," with its ritualized mourning, its symbolic "trinity
sure" of flower-bird-star, and its allusive evocations of the Egyp-
tian *Book of the Dead,* the regenerative power of the earth, the
comradeship of fathers and sons, and the "wondrous chant" of
brother poets. For although Whitman here appears at first to
stroll his own generically idiosyncratic route toward the unknown, "with the knowledge of death as walking one side of
me, / And the thought of death close-walking the other side of
me," the path he follows, as many critics have observed, clearly
parallels the course that shapes the traditional pastoral elegy.
Indeed, from his opening lament for the "powerful western
fallen star" that emblematizes Lincoln and his first complaint
against the "harsh surrounding cloud that will not free my soul"
to his ceremonial offering of lilacs to the journeying coffin, his
identification of himself as priestly spokesman for "my cities"
and "the large unconscious scenery of my land," his visionary
reconciliation with the armies of the dead, and his final appeased
perception of the fallen president as a "comrade lustrous with
silver face in the night," Whitman might almost be rewriting
and revising such a more obviously conventional pastoral elegy
as Shelley's "Adonais," with its movement from mourning for
the fallen "star" of Keats ("Thou wert the morning star among
the living / Ere thy fair light had fled") to joy that "the soul of
Adonais, like a star, / Beacons from the abode where the Eternal are."

That so many critics have found "Lilacs" Whitman's most
teachable and "coherent" poem testifies to the intensity not
only of their own yearning for generic familiarity but also of
the poet's need for a structural identification with the tradition
against which he claimed to set his individual talent. Further,
that in the view of some Whitman scholars "Lilacs" signals an
end to the writer's great phase of innovation suggests, again,
the possibility that even this self-defined bard of the new could
go only so far and no further in his journey away from "poetry."[33] Having at first found the "spermatic" language of which
he (like Emerson) dreamed in a "rough" speech of filial rebel-

33. See, for instance, Black's discussion of "Lilacs" in the concluding chapter
of *Whitman's Journeys into Chaos.*

lion, he finally had to fortify his increasingly imperilled masculinity through a deployment of the more strongly, because more paternally, "spermatic" language of genre.[34] Moreover, though it may well be that the frankness with which "Lilacs" insists on achieving consolation through learned formal patterning signals a definitive Whitmanesque turn from an unprecedented "not poetry" to a "not poetry" that is haunted by the claims of "poetry," I would suggest that the generic outlines of "poetry" had always in some sense structured this artist's major texts.

It has long been clear to many readers, after all, that such works as "Out of the Cradle," "Crossing Brooklyn Ferry," and "As I Ebb'd with the Ocean of Life" have deep affinities with high Romantic odes. "Out of the Cradle," for instance, is plainly a poem about the poet's fall from innocence to experience and consequent accession to, or more accurately initiation into, his art, and thus it has much in common with Wordsworth's "Ode: Intimations of Immortality." Similarly, "Crossing Brooklyn Ferry," with its grammatical enactment of physical/spiritual death, rebirth, and godly empowerment ("I too *lived* . . . I too *knitted* the old knot of contrariety . . . What gods can exceed these that *clasp* me by the hand . . . *Flow* on, river!"), depends upon a trope of poetic resurrection and potency not unlike the one that resolves the aesthetic crisis at the center of Coleridge's "Dejection: An Ode." Finally, "As I Ebb'd," elaborating as it does a deadly skepticism comparable to that which informs Keats's "Ode to a Nightingale," achieves meditative grandeur through a comparably searching exploration of epistemological uncertainty. But even the apparently loose-jointed, "formless" and "sprawling" "Song of Myself" is also, after all, held together by crucial moments of poetic disintegration and reintegration (notably sections 28–29 and 38) in which the speaker loses and regains the "supreme power" of his voice through a negotiation with experience that parallels the transactions with death which lie at the heart of the pastoral elegy and the Romantic ode. In becoming the New World's representative man, Whitman al-

---

34. Emerson exclaimed "Give me initiative, spermatic, prophesying, man-making words" in his journal written at Concord in November-December 1841.

ways, evidently, had to certify his poetic identity through covert repetitions of the aesthetic maneuvers which characterize the old world's male tradition of poetic representation.

If we search Dickinson's oeuvre for similar examples of poems implicitly structured through strategies borrowed from such ceremonial genres as elegy and ode, it seems to me plain that we will not find any. At most, we may encounter groups of verses that disperse among themselves the enactments of death and resurrection, of knowledge and power, which works like "Lilacs" integrate into unified coherent structures, or we may (very occasionally) discover single poems which offer dark and elliptical parodies of such enactments. Dickinson's poetic idiosyncrasies are stigmata of her inability—or her refusal—to deploy the major generic features that distinguish the lyric as a genre. What single work of hers, after all, could we set against "Lilacs"? If we look at J. 731, a fairly representative though not startlingly superior Dickinson elegy whose date of composition Johnson places some two years before that of "Lilacs," we must at once note the severity with which this poet rejects, or *overlooks,* every step of the quasi-official ritual process by which Whitman confronts and confounds grief.

> "I want"—it pleaded—All its life—
> I want—was chief it said
> When Skill entreated it—the last—
> And when so newly dead—
>
> I could not deem it late—to hear
> That single—steadfast sigh—
> The lips had placed as with a "Please"
> Toward Eternity—

Reducing the dead subject from a powerful fallen star to a mere yearning object—an "it" whose wants are both hopeless desires and helpless lacks—Dickinson allows herself no role as potent mediator, no triumph of hopeful perception. Rather, she is herself little more than an ear which hears the "single—steadfast sigh" of the dead, a sigh uncannily prolonged toward an "Eternity" which is neither obscurely blissful (like Whitman's) nor redemptively radiant (like Shelley's). Nor does this poet contextualize the scene of mourning—if her flat account of "its" decease can be called "mourning"—in terms of a communal grief. Her slight, two-stanza-long encounter with "its" assimilation into "Eternity" occurs in a setting of absence, blankness: the little that the poet speaks about death as an event is spoken nowhere and for nobody, in an atmosphere of bleak skepticism which she was more sardonically to elaborate a year later in J. 892 ("Who occupies this House?"), a piece in which both the dead citizen of the graveyard and the transfigured soul in eternity are presented as equally alien:

> The Owner of this House
> A Stranger He must be—
> Eternity's Acquaintances
> Are mostly so—to me.

The fluidity of ego which gives Dickinson's rejection of genre its special fluency can be witnessed in countless poems—verses whose daring experiments with oblivion or assertions of alternative identity signal a rejection of tradition as surely as do their proliferating pronoun shifts. For instance, if, in an attempt to discern parallels between Whitman and Dickinson, we set "I heard a fly buzz when I died" against "Crossing Brooklyn Ferry," we must obviously conclude that Dickinson's speaker-from-beyond-the grave does not require, or cannot imagine, the interactive resurrection on which Whitman relies. His accomplishment is simply foreign to her. Her sepulchrally enduring voice might seem to be a guarantee of survival, but her sense of an ending— "I could not see to see"—elides the epistemology that precedes coherent language.

Similarly, if we define "My Life had stood—a Loaded Gun" (J. 754) as a poem of aesthetic initiation comparable to works like "Out of the Cradle," we may conclude that Dickinson's verse has several features in common with Whitman's, specifically the paralleling of an account of self-discovery with an account of accession to poetic power through a confrontation of the murderousness of experience. Yet we cannot fail to note that Dickinson's gun/speaker is drained of precisely the consciousness, the "cries of unsatisfied love," that in Whitman accompany, and indeed constitute, linguistic desire. Anaesthetized, instrumental, "without the power to die," her speaker is a mind-

lessly "deadly foe" to foes of the Master/Muse, but she has in
a sense lost the loss—the awareness of vulnerability—which the
ode of aesthetic initiation defines as preliminary to poetic gain.

Split off from the generic framework that would, for male
artists, have contained and transformed it, such consciousness
of originary pain becomes for Dickinson the subject of separate
poems in which, bleakly articulated, it is defined as simply a
condition of life rather than as a precondition of art. "The first
day that I was a life" (J. 902), for instance, toys riddlingly with
temporality to question the ideas of orderly awakening implicit
in Whitman's poem:

> The first Day that I was a Life
> I recollect it—How still—
> That last Day that I was a Life
> I recollect it—as well—
>
> 'Twas stiller—though the first
> Was still—
> 'Twas empty—but the first
> Was full—

With equal austerity, "A loss of something ever felt I" (J. 959)
begins by describing a visionary desolation not unlike Whitman's
"unknown want" (or Wordsworth's "There hath passed away
a glory from the earth"). But the yearning for "Delinquent
Palaces" is presented as perpetual; no movement from *having*
something to *losing it* to *gaining* something else structures the
poem.

Finally, if we compare what we might call Romantic crisis
poems with such a work as Dickinson's "This Chasm, Sweet,
upon my life," we find few traces of the orderly and meditative,
if skeptical, listing of alternatives that characterizes "As I Ebb'd."
Rather, the self that must encounter and struggle to resist the
mortality which threatens to dissolve identity has already dis-
integrated under the pressure of pain.

> This Chasm, Sweet, upon my life
> I mention it to you,
> When Sunrise through a fissure drop
> The Day must follow too.

If we demur, its gaping sides
Disclose as 'twere a Tomb
Ourself am lying straight wherein
The Favorite of Doom.

When it has just contained a Life
Then, Darling, it will close
And yet so bolder every Day
So turbulent it grows

I'm tempted half to stitch it up
With a remaining Breath
I should not miss in yielding, though
To Him, it would be Death—

And so I bear it big about
My Burial—before
A Life quite ready to depart
Can harass me no more—

Shifting pronouns (I, we, ourself, it, him) and linking them, as she often does under stress, with the "wrong" verbs ("Ourself am"), Dickinson's speaker enacts precisely the catastrophe— the engulfment by "fathomless workings"—that Whitman wards off through contemplation. Indeed, where the imperatives of genre toll Whitman back at least to the triumphant autonomy of a sole self in lucid revery, the abandonment of genre, in Dickinson's poem the absence of a need to find a way out of the chaos of the womb/tomb, leaves consciousness dramatically buried in a "Burial—before."

What implications for the analysis of American poetic modernism can we derive from an understanding of the distinctive psychosexual needs which impelled Whitman and Dickinson to shape their drastically innovative "not poetry" in such notably different ways? To explore the question properly would require another essay, but I will end with a few questions which might serve as prolegomena to such a meditation. In 1856, at the height of his innovative powers, Whitman wrote a poem entitled "Unfolded Out of the Folds" in which he seems completely to acquiesce in a female potency and priority against which no identification with patriarchal tradition can defend him. Declaring that "Unfolded out of the folds of the woman man comes unfolded, and is always to come unfolded," he goes on to insist that "Unfolded only out of the inimitable poems of woman can come the poems of man, (only thence have my poems come)" and "Unfolded out of the folds of the woman's brain come all the folds of the man's brain, *duly obedient . . ."* (italics mine). Given the anxieties that such a vertiginous, if momentary, admission of dependence on matrilineage and such a floating free of patrilineage might elicit in the son/poet, it is not surprising to find that, in the same year, Whitman had both covertly and overtly to reestablish his bond with the father, covertly through the generically prescribed victory he achieved in "Crossing Brooklyn Ferry" and overtly through the definition of defiant masculinity (or assertive not-femininity) outlined in the passage from "A Woman Waits for Me" that I have used here as one of my epigraphs: "It is I, you women, I make my way . . . I brace myself effectually, I listen to no entreaties."

Threatened with the same alienation from paternal authority, did Whitman's descendants have to seek similar ways of bracing themselves? Wallace Stevens' late despairing "Madame La Fleurie," a dirge that dramatizes the aesthetic horror with which the male poet confronts that fierce old mother, Death, implies that they did. Describing the engulfment of male consciousness by the female earth, "a bearded queen, wicked in her dead light," Stevens mourns that "His crisp knowledge is devoured by her, beneath a dew," and concedes that "her" voracity even interrogates the authority of that knowledge, for his dead subject had only "a language he spoke, because he must, yet did not know," and the text of his perception was no more than "a page he had found in the handbook of heartbreak."[35] To be sure, the wicked, word-eating queen who dominates this poem took a long time to unfold so nakedly out of the folds of Stevens' brain, but surely, too, she was there all along, and it was within her "burning bosom"—a flash of which was revealed in "Sunday Morning"—that, like his precursor, Whitman, Stevens sought

35. *The Collected Poems of Wallace Stevens* (New York: Alfred A. Knopf, 1955), p. 507.

to brace himself by covertly constructing the supreme fictions of ceremonial genre (ode and elegy, philosophical essay and epistle) which fortify his work.

For Stevens' female contemporaries, Dickinson's descendants, however, such bracings appear to have been either impossible or unnecessary. Perhaps the most ambitious of them, H.D., also did contrive her own supreme fictions—meditative masterpieces and quasi-epics like *Trilogy* and *Helen in Egypt*. Yet just as her long poems increasingly focus on narrative and eschew ceremonial poetic assertion, so they also oscillate between a "mother-father," an "unsatisfied duality" that implies a fluid identification with all tradition—or none. In fact, the most striking episode in *Trilogy* is probably the moment when the ritual evocation of celestial presences that was, according to the poet herself, intended to structure *Tribute to the Angels,* is interrupted and disrupted by the appearance of an unprecedented lady, seen as no one before has ever seen her, who carries "the unwritten volume of the new," the book, we might suppose, of antitradition, revisionary genre. Yet although this epiphany inspires the poet to utter a paean to new life comparable in tone to some of Whitman's work *("we pause to give / thanks that we rise again from death and live"),* H.D.'s evidence of resurrection is not drawn from meditation but mediated through narration, specifically through the "tale of a jar or jars" which will constitute Book 3 *(The Flowering of the Rod)* of *Trilogy* and whose outlines the poet dimly intuits in her female muse's "blank pages."[36]

Perhaps, from a female perspective, some of the most crucial male-defined genres constitute what, quoting Adrienne Rich, we might call "a book of myths / in which / our names do not appear."[37] Clearly, the composition of "not poetry" has facilitated composition for both male and female Americans during the last century. But it seems just as clear that that work has been structured for men through allusions to genres whose contours reemphasize the winning of art. Has it, at the same time,

---

36. H.D., *Trilogy* (New York: New Directions, 1973), pp. 72, 103, 110, 103.

37. "Diving into the Wreck," in Adrienne Rich, *The Fact of a Doorframe: Poems Selected and New, 1950–1984* (New York: Norton, 1984), p. 164.

been further deconstructed for women because, from the vantage point of the female imagination, "the art of losing," as
Elizabeth Bishop puts it, "isn't hard to master"?[38] Or has it
been revised by women because losing and winning are simply
a set of different stories about the world, fascinating enactments
of—in Dickinson's words—triumphant "splendors" that are all
"menagerie"?[39]

   38. "One Art," in Elizabeth Bishop, *The Complete Poems, 1927–1979* (New
York: Farrar Straus & Giroux, 1983), p. 178.
   39. As in so much of my work, I am in this essay indebted to the ideas and
suggestions of Elliot L. Gilbert and Susan Gubar. In addition, I have profited
from the thinking of Joanne Feit Diehl and (particularly on Whitman) of Roger
Gilbert, and I have also learned a great deal from discussions with members
of my seminar on American sexual poetics at the School of Criticism and Theory,
Northwestern University, in the summer of 1984.

PHILIP FISHER

Appearing and Disappearing in Public: Social Space in Late-Nineteenth-Century Literature and Culture

High visibility like most light comes in a variety of colors. To be notorious or to be infamous may be no more than shortcuts to that final moral neutrality of fame, and as such, more efficient uses of the machinery of fame. As many muckraking journalists at the turn of the century knew very well, a by-product of making someone else notorious was making themselves famous. The owners of the papers in which the great civic exposés of the 1880s and 1890s appeared, Dana, Pulitzer, and Hearst, could also see that once the newspaper fills its front page with the fame-making and notoriety-making process, the newspaper itself becomes news and its daily appearance, shouted from street to street, becomes the most exciting daily event in the lives of many of its readers.

By means of the Armory show of 1913, modern art became notorious in America long before it was in any ordinary sense well-known. Scandal is not the most refined form of publicity, but it does conveniently insert a fact, a name, a product solidly into the space of appearance. The remark of Roscoe Thayer that the most representative man of the third quarter of the nineteenth century was P. T. Barnum should remind us that the public realm in the years following the Civil War was giddy, intoxicated with the newly available energies for the magnifi-

155

cation of personality that had been discovered in the economic and political realms.[1] The force of the mass circulation newspaper to create ever new overnight sensations, or faces instantly recognizable to millions of people, permitted the newspapers to create a common focus of attention—the Philippines, a shipwreck, a baseball star, a political scandal—and then to rotate this massive attention from one event to another, from one personality to another.

In the same period, ideas, or "movements" as they significantly came to be called, had available the amplification of voice and message offered by the personal appearance of a charismatic lecturer on a platform before a crowd. The platform had taken on a new importance thanks in part to the successful use of emotional oratory and staged events in the abolitionist movement and then by the temperance movement with its dramatic oratory, its repentant drinkers, and its ceremonial signing of the pledge. In late 1875, the religious revivalist meetings of Moody and Sankey in Philadelphia that assembled crowds of thousands night after night for two months convinced the merchant John Wanamaker that, by means of carefully crafted events, city-wide crowds could be brought together, for example, for a dry-goods store. His biographer has written, "No memory of his crowded life was more precious to the great merchant than this revival. No event had a more far-reaching effect upon his business and religious activities, always closely related."[2]

John Wanamaker's store set the pattern in America for the successful use of newspaper advertising, periodic sales events, high-cultural entertainment, the theatricalization of Christmas, and the enormous crowds of shoppers and the carefully staged display of merchandise that made the department store the most important and exciting theatrical space in every major American city in the final decades of the nineteenth century. Not even Booth's Hamlet could draw crowds and excite public attention

1. Stuart P. Sherman, "Roosevelt and the National Psychology," reprinted in Morton Keller, ed., *Theodore Roosevelt, A Profile* (New York: Hill and Wang, 1967), p. 37.
2. Herbert Adams Gibbons, *John Wanamaker* (New York: Harper & Brothers, 1926), p. 133.

like a Wanamaker White Sale or the unveiling of Macy's Christmas windows.
The platform from which moral or political emotion sensationalized ideas, just as the newspaper did events or the department store did merchandise, had also made possible the appearance of an author before the no longer invisible audience. Now the public might have him "in person" while he would enjoy the visceral attention and emotion that his words might, ordinarily in private, evoke. In 1867 Charles Dickens earned more than $100,000 for a series of crowded readings that made author, book, and audience—"live and in person"—performances that would pose the challenge of celebrity to American authors of the next generation, a challenge that was the despair of Henry James as well as, finally, the source of one of his richest topics. The space of performance invited the writer or artist to imagine, at once, a high cultural form of celebrity and a personal hold on his audience. Mark Twain, with his lecture style and his appearance carefully chosen to create an iconographic display of his role as performer, actor, and artist all in one, was the writer who grasped and managed the intoxication of the magnified and performed self. For thirty years, from the time of his first lecture tour in the late 1860s to his World Tour of 1895–96, Twain was the first major American writer as "star," a position only approximated after Twain by Hemingway.[3] On a plane beyond Dickens or Twain, Emerson had, in the previous generation, created American philosophy in public as the performance of philosophy and thought before the lecture hall crowd.

The Performance of Mastery

The space of performance is itself the subject of the most important and in some cases most notorious paintings done in America between 1870 and 1900, those of Thomas Eakins. Many of Eakins' greatest paintings depict the performance of a skilled master before an audience—an opera singer on a stage, a rower

3. Fred W. Lorch, *The Trouble Begins at Eight: Mark Twain's Lecture Tours* (Ames: Iowa State University Press, 1968).

before the crowd that we assume lines the banks of the river, a boxer in a ring surrounded by fans, or a professor of surgery before an audience of students. In Eakins' "The Gross Clinic," certainly one of the very greatest of nineteenth-century works and, arguably, the single most important American painting between the Civil War and the First World War, what is performed is surgery and the surgeon is seen as a noble celebrity in a world of acclaim that we see made visible in the internal audience of students and professional observers.

Surgery differs from Eakins' other subjects such as boxing or rowing because it is normally a socially invisible act that has for most people an aura of mystery and fear. Eakins brings surgery into public view by means of this painting in the same way that the novelists of Realism and Naturalism or the journalistic muckrakers would bring into the light of public scrutiny the normally invisible and often deliberately concealed affairs of political and economic life. To be prepared to look at this act of surgery was the mark of a society that had set out to face everything. Narrative Realism, the new photography as used, for example, by Jacob Riis in the slums of New York, the newspaper exposé—all had mastered the techniques of seizing attention by means of daring and shock and then sustaining attention by narratives that seemed to permit the public to educate itself about the realities of its own life and times. As Eakins' medical paintings illustrate, that process of gaining attention cannot be done merely by the appearance of what had until then been invisible. What is required is the highest key of appearance: not surgery, but the performance of surgery as though on a stage with a spot-lit star, a supporting cast, a visible audience, and the melodramatic clues of knife and blood, a horizontal, unconscious body, and its proud, vertical assailant. When surgery is not only permitted to appear, but is depicted as performance, the viewer of the painting is asked to regard himself or herself as part of an audience and to become aware, even morbidly self-conscious, of both the details of surgery and the details of observation, of attention, of the respect that creates the star-system of professional experts, and of the great civic drama of the one and the many, the leader and the people.

Dr. Gross himself is illuminated as if he were the star of this medical theater, isolated, erect like a soloist or conductor. The students whom we see are one half of a symmetrical audience. We viewers of the painting are the other half of the circle, but we are witnesses to two superimposed demonstrations of mastery: that of the surgeon Dr. Gross and that of the painter Thomas Eakins, both of whom work with an extended hand holding scalpel or brush covered with the brightest of crimsons, paint or blood.[4] We, as the audience for two performers, also have before us an audience—the students—who instruct us in the intensity of attention that should be given to the scene, to surgery, and to painting. As Gross instructs them in surgery, they instruct us, by their variety of expressions and postures, in the art of observing and witnessing, learning from skill and repaying skill with the reverence and attention that it has earned. What we learn from them we apply to the equally visible (to us) skill of the painter Eakins, who, although no longer standing there in front of the finished painting, is still visible in his surrogate Dr. Gross.

Between "The Gross Clinic" of 1875 and "The Agnew Clinic" of 1889 Eakins, returning to surgery as his metaphor for the performance of the artist, increased his emphasis on the audience that we can see behind the surgeon, his patient, and his assistants. Now almost a wallpaper of faces, the thirty or so observers spell out the painter's instructions to his own observers. The colorless technique with which the audience is painted increases our feeling that this is a scene in a theater because the audience seems like one of those painted drop scenes of landscape or train station that so crudely set out the frame of reality in a play. At the same time, the audience of students is rendered in so different a technique that they seem to have only a half reality, as though full personal being were denied to spectators. Their uniformity, colorless in shadow, makes of them a mass rather than an audience, almost a science fiction cartoon of efficient and decent mass men.

The striking ontological distinctions made in Eakins' painting

4. For an extraordinary analysis of the physical and structural reality of Eakins' "The Gross Clinic" see the essay by Michael Fried in *Representations*, 9 (Winter 1985), 33–104.

between the thing-like existence of the anesthetized, faceless, uncovered body and, secondly, the massified realm of spectatorship thrown into shadow almost as a visual equivalent for the anesthesia, and, finally, the full and singular humanity of the performer is a set of distinctions with profound implications for the larger social world. These ontological levels are given in several other structural ways in the social design of the painting. In "The Agnew Clinic" we see the three-part progression: the nakedness of the patient; the business suits or social dress of everyday street life of the audience of students; and, third, the white uniforms of the doctor and his assistants. Uniforms here are part, as costumes in a theater, of a higher reality than the social, which is, in its turn, higher than the nakedness of the patient. The patient is unconscious; the audience is alert and attentive; but the doctor and his assistants act and move freely in space—once again a third level beyond spectatorship just as observation and attention are beyond the sleep of ether. The patient is faceless. The audience is a screen of faces seen frontally. The doctor, however, is in profile; only half of his face can be seen, and his hands are given equal standing with his face as centers that draw our attention. His hands are, literally, the other side of his face, his humanity. His assistants are seen from a variety of incomplete angles that deprive us of their facial expressions while reminding us of their activity. Finally, the patient lies down in the position of death or sleep or receptivity; the audience sits; the doctors stand, often bent over the patient. Only the star performer, Dr. Agnew or Dr. Gross, is given that final position of full humanity—homo erectus—here defined as the ontological opposite to unconscious, horizontal nakedness.[5]

These spiritual distinctions made in technique, in posture, in human presence are clearly deliberate, even pedantic. We see here a reality that is hierarchical, no longer democratic. It is

5. The physical presence of the painter within the scene of the painting and the interpretation of action given by the parallels between the physical acts of surgery and painting are major points made by Fried. For the use of the body to certify and make real political and other socially abstract facts, see the brilliant analysis of war and torture done by Elaine Scarry in *The Body in Pain: The Making and Unmaking of the World* (New York: Oxford University Press, 1985).

one of the many images by which the late nineteenth century seemed to be memorizing a new social aggregation for which professionalism, expertise, and performance offered key models. Eakins' paintings remind us of those many civic symphony orchestras, among them the Boston Symphony or the New York Philharmonic, that came to be a key image and ritual of society in late nineteenth-century American cities. The symphony is made up of the conductor—standing just as Eakins' doctor does; the soloist—parallel to Eakins' patient; the musicians—making up the group of assistants and experts; and, finally, the audience of observers or listeners. This configuration also describes the corporation with its great founder or leader, its managers, the product, and the great audience of consumers. The social fracture of reality into layers marked by diminishing degrees of reality that is given so richly in Eakins' clinic paintings makes available, as though for practice and memorization, the elements of a new order.

In "The Agnew Clinic" Dr. Agnew's right hand is raised and flat, extended in gesture toward our half of the audience. His hand is in the familiar religious sign of Renaissance painting: Behold! What is beheld in Eakins' pair of paintings is both surgery and the teaching of surgery. The audience is not a mob of the curious, but those who watch in order to learn to perform themselves at a later time. Eakins too is a teacher of artists, as head of the Philadelphia Academy. One reason to expose in public not only surgery but the teaching of surgery is to insist that the audience for art is not the audience that gapes and stares at wonders or sensations but the alert, serious bank of students whose intelligence and learned respect for the skilled hand translates back into veneration for the grey-haired master who commands the performance.

The crafts of rowing, boxing, and surgery that Eakins portrayed as performances were all highly visible physical skills. The boxer's jab, the rower's stroke and turn, the surgeon's cut— each made visible to the trained eye under the pressure of a race, a boxing match, or a life or death surgical act, the pose of assurance and economy that would triumph in circumstances where even the smallest clumsiness would invite defeat. That Eakins considers these to be metaphors for the heroism of the painter who applies his careful strokes to the canvas as the rower does to the river or the doctor to the patient, is obvious. In American painting from Eakins to Jackson Pollock an unusual awareness has been present in the paintings themselves of the dangerous and elegant skills of the artist risking himself in full view before his audience. Hemingway's life-long analogy between writing and bullfighting was another version of this life or death account of the performance of art.

Within the two clinic paintings that exhibit the arts of surgery, teaching, painting, and observing, we find one final and startling exhibition: the exhibition of privacy. The naked and surgically opened body, a breast in "The Agnew Clinic," offers as the ultimate material of the crowded and surrounded public stage, the most intimate and private physical self. Surgery, by making for a moment the inside of the body appear in a visible space, has in its power a greater nakedness than that of the merely social nude. It is the cut flesh that makes painting and performance notorious.

In "The Agnew Clinic" the female breast is desecrated both by surgery and by the imputation of disease that surgery implies and then by painting that exposes not only the breast but the body within the breast. What Eakins has done is to install his own performance as a painter onto the double energy of a newly composite public space, one that saw complex undercurrents that linked fame and exposé. The heroic celebrity of the surgeon transmits one half of this composite energy. The surgeon and with him the painter Eakins are seen as stars subject to an extraordinarily reverent treatment that magnifies the greatness of the skilled practitioner. But alongside the energy of enchantment and professional mystification occurs the demystification of the body, of privacy, the de-idealization of breast and groin. The energies of mystification and demystification, of star-making and muckraking, of celebrity and exposé are simultaneous and draw their energy from one another. The collision of fame and privacy that takes place in Eakins' paintings of medical performance installs American art on a paradoxical and very knowing moral terrain.

The naked body that would in any painting catch the eye at once is made shocking and conspicuous by the surgeon's bloody hand and scalpel. In the delirious years of the sensational press, Eakins had produced the first great American paintings whose psychology was grounded in the avant-garde tactic of shock. Appropriately enough, Eakins' first masterpiece that had so deeply meditated on the appearance in public of the most private and the most famous (of the body and the surgeon and the painter himself) itself first appeared at the Philadelphia Centennial Exposition of 1876, the same event that saw the appearance of John Wanamaker's giant store. Eakins' painting was also on view at the later Columbian Exhibition at Chicago in 1893 and at the Universal Exposition in Saint Louis in 1904. In these World's Fairs of marvels and technological breakthroughs, stunt and county-fair atmosphere, this Bon Marché of civilization that counted its crowds by the hundreds of thousands, "The Gross Clinic" offered the first great account in America of the idea of exhibition itself, of what might be exposed in public, and of how the energies of exposure might be accumulated and directed.

Conspicuousness

One of the most striking phrases of the newly emergent American sociology, a discipline that implies a conception of social life as role and performance (as can easily be seen in the later work of Goffman and the convergence of sociology and anthropology in recent years), was the phrase Thorstein Veblen coined in 1899, "conspicuous consumption." The first of these two words is the more important to us because it invites us to imagine all life directed toward an audience. In 1899 this word "conspicuous" arrived just in time to describe the ten-year domination of public life by Theodore Roosevelt, who has been described by John Chamberlain as "a careerist, a showman of his own personality."[6] As Dixon Wecter put it, "Roosevelt created a character and lived up to it with winning consistency."[7] He did so, we might add, in public, brought into focus for the national and world audience by the daily newspapers for whom his exploits and performances were the kind of godsend usually

6. Keller, p. 67.
7. Keller, p. 100.

guaranteed only by the hurricane and baseball seasons. The newspapers require, oddly enough, predictable sensational events that arrive just as regularly as the paper itself does each day. In his recent book, John Milton Cooper, Jr., has described Roosevelt's career as "the first major career in American politics to be conducted wholly within the era and under the influence of modern journalistic media."[8]

Between the Civil War and the First World War, the mass circulation newspaper had become one of the dominant and novel set of spaces within which public reality appeared. Today, television with its very different pressure on and drive toward certain types of events and personalities plays an equivalent part. Even a different type of face is required once the change from the newspaper to television has taken place, just as a different voice was made necessary once radio had replaced the lecture platform. The newspaper circulation wars of the 1890s in New York had as their agenda readerships that could finally reach the millions. The new materials of personality and action suitable to be made conspicuous were only slowly discovered in the different realms of culture. We might describe the years between 1890 and 1910 as a series of experiments in the modeling of a highly visible structure of identity under the new circumstances of conspicuous performance.

These conditions of identity writ large would be appropriate for the "most famous man in the world," as Roosevelt had been called, but they would equally describe the very structure of character for the novel that gives the richest account of this new world of fame, Dreiser's *Sister Carrie*.[9] In Dreiser's novel the Broadway career of the youthful, energetic, but relatively talentless Carrie who rises to be, at last, a "somebody" is played off against the alternative descent of a man on his way to being that great American dread, a "nobody."

8. John Milton Cooper, Jr., *The Warrior and the Priest: Woodrow Wilson and Theodore Roosevelt* (Cambridge, Mass.: Harvard University Press, 1983), pp. 28–29.

9. For an analysis of Dreiser's *Sister Carrie*, see the final chapter of Fisher, *Hard Facts: Setting and Form in the American Novel* (New York: Oxford University Press, 1985). The concept of performance and its consequences for a social account of personality are given there in detail.

The very same conditions lay behind the fame of the writer whom we might call America's first coast-to-coast literary figure, Samuel Clemens, whose better known name, Mark Twain, should be seen not so much as a pen name but as a trademark (as it always appears on the copyright page of his works), a brand name for the various enterprises of lecturing, door-to-door subscription sales of novels or travel books, printing investments, and public appearances, all headquartered in that gaudy Hartford mansion that would, like his name itself, come to be seen as part of his identity. Twain's appearance had even turned his own features and clothes into elements of his performance.

Howells in the reminiscences that he published in *My Mark Twain* described his meeting with the man whose very hair and mustache seemed already part of a costume. Twain was wearing a sealskin coat, fur-side out. He had a "crest of dense red hair," and Howells noticed the "wide sweep of his flaming mustache." To Howells this conspicuous sealskin coat, however warm Twain found it, "sent the cold chills through me when I once accompanied it down Broadway, and shared the immense publicity it won him. He had always a relish for personal effect, which expressed itself in the white suit of complete serge which he wore in his last years, and in the Oxford gown which he put on for every possible occasion and said he would like to wear all the time."[10]

In the same period the laws of conspicuous and performed identity were even more fundamental for that abstract person, a corporation. The historian of technology David Nye has recently written an analysis of the more than one million photographs in the archives of the General Electric Company.[11] Nye has shown that between 1890 and 1940 the corporation represented itself to itself and to the public that it was constructing into its pool of customers by means of a segmented performance. The internal magazines for managers that pictured the teamwork and good times of the summer camp at Association Island differed from the newsletter for workers, the journal for sci-

10. William Dean Howells, *My Mark Twain,* ed. Marilyn Austin Baldwin, (Baton Rouge: Louisiana State University Press, 1967), p. 6.
11. David Nye, *Image Worlds: Photography at General Electric, 1890–1930* (Cambridge, Mass.: M.I.T. Press, 1985).

entists, and the news ads aimed at the general public. Yet the
corporation was in the process of setting in place, inventing we
might say, three realities: the product itself projected through
advertising, brand names, and corporate imagery; the company
seen as a hierarchical and yet interdependent family through
newsletters and other internal publications; and the consuming
public, national in scale, eager for the new electrical way of life,
loyal to General Electric products. Both the new public and the
new corporation were geographically so extensive, so great in
numbers, that to manufacture the corporate patriotism or what
came to be called "consumer loyalty" among people numerous
enough to form an army required the constant newspaper-like
and newspaper-dependent diet of visual and narrative reminders
that created the uniqueness and conspicuousness of the company. To create corporate identity, brand-product identity—
such as the Mazda light bulb—and the identity of a purchasing
public, required the one million photographs as tokens of a
world that needed to make itself visible in order to remember
that it existed. Just as in Eakins' paintings of performance, the
three realities, that of performer, act or product, and public,
all come into simultaneous existence by a process of mutual
conferring of reality.

It was also by means of photography in the 1890s that Jacob
Riis had made America aware of how the other half lived. The
same camera that played so large a part in the creation of reality
for the modern product and corporation also brought into focus
suppressed and forgotten social facts. The machinery of fame
and exposé were once again the same.

The phrase "larger than life" or a "giant among men" so
often used to describe Teddy Roosevelt implied not so much
the traditional rhetoric of the heroic as a more diffusely available, heightened reality. It was a version of this enhanced, speeded
up, intensified reality that newspaper headlines or advertisements and mass public events, whether the newly crowded baseball games or the sales days at stores like John Wanamakers,
made convincing. A certain transfer of reality takes place for
someone lucky enough to be in the presence of Eakins' Dr.
Gross, an actress like Dreiser's Carrie, or for a ticket holder
for one of the lectures of Mark Twain's World Tour of 1895–

96. The atmosphere of this surplus reality is captured in a description of the department store in a recent book on the Bon Marché, the Parisian equivalent to Wanamakers.

Dazzling and sensuous, the Bon Marché became a permanent fair, an institution, a fantasy world, a spectacle of extraordinary proportions, so that going to the store became an event and an adventure. One came now less to purchase a particular article than simply to visit, buying in the process because it was part of the excitement, part of an experience that added another dimension to life.[12]

The democratic right to enter such heightened spaces was equally available to the common man in his access to famous and talked about things in the new brand name products which were, on one level, no more than a common sense solution to the new national market, as Twain's lectures were. The Singer sewing machine, the Kodak camera that swept the nation in the 1890s, or Coca Cola, a brand name so successful that it would come to stand for America itself—these were what we might call "famous" objects. As things they differed from ordinary goods just as a star does from a person, or a trip to Wanamakers from just going out to the store. The overall creation of this surplus reality for persons, things, or events defined by inversion the newly negative condition of being a "mere camera," a "mere doctor," or a "mere human being," meaning that it was not a Kodak, not Dr. Gross, not Teddy Roosevelt. Everyday reality comes to be "merely" so, once a higher dimension of conspicuous and performed reality has been added, like a new economy of being, on top. The star and what came to be called the "little man" or, as I am calling him here, "mere" man, are created at the same moment.

The public world that trained its eyes to see that the headline of the newspaper, since it was an eye-catching fact, stood at the top of the pyramid of news, being the "star" event of the day, was also a public world that had developed, in its explosive building technology, the skyscraper, the most deliberately theatrical and conspicuous building type since the medieval cathe-

12. Michael B. Miller, *The Bon Marché: Bourgeois Culture and the Department Store, 1869–1920* (Princeton: Princeton University Press, 1981), p. 167.

dral. Thanks to the Otis elevator and the high cost of inner-city land, the years between 1880 and 1920 saw the first classical phase of the Chicago and New York skyscraper. The Woolworth Building, built in New York in 1913, has been called the first skyscraper as advertisement.[13] The skyscraper is the star on the stage of the city streets, the conspicuous sign of the prestige and importance of the company. Just like the mansions of the rich that were rising along Fifth Avenue or the eccentric and grandiose mansion of Twain, the skyscrapers naturally appealed to the newspapers housed in some of the most striking of the new buildings.

The refinement and sophistication of high visibility as well as the development of new techniques to dramatize and convert into events even the most static or abstract of facts were cultural accomplishments that came to a climax in the great national expositions which were, after London's Crystal Palace Exposition of 1851, a periodic and prominent fact of the years up to the First World War. The Philadelphia, Chicago, and St. Louis fairs permitted the industrial world to convert its machinery into exhibitions that, by speeding progress up, made progress itself visible, invention and national power visible.

Alongside these many experiments that converged finally toward a national strategy of celebrity, product promotion, political fame, and high visibility of a kind available to persons, places, things, and ideas, the cultural period between 1880 and 1910 also produced an ongoing meditation, often filled with anxiety and strident anger, that struggled with the psychological and social consequences of the new power. The predictable autobiography for this period, *The Education of Henry Adams*, put on display, once the book was no longer privately circulated among friends, the hesitations of a public actor convinced that he had never found the right role and so must exhibit his awkwardness and failure as substitutes for the display of what Eakins had put on view: the pleasures of mastery. The costs and distortions built into this centralized, national space of appearance, for which the newspaper was only one expression, and the na-

13. Daniel J. Boorstin, *The Americans: The Democratic Experience* (New York: Random House, 1973), p. 115.

tional market as symbolized by the Sears catalogue, another, were tallied and recomputed by writers as different as Henry James, Mark Twain himself, and Theodore Dreiser.

The counterweight to this novel, economically driven blend of identity and product that I am calling "conspicuousness" was a new and profound regrounding of privacy. The greatest domestic architecture of the years 1890–1910 were the houses built by Frank Lloyd Wright in the Chicago suburb of Oak Park. These houses create a new internal openness by breaking down the cell-like home of the Victorian middle class. At the same time Wright's houses present to the outer world a mysterious, low-slung privacy. The very feature of a house that announces in capital letters the wealth and importance of the family within, the entrance, often posed on its pedestal of unnecessary steps and flanked by pillars as pompous and grand as funds permit, is absent in the new Wright homes. It is often difficult to see where to enter these homes, as though they did not wish to invite strangers at all. The facade, that upright, decorative statement facing the street, disappears in favor of a three-dimensional form, equally rich and interesting on all sides. The houses hug the ground almost in disdain of the visibility that the vertical dimension commands. In an age of skyscrapers, Wright reclaimed the symbolically "low" territory for its advantages for privacy. His houses protect inner life and they renew it. The Robie House, to take only the most famous example, could be said, in traditional terms, to have not only no facade but not even a front. It refuses to address the street, to announce the family within, to be their social face or at least the outer face of their prestige and wealth. It is nearly impossible at first glance to see how to approach the house or to enter it, both normal and conspicuous features of the facade.

Like all of Wright's work, the outside of the Robie House makes a stranger, a viewer, feel excluded rather than a partner in a performance. The observer is mainly aware of an inner life that is self-contained and has no need of observers, visitors, or admirers, an inner life that is rich, mysterious, and detailed. About this inner life, the Chicago houses, as later the Kaufman House or the Guggenheim Museum, remain silent except to make us aware of its spirituality, nobility, and uniqueness. Within this space, Wright designed the materials for a new democratic intimacy and privacy, one of the fundamental cultural achievements of the last hundred years, an achievement dependent not only on artists like Wright, but equally upon the developers of the suburb as a way of life and on the invention of, first, the radio and, then, the television as spaces of appearance that replaced the newspaper and the crowd-surrounded public stage as the intimate devices for the transfer of events and personalities.

The honesty of materials that Wright stressed was part of the obverse side of high visibility. Here Wright joins forces with the Realists in literature who tested and revealed the dishonesty and idealism that lay concealed in many descriptions of reality. The requirement that we see and value the stone, wood, tile, and fabric of the house is like a pure food and drug act for architecture. Wright's demand for honest, natural materials, never covered or disguised, is parallel to the exposé of adulteration and fraud in food and medicine, or of corruption and deceit in government. Lincoln Steffens' *The Shame of the Cities*, as well as the muckrakers and writers of Naturalism, share Wright's goals of visibility and naturalness.

Signature and Memorability

Veblen, whose *Theory of the Leisure Class* of 1899 remains one of the classics of the remote and estranging stare of late Victorian anthropology, described the conditions under which conspicuous consumption would overtake conspicuous leisure as a strategy. He wrote that the new techniques would work best in "those portions of the community where the human contact of the individual is widest and the mobility of the population greatest."[14] As Veblen wrote,

The exigencies of the modern household system frequently place individuals and households in juxtaposition between whom there is little contact in any other sense than that of juxtaposition . . . In the modern

14. Thorstein Veblen, *The Theory of the Leisure Class* (New York: Macmillan Company, 1899), p. 71.

community there is also a more frequent attendance at large gatherings of people to whom one's everyday life is unknown; in such places as churches, theaters, ballrooms, hotels, parks, shops and the like. In order to impress these transient observers, and to retain one's self complacency under their observation, the signature of one's pecuniary strength should be written in characters which he who runs may read.[15]

The signature that Veblen speaks of here is the brief token of an identity, the minimum of legible individuality. That it must be written on a scale that he who runs may read is a requirement not only for the display of wealth, but for the production of public reality no matter what the realm. The new chain stores, The Atlantic and Pacific Tea Company or the Woolworth's 5 & 10 Cents Stores used the colors and design of the facade of the store itself to package the store's identity as a signature. The red sign and the old-fashioned gold-painted wood letters of the Woolworth's sign are still in use from Two-Forks, Iowa, to Berlin. To this day the advertisements for the John Wanamaker store carry the literal signature of the founder in bold type across the full page. The signature within this period takes on the scale of the headline. To consider for a moment the champion headline maker of all times, Teddy Roosevelt, the description of the man himself by William Allen White illustrates the conversion of physiognomy into signature. White begins by saying, "Theodore Roosevelt was a giant, an overgrown personality."[16] The physical description that follows has the exaggerated quality of a blown-up photograph or what we would now call a Super Realist painting. The features are distinct enough and of a size to be seen in a crowd of 50,000, half a mile from the platform. It is personality projected onto the scale of skyscrapers.

His walk was a shoulder-shaking, assertive, heel-clicking gait, rather consciously rapid as one who is habitually about his master's business. He shook hands vigorously with a powerful downward pull like a

15. Ibid., pp. 71–72.
16. William Allen White, "Theodore Roosevelt," *Masks in a Pagent* (New York: Macmillan, 1928), p. 283.

pumper, with a firm but never rough handclasp. His shoulders sloped a little off the square line, and his head often, perhaps generally, was thrust forward from the neck, a firm short pedestal for his face, which jammed his head forward without ever requiring a stoop of his shoulders. His countenance was dominated by a big, pugnacious nose, a mustache drooped to cover a sensitive mouth in which a heavy underlip sometimes protruded, indicating passion. Occasionally, he used the lip as a shutter, purposely to uncover a double row of glittering teeth that were his pride.[17]

The lip that rises like the curtain of a theater to show off the bright teeth uncovers the cartoonlike signature that came to be recognized as the visual summation of the man. Howells describes a similar theatrical unveiling of signature by Mark Twain. "Nothing could have been more dramatic than the gesture with which he flung off his loose overcoat, and stood forth in white from his feet to the crown of his silvery head. It was a magnificent coup."[18] Each of the features of White's description of Roosevelt is seen close-up and seen in vigorous action. Each detail is immediate. We seem to be seeing the action of the lip or the teeth from less than three feet away. The vigor of the description of Roosevelt turns him into a character from a tall tale. He is close-up the way the front of a train running toward us down the track would be.

To locate the tradition of White's picture, in which the appearance is made up of disconnected, oversized details, almost like the faces in nightmares, we would have to go back to Dickens and his lurid but comic style in which faces and personalities are designed, like the odd Dickensian names, to make a character unforgettable even over a crowded novel of 900 pages and fifty competing personalities. Mark Twain's first description of Huck Finn's father as he appears to the frightened boy has exactly the same quality of White's Roosevelt.

He was mostly fifty and he looked it. His hair was long and tangled and greasy, and hung down, and you could see his eyes shining through like he was behind vines. It was all black, no gray; so was his long, mixed-up whiskers . . . He had one ankle resting on t'other knee; the

17. Ibid., p. 284.
18. Howells, p. 80.

boot on that foot was busted, and two of his toes stuck through, and he worked them now and then.[19]

The bold verbal sketch that invites the illustrator's pen or the cartoonist's few witty strokes had been the essence of Dickensian characterization. Whether in Twain's physical melodrama or the actual cartoonlike appearance of Teddy Roosevelt, an appropriate descriptive rhetoric had been invented for the rapid attention of a public that had to be seen in terms of a crowd. Roosevelt's words themselves were sometimes prewritten cartoons—"Talk softly and carry a big stick!"—in which the thousands of cartoons are already present in the words and bearing of the man. The most famous package ever invented— to use the language of advertising—was the Coca Cola bottle of 1916, an ingenious container that provided the costume in which the liquid within performs in public, the bottle or the appearance being the signature of identity forced into a conspicuous scale.

Eakins' painting of Dr. Gross will provide a final technique for the signature of conspicuous identity. By his spot-lit, isolated position, his erect, vertical bearing, his dignity, his domination of the scene, Dr. Gross is already highly visible. But by means of the bloody hand and knife he is made conspicuous and unforgettable. The bloody hand is what we might call Eakins' device, even his gimmick. He uses the poetics of intensification that we have come to identify with advertising. The bloody hand and knife or the cut breast of "The Agnew Clinic" seize upon deeper layers of feeling than mere respect or professional awe can command. As in advertising where fear or sexual desire, competitive triumph or social anxiety can be generated and then linked to the product or surface of belief that is the topic of the advertisement, or in this case, the painting, the shock or fear confer unforgettability on both Gross and on the painting itself, thus seizing a permanent hold on the memory. Eakins, by this device, has guaranteed that his painting will be talked about

19. Samuel Clemens, *The Adventures of Huckleberry Finn,* edited and with an introduction by Lionel Trilling (New York: Rinehart and Company, 1948), p. 19. All further references to the novel will be indicated by page number parenthetically at the end of the quotation.

and notorious, eye-catching and controversial. Most important
of all, once seen, it will be unforgettable. The taboos of sexuality, nakedness, violence, the excavation of irrelevant fear or
shame that can then be harnessed to the object or idea in search
of high visibility—these become an underlying factor in the
creation of signatures and conspicuous identities.

Disappearing in Public

The magnification of personality under the new conditions of
appearance and performance, its morally corrosive relation to
the simultaneous need to fashion and defend a private personality geared to the domestic and intimate realms of life, its
treacherous dynamic of rise and fall, overnight sensation and
overnight collapse, its displacement of the conversational and
the personal—even in the erotic sphere—by the mass psychology of the platform and the crowded hall with their public se-
duction of voice and spirit: these features of a potent and expansive
public life were subject to an unusually profound and hesitant
analysis in three of the greatest novels of the 1880s—James's
The Bostonians, Howells' *The Rise of Silas Lapham,* and Twain's
The Adventures of Huckleberry Finn.

Howells' novel begins with its millionaire businessman going
public, submitting to an interview with a newspaperman. The
interview looks back over Lapham's early life, his rise to success,
and then pictures for the public his anecdotal, down home side,
making him both famous and human at the same time. Lapham
consents to be made into a type. Now as one of the "Solid Men
of Boston" series he not only *is* a successful entrepreneur, he
stands for those facts just as Edison stands for the inventor;
Einstein, the scientist; or Twain, the new Western literature.

The close relationship between what interests the newspaper
public and the novel reading public becomes obvious when we
see that Howells himself, just like the reporter, is writing about
Lapham in order to describe a new phenomenon of wide social
meaning, and, at the same time, to satisfy the curiosity of the
public about such new self-made millionaires. Where do they
come from? How do they live? What are their ethics? The self-

made man is a new social type, like the new American girl that writers from Henry James in *Daisy Miller* to Dreiser in *Sister Carrie* defined and exhibited as a type. With his opening chapter Howells defines himself and his project as parallel to the new publicity of the newspapers, yet deepened by the energies of self-consciousness about the machinery of making known, exposing, exhibiting, and locking into place a new type.

The machinery of fame in its close ties to representability and typicality, and in its hidden affinities for exposure, collapse, and the shredding of public identity are common central features of the rise and fall of Verena Tarant in James's *The Bostonians,* the fall and collapse of Silas Lapham that is, of course, in Howells' title, his rise, and, finally, those chapters of *Huck Finn,* nearly a third of the whole, in which Huck and Jim play servants and supporting actors to those two masters of the public space, the Duke and the Dauphin, whose many performances elude only by seconds and well-timed flight the exposure and disgrace that the unwanted costume of tar and feathers finally makes into a final act to their flimsy, but almost lucrative, self-exhibition.

The full intensity with which Mark Twain had laid siege to the new public world in his greatest novel can be seen when the fundamental premise of his novel is made clear: Huck and Jim are two heroes who cannot appear in public, the one because he is supposed to be dead, the other because he is a runaway slave. For Huck, who does not yet know that Pap is dead, and Jim, unaware that he has been legally freed, to appear in public without an alias, a story, a false identity, is to risk the loss of all freedom. Even the normal social space of homes, of streets, of conversation and recognition is for them a space of danger. Yet superimposed upon the violent but ordinary public world of lynchings and feuds is the additional set of claims of the magnified space of performance and crowd, actor and preacher, billboard announcement and rented hall.

To hide from even the routine of social recognitions implies that one is captured rather than presented in public. Once Silas Lapham begins his appearances—in the newspaper by means of the interview; in the social geography of the city by means of the striking house that he is having built to represent his prestige; and in polite society by means of his family's bungled appearance and his own self-exposure, once he has drunk too much at the Coreys' dinner party—he is risking the great public fall that his bankruptcy will climax as the death-blow to his "run" in the public eye.

James, too, in posing the career that Verena Tarant might have had on stage as the alternative to the hidden, silent marriage in which her charm and smile would be redesigned for the domestic audience of one, her voice lowered, implies that this is also a choice to live or to die. The public self of the star, or of the type, crowds out and extinguishes a pre-social or a pre-public self that finds itself unusually fragile once it accepts the seductions that drive it to appear and to perform.

Since both James and Twain are openly concerned with the literal performances of hired halls and hissing or applauding audiences, it might seem that Howells' more old-fashioned social novel is only obliquely aware of the new landscape of appearance. But, what is the whole of *The Rise of Silas Lapham* but a series of moments of exhibition brought about by that moment in a man's life when, with two marriageable daughters who must be put "on show," his entire life must be exhibited, not only *their* accomplishments and beauty, but his total, earned social standing? The house which Lapham sets out to build and then accidentally burns is a stage on which to mount, for public view, his social worth at the key moment of his daughters' marriageability. Appropriately, Lapham's fortune has been made in paint, a surface that, as Frank Lloyd Wright would point out, conceals the nature of the substance that it covers.

Howells' novel itself, while being about exhibition and visibility, is one of the first major novels of American Realism, a form devoted to placing on public view accurate accounts of social life without either idealization or the moralizing distortion of fact. The power of the author's privilege under Realism to let social life be seen and to let wider ranges of experience appear and be included within the line of vision of the novel can be felt in Howells' inclusion of the scene of Laphams' visit to Mrs. Dewey. Howells puts on view, as Jacob Riis would do photographically, the sordid urban scene, letting it stand adjacent to the life and settings of the Coreys and the Laphams. Howells' own exhibition of the two Lapham daughters becomes an investigation into the phenomenon of the new American woman. Beginning with the superficial contest between beauty and wit, his novel turns, in its marriage plot, on the question of just what feature of rising wealth the old aristocracy will find irresistible. The progression of the novel is to widen or deepen what is on exhibit and to postpone the question of marriage by asking exactly what, once exhibited, will make such a socially unequal marriage acceptable. After beauty and intelligence—themselves a second layer of attraction after the presumed lure of mere money—both girls, because of the confusion over Corey's choice, exhibit two styles of suffering. Each seems prepared, in the noble style of sentimental heroines, to fall back on a life of injured penitence or hurt pride. This only prepares the way for both sides of the couple, male and female, during the course of Lapham's fall, to exhibit generosity, moral tact, resourcefulness, and resilience: the moral virtues which are held—at least here—to be the property of both rising and established varieties of wealth. The novel, in other words, peels away a series of exhibited surfaces, each of which reveals the differences between Penelope Lapham and her suitor until a layer is found where genuine similarity exists at last.

It may seem distorting to speak of the novel as a series of acts of exhibition, but that it is just that becomes clear once the events outside the marriage plot are considered. In bringing together two families from distinct social worlds in a series of visits, dinners, and office meetings, what occurs is that they are placed on view for one another. Their language, styles of decoration, sense of manners—as when one Lapham daughter does not show up for the dinner party without even a prior excuse—create, by means of contrast, a co-visibility. They make each other conspicuously what each is. Lapham exposes himself, once drunk, and reveals the bragging upstart that the Coreys had anticipated. His wife lives in fear that she will make mistakes that will expose her unfamiliarity with society. The small piece of paper that Mrs. Lapham finds that exhibits to her what she imagines is her husband's infidelity turns out to reveal only his nobility. Bankruptcy reveals or exhibits the true financial worth of an otherwise speculative set of facts—Lapham's wealth.

Howells' novel is through and through concerned with the dangerous paths of exhibition and with a world that exhibits itself, only to then be exposed, until, finally, the exposure itself is torn aside to reveal a further surface beneath. Lapham, who is displayed in the newspapers as solid and rich, is progressively revealed as insubstantial, then as noble in refusing to transfer his losses to innocent investors, finally as solid and vigorous on the smaller scale of his final decline, reduced to a single line of paint and a small country life.

The society of cautious and incautious self-display that is Howells' Boston has not yet swept out into the melodramatic and political society of the lecture platform and crowded hall that make up the Boston and New York of James's *The Bostonians* with the intensified possibilities of celebrity and stardom as a way of life. Only Dreiser's *Sister Carrie,* published some fifteen years later, would produce an account equal in intelligence and scale to James's romance of fame.

James's plot is shaped around three performances: Verena's trancelike, naive, and fervent speech in the crowded, shabby room filled with the odd-lot society of Boston reformers and spiritualists; secondly, her more polished debut as a lecturer in the select New York Society of Mrs. Burrage's Wednesday Club; and, finally, in the extraordinary scene that ends the novel, the performance that does not take place, the empty stage of the sold-out music hall, crowded with the stamping and the whistling of the disappointed crowd. Her photographs and life story sold in penny versions, her name on all lips, her pictures in the windows of the stores, and her name on handbills plastering the theater, Verena is prepared for launching. Yet the final scene invites us to imagine a last-minute escape from a life of performance.

While Olive Chancellor faces the public that she cannot satisfy and takes on herself the anger of their feeling that they have been, as we say, "had," Verena steals away. The climactic act that asserts the full possession of an individual self is the act of disappearing. Concealed in a cloak, Verena vanishes just when the sold-out house guarantees the cranking up of the machinery of high visibility. The smaller steps toward this full private self were earlier based on small acts of disappearance and invisibility—having secrets, for example, or withholding information from Olive, practicing reticence or leaving the house for long, intimate walks. These earlier steps made up a series of domestic acts of not speaking, not letting the facts appear, not being entirely visible to another person. By this strategy of negation a private self is born and sheltered in the novel.

James is underlining a strategy of self-creation that inverts the strategy of publicity and visibility that are the machinery of celebrity. The tactics for resisting a world that so strenuously discovers and publishes the self go far beyond reticence. Active countermeasures, like the lies of Huck Finn, are invented and the costs are paid. Verena must negotiate and demand the hours of private conversation with Basil after the first walk that she had kept so long as her secret. In the end she must not only *not* perform, she must refuse to perform. She must become self-silencing.

The starting point for James's account is not the fashioning of a public form for ordinary personality, but rather the question of the appearance of instinctively public personalities. For these natural performers the reverse question must be put: how might a genuinely private self ever be fashioned out of personalities that seem to arrive written in headlines? Faces born to adorn billboards? With the coming of photography we arrived at the very important concept of the photogenic. Some variant of this notion applies to every form of representation or appearance. The photogenic is that which seems born to be photographed, most real in pictured form, most present not in person but in images of itself. Verena Tarant is "genic," in this sense, to the world of publicity, just as Mark Twain, Charlie Chaplin, or Thomas Edison were, or as the voice and manner of FDR were "genic" to the new radio culture of the 1930s.

Verena's father Selah, by contrast, shows us the ordinary and shabby material of personality now frayed and tattered by too many hours in the bright lights of the public space. James describes him, through his wife's eyes, as one of those whose intimate self has been eroded by years of keeping his gaze and his voice pitched to the scale of the crowd. "Even in the privacy of domestic intercourse, he had phrases, excuses, explanations, ways of putting things, which, as she felt, were too sublime for just herself; they were pitched altogether in the key of public life."[20] Verena herself, as Basil, who first sees her and falls in love with her in the public setting of one of her performances, comes to see once he has her alone and has begun to develop an intimacy with her, projects herself on the grand scale. "There was indeed a sweet comicality in seeing this pretty girl sit there and in answer to a casual, civil enquiry, drop into oratory as a natural thing. Had she forgotten where she was, and did she take him for a full house? She had the same turns and cadences, almost the same gestures as if she had been on the platform" (p. 232). Her voice, which we might expect on occasion to forget that it was now aimed at a smaller audience, is only one part of a thoroughly conspicuous personality, one that, we might say, you can see for miles. When Ransom first catches sight of her, he is struck by the melodrama of her appearance. "She had the sweetest, most unworldy face, and yet, with it, an air of being on exhibition, of belonging to a troupe, of living in the gaslight, which pervaded even the details of her dress, fashioned evidently with an attempt at the histrionic" (p. 58). She is so gaudy that, as Ransom says, "If she had produced a pair of castanets or a tambourine, he felt that such accessories would have been in keeping" (p. 59). Her clothes seem more a costume, like the white serge suit that, once his hair had turned white, became Mark Twain's signature. "She wore a light-brown dress, of a shape that struck him as fantastic, a yellow petticoat, and a large crimson sash fastened at the side; while round her neck, and falling low upon her flat young chest, she had a double chain of amber beads" (p. 59). She seems packaged for recognition at a distance and her appearance itself is the start of her performance.

The genius of James's novel is not to ask the question of how, out of normal human materials, such blatant, performing personalities are made. Instead he begins with Verena's instinctively public self and asks how, out of this, an intimate and human-scale personality might be won. It is this reversal of terms

20. Henry James, *The Bostonians* (New York: Modern Library, Random House, 1956), p. 74. All further references to the novel will be indicated by page number parenthetically at the end of the quotation.

that generates the progression of Howells' and Twain's novels as well. Lapham begins in the newspaper, but by the end of the novel he has crafted a small-scale dignified obscurity. He has miniaturized his fate, as Verena has. In *Huck Finn* the winning back of small-scale intimacy—for which Jim's calling Huck "honey" is one of the tokens, and their nakedness on the raft another—from a world that conscripts them into performances and overcrowded and dramatic public realities lies at the heart of the novel. To put it paradoxically, all three novels turn on the complex victory brought about by disappearing in public.

Intimate Performance

James, like Twain, was concerned with the paths of power over another person. In America the relation of slavery set an outer limit to the more restrained or concealed models of domestic power, since in slavery the other is owned, his will suspended. But to be the manager of a rising celebrity whose every detail of appearance, every public statement, gesture, and idea must be planned might also be seen as an absolute form of power not far from the slave-relation. The choice between the life of celebrity and that of marriage could be posed, as James saw, in terms of the inevitable, central intimate relationship of each way of life—husband and wife for marriage; manager and star, promoter and star, for the public realm. The molding of another person in education, as Olive does for Verena, is, in this context, a somewhat sinister power, as is the mesmerizing process by which Selah Tarant starts his daughter's performances. He acts out the parental "gift" of life and talent to a child, but in so literal a way that the umbilical cord seems as yet uncut.

James has placed at the center of his feminist novel, with its natural question of what it would mean for a woman to be free, the purchase of Verena from her parents by Olive Chancellor. Olive pays off the parents, almost seeming to rent their daughter on a year-to-year basis, or at least she buys off their own disappearance from the scene of Verena's life. She buys the right to become her framing influence. Educating, marrying, managing, owning, and inspiring are all relations of power that occur within intimacy. All are asymmetrical: that is, they are not relations of mutual action and control, but rather examples of complementarity, like the parent-child relation. James's reactionary hero speaks out for the traditional complementary relation of man and woman, but Olive and Verena, too, are a complementary and not an equal pair. Olive will provide the money, the social access, the education, the will, and the anger. Verena will speak, enter the public world, provide the youthful and sweet-tempered vehicle, the spirit and the beauty through which Olive's ideas, resources, and energy will appear in public.

What does, finally, appear in public is an eroticized privacy that, like the naked body in each of Eakins' clinical paintings, charges the public space with its crowded intimacy. The description of Verena's first lecture in *The Bostonians* is a careful and profound analysis of the public self. Verena is worked into her state or inspired as though by hypnosis. A nearly identical scene occurs in *Sister Carrie* when Drouet comes backstage to save Carrie's first dismal performance by breathing a confident self into her. The gap between Verena's self and her performance is that between a vehicle and a source.

She began incoherently, almost inaudibly, as if she were talking in a dream . . . She proceeded slowly, cautiously, as if she were listening for the prompter, catching, one by one, certain phrases that were whispered to her a great distance off, behind the scenes of the world. Then memory, or inspiration, returned to her, and presently she was in possession of her part. She played it with extraordinary simplicity and grace. (pp. 60 61)

The performed self is at so great a distance from the intimate self that hypnotism, dream, trance, the memorization of a role by an actress are all needed to make the distance and the moral peculiarity felt. Each of her gestures becomes suspect. After the lecture Ransom notices the odd character of her smile. "Yet she smiled with all her radiance, as she looked from Miss Chancellor to him; smiled because she liked to smile, to feel her success—or was it because she was a perfect little actress, and this was a part of her training?" (p. 68). It seems impossible to distinguish these two alternatives because the most prized form of acting is the fresh, the naive, the apparently natural. Although he sees that Verena smiles universally, Ransom is caught up in the illusion of individual notice. "So he only smiled at her in silence, and she smiled back at him—a smile that seemed to him quite for himself" (p. 69).

Ransom is aware that the effect of Verena's performance has nothing to do with the argument or the ideas. "It was simply an intensely personal exhibition" (p. 61). The device lies in the offering of a nakedness and the use of it to authenticate ideas, as a person used to be sacrificed when a city was founded, the reality of death conferring reality on the abstract civic fact.[21] James describes a world of ideas given immediacy by a trans-posed intimacy and sexual energy. Later, in his stories of the 1890s he would picture the modern literary world as one in which the artist is asked to make genuine his works by appearing in public and producing his own personality as a performance that gives "interest" to his works.

Verena, at the end of her speech, "turned away slowly to-wards her mother, smiling over her shoulder at the whole room, as if it had been a single person" (p. 63). A sexual vocabulary surrounds the talk, from Ransom's feeling that Verena's father's hands placed on her head to inspire her are a "dishonor to the passive maiden" to the conclusion when Ransom laughs at "the sweet grotesqueness of this virginal creature's standing up be-fore a company of middle-aged people to talk to them about 'love' " (p. 64).

Each of those present attempts, as a result of the perfor-mance, to set up a more intimate connection. Olive adopts her and buys her from her parents. Ransom begins his courtship by seeking an introduction. The newspaper reporter, Mathias Par-don, seeing the effect she has made, says, "There's money for some one in that girl; you see if she don't have quite a run" (p. 64).

If we ask what the intimate power of Verena consists in, it lies in the fact that she is herself both the speaker of the ideas and a personal allegory of them. She is the enactment of the yearning for freedom, including the paradoxes of freedom: that she is mesmerized into a performance about freedom for women

21. For an account of the transfer of reality between the physical and the political realms, see Scarry, *The Body in Pain*.

by her father; that she is bought and sold, managed and produced for the public like a traveling Indian on show; that she is hidden away and then displayed with tickets sold, passed from sponsor to sponsor. She is the iconography of her ideas as Theodore Roosevelt was for the strenuous life that he promoted and lived. The ideas take visual form in the materials of personality.

Just as ideas such as feminism or the vigorous life were given performance in publically memorable dramas—the Rough Riders at San Juan Hill, for example—so, too, the performances of small dramas or tests of inventions or products came to be part of their dissemination within the economy. San Juan Hill is, so to speak, the publicity for the Roosevelt ideas. Daniel Boorstin has described a key moment in the publicizing of the sewing machine, that instrument that became the first of the household appliances that penetrated and reshaped domestic life.

To persuade the public that his machine would really work, Howe took it to the Quincy Hall Clothing Manufactory in Boston, seated himself before it and offered to sew up any seam that anyone would bring. For two weeks he astonished all comers by doing 250 stitches a minute, about seven times the speed by hand. He then challenged five of the speediest seamstresses to race his machine. The experienced tailor whom he had called in as umpire announced Howe's victory and declared that "the work done on the machine was the neatest and strongest."[22]

The inventor dramatizes his machine in this heroic round of challenges and boasts, umpire and victory announcements. The public in the form of the spectators around the stage and then, through word of mouth, newspaper reports, or handbills that recount the event, the larger buying public that is the ultimate audience, receives the machine by means of its ability to perform in public, to become as we say, a commercial. Verena's speech, too, is not an argument for feminism, but an endorsement of it, a commercial for it.

Alongside his display of the varieties of publicity and performance, James must describe the varieties of privacy from

22. Boorstin, pp. 93–94.

Basil Ransom's reserve to Olive Chancellor's abashed, tense, and sexualized shyness. One of James's greatest accomplishments in his novel is the notation of the painfully physical shyness that is Olive's one performance. Her white-lipped anger, her sudden tears, her tense expectation, as well as her passion are all transparent in her face and tense bearing. For such a person, although she dreads being in public, there is never any genuine privacy, because her aspect broadcasts her mood in spite of her will. Blushes, frowns, clipped-off words, breathlessness, blazing eyes—she has no hidden feelings at all. She is a martyr of involuntary publicity. Her moods are written all over her face.

Opposed to this high-strung, almost hysterical privacy are the silence and reserve of Ransom. When asked, at the meeting that opens the novel, to say a few words about the condition of the south, Ransom refuses politely, but fumes inwardly. "To talk to these people about the south—if they could have guessed how little he cared to do it! He had a passionate tenderness for his own country, and a sense of intimate connection with it which would have made it as impossible for him to take a roomful of northern fanatics into his confidence as to read aloud his mother's or his mistresses' letters" (p. 50). His political vocabulary is that of love. For the south he feels "passionate tenderness" and "intimacy." Those feelings are as private as the letter of a mistress or a mother. When he speaks in public he thinks of it as taking others "into his confidence." The sexual and the intimate are the model for the political and not vice versa.

The political realm as Ransom embodies it is not yet distinct from loyalty or from the passionate realm of feelings. James has injected Ransom into a new social and political world in which the political has become distinct and public. Even more, it has turned back to appropriate for its own uses those private energies that are intimate and sexual so as to display them as charisma. The final step of the public realm is exactly to read in public the letters of the mistress or mother, and it is this step that James can study in the young girl whose beauty and rhapsodic feelings are placed on the platform to burn in public under the costume of politics the energies of fervor and passion.

The Masters of Performance

The full encounter between the public and the sexual that might seem at first to be one of the strongest and darkest elements of both James's and Howells' account of performance and exhibition turns out to set a sharp limit. Because both James and Howells require the marriage plot for an analysis of social fact, the notion of privacy has in advance a specific and privileged content. Throughout James's work the erotic had always entailed not only the private, but to some extent the secret. The most famous single scene in all of James is the appearance in public together of Chad and Mme. de Vionnet, an exhibition of their intimacy that is, in the novel's terms, a catastrophe. In *Daisy Miller* the public appearance of Daisy at night in that most historical theater of western history, the Coliseum, is fatal. In the late story "The Death of the Lion" the public days of the newly celebrated author give him time to perform in public only the act of dying, a performance that mainly serves to ruin a country weekend at which he was to serve as the latest celebrity. By posing the new public world in terms of the sexual and the rather special matter of the private life of the artist, both James and the Howells of *The Rise of Silas Lapham* distorted the nature of the new energies and the dangers totally unrelated to the guiding form of marriage and sexual intimacy.

What is usually taken to be one of the defects of Twain and particularly of *The Adventures of Huckleberry Finn,* that Twain avoids any account of sexual relations or even adult relations between men and women, turns out to be one of the greatest strengths of his novel in permitting him to display the full energies of the new public world, one to which he, unlike Howells or James, was drawn in his self-imagination and of which his entire career is an instance as complex as any in his fiction. In the purely male world of the raft Twain can construct the actual texture of late nineteenth-century public space, a space of power and deception whose final topic is not intimacy but survival.

In the Duke and the Dauphin Twain parades the range of performances and frauds, lies and scams that make the amateur lying of Huck reveal itself as the defensive tactic that it is. The Duke is the master of the Temperance meeting, the Revival

camp, the traveling Shakespearean performance, and the car-
nival sideshow. The professions of these two scoundrels—actor,
revivalist, preacher, printer—cross the field of public appearance. They turn the raft itself into a practice hall, stock it with
costumes that replace the nakedness of Huck and Jim, and break
down the great division that Twain had so carefully invented in
which the land was the world of deceptions and lies while the
raft was conversational and intimate, naked and exempt. With
the Duke and the Dauphin come the framing lies about their
own identities—as royalty fallen on hard times—and the per-
fected staging in which Jim, tied up with ropes, plays just what
he turns out to be, the already recaptured runaway slave.

With his two great symbols of the underbrush of culture that
Twain as the American master of the one-night performance in
a rented hall knew very well, he can imbed dizzying layers of
role and performance. The old man who, in order to seize
position on the raft, passes himself off as "the wanderin', exiled,
trampled-on and sufferin', rightful King of France" (p. 124),
must practice, on that raft, the role of Juliet. The playbills
announce him as "The Illustrious Edmund Kean the Elder." In
total he is the old man playing the Dauphin, pretending to be
Edmund Kean who is in the role of Juliet.

The failure of this too richly layered offering, leads to the
second night's performance in which the king comes out prancing on all fours, naked. Although the skit is too short for the
audience's taste, they love it enough to have it repeated. As
Huck says, "The people most killed themselves laughing" (p.
151). Instead of the high cultural language and costumes of
Shakespeare, this audience turns up in droves to see the naked
human animal, prancing around the stage. Unable to perform,
they expose. Unable to rise, they descend. The naked, capering
old fool sells the ridiculousness of his own flesh, taking in four
hundred and sixty-five dollars in three nights.

Just as the Duke had successfully disguised Jim as what he
actually was by printing up a bill identifying Jim as a runaway
slave, so too the old man in his performance makes public only
his naked foolishness. What is performed by Jim or by the king
is privacy itself. The secret is exposed. Twain, like Eakins in
his clinical paintings, and James in his metaphoric exposure of

the private self in Verena's performances, has tied the space of performance to self-exposure—the surgically opened breast, the capering old man, the rapture of the virginal girl.

Free of the Duke and the Dauphin, Huck and Jim alone on the raft are engaged in the tender and risky experiments in feeling that, taking place between a boy considered dead and a vanished slave, occur in spite of and at the mercy of a public world to which they must lie and perform. Twain's novel, like James's, gives off the electricity of experimental intimacy within a private world only occasionally free from invasion or conscription. The uncomfortable moral improvisations of Huck in his feelings for Jim are stuttered through with a necessity that, in James's novel, can be felt in the high-strung affections and fears of Olive Chancellor as she designs euphemistic notations to account for her feelings for Verena. In James's case even the romance between Basil and Verena, for which neither northern nor southern societies provide a code of courtship, asks us to picture lovers improvising their way across an unmarked social terrain of intimacy where "mates" are captured almost in a primitive recreation of male and female sexuality. That each of these novels revolves around the strategies of escape, mystification, outwitting of the public world's styles and performing claims, and disappearances done by characters who are spontaneous masters of lying and performance, as both Huck and Verena are, invites us to imagine that the primary victims of this world are not its failures but its apparently triumphant artists of performance. Only with Dreiser's *Sister Carrie* would this world receive at last its heroic tribute.

Corporate Fiction: Norris, Royce, and Arthur Machen

Toward the end of *The Octopus*—after the shoot-out between the railroad and the ranchers, and after the railroad has put its "dummy buyers" in possession of the ranchers' property—Norris contrives a dramatic way of illustrating some of the consequences of this event. He cuts back and forth between scenes of the immigrant rancher's widow Mrs. Hooven and her daughter starving in the streets of San Francisco and scenes of a fashionable dinner party at the home of the railroad magnate Gerard. The contrast is crude but powerful. The "wrecked body" of Mrs. Hooven "clamor[s] for nourishment; anything to numb those gnawing teeth—an abandoned loaf . . . a half-eaten fruit."[1] Mrs. Gerard describes how her asparagus is brought in fresh every day by a "special train": " 'Fancy eating ordinary market asparagus,' said Mrs. Gerard, 'that has been fingered by heaven knows how many hands.' " (p. 430). By the time the dinner party ends, Mrs. Hooven is dead.

But stark as this contrast is, it is compromised by Norris' depiction of what Mrs. Hooven actually experiences in the moment of starving to death. The "numbness" she had yearned

---

1. Frank Norris, *The Octopus* (New York: Signet, 1964), p. 427. Subsequent references are cited in parentheses in the text.

189

for now begins "to creep over her" and the "torture" of "famine" begins to fade. "She no longer felt the pain and cramps of her stomach"; the moment when starving becomes starving to death is here depicted as a curious form of satiation: "Even the hunger was ceasing to bite" (p. 430). It is almost as if starving to death represents somehow a failure to be hungry enough and hence as if Mrs. Hooven's final experience of her body is in some sense comparable to the satisfaction experienced by the Gerards and their guests. " 'We aindt gowun to be hungry enymore,' " Mrs. Hooven has promised her daughter, " 'we gowun to die' " (p. 429). Norris seems to imagine satiation not as a pleasurable sensation but as the beginning of the end of sensation, "a pleasing semi-insensibility" (p. 430). The moment in which one ceases to feel hunger becomes the moment in which one ceases to feel anything at all and the body, becoming insensible, becomes "inert"; a good meal is a harbinger of mortality.

Lest this account of death (even death by starvation) as a form of satiation seem implausible, it is worth noting that Dreiser in *Sister Carrie* associates Hurstwood's death with the failure of desire"[?] (Norris had read *Sister Carrie* in manuscript for Doubleday, Page). Perhaps more to the point, it is worth noting that satisfaction in *The Octopus* is also a sure sign of mortality. The "picture of feasting" (p. 428) at the Gerards' party is anticipated by the self-consciously Homeric barbecue on Annixter's ranch, "a feeding of the people, elemental, gross, a great appeasing of appetite, an enormous quenching of thirst" (p. 355). "Everyone had his fill," Norris writes, and while the people feast, the railroad takes possession of their ranches and within hours the ranchers have been killed. " 'Dabney dead, Hooven dead, Harran dead, Annixter dead, Broderson dead, Osterman dying' " (p. 378), writes the poet Presley. More striking still, the "immense satisfaction" (p. 434) of S. Behrman, the railroad agent who takes possession of the Rancho de los Muertos, turns out to be only a foretaste of his own extinction. Examining the wheat—once the ranchers', now his—being

---

2. For further discussion see Walter Benn Michaels, "*Sister Carrie*'s Popular Economy," *Critical Inquiry*, 7 (Winter 1980), 373–390.

shipped to the "starving bellies" of Asia, Behrman falls into the hold and, "deafened with the roar of the grain, blinded and made dumb with its chaff" (p. 454), is, like Mrs. Hooven, exhausted and rendered insensible. "The wheat leaping continuously from the chute, poured around him. It filled the pockets of the coat; it crept up the sleeves and trousers legs; it covered the great protuberant stomach; it ran at last in rivulets into the distended, gasping mouth." The cause of Behrman's death is, no doubt, suffocation but Norris manages to make it sound like he has eaten too much, or rather, like he has been unable to eat enough. Even the gluttonous Behrman isn't hungry enough to eat his way out of the wheat, and his death too is imagined as a moment in which appetite fails.

Despite its place as the first novel in Norris' projected trilogy dealing with "(1) the production, (2) the distribution, (3) the consumption of American wheat," *The Octopus* is much less concerned with its presumed subject (production) or even with its titular subject (the railroad, hence distribution) than with the final stage in Norris' economic cycle—consumption, the imagination of an appetite for American wheat. "The great word of this nineteenth century has been production. The great word of the twentieth century will be . . . markets" (p. 216). Set in the early 1880s, the novel, in traditional agrarian terms, imagines the railroad as an obstacle between producers and their markets:

between the fecund San Joaquin, reeking with fruitfulness, and the millions of Asia crowding toward the verge of starvation, lay the iron-hearted monster of steel and steam, implacable, insatiable, huge . . . its ever hungry maw glutted with the harvests that should have fed the famished bellies of the whole world of the Orient.   (p. 228)

But, written in 1900, in the wake of Populism's spectacular rise and fall, the novel begins to imagine not only production but also the opposition between producers and distributors as something of an anachronism. The Populist dream of "the farmer and manufacturer" is to do away with the "middleman" (pp. 216–217), to "free" themselves from the "speculator" and the "trust" (p. 226), and, "acting for themselves," to sell their own wheat in the "markets" of the Orient. The title of *The Octopus* marks the failure of this dream but not, by the same token, the triumph of the middleman. For instead of describing the railroad as controlling the flow of wheat from producer to consumer, Norris describes it as if it were itself the consumer, competing with rather than profiting from the hungry Asians, replacing their "starving bellies" with its own "ever hungry maw." Rather than dramatizing the customary agrarian fear of the middleman, the novel here transforms distribution into consumption and, indeed, throughout *The Octopus*, the final stage in Norris' cycle seems on the verge of swallowing up the first two. The railroad that distributes the wheat turns out to be imagined as consuming it; even the machine that harvests the wheat is a "monster, insatiable, with iron teeth . . . devouring" (p. 433) it.

Finally, the "insatiable ambition to write verse" of the poet Presley who (like Norris) will seek to produce an "Epic of the Wheat," is identified with the fact that he is "threatened with consumption" (p. 13). He comes to California in search of his health and a "subject" and leaves having found the subject— he has written "The Toilers"—but not his health. For what is truly insatiable in Presley is the hunger that drives his body to consume itself, his "vast desire" for "some terrifying martyr-dom, some awe-inspiring immolation, consummate, incisive, conclusive" (pp. 397–398). Presley's poem of production, his own productivity, is depicted as an epiphenomenon of his con-suming desire to be consumed. Putting him, at the end of the novel, on a ship loaded with wheat for "the hungry Hindoo" (the wheat belongs to Behrman and the ship carries him too, dead, in its hold), Presley's friend Cedarquist urges him to "get fat yourself" (p. 455). But all the wheat in the San Joaquin couldn't make Presley fat. Indeed, shipping both the wheat and Presley to the Orient, it isn't clear whether Cedarquist is ex-porting food or hunger; given Norris' account of production as a byproduct of the desire to consume, it isn't even clear whether the difference between them survives. What is clear is that in the market of the twentieth century, as Norris foresees it, there will be no place for the too-easily-satisfied appetites of the wheat farmers. Only "insatiable" poets like Presley and "ever hungry" corporations like the Southern Pacific Railroad will survive.

The Octopus thus displaces what Tom Watson characterized

as labor's fundamental question to capital—" 'Why is it you
have so much and do so little work, while I have so little and
do so much?' "³—with a question that was in some respects
more puzzling: why, having so much, do you want still more?
"A man cannot wear more than one suit of clothes at a time,"
as Ignatius Donnelly put it; the spectacle of "the Goulds and
the Vanderbilts and the Rockefellers" spending "nights and
days of ceaseless labor"⁴ in pursuit of fortunes they could never
live to spend was more perplexing and ultimately more terrifying
than Watson's imagination of the idle capitalist. What did these
men want? Or, to put the question in terms more appropriate
to *The Octopus,* how, having everything they wanted, did they
manage to keep on wanting? Donnelly's answer to this question
took the form of a parable about "the hog in human nature."
A farmer out to raise prize-winning pigs would feed them all
they could eat, but "at a certain point they stopped laying on
fat. Nature had got all it wanted and would go no farther."⁵
Then, to get his best pig eating again, the farmer would put "a
poor, half-starved, hungry shoat" into the pen, arousing in "the
porcine bosom" all the "instincts of the millionaire." "It turns
and gorges the food for which before it had no appetite."⁶ In
this analysis, the natural limits on desire can be transcended by
supplementing the desire to eat with the desire to keep someone
else from eating. But why anyone should want *that* remains a
mystery: "It is a thing no man can understand."⁷

But its ultimate failure to explain was not the only unsatis-
factory aspect of Donnelly's explanation. Eventually even the
prize-winning pig, like Norris' S. Behrman, can eat no more; it
runs up against nature in the form of its own body and of that
body's inability to consume all the food around it. For Behrman,
in the ship's hold, this food comes to constitute his entire environment, as if the world contained nothing but men and food

3. Tom Watson, "A Labor Day Message" (1891), reprinted in *The Populist Mind,* ed. Norman Pollack (Indianapolis: Bobbs-Merrill, 1967), p. 424.
4. Ignatius Donnelly, *The American People's Money* (1895; rpt.: Westport, Conn.: Hyperion, 1976), p. 100.
5. Ibid., p. 99.
6. Ibid., p. 100.
7. Ibid., p. 101.

and as if the identity of a man—the difference between him and his food—depended on the moment in which he was unable to make his food a part of himself, unable to incorporate the world into himself. The mere fact that S. Behrman has a body seems, from this standpoint, a mark of what must be a principled satiability, since the fact of his body being his body (as opposed, say, to just being the world) requires a world outside his body, a world, in the ship's hold, of food that he has failed to consume. To imagine insatiability seems then to involve not imagining an insatiable body but something that is not a body at all, something that really is as "intangible" as S. Behrman ("there ain't nothing can touch me") mistakenly imagines himself to be. And, of course, in *The Octopus* itself, as in the polemical literature of Populism, it is the corporation, "a mere ideal being, an artificial creation of imaginary workmanship, set up as a person . . . to move among natural persons,"[8] that embodies, if that's still the right word, the possibility of such an "intangible" person and hence of a truly "exhaustless greed for lucre."

To writers like James "Cyclone" Davis and Henry D. Lloyd, it was this combination of personhood and intangibility that conferred upon corporations "unprecedented" powers—above all, the "power to act as persons, as in the commission of crimes, with exemption from punishment as persons."[9] As persons, corporations, like natural persons, could cheat or steal; but as intangible persons, corporations, unlike natural persons, could not be sent to jail. To writers like Josiah Royce, however, the great philosopher of American corporate life, the perfection in commercial life of the intangible person seemed a practical fulfillment of the promise of Absolute Idealism. Thus in his last book, *War and Insurance,* Royce took the insurance company, consisting, in its most stripped-down form, "of what is usually called a *principal,* of an *agent,* and of a *client . . . to whom the agent represents the principal"* as a model for the *"Community of Interpretation"*[10] whose epistemological importance he had

8. Judge A. W. Terrell (of Texas), quoted in James H. Davis, *A Political Revelation* (Dallas: Advance Publishing Co., 1894), p. 240.

9. Henry D. Lloyd, *Wealth Against Commonwealth* (New York: Harper & Bros., 1894), p. 519.

10. Josiah Royce, *War and Insurance* (New York: Macmillan, 1914), p. 47.

discovered in reading the early essays of C. S. Peirce. An "international corporation" constructed along the lines of a "community of insurance" would constitute, Royce thought, "a distinctively new entity which would be neither a nation, nor a court of arbitration, nor an international congress, nor a federation of states, nor any such body as at present exists."[11] As a corporation designed to insure against risk, this international body, in order to be free itself from the risks besetting comparatively more material corporate bodies (such as nations), would itself be finally separate from any body at all: "it would possess no territory which could be seized, it would lay claim to no neutrality which could be violated . . . Its individual trustees might be made prisoners or executed; but such efforts might well kill its body without touching its essentially intangible soul."[12]

From Royce's standpoint, the ultimate immateriality of the international insurance corporation was the necessary condition of its success in preventing war. Writing in August 1914, he was only too aware of the failure of international courts to maintain peace and of the susceptibility of such institutions to political pressures and military threats. Even the neutrality of a nation can be violated since even a neutral nation, like a body, has borders and those borders can be crossed. His solution was to imagine an utterly disembodied entity, to think of the relation of the corporation to its employees, its board of directors and its shareholders as the relation of soul to body. Whereas in a partnership the death of a partner dissolves the partnership, in Royce's model of the corporation, no physical event can jeopardize the existence of the corporate entity—its soul is immortal. If it is the fact that persons have bodies that makes insurance desirable, it is the possibility of a person without a body that makes the absolute insurance of Absolute Idealism possible.

Both the promise and the threat of corporate personality are thus linked to idealism, an idealism that must itself be defined in opposition to the organic materialism of the body and, even-

11. Ibid., pp. xix–xx.
12. Ibid., pp. xxvii–xxviii.

tually, to the mechanical materialism of the automaton. And despite its materialist subject (or, rather, by way of it), this idealism finds its way into the "Epic of the Wheat." Imagining "the very first little quiver of life that the grain must feel after it is sown," the shepherd Vanamee insists that this "premonition of life" must take place "long, long before any physical change has occurred—long before the microscope could discover the slightest change" (p. 155). The novel's central image of materiality is here converted into an emblem of the immaterial, a conversion authorized by the Pauline sermon of Father Sarria: " 'Your grain of wheat is your symbol of immortality'; 'It is sown a natural body; it is raised a spiritual body' " (p. 106). The corporate enemy of producers in *The Octopus* thus turns out to be present from the start in the object that is produced, present in fact in the utterly idealized possibility of production. For in identifying the germination of the wheat with the emergence of a spiritual out of a natural body, Norris describes production itself as the transcendence of the material. The moral of this description according to Vanamee is that "evil dies" but "the good never dies" (p. 447). We might say that in moralizing the process of production, Vanamee removes it altogether from the sphere of economy, that he speaks in Royce's voice, a voice that Norris also attempts to make his own when, distinguishing between the "individual" who "suffers" and the "race" that "goes on," he ends by asserting that the "larger view . . . through all shams, all wickednesses, discovers the truth that will, in the end, prevail, and all things surely, inevitably, resistlessly work together for good" (p. 458). The cheerless optimism of this passage seeks to override the troublesome character of its distinction between the individual and the race. Is the individual's relation to the race that of part to whole? Body to soul? Natural person to corporate person? A race would seem to be made up of individuals but a soul could never be described as made up of a body. Was a corporate person, like a race, composed of natural individuals? Or did it, like the soul, have an independent, intangible existence?

Royce's commitment to the priority of the social, to the "community of interpretation" as a "corporate entity" "more concrete" than "any individual,"[13] was virtually lifelong, finding expression not only in minor pieces like *War and Insurance* but in his major philosophical works, *The World and the Individual,* and *The Problem of Christianity.* Even the early history, *California,* taught "the sacredness of a true public spirit."[14] But the particular place of the corporation in this ontological hierarchy was not always as unequivocal as it came to be in the later writings. And, interestingly enough, what unease Royce felt about the ontology of the corporation surfaces most explicitly in his only novel, *The Feud at Oakfield Creek,* written in 1886 (just after the history of California) and based, like *The Octopus,* on the land dispute at Mussel Slough.

But there are important differences. *The Octopus* is set, like the original dispute, in the San Joaquin valley; Royce's *Feud* takes place almost entirely in San Francisco and the hills of the East Bay. Although Norris converts the dirt-poor farmers of Tulare county into facsimiles of the wealthy ranchers of Santa Cruz, he at least recreates the economic struggle between the farmers and the railroad. Royce leaves the railroad out and turns the whole affair into the aftereffect of a soap opera quarrel between two old California pioneers, the rich landowner, Alonzo Eldon, and the poor poet-professor, Alf Escott. Indeed, early on in the novel, Royce makes a point of the unbusinesslike and economically trivial nature of the feud. " 'Men are so strange,' " remarks Alonzo's daughter-in-law, Margaret:

You call us women mere creatures of feeling. But dear me, the thing seems easy enough to me. Perhaps it's all my womanly stupidity, but if the poor people have their rights, and you know it, why do you want to turn them out of house and home, just for a mere matter of pride? I think men are the least rational beings on earth. Women wouldn't have such troubles with settlers, I know.[15]

13. Josiah Royce, *The Problem of Christianity* (1918; rpt.: Chicago: University of Chicago Press, 1968), p. 93 and passim.

14. Josiah Royce, *California* (1886; rpt.: Santa Barbara: Peregrine Smith, 1970), p. 366.

15. Josiah Royce, *The Feud at Oakfield Creek* (1887; rpt.: Upper Saddle River, N.J.: Gregg Press, 1970), pp. 28–29. Subsequent references are cited in parentheses in the text.

The moral tone of this passage suggests an opposition between justice (the settlers' rights) and business (Alonzo's attempt to claim the land for himself and his "Land Improvement Company"); its real target, however, is not business but the irrationality and sentimentality of businessmen. From the standpoint of what Royce elsewhere calls "pure business," the Oakfield Creek (unlike the Mussel Slough) affair is not a difficult one—the differences between the settlers (who claim squatters' rights to the property) and Eldon (who claims legal title) might easily be adjudicated. But the settlers are now led by Escott who, having bought up some of their claims out of "enmity" to Eldon, sees the "business" as one of "eternal justice" (p. 31). Escott is a "confirmed romancer"—by which Royce turns out to mean that, unlike the settlers, he has no real interest in the land: "Escott has lived on one of the tracts twice or thrice since he purchased the claim, though always for short periods. Part of the land he has lent, without rent, to poor families. At other times, he has employed two men to take care of some of it for him" (p. 41). Escott is thus an absentee squatter. The structure of his commitment to the settlers' claims undermines the basis for those claims, and the intensity of his commitment to justice makes an equitable adjudication impossible. This is not to say that Eldon has any interest in the land either or even, finally, in the money that might be made from selling it. "In the course of the controversy," he has become "so much wrought up" that he has declared he will "never settle with the old claimants at any price" (p. 39). " 'For the money he doesn't care now' " (p. 40). Like Escott, he is motivated by something beyond self-interest. Indeed, he is willing to take a loss to get rid of the settlers: " 'he would eject them, if it cost him half a million.' "

Alonzo's son Tom dismisses such threats as " 'the words of passion' " and asserts what the novel continuously seeks to demonstrate, " 'Father is not so bad as that.' " But neither the contrast between Escott's noble purposes and Eldon's ignoble ones nor Royce's and his family's attempts to rehabilitate Alonzo should be allowed to obscure the essential "irrationality" of their positions: the champion of squatters' rights is a kind of absentee landlord; the land-grabbing capitalist is willing to lose money to assert his rights. " 'A woman simply can't understand such passions,' " says Margaret. She is speaking of Alonzo's vindictiveness but in effect she characterizes what is most puzzling about the Oakfield Creek situation and especially about Royce's representation of it. The "whole question of California land titles," Royce had written in 1885, was "a critical one" for "the new community," involving the "universal question of the conflict between abstract ideas and social authority, at a moment when the order of a new society, and the eternal conflict between the private and the universal Selves had to be settled."[16] And yet, in *Feud,* the struggle over land titles is represented as a struggle between two men with absolutely no interest in the land or in the "abstract question" of legitimate title. And, despite Royce's claim that the history of California teaches only one "lesson"—"We are all but dust, save as this social order gives us life"[17]—*The Feud at Oakfield Creek,* by its very mode of narration, resolves the eternal conflict of private and universal in favor of the private, thus transforming public events, at every opportunity, into private ones. It is as if the genre of the novel seemed to Royce to require a valorization of the individual that as a historian and philosopher he would have found intolerable. Converting the struggle between the settlers and the railroad into a quarrel between two old men caused by the son of one having jilted the daughter of the other, Royce turns a political and economic dispute over "abstract principle" and "social authority" into "a personal and private fight" (p. 470) over a girl.

One way to account for this anomaly might be to note, with R. Jackson Wilson, that Royce's "critique of individualism was psychological and metaphysical, not economic or political."

Royce's political and economic ideas always remained essentially those of the Berkeley and San Francisco businessmen who had financed his year in Germany . . . In the main, he was simply frightened by turn-

16. Josiah Royce, "An Episode of Early California Life: The Squatter of 1850 in Sacramento" (1885), reprinted in *The Basic Writings of Josiah Royce,* vol. 1, ed. with an intro. by John J. McDermott (Chicago: University of Chicago Press, 1969), pp. 126, 122.

17. Royce, *California,* p. 394.

of-the-century America, and fright provoked the usual conservative response, a reassertion of what he thought were the traditional concepts of property and obligation.[18]

Transposing this account of Royce's politics to *The Feud at Oakfield Creek,* we might argue that the requirements of the sentimental novel as Royce understood them—"two bloody fights, three heroes, two heroines, several villains, and almost no morals"[19]—provided him with an opportunity to defuse the threat to the self: the threat, that is, to "traditional concepts of property and obligation" posed not only by developments in American political and economic life but by the tendencies of his own philosophical work. Eventually, Royce would come to regard the individual as "essentially defective," and to equate "the very form of his being as a morally detached individual" with "original sin."[20] From the radically Pauline perspective of *The Problem of Christianity,* only the "destruction" of the "natural self" could make "salvation" possible. But the Royce of the mid 1880s was as yet unable to seek the solution to social problems in the miraculous subsumption of the individual by the "corporate entity" embodied in "the Christian community," and as yet unwilling to identify the business corporation with that Christian corporate entity. The "personal and private" life of the novel might well have seemed the saving grace of the business life of California. We might say that the political and economic had first to be reduced to the personal so that later they might be transformed into the religious.

But the novel itself, concerned though it is to represent the public history of California as an epiphenomenon of the private lives of some of the state's more prominent citizens, nevertheless experiences some difficulty in separating the private and personal from the public and political. To some extent, this is probably due to Royce's incompetence as a novelist. Virtually all the action of the novel consists of secret intrigues designed

18. R. Jackson Wilson, *In Quest of Community* (New York: John Wiley & Sons, 1963), p. 163.

19. Josiah Royce, *Letters,* ed. with an intro. by John Clendenning (Chicago: University of Chicago Press, 1970), p. 202.

20. Royce, *The Problem of Christianity,* p. 194.

to avoid a violent confrontation between settlers and landowners at Oakfield Creek; and the people engaged in these intrigues are so clever, so dedicated and noble, that it begins to seem (about three quarters of the way through) that their plans must succeed. But they can't succeed if the novel is to end in the required tragic manner. So Royce causes an evil newspaperman miraculously to hear of some private interviews between the unmarried hero and the married heroine; the newspaperman publicizes this information in the appropriate places and attributes the publicity to the boasting of the hero. Since the interviews were secret, who else could be the source? Having thus managed, in the most arbitrary manner, to revive old enmities, Royce pushes the story on to the violent climax demanded by the Mussel Slough affair.

Something more than incompetence, however, is involved in this arbitrary authorial intervention. For Royce has managed things so that the narrative insists on the sanctity of emotions so personal that they never can be and never are revealed ("Their secret was safe, their mutual understanding perfect." [p. 398]), while at the same time it inexplicably reveals them. And this inexplicability is, in a certain sense, necessary, since any plausible account of how the secret and ultimately innocent love of hero and heroine was made public would compromise both the integrity of the secret and the innocence of the love. By means of this hole in his plot, then, Royce asserts simultaneously the absolute primacy of the private and the absolute impossibility of keeping anything private. There is a gap between the world of persons and the world of politics, a gap that must be left unbridged if persons are to be saved from politics while it must at the same time be constantly crossed if politics are to be causally accounted for by reference to persons. Thus the formal incoherence of Royce's plot corresponds to an incoherence in his conception of the relation between public and private, an incoherence the novel serves above all to defend.

These uneasy relations between public and private emerge as thematically central to the novel in Royce's even more uneasy introduction of what was, after all, the central character in the Mussel Slough affair, the Southern Pacific Railroad. The railroad turns into a "Land and Improvement Company" and, instead of being, as Norris would describe it, "huge," a "colossus" (p. 42), it is only, as Margaret Eldon puts it to her father-in-law, its chief stockholder, "something about as big as your own thumb" (p. 264). Nevertheless, it presents a serious obstacle to resolving the feud, since while Alonzo Eldon professes himself willing "in my private capacity as his old friend" (p. 259) to settle things with Alf Escott, he reminds his daughter-in-law that as president of the company he "can't act alone" but must bear in mind the "capital of innocent shareholders" (p. 258). Not Eldon but the Land and Improvement Company owns the Oakfield Creek property. To his listeners this "explanation" seems "to have a certain hollow sound," but Eldon insists on the distinction between himself and the company: "a man isn't a corporation."

Margaret Eldon responds to this argument by urging him to make the corporation private. She tells him to buy back the rights he ought "never" to have sold so that "all will be in [his] hands again" (p. 264). Having thrown this sop to the "miserable little monster" of the corporation (since what he claims to "fear is *its* bitterness of feeling towards Escott"), Eldon can then go ahead and deal fairly with the settlers. And with Eldon holding all its shares, the corporate "monster" will be reduced to the man (Eldon himself) that Margaret already understands it to be. The "hollow sound" of a corporate body will be replaced by the sound of flesh and blood.

The only difficulty here is that what Margaret has proposed, as a "woman of business," is too businesslike for the corporation—"the passions that had been aroused couldn't be allayed today or tomorrow" (p. 267). The shareholders don't want their money, they want to know that the settlers have been "beaten in the courts" (p. 266). The corporation is here identified with the irrationality and sentimentality of the original quarrel between Eldon and Escott, and the difference between a man and a corporation begins to blur. "A woman simply can't understand such passions." Men and corporations both are too passionate for "pure business"; the "miserable little monster" of a corporation is doubled by Margaret's "powerful, capricious monster of a father-in-law" (p. 270). Where the novel's plot requires miracles, its cast of characters requires monsters, and what's most monstrous is finally the difficulty of saying exactly why and in what way a man isn't a corporation.

In effect, Alonzo Eldon asserts what most writers of the period were coming to recognize as "the theory of the existence of the corporation as an entity distinct and separate from its shareholders,"[21] when he distinguishes between a man and a corporation. What he means, of course, is that, even as the chief shareholder in the Land and Improvement Company, he can't be held personally responsible for that company's actions. His daughter-in-law expresses a skepticism about this difference that goes hand-in-hand with the developing doctrine of corporate entity. If the chief officer and/or the chief stockholder isn't responsible for the corporation's actions, who is? It is sometimes necessary, as one writer put it, to "pierce the veil of corporate entity"[22] in order to get at what another writer called "the human beings who are behind the entity."[23] The quarrel between Margaret and Alonzo is thus a quarrel between two different legal theories of the corporation: the theory of the corporation as one mode among others of organizing a "group of natural persons"[24] and the theory of the corporation as not simply a group but a "group" "which is recognized and treated by the law as something distinct from its members."[25]

In retrospect we can see that to characterize the dispute in this way is to miss its real point. The question of whether corporations existed independent of the persons who owned and operated them had already been decisively answered by the time *The Feud at Oakfield Creek* was written. In what legal writers characterized as the "leading case" of Button v. Hoffman (1884), the sole owner of all the shares in a corporation brought suit

21. I. Maurice Wormser, *Disregard of the Corporate Fiction and Allied Corporation Problems* (New York: Baker, Voorhis & Co., 1927), p. 43. The essay from which this remark is drawn, "Piercing the Veil of Corporate Entity," was first published in 1912.

22. Ibid., p. 30.

23. Arthur W. Machen Jr., "Corporate Personality," *Harvard Law Review,* 24 (1911), p. 265.

24. John P. Davis, *Corporations* (1905; rpt.: New York: Capricorn, 1961), p. 13.

25. George F. Canfield, "The Scope and Limits of the Corporate Entity Theory," *Columbia Law Review,* 17 (1917), p. 128.

"to recover certain personal property which had been unlawfully taken from the corporation's possession."[26] The plaintiff thought himself entitled to recover the corporation's property because, as he put it, "I bought all the stock, I own all the stock now, I became the absolute owner of the mill. It belonged at that time to the company, and I am the company." The Wisconsin court, however, was unpersuaded by this Margaret Eldon-like account of corporate ontology. "The owner of all the capital stock of a corporation does not own its property," wrote the court, "and does not himself become the corporation, as a natural person, to own its property and do its business in his own name. While the corporation exists he is a mere stockholder of it, and nothing else."[27] The man is not the company and the company is not the man because the company is, "by a fiction of law," another man. Royce's rhetorical doubling of the monster corporation (Davis calls it the "man in law") by the monster Alonzo Eldon (Margaret's "father-in-law") thus invokes the disconcerting possibility that the struggle between man and corporation at Mussel Slough can be transformed into a struggle between man and man not because the corporation is a veil concealing a man but because the corporation is itself a new kind of man.

But what kind? "The orthodox American lawyer," wrote Arthur Machen in his frequently cited "Corporate Personality," "would be apt to say, 'A corporation is a fictitious, artificial person, composed of natural persons, created by the state, existing only in contemplation of law, invisible, soulless, immortal.' "[28] According to Machen, however, this definition is nothing but a "*congeries* of self-contradictory terms" (p. 257). It asserts both that a corporation is "artificial" and that it is "imaginary or fictitious," when, in fact, what is "artificial is real, and not imaginary: an artificial lake is not an imaginary one"; it asserts that a corporation is "created by the state" and "fictitious," whereas something that has been created must be "real"; and it asserts that a corporation is "composed of natural persons" and is "imaginary or fictitious," whereas "Neither in mathe-

26. Wormser, *Disregard of the Corporate Fiction*, p. 17.
27. Quoted in ibid.
28. Arthur W. Machen Jr., "Corporate Personality," *Harvard Law Review*, 24 (1911), 257. Subsequent references are cited in parentheses in the text.

matics nor in philosophy nor in law can the sum of several actual, rational quantities produce an imaginary quantity." All these contradictions revolve around what is said to be "fictitious" in the corporate identity, and since what is "fictitious" is the characterization of the corporation as a person, the way to eliminate the contradictions, Machen argues, is to try to hang on to the notion of the corporation's real and independent existence while getting rid of the idea that this independent existence is personal. He thus distinguishes between two "propositions" about the nature of corporations: "(1) that a corporation is an entity distinct from the sum of the members that compose it, and (2) that this entity is a person" (p. 258). The first of these propositions seems to him true and the second false.

By way of argument for the real existence of the corporate entity, Machen adduces a series of analogies, from a bundle of faggots (the "bundle" being "something distinct" from the faggots) to a school ("something distinct from the boys that constitute it" [p. 259]), to a "voluntary association" for doing business: "It is hard to convince a sensible businessman that when a senior partner gives his son on attaining majority a small interest in the firm, an entirely new firm is thereby created" (p. 260). The "ordinary layman" can see that the identity of the firm is not changed just because a new owner has been added. Hence the identity of the firm is not dependent on the identity of its owners. And following this model, the existence of the corporate entity "is precisely as real as the existence of any other composite unit."

If a corporation is fictitious, the only reality being the individuals who compose it, then by the same token a river is fictitious, the only reality being the individual atoms of oxygen and hydrogen. The only difference is that one of the essential elements of . . . a river, consists in juxtaposition in space of . . . the molecules of water, whereas the bond of union in the case of a corporation is less material. (p. 261)

This real existence of the corporation as an entity does not, according to Machen, make the corporation really a person. He acknowledges that the two propositions have been "often confused" so that, for example, theorists in Germany, correctly asserting the real existence of corporations, have supposed that this assertion committed them also to thinking that corporations are real persons. They have actually carried this commitment to "grotesque lengths," describing the "corporate organism" as an "animal," claiming that "it possesses organs like a human being" and "even possesses sex" (churches are feminine, states masculine [p. 256]). But, Machen points out, there is no logical connection between the claim that corporations are real and the claim that they are persons; rivers are real but rivers are not persons. A "corporate entity," like a river, "is not a rational being, is not capable of understanding the law's commands, and has no will which can be affected by threats of legal punishment"; hence, "a corporation is not a real person" (p. 265). It is "personified" (that is, "regarded as having rights and liabilities" [p. 266]) only "for the sake of convenience"; in reality only "men of flesh and blood, of like passions with ourselves . . . enjoy the rights and bear the burdens attributed by the law to the corporate entity." Only corporate *entity* is real, then; corporate personality is a fiction.

Understanding the corporation as a real thing but not a real person, Machen suggests a difficulty with our earlier characterization of the corporation as a figure for intangible insatiability. Machen's corporation, because it isn't "flesh and blood," can experience no "passions"; and, although Cyclone Davis characterizes the corporation as "moved only by an exhaustless greed for lucre,"[29] for him too it is "without one human sympathy." Furthermore, its effect on the human beings who own it or who are employed by it is to recreate them in its own image—to deprive them of their "sympathy." These "natural persons" come to "feel no personal concern for the moral quality of the acts which produce money" and eventually cease to be persons at all. "The individual is merged in the money-machine of which he is an integral part."[30] So for Davis, as for Machen, the corporation is finally not a person but a thing, an "entity" or a "machine." But Davis goes one step farther than Machen, understanding corporations not only as different from but as threatening to "natural persons." And Norris' Shelgrim, the

29. Davis, *A Political Revelation*, p. 242.
30. Ibid., p. 245.

president of the railroad, goes farther still, telling Presley that "when you speak of wheat and the railroads," "you are dealing with forces . . . not with men." Here what Mark Seltzer has called naturalism's "discourse of force"[31] not only imagines a world of "entities" competing with men but imagines that men, properly understood, already have been reduced to the things ("brutes," "machines") they are said to be competing with.

In fact, following Seltzer's lead, we can say that the "discourse of force" not only undoes the opposition between body and machine but, perhaps more surprisingly, undoes the opposition between the body/machine and the soul, between something that is *all* body and something that is no body at all. Thus Davis can think of the corporation as simultaneously "intangible" (no body) and a "machine" (all body) not because he is inconsistent but because these two conditions are more like one another than either is like the alternative, a soul in a body. And much the same may be said about *The Octopus*. Norris' utterly idealized account of the production of wheat as the emergence of a spiritual body out of a natural one can coexist peacefully with an utterly materialist account of the growing wheat as a mechanical "force"; "indifferent, gigantic, resistless, it moved in its appointed grooves" (p. 316). Furthermore, the problem of insatiability with which I began gets rather elegantly solved by this double reduction to ideal and to material. Insofar as men are really souls, they don't desire at all. To participate in the spiritual life of nature is to become, like the grain of wheat, like life itself, immune to loss. "Life never departs. Life simply *is*" (p. 447). A world where nothing can be absent leaves nothing to be desired. And insofar as men are really bodies, they don't desire either; nothing can stop natural "forces," not because they are insatiable but—just the opposite—because they are "indifferent." Separating consumption from desire, the logic of material forces liberates men from the constraints of human embodiment just as surely as the logic of Pauline spirituality.

What Norris calls "human agency" is thus effaced by the

31. Mark Seltzer, "The Naturalist Machine," forthcoming in *Selected Papers from the English Institute* (Baltimore: Johns Hopkins University Press, in press), ed. Ruth Yeazell.

double reduction to ideal and to material—which is to say, to a natural ontology of bodies and souls: "As if human agency could affect this colossal power!" (p. 316). The point is not simply that human agents are less powerful than nature but that, reduced to the "forces" they really are, human agents are not agents at all. To recall Machen's terms, they are more like rivers than persons. His claim that corporations are "entities" appears now as simply a version of the more fundamental naturalist claim that "persons" too are really entities and hence that natural persons are as fictitious as corporate ones. From this standpoint, however, to characterize corporate personality as a fiction is not to dismiss it any more than to characterize numbers as imaginary is to dismiss imaginary numbers. American courts, more skeptical than German philosophers of the reality of corporate personality, had been "troubled" by the "old difficulty" of finding corporations guilty of "fraud, of malice, or of crimes involving a particular mental state" (p. 348); since "a corporation has no mind and is therefore incapable of entertaining malice," how can it be capable of "contriving a fraud or of doing any other act involving a mental state?" But according to Machen, this reasoning is "illogical." The fact that corporate personality is imaginary constitutes no obstacle to treating corporations as if they had minds. On the contrary: "if the corporate personality is imaginary, there is no limit to the characteristics and capacities which may be attributed to that personality." In particular, "if you can imagine that a corporate entity is a person, you can also imagine that this person has a mind." And, having imagined that it has a mind, you can hold it responsible for "crimes involving a particular mental state." In fact, Machen suggests, with a flourish that might dazzle even a German philosopher, "To take the opposite view would be like arguing that Hamlet must have been insane, because he was a fictitious person and could therefore have no mind."

What is dazzling here is the way in which the attempt to apply "sturdy common sense" (p. 365) to the doctrine of corporate personality, denying the German theory that the corporate person is real and thus has real characteristics ("will," "sex") has turned into the claim that because the corporate person *isn't* real, we are justified in attributing to it any characteristic we like: a mind, a soul (Sir Edward Coke and Cyclone Davis to the contrary notwithstanding), even a body, although it may be that "to carry the metaphor so far would provoke a smile, and would serve no good purpose" (p. 349). Common sense dictates that the "legal imagination" can attribute to corporations any characteristic of persons it chooses. The restraints lie not in any "logical" considerations but only in the demands of something like good taste.

But why should we want to think of corporations as persons? If common sense tells us that corporate entities are real and corporate persons are not, why don't we just treat corporations as things and forgo the fiction of personality? Machen's answer to this question is that it would be inconvenient and unnatural to do so. It is inconvenient because the law has given corporations as entities some of the powers of persons (the right to sue and be sued, for instance); thus the lawyer may think of the corporation as a person in the same way that a mathematician may call a "complicated expression such as $x^2 + 3ax + b^2$" equal to "y" and to use "y" in his calculations "instead of the longer and more cumbrous expression" (p. 353). It is unnatural because "the human mind is so constituted" that it finds it difficult "not to personify" "close organization[s]": "We instinctively speak and think of [such an] organization as a person; and the law finds it difficult or impossible to refrain from doing the same" (p. 349). As if he were parodying naturalism's reduction of persons to personifications, Machen identifies the desire to personify as itself one of those "instincts" that mark the replacement of persons with brutes.

Neither the appeal to convenience nor the appeal to nature is entirely satisfactory, however, for reasons having to do not so much with the distinction between (real) corporate entity and (fictitious) corporate personality as with the retroactive questions raised by such appeals about the nature of the corporate entity in the first place. For if a corporation created by the state is real and not imaginary in the same way that "an artificial lake is not an imaginary lake," and if that corporation is endowed by the state with many of the powers of persons, why isn't it a real, albeit artificial, person? The answer to this is presumably that we find it more difficult to conceive of artificial persons than of artificial entities; indeed, our very notion of a person seems to require that it not be artificial. But why then is it more "natural" to personify a corporation than it is to personify another artificial entity like an artificial lake or river? If real persons are "men of flesh and blood, of like passions with ourselves," why is it natural to think of corporations as real persons?

The answer to this question is implicit in the account I noted earlier by Machen, concerning the reality of the corporate entity. The corporate entity is real instead of fictitious, by analogy with a river or with an army:

> If a corporation is fictitious, the only reality being the individuals who compose it, then by the same token a river is fictitious, the only reality being the individual atoms of oxygen and hydrogen. The only difference is that one of the essential elements of an army, or of a river, consists in juxtaposition in space of the members, or of the molecules of water, whereas the bond of union in the case of a corporation is less material. (p. 261)

The identity of a river, according to Machen, is a function of the "juxtaposition in space" of its molecules, but the "members" of a corporation, unlike the molecules in a river, are not juxtaposed in space; their "bond of union" is "less material." The relation between corporate entity and corporate person is understood along the same lines. "*In rerum natura* there is no distinction between a personified entity and an entity not personified" (p. 349). The distinction between a personified entity and an entity not personified, like the bond of union between the members of a corporation, is immaterial.

In the case of corporate entity, Machen argues, the difference between material proximity and "less material" proximity is "not fundamental," but, as the parallel with personification suggests, it must by his own logic be at least as fundamental as the difference between a thing and a personified thing—indeed, between a thing and a person. The differences between persons and things, like the differences between personified entities and entities not personified, are not material. The transformation of thing into person involves, as it were, the addition of a certain immateriality. Conceiving this immateriality as fictional, corporate theorists repeat the naturalist gesture of imagining persons as personified things. But, unlike rivers, the corporate entity requires the fiction of immateriality even to qualify as a thing. Without the "less material" "bond of union" that identifies the individual members of a corporation, there would be no body. Unless the individual members belonged to the same body, there would be no corporation. Hence the corporation comes to seem the embodiment of figurality that makes personhood possible, rather than appearing as a figurative extension of the idea of personhood. The corporation serves as a kind of model for personhood precisely because it finally makes no sense to think of it as a thing that has been personified (in the way that the ancients might have thought of a river, or in the way that naturalism might think of a human body). The corporation cannot be a personified thing because to be a thing at all it must already meet the conditions of being a person; its material identity as a thing is thinkable only in terms of the immateriality that constitutes its identity as a person.

"The doctrine of corporate personality is a natural though figurative expression of actual facts" (p. 363). Machen opposes nature to figuration, conceiving the actual fact of corporate entity as ground for the legal fiction of corporate personality. But the commonsense difference between natural entity and fictional personality turns out to be unthinkable in the case of corporations, and the blurring of that difference turns out to be inevitable: "We do not need to be instructed to regard a corporation as an entity and to regard that entity as a person: our minds are so constituted that we cannot help taking that view." The point here is not, as before, that we instinctively personify but, more radically, that the possibility of personification depends on there already being persons.[32] In other words, corporations must be persons even if persons aren't. Or, to put this still another way, what I have described as the naturalist reduction to body and soul becomes impossible for the corporation which, as an entity, must have a body, and which, to be

---

32. I am led to this way of putting the point by Frances Ferguson's remark that the cottage girl in Wordsworth's "We are Seven" pushes personification "to such an extreme that it becomes a virtual anti-type to personification. This girl personifies *persons*"; *Wordsworth: Language as Counter-Spirit* (New Haven: Yale University Press, 1977), pp. 26–27.

the entity it is, must also have a soul. The scandal of the corporation, then, isn't that it's a new kind of man; the scandal is
that it's the old kind. If what seemed monstrous to Royce in
The Feud at Oakfield Creek was the discovery that Alonzo Eldon's declaration—"a man isn't a corporation"—was only true
because the corporation was *another* man, what seems monstrous now is the discovery that for a man to be a man he must
also be a corporation—a man *is* a corporation. The monstrosity
of the father-in-law, the monstrosity of the Land Improvement
Company, is the monstrosity of personhood, the impossible and
irreducible combination of body and soul.

   In *The Octopus,* the monster is the railroad, the "leviathan"
(p. 130), the "colossus" (p. 42), the "ironhearted monster of
steel and steam" (p. 228). But the corporate moment, the moment when the nonidentity of material and ideal constitutes the
identity of the person, is disseminated throughout *The Octopus.*
When, for example, seeking to recall his dead lover, Vanamee
begins to exercise his telepathic powers, his "body" and "mind"
come literally, if temporarily, apart as his "imagination" reshapes itself to encounter the "intangible agitation" (p. 273) of
Angele's spirit becoming the "tangible presence" of her daughter's body. By the same logic, Annixter's love for Hilma
Tree involves what Norris characterizes as the fusing together
of "things as disassociated . . . as fire and water" (p. 258),
the "tangible, imminent fact" of Hilma herself and the "formless . . . abstraction" of marriage. On the night the wheat comes
up, Vanamee calls Angele back and the "tangible fact" and the
"abstraction" are "melted into one" (p. 259), turning Annixter
from a "machine" into a "man" (p. 329). The transformation
from machine to man suggests here the customary opposition
between mechanical and organic with the customary preference
for the organic. But, as we have already seen, the sprouting
seed makes a bad symbol of organic growth; what it emblemizes
for Norris is the dispossession of the "natural body." And,
following the same scenario, the machine becomes a man not
because iron is made flesh (flesh can be the material of machines)
but because the body acquires a soul. Just as the novel's chief
symbol of organic materialism, the wheat, is made into the body
of the immaterial, its chief symbol of mechanical materialism,

the steam engine, is made into the site where material and immaterial intersect. Annixter, like the engine, is the place where the tangible and the intangible, "things as disassociated as fire and water," get mixed into one—steam. Re-imagining the mixture of elements that produces thermodynamic energy as the mixture of tangible and intangible that produces human actions, Norris, like Machen, turns the emblem of the entity into the emblem of the person.[33]

Hence the monstrosity of the "ironhearted monster of steel and steam"; the point is not only that its heart is made of iron but that its body has a soul. When Presley visits Shelgrim, it is not "a terrible man of blood and iron" (p. 404) he meets, but "a sentimentalist and an art critic," a man as passionate as Royce's Land Improvement Company. Expecting (perhaps hoping) to find a machine, something that is all body, Presley finds a body that, "enormous" though it is, is still not quite equal to "the head" of the railroad. Presley has never seen "a broader man" (p. 402) but what really astonishes him is that "Shelgrim did not move his body. His arms moved, and his head, but the great bulk of the man remained immobile" (pp. 403–404). Eventually Presley begins "to conceive the odd idea that Shelgrim, as it were, placed his body in the chair to rest while his head and brains and hands went on working independently" (p. 404). Reversing the charges of body and soul, it is tempting to see Shelgrim here as a figure for corporate disembodiment, his body even bigger than the "gross" S. Behrman's but at the same time more corporate, more truly "intangible." The railroad gets its way, after all, not by acts of physical violence but by changes in the freight rates which, intangible themselves, can nevertheless leave as strong a man as the engineer Sykes—"a veritable giant, built of great sinews, powerful" (p. 250)—"absolutely crushed" (p. 252).

At the same time, however, even grain rates have a certain materiality; they are produced by "a turn of the hand" (p. 251), "inscribed" on a piece of "yellow paper" (p. 245). And in *The*

33. For a different reading, emphasizing the "impersonal" and "indifferent" character of what he calls the "nature-machine," see Ronald E. Martin, *American Literature and the Universe of Force* (Durham: Duke University Press, 1981), 146–183.

Octopus, it is Shelgrim, "the head" of the railroad, whose hands set the rates. In fact, like the octopus he heads, Shelgrim, his body placed in the chair to rest, is all head and hands, a cephalopod. With his "great bulk" set to one side, he is, like the corporation, something more than his body. But with his "head, brains and hands" all working, he is never, again like the corporation, independent of his body. Rather, everything that the corporation does must be done with its hands—from fighting for its property (the hired guns, Christian and Delaney are "S. Behrman's right and left hands" [p. 344]) to receiving that property ("Quien Sabe was in the hands of the railroad" [p. 377]) to legitimating and consolidating its title to the property (by the time the "Supreme Court hands down a decision" [p. 344], all political resistance will have been crushed by "the great iron hand" [p. 379] of the trust). These metaphors, in their ordinariness, get at the causal connection between grain rates and bodies—no action can be performed without a body—while at the same time suggesting—since as ordinary as they are they are still metaphors—that no action can be performed just by a body. The nonphysical notion of the person is required to make the bodies of Christian and Delaney, for example, the hands of the corporation. Irrevocably in his body without being entirely of his body, Shelgrim embodies this constitutive discrepancy between material and ideal. Acting in the world with "a turn of its hand," the octopus embodies embodiment.

Versions of Dyke's complaint were, of course, traditional in populist attacks. Corporations "wield no weapon more alarming than the little pencil";[34] they destroy the farmers with "a single stroke of the pen."[35] Writing here is an emblem of the ideal and as such, given the reversibility of material and ideal, it can easily be made mechanical. Cyclone Davis worries that because so much is published, "busy people are disposed to pass by a new book without stopping to even read the title." They "would not be surprised to hear that some man had invented a machine for

34. Edward Winslow Martin, *History of the Grange Movement* (San Francisco: National Publishing Co., 1873), p. 327.

35. W. Scott Morgan, *History of the Wheel and Alliance* (1889), reprinted in part in *The Populist Mind,* ed. Norman Pollack, p. 274. Morgan here is actually quoting Jeremiah S. Black.

making books that dispensed with [the] author . . . and ground out paragraphs by steam."[36] Tales of "automatic writing" were common in the literature of psychology. Just as Shelgrim invokes the mechanical laws of supply and demand ("forces" instead of "men") to describe the setting of grain rates, so Norris flirts with automatism in his description of Presley writing the poem that will make him famous, *The Toilers:* "For a time, his pen seemed to travel of itself; words came to him without searching, shaping themselves into phrases" (p. 262).

But what we might call Shelgrim's mechanical alibi[37] won't work. For one thing, the law of supply and demand is the law that sets rates in a free market, but the railroad, as a monopoly, doesn't operate in a free market. As Alfred D. Chandler Jr. has put it, "The operational requirements" of the railroads "had made obsolete the competition between small units that had no control over prices—prices that were set by the market forces of supply and demand."[38] The whole point of monopolies, like the railroad (what makes them "monstrous"), is that they transcend the mechanical laws of the market; they are "no longer regulated by market mechanisms."[39] Furthermore, while business conditions were undermining the transposition of thermodynamic laws into economics, developments in physics seemed to be undermining the very notion of a thermodynamic law."[40] Thus, in a paper called "The Mechanical, the Historical, and the Statistical" (1914), Royce pointed out that recent work by

36. Davis, *A Political Revelation,* p. 4.

37. This phrase is adapted from Leo Bersani. Describing the turn toward the family at the end of *War and Peace,* Bersani calls Tolstoy's appeal to "the obvious foundation of the family in nature" a "biological alibi for social conformity"; *A Future for Astyanax* (Boston: Little, Brown, 1976), p. 63.

38. Alfred D. Chandler, Jr., *The Visible Hand: The Managerial Revolution in American Business* (Cambridge, Mass.: Harvard University Press, 1977), p. 203.

39. Ibid., p. 204.

40. Seltzer's description of the naturalist text as the naturalist "machine" and his claim that the laws of thermodynamics constitute a "mechanics of power" which "govern" that machine thus seem to me questionable. His appeal to Deleuze and Guattari's notion of the "desiring-machine" is illuminating in this regard, since the whole point of that notion is to do away with persons and its ultimate effect (like that of the double reduction to body and soul) is to do away with desire itself.

Boltzmann and Arrhenius suggested the possibility of "the occasional if not the general reversal of the second law of the theory of energy," a reversal impossible in the mechanical view of nature but not in "the statistical view of nature."[41]

For Royce, the consequences of such reversals were profound:

Suppose an aggregate of natural objects which contains a very great number of members . . . These objects may be things or events, at your pleasure. They may be molecules or stars . . . or literary compositions or moral agents or whatever else you will.[42]

Such an aggregate is utterly indifferent to the apparently crucial distinction between the "vital" and the "mechanical." The laws of probability apply to it no matter what its members are. Hence the statistical aggregate constitutes an entity quite distinct from an organic whole or a mechanical system. It is made up of natural objects—whether these objects be understood biologically or mechanically—but the laws of its behavior are neither biological nor mechanical and, as a statistical aggregate, it is itself neither a biological nor a mechanical object.

This is not to say that for Royce the statistical aggregate independent of the identities of its members and indifferent to their status as "molecules" or "agents" is itself neutral with respect to agency. For one of the "most widely applicable laws of nature," he thinks, "wholly indefinable in mechanical terms, but always expressible in . . . statistical tendencies" is the "law that aggregation tends to result in some further and increasingly mutual assimilation of the members of the aggregate."[43] Thus, in what would seem like a bizarre parody of naturalism's rhetoric of biological force were it not so clearly an earnest extension of that rhetoric, Royce speaks of the "law of the fecundity of aggregation" as expressing "what seems to be a sort of unconscious teleology in nature." Natural objects—moral agents or molecules—may or may not have their purposes, but nature

41. Josiah Royce, "The Mechanical, The Historical, and the Statistical" (1914), reprinted in *The Basic Writings of Josiah Royce*, vol. 2, ed. with an intro. by John J. McDermott (Chicago, 1969), p. 726.
42. Ibid., pp. 728–729.
43. Ibid., p. 729.

itself, embodied not precisely in either the molecules or the moral agents but in the abstract principle of "statistical fecundity," has a purposiveness of its own, "a purposiveness whose precise outcomes no finite being seems precisely to intend."[44] It is thus the discrepancy between the behavior of individuals and that of aggregates that constitutes the personhood of nature, and the indifference of statistical laws to the question of whether *anything* really is a person turns out to be nature's way of guaranteeing that ultimately *everything* will be a person.

For Norris' Presley too, despite the touch of automatism in his inspiration, nature is a person. The "gigantic sweep of the San Joaquin" is a "mother" (p. 39), like Royce's nature, "illimitable, immeasurable" (p. 260). But as Norris describes it, the "romance" Presley wants to write in celebration of her, the "Song of the West," is "shattered" against the stubborn iron barrier" (p. 16) of the railroad. Dreaming of "things without names—thoughts for which no man had yet invented words, terrible, formless shapes, vague figures, colossal, monstrous," Presley is brought down to earth by the "realism" of the "commonplace" (p. 15): "He searched for the true romance and, in the end, found grain rates and unjust freight tariffs" (p. 16). From our perspective, however, it is easy to see how false this opposition between romance and realism, mother nature and the railroad, really is.[45] Dreaming of the "monstrous," Presley is already dreaming of the corporation. Imagining the valley as a "gigantic scroll" (p. 260), he is already putting pen to paper, reproducing with the turn of the poet's hand the turn of the hand that sets the grain rates.

The poet, then, is the paradigm of the corporate person, writing the paradigmatic corporate act. When Vanamee urges Presley to "live" the "epic" life of the west rather than "write" about it, Presley responds that its "vastness" would "suffocate" him if he couldn't "record" his "impressions" (p. 36). But Presley, unlike S. Behrman, is in no danger of suffocation. The

44. Ibid., p. 731.

45. Although for a different view, see Donald Pizer: "The monopoly is the soulless Force whose practices, spreading death and destruction, are opposed to the landscape"; *Realism and Naturalism in Nineteenth-Century American Literature* (Carbondale: Southern Illinois University Press, 1984), pp. 160–161.

wheat kills Behrman, forcing its way in from the outside just as Presley imagines himself "overwhelmed" by his "impressions." But the wheat is already inside Presley: "his mental life was not at all the result of impressions and sensations that came to him from without, but rather of thoughts germinating from within" (p. 13). And when Presley *is* "all but suffocated," the cause is "the repression of his contending thoughts" and the cure is indeed literature—"he flung himself before his table and began to write" (p. 262). Imagined simultaneously as consumptive (taking wheat in without losing his hunger) and productive (writing out his "germinated" thoughts), Presley and his "insatiable" desire "to write verse" (p. 13) combine in one person the monstrous productivity of the valley and the monstrous appetite of the railroad.

In the Song of the West, the epic life doubles the corporate life, production doubles consumption, the "fecundated earth" (p. 152) doubles the "fecundity of aggregation." They are all, as Royce and Norris variously put it, "immeasurable," "illimitable," "immortal," "infinite," "insatiable." The corporation, the "artificial person," incarnates (for better or for worse) this transcendence of the limits that make up "natural" persons. And in doing so, it represents what I take to be a central problem for naturalism, the irruption in nature of the powerfully unnatural. The rhetoric of "force" tries to solve this problem. Substituting machines for men, it resolves the anomaly of the corporate person by turning all persons, corporate and natural both, into entities. But just as Machen's common sense reduction of person to entity turned out to involve an irreducible and immaterial fictionality that produced instead a dazzling legitimation of corporate personality, so the corporate fiction of Royce and Norris continually produces persons out of material as unpromising as statistical aggregates or the "limitless" "monotony of the . . . wheat lands" (p. 229). It accomplishes this not by personification—treating the thing as if it were a person—but by seeing the immaterial in the material, seeing the person who is already there. While the word "monopoly" appears only once in the 450-odd pages of *The Octopus,* the word "monotony" appears over and over again, almost always describing the fields of wheat, "bounded only by the horizons": "there was something inordinate about it all, something almost unnatural" (p. 48). What is "inordinate" and "unnatural" is the monopoly behind the monotony, the artificial person behind the natural one. Here is perhaps the deepest complicity between naturalism and the corporation. In naturalism, no persons are natural. In naturalism, personality is always corporate and all fictions, like souls metaphorized in bodies, are corporate fictions.

FRANK LENTRICCHIA

On the Ideologies of Poetic Modernism, 1890 – 1913: The Example of William James

When George Santayana was appointed to the philosophy department at Harvard in 1889, just one year after finishing his doctorate there, he became the junior colleague of William James and Josiah Royce, who were not only his former teachers but also strong backers of his appointment, and the three together, over the next two decades—in relationships at once supportive, competitive, and critical—collectively defined the shapes and limitations of what would come to be understood as poetic modernism in the United States: its desires and values, its literary and philosophical genesis and ground, and the sometimes stinging antithetical force of its cultural and social commentary. In different ways Santayana, James, and Royce each addressed the future of philosophy and poetry as if, at the same time, they were addressing the future of society, as if the shape of things to come in some crucial part depended on the way intellectuals conducted themselves.[1] The landmarks of modernism established by the group are easy to identify: James's *The Principles of Psychology* in 1890, a work which among its other

1. See part 4 of *Criticism and Social Change* (Chicago: University of Chicago Press, 1983). Also see Edward Said, "The Future of Criticism," *MLN*, 99 (September 1984), 951–958.

220

accomplishments gave us both the term and the theory of "stream of consciousness"; Royce's *The Spirit of Modern Philosophy* in 1892; Santayana's *The Sense of Beauty* in 1896 and his pivotal *Interpretations of Poetry and Religion* in 1900; James's *Pragmatism* in 1907 and, finally, one year after Harriet Monroe founded *Poetry: A Magazine of Verse,* three years before Santayana would leave Harvard and the United States for good, and three years after the death of James, Royce's *The Problem of Christianity* in 1913.

If the years between 1890 and 1913 mark the most energetic period of American philosophical modernism, that same period represents, as more than one historian of American literature has implied by word and by silence, the big blank of American poetic history. Bryant died in 1878, Longfellow in 1882, Lowell in 1891, Whittier in 1892, and Holmes in 1894. When we correlate these end-dates with their respective beginnings—Bryant was born in 1794, Whittier and Longfellow in 1807, Holmes in 1809, and Lowell in 1819—in other words, when we add the fact of biological endurance to the fact of unprecedented popular acceptance, we are pressed to conclude that the dominance of America's "Fireside" poets, who were published in the later nineteenth century in "Household" editions, is a literary reality of long and perhaps even of oppressive extraliterary reach. (Imagine, if you can, a "household" edition of *The Cantos.*) The Fireside poets were among the chief cultural powers of our nineteenth century: they stood for poetry. By their lives as well as by their practice as writers they defined, however conservatively, a broad-ranging cultural (educative) function for the man of letters: they translated Homer and Dante, they held chairs in romance languages at Harvard, they edited influential newspapers, they were foreign diplomats, they gave well-noted and well-attended speeches on the controversial affairs of the day. Whitman, a visible dissenter from Fireside forms and morals (though not from its cultural ambition) died in 1892, a year after the publication of the tenth edition of *Leaves of Grass;* Emily Dickinson, another qualified dissenter, died without fame in 1886.

Looking back at the early days of his poetic development, in the first decade and a half of this century, T. S. Eliot reflected on the literal and anxious truth of his poetic origins when he said that there was not "a single living poet, in either England or America, then at the height of his powers, whose work was capable of pointing the way to a young poet conscious of the desire for a new idiom."[2] Long after the fact, Eliot was rationalizing his interests in continental literatures and in the older periods of English literature. (American literary history would, however, exact its revenge: Eliot became the high modernist representative of the traditional New England poets.) Wallace Stevens added a concurring and decadent note to Eliot's testimony when he wrote that when he was a student at Harvard, "it was commonplace to say that all the poetry had been written and all the paintings painted."[3] Feeling the familiar romantic burden, the embarrassment of tradition, Stevens moved in his young manhood into self-consciously avant-garde styles in an effort to accentuate his difference and originality. Like Eliot, however, he was also decisively marked by his American poetic inheritance—hence his self-definition in "The Comedian as the Letter C" as a poet of "disguised *pronunciamento,*" a writer of "anecdotes" which he characterized as doctrinal not in form (no Longfellow or Bryant he) but in intention: Stevens as closet Fireside poet, as it were. On the other hand, Robert Frost, who was never embarrassed by the American literary heritage of popular poetry, paid open tribute to his Fireside predecessor, Longfellow, when he titled his first volume *A Boy's Will.*

E. A. Robinson, Stevens, and Frost were all "special" students at Harvard in the period in question: Robinson from 1891 to 1893, Frost from 1897 to 1899, Stevens from 1897 to 1900. Eliot, from 1906 to 1914, was a genuine article at Harvard, taking a B.A. in 1910, an M.A. in 1911, and doing advanced work for the Ph.D. in languages and philosophy before settling in London in 1914, dissertation completed, but by choice no Ph.D. in hand. So the apprenticeship of what we know as modern American poetry coincides both with the big blank of American poetic history and the big bang of modernist American

2. T. S. Eliot, *To Criticize the Critic* (New York: Farrar, Strauss and Giroux, 1965), p. 58.

3. Wallace Stevens, *Opus Posthumous,* ed. Samuel French Morse (New York: Alfred A. Knopf, 1957), p. 218.

philosophy. And the site of emerging modernist poetic idioms and of an authoritative philosophical discourse was Cambridge, Massachusetts at the turn of the twentieth century. Both in personal ways and in the prescribed academic fashion, Robinson, Frost, Stevens, Eliot, and Radcliffe's amazing modernist, Gertrude Stein, encountered the Harvard philosophers. In the conventional sense of what we mean by "influence" and "source," these philosophers were influences and sources. It is not hard to trace links between sentences in Santayana and James and specific poems and phrases in Stevens, Frost, and Eliot. But those are the footnotes to our modern poetic history. The main text must put into the foreground the philosophical works written in Cambridge in the last decade of the nineteenth and first decade of the twentieth century: those works, despite the attitude of traditional literary history, are not background. As more expansive, detailed, and precise expressions of theory than anything written in prose by any of the important modern American poets, either in that period or thereafter, the works of Santayana, James, and Royce are themselves collaborative modernist texts, the original metapoetic idiom of the youth of Eliot, Frost, and Stevens, both reflections and criticisms of the ideologies of modernist poetry before the fact.

Despite the wisdom that says that categories as well as arteries start hardening after thirty, the senior member of the Harvard philosophical modernists, William James (1842–1910), was to the end its most relevant as well as its maverick thinker, even though the canons of social responsibility accepted by Santayana, Royce, and the main line of Marxism that comes down to us through the Frankfurt school say that James is not responsible, that he lacks something in genuine seriousness. What these canonical standards declare that James lacks is nothing other than the proper sense of "theory," which Santayana explicitly defined in its traditional (Arnoldian) setting when he wrote that theory is "a steady contemplation of all things in their order and worth. Such contemplation is imaginative. No one can reach it who has not enlarged his mind and tamed his heart. A philosopher who attains it is, for the moment, a poet;

and a poet who turns his practice and passionate imagination on the order of all things, or on anything in the light of the whole, is for that moment a philosopher."[4] To think theoretically is to think beyond the parochialisms of the schools, to achieve some ultimate humanity of inclusive broadmindedness and to rise above the particular involvements of passionate commitment. From out of this serene, epistemologically and morally secure space, where one has knowledge rather than opinion or ideology, one produces the superdiscourse of theory which obliterates the boundary of philosophy and poetry and makes itself transparent to the ultimate referent, the real order and value of all things. Early philosophical defenders and detractors of this view of theory called it "absolute," Marxists and anti-Marxists alike say "totalizing," and most recently (after Richard Rorty) the tendency is to call it "foundational." James's coded synonym is "rational," a close cousin of his pejorative of all pejoratives— "abstract." For James there may be nothing more ugly than theoretical consciousness in the practices it authorizes.

The lectures James delivered in late 1906 and early 1907 in Boston and New York, and then shortly after published as the book *Pragmatism,* bear the mark of a decisive moment in U.S. history: our first fully launched imperialist adventure, in the last years of the nineteenth century, in Cuba and in the Philippines. Among the prominent protesters against our lurch toward empire, James was then and remains today one of our most distinguished intellectuals. His philosophy of concreteness and action, though inchoately present in his *Principles of Psychology,* knew itself as pragmatism only after he found the political terminus of his thought in his anti-imperialist activism at the turn of the century. In the New England Anti-Imperialist League James experienced a direct connection between his philosophical principles and his political life. It was at that point, and not before, when it was abstractly possible for him to do so, that he began freely adapting from C. S. Peirce.

4. *Selected Critical Writings of George Santayana,* ed. Norman Henfrey (Cambridge: Cambridge University Press, 1968), I, 149–150 (introduction to *Three Philosophical Poets*).

James's anti-imperialism became the first effort in a hidden history of American intellectual resistance, the first effort in an odd series of literary refusals of imperialism. The second effort was Wallace Stevens' "Anecdote of the Jar" of 1919 as read by a third effort, that of Michael Herr in his book on Vietnam of 1970, *Dispatches,* in which the entire focus of American military power that was concentrated in the fortification of Khe Sanh was crystallized by Herr for his readers with, of all things, Stevens' poem. Stevens, who spoke casually of "coons" and "polacks," and who found Dwight Eisenhower radical, is made by Herr to speak directly against the ideology of imposition and obliteration coterminus in Vietnam with a strategy of defoliation. The textual expression of that strategy is the literal remapping of a country—"the military expediency," in Herr's ironic reflection on the sometimes deadly relations of sign and referent, "to impose a new set of references over Vietnam's truer, older being, an imposition that began most simply with the division of one country into two and continued . . . with the further division of South Vietnam into four clearly defined tactical corps."[5] Herr concludes by glossing Khe Sanh via the imaginative imperialism that was activated and evaluated in "Anecdote of the Jar." "Once it was all locked in place, Khe Sanh became like the planted jar in Wallace Stevens's poem. It took dominion everywhere."[6] The Vietcong and the North Vietnamese regulars, however, like the stubborn Tennessee in Stevens' poem, had a different view. In the end, Khe Sanh would represent both the expression and the thwarting of imperial will.

James had written his own anecdote of the jar in the opening lecture of *Pragmatism:* "The world of concrete personal experiences to which the street belongs is multitudinous beyond imagination, tangled, muddy, painful and perplexed. The world to which your philosophy professor introduces you is simple, clean and noble. The contradictions of real life are absent from it. Its architecture is classic. Principles of reason trace its outlines, logical necessities cement its parts. Purity and dignity are

5. Michael Herr, *Dispatches* (New York: Alfred A. Knopf, 1977), p. 92.
6. Ibid., p. 107.

what it most expresses. It is a kind of marble temple shining on
a hill.'"[7] The marble temple shining on a hill is James's metaphor
for traditional philosophy in its traditional project of representation: mind as correspondence—thought as reflection of real
ontological structure and therefore thought emptied of the messes
of social time, thought uncontingent. Philosophy so conceived,
James says, is not an "account of this actual world" but an
"addition built upon it": a "sanctuary," a "refuge," a "substitute," a "way of escape," a "monument of artificiality"—"clois-
tral and spectral" (p. 18). All negative qualities, of course, but
quite harmless until we add one other characteristic which gives
ominous point to all the others—the shining marble temple,
like the jar, like Khe Sanh, is also a "remedy" (p. 18). In this
early dismantling of the classic project of reason, what James
wishes to show is that the product of rationalist method is not
cool, contemplative representation—"theory" above the battle:
it is *purity in action.* The shining marble temple is "round upon
the ground" and it does not give "of bird or bush." Instead, it
gives of death. Like the defoliating jar in Stevens' Tennessee,
or the imposed references of military need in Vietnam which
attempt to recreate the referent (we had to destroy that village
in order to save it), classical theory is the desire for a "refined
object." And refinement is a "powerful . . . appetite of the mind"
(p. 18) which gets expressed as the *will to refine:* a chilling
process when considered in the existential and political contexts
within which James writes. In an eerie prolepsis of Stevens'
poem and Herr's reading of Khe Sanh as the planted jar, James
evoked his sense of the perverse American presence in the
Philippines with an oxymoron— it is a "planted order."[8]

Independently of Marx, then, James makes something like
the point of the most famous of the theses on Feuerbach—that
philosophy should be trying to change, not interpret the world—
but he is, in effect, out-Marxing Marx by saying that all the

7. William James, *Pragmatism* and *The Meaning of Truth,* introduction by
A. J. Ayer (Cambridge, Mass.: Harvard University Press, 1975), pp. 17–18.
Further references will be to this edition, by page number in the text.

8. Quoted in F. O. Matthiessen, *The James Family: A Group Biography*
(New York: Alfred A. Knopf, 1961), p. 626: "We must sow our ideals, plant
our order, impose our God."

interpretive efforts of philosophy, including rationalism, are always simultaneously efforts to work upon and work over things as they are, that interpretation is always a form of social activity. The recurring double point of James's *Pragmatism* is that all theory is practice (situated intellectual involvement with real local effects) and that all practices are not equally worthy (one at least, rationalist practice, James views as necessarily inhuman). If all thought is a mode of action, then the key consequence forced upon us by this philosophy of consequences would not be the recognition that there is nothing but practice—that is only James's banal and potentially dangerous starting point—but the urgent directive that we attend to the different consequences of different practices, for only in their different consequences can we know and evaluate such practices as different. No difference in consequence, no difference in practice: that is one major corollary stated early on by James. An attendant point is that "belief"—which is what a pragmatist has instead of "theory"—is a "set of rules" for action (pp. 28–29). Belief shapes conduct and conduct is the sole significance and real content of belief. But as a "set of rules" belief is open to critical reflection, and whether the set of rules is knowable in advance of the conduct it shapes, or whether such rules are extrapolated from conduct, after the fact, what is forced upon us is the obligation to evaluate the consequences of belief—action in the world—by evaluating the conduct-structuring rules of belief—and in doing that, we act upon (by evaluating) the future of a belief (the conduct that belief *will* produce), not from some transcendental standpoint in "theory" but from within some other set of rules. So the fully articulated pragmatism we find in James says that there is not only nothing but practice, but that *there is no escape from reflection on practice,* that practice should be accompanied by constant scrutiny of one's own position (belief, conduct) and constant scrutiny of the positions of others. When not so accompanied, practice becomes mindless work, like Charley Marlowe's with his rivets: which is to say that such work is not really mindless, but a hopeless effort to escape from reflection and a form of intellectual and moral cowardice. When not accompanied by a critical consciousness, the sort of "practice" synonymous with pragmatism can become

a justification of the politics of Benito Mussolini, who was perhaps the most famous proponent of the position "against theory" in our century—an enthusiastic reader of James who found
in his writings an apologia for the belief that the ends sanction
the means, and who, in his own words, was quickened in "that
ardent will to live and fight, to which Fascism owes a great part
of its success."[9]

James's vision of pragmatism is irreducibly a vision of heterogeneity and contentiousness—a vision always strong for criticism and self-scrutiny that never claims knowledge of a single
unfolding human narrative because it refuses the belief and it
refuses the often repressive conduct resulting from the belief in
a single human narrative. James's fully committed pragmatism
has no way of settling, once and for all, therefore, the question
it constantly asks: Does the world rise or fall in value when any
particular belief is set loose in the world? when any mode of
conduct is engendered upon us? (pp. 122–123). By insisting that
the question of value be posed so broadly (Does the *world*, not
literature or philosophy, rise or fall in value?), James is insisting
that the consequences of belief reveal themselves most fully
outside the immediate domain (in his case, the discipline of
philosophy) of any particular belief's application. Like the father
of pragmatism, C. S. Peirce, James acknowledges the sobering
social impulse: no philosophical ostrich with its head in the sand,
pragmatism starts from critical self-consciousness, recognizing
that others believe differently and just as strongly.[10] James would
put us in a world of different and sometimes competing con-
ducts, and different and sometimes competing stories, a world
in which resolution could be achieved only in a final solution
of criticism: by the forcible silencing of the competitor.

The world according to James is (or should be) a geography
of practices adjacently placed; a heterogeneous space of dis-
persed histories, related perhaps by counterpoint, or perhaps
utterly disrelated—a cacophony of stories—but in any case never
related in medley. "The world we live in exists diffused and

9. Ibid., p. 677.
10. C. S. Peirce, *Selected Writings*, ed. Philip P. Weiner (New York: Dover
Publications, 1966), p. 103.

distributed, in the form of an indefinitely numerous lot of *eaches*"
(p. 126). The overarching Hegelian and Marxist schema which
would make all the "eaches" cohere never tempts James, though
it does interest him. For he believes that history conceived as
telcological union is a late and nostalgic expression of classical
aesthetics—the proleptic imaging forth, in the rigorous perfec-
tions of Aristotelian plot, of desired historical order, the harmony of time itself. Better to think against Aristotle's preference
for drama over epic, better to prefer epic to drama, better to
think that the "world is full of partial stories that run parallel
to one another, beginning and ending at odd times. They mutually interlace and interfere at points, but we cannot unify them
completely" (p. 71). Alongside his metaphor of epic as a tool
to resist the dogmas of monism, James—in sweet reasonable-
ness—offers us this metaphor bearing on temporal as well as
on geographic plurality: "It is easy to see the world's history
pluralistically, as a rope of which each fiber tells a separate tale;
but to conceive of each cross-section of the rope as an absolutely
single fact, and to sum the whole longitudinal series into one
being, living an individual life, is harder" (p. 71).

History in James, as in Emerson, is no monumental text that
demands our mimetic fealty. In a final, difficult refiguring, James
gives us history as both text and as the liberation of textual
work—a text in "only one edition of the universe, unfinished,
growing in all sorts of places, especially in the places where
thinking beings are at work. On the rationalist side we have a
universe in many editions, one real one, the infinite folio, or
edition de luxe, eternally complete; and then the various finite
editions, full of false readings, distorted and mutilated each in
its own way" (p. 124). If there is only one text, and it is the
text of history—forever unfinished, new chapters being written
in all sorts of places by all sorts of people not especially in touch
with one another—then there is no unhistorical text, whatever
else poetry and philosophy are to be called, and the distinction
between commentary and creation cannot long be sustained
except in a rationalist vision. James's point about history as text
does not, however, anticipate the critical polemic of the 1970s.
His textual metaphor is an effort to speak not against the authority of a self-styled "literary" creativity to which modern

"critics" have paid long and often self-flagellating veneration,
but against the political authority which masks itself in rationalist certitude and self-righteousness, and which he specifically
and frequently evokes after his involvement in the New England
Anti-Imperialist League in royalist, militarist, aristocratic, and
papal terms.[11] James's textual metaphor speaks *for* the liberation
of the small, the regional, the locally embedded, the underdog.
His unfinished text of history, authorized by no single author,
is the expression of his American ideology, the text of American
history as it ought to be—the multi-authored book of democracy
in its ideal and wild antinomian form. For James, American
imperialism is the foreign policy of the unionist impulse, or what
he called in another context "the big organization." "The bigger
the unit you deal with, the hollower, the more brutal, the more
mendacious is the life displayed. So I am against all big orga-
nizations as such, national ones first and foremost . . . System,
as such, does violence whenever it lays its hands upon us. The
best Commonwealth is the one that most cherishes the men who
represent the residual interests, the one that leaves the largest
scope to their peculiarities."[12]

The moral and political authority behind James's pragmatism
is Emerson—more exactly James's reading of Emerson, so that
James and Emerson become twined ideological agencies within
American literature. The Emerson/James connection may constitute the most influential enhancement of intellectual force in
American literary history, for their own time and for the time
of modernism and beyond. The connection, moreover, seems
to have derived its power from its mediation in the great inter-
biography of American literary culture. I refer not only to the
interrelations of Henry Jr., William, Alice, and their redoubt-
able father, easily the first family of American intellectual history, but also to the larger cultural family composed of Emerson
and the Jameses, with particular emphasis on Emerson's rela-

---

11. See, for example, *Pragmatism*, pp. 31, 40, 125, and *The James Family*,
p. 633.
    12. Quoted in *The James Family*, pp. 633–634.

tions to the novelist, the philosopher, and to Henry Sr.: relations which at different times, both in his lifetime and after, cast Emerson in roles ranging from older brother, teacher, culture hero, and father, to godfather, priest, and deity.

On 3 March 1842, Henry Sr. heard Emerson lecture in New York and later that evening wrote him a letter which combined the sympathy and honor that can only be bestowed by a cold-sober admirer with the spunky impudence and independence of a younger brother (eight years Emerson's junior) determined to contest his older sibling in a similar vocation and with identical ambition.[13] The same letter warmly invited Emerson to visit; Emerson accepted shortly thereafter. According to James family legend— it became a favorite anecdote— Henry Sr., immediately after Emerson's arrival, with the enthusiasm appropriate to a proud father, ushered his guest upstairs into the nursery to see his infant son, William, then about three months old. Henry Jr. tells us that "it remained a tradition" with William that "our father's friend" gave "his blessing to the lately-born babe."[14] It remains a psychoanalytically resonant fact that only six weeks before his first visit to the New York home of the Jameses and the bestowal of his mythic blessing, Emerson had been decisively devastated by the death of his first son, Waldo. And it remains forcefully significant for American literary and philosophical history that, though Henry Sr. was a central man for his more famous sons, Emerson became for them an alternative, perhaps even a competing father—in Henry Jr.'s memory, a "center of many images."[15]

The most extraordinary of the many provocative expressions of this culturally provocative family romance, from among the participants themselves, came from the novelist, and again from his recollections:

I 'visualize' . . . the winter firelight of our back-parlor at dusk and the great Emerson—I knew he was great, greater than any of our friends— sitting in it between my parents, before the lamps had been lighted

13. Ibid., p. 40.
14. Henry James, *Autobiography,* ed. Frederick W. Dupee (New York: Criterion Books, 1956), p. 7.
15. Ibid.

. . . affecting me the more as an apparition sinuously and . . . elegantly slim, benevolently aquiline, and commanding a tone alien, beautifully alien, to any we had heard round-about, that he bent this benignity upon me by an invitation to draw near to him, off the hearth-rug, and know myself as never yet . . . in touch with the wonder of Boston . . . just then and there for me in the sweetness of the voice and the finish of the speech—this latter through a sort of attenuated emphasis which at the same time made sounds more important, more interesting in themselves, than by any revelation yet vouchsafed us. Was not this my first glimmer of a sense that the human tone *could,* in that independent and original way, be interesting? It had given me there in the firelight an absolutely abiding measure . . . the truth of which I find somehow reflected in the fact of my afterwards knowing one of our household rooms for the first time . . . as "Mr. Emerson's room."[16]

This appearance in the fading light of dusk of a benign father, this parent who sits "between" the actual parents, bears the gift that is wholly and originally *himself.* It is he who commands the alien yet beautiful tone, inviting intimacy and the knowledge of the wonder of his difference; an "absolutely abiding measure" who set the standard for what is not subject to standards: the unrepeatable individual self. For the novelist, long after the fact to which his memory, no doubt creatively, referred, the great Emerson returns in splendid individual perfection as the apparition who sanctions his art of the novel.

For James Sr., on the other hand, what Emerson represented philosophically was simply the curse of selfhood. The "sphere of redemption" for James *père,* according to son William, was society with a capital letter, while for Emerson redemption lay precisely in "resolute individualism" (William's phrase), which could be felt even in the aesthetic texture of his writing. In a headnote to an essay written by Henry Sr. on Emerson, but not published (in the *Atlantic*) until long after the death of both (when neither could respond), William set forth this fundamental dispute between his father and Emerson and then adjudicated it in favor of Emerson. In favor, to be exact, of William's own reading of Emerson. In the sentence which I am about to

16. Ibid., pp. 358–359.

quote it is important to see William the adjudicator dramatizing himself as critical audience in the back-parlor theater at 58 West Fourteenth Street: "Emerson would listen, I fancy, as if charmed, to James's talk of the 'divine natural Humanity,' but he would never *subscribe:* and this, from one whose native gifts were so suggestive of that same Humanity, was disappointing." Against his father, William in effect took the side of Henry Jr., who in this family fight over the meaning of Emerson wrote that the heart of Emerson's genius was "for seeing character as a real and supreme thing."[17] But the James brothers should have known better than to make him into a single-visioned champion of the liberal individual. It was their father, after all, who had called Emerson a "man without a handle." For their part the brothers were not interested in producing a picture of an uninterpretable "man without a handle."[18] They were seeking to create a cultural authority who prefigured—I mean hinted at—what they would become.

The antidote to the philosophy of atomic selfhood attributed to Emerson (a curse or glory, depending on whether we listen to Henry Sr. or to William) was James Sr.'s American brand of institutionally innocent socialism, a vision which James Sr. repeatedly set against the traditional liberal vision that he aligned with class-conscious England. By socialism he meant "not any special system of social organization, like that of Fourier, Owen, or St. Simon, but what is common to all these systems, namely, the idea of a perfect fellowship or society among men."[19] Socialism so defined he even found to be the deep message of the Declaration of Independence and so argued at a Fourth of July speech. The true American vision he believed to be of original community from which the liberal ideal of a sanctified original individual is merely derivative. The great enemy of the original community and of the individual freedom grounded thereon is of course the central institution of limited property and all the coordinating institutions whose social purpose is to accredit,

17. Quoted in *The James Family,* p. 429.
18. Ibid., p. 43.
19. Ibid., p. 49.

enforce, and idealize property so that all selfhood is ultimately identical with its various, limited, and *external* forms. James Sr. was saying, without access to a later jargon, that the self had become reified—it had become a commodity: "The more external property it gives him, the more houses, lands, flocks, and perishable goods of all sorts, the more society finites him and renders him dependent on itself."[20] The source of idealist liberation for James Sr. is no material, external reorganization of society, which would render limited property nonexistent, but the spiritual infusion of God into the interior terrain of the subject, which would render the subject infinite. James Sr.'s God is the heroic bearer of liberation who must struggle against what man hath made. If limited property imposes a finite, external, possessive, and reified selfhood, then true selfhood (what God gives) must be internal and it cannot be personal. In a passage whose oblique cultural and social commentary on the capitalist system in its strong commodity and sexist form is acute, whose specific rhetoric and implications would later haunt his son William's conception of the self in *Principles of Psychology,* and which perhaps energized his son the novelist's social criticism in a work like *The Portrait of a Lady,* James Sr. wrote: "You know that you never find perfect peace or contentment in your outward and finite *proprium.* You know by experience that you cannot set your life's happiness upon any outward possession, be it wife or child or riches, without an incessant and shuddering dread of betrayal . . . [W]e degrade and disesteem whatsoever we absolutely own . . . [W]e degrade and disesteem . . . every person bound to us by any other tenure than his own spontaneous affection."[21]

Henry Sr.'s brilliant friend himself struggled against the commodified ideal of the self produced on capitalist social ground. In his essay "Politics" (1844), Emerson wrote that "whenever I find my dominion over myself not sufficient for me, and I undertake the direction of [my neighbor] also, I overstep the truth, and come into false relations with him . . . This is the history of government—one man does something which is to

20. Ibid., p. 50.
21. Ibid., p. 57.

bind another.''[22] Emerson found the history of the word "politics" to be the history of a pejorative, coincidental with "cunning," the indenturing of others to the imperatives of power not their own, and (as Stevens would put it) the taking of dominion everywhere. In the essay "History" (1841), he argued by metaphorical sleight-of-hand that in the self's true domain there are no medieval relations of economic and political coercion, and that the privileges of spirit are radically open to all: "There is one mind common to all . . . He that is at once admitted to the right of reason is made a freeman of the whole estate. What Plato has thought, he may think; what a saint has felt, he may feel; what at any time has befallen any man, he can understand; who hath access to this universal mind is a party to all that is or can be done, for this is the only and sovereign agent"(p. 123). And with punning agility in "Nature" (1836), Emerson trained his wit on private property in the capitalist system, writing that though Messrs. Miller, Locke, and Manning may claim ownership to the physical property of their farms, the very best part of those farms their warranty deeds give them no title to: the "property" of vision is "owned" by the integrating eye of the poet who alone can possess, because he creates, the landscape (pp. 5–6).

For Emerson the great human values are preserved only in the world of culture, because in that world the power that accrues from economic privilege—whether lordly or bourgeois—is presumably annulled. But apparently culture can at no point annul the actual unfreedom and oppression that obtains in material society which, in Emerson's memorable phrasing, "everywhere is in conspiracy against the manhood of every one of its members." "Society" for Emerson is synonymous with the surrender of "liberty and culture," with a process of coercion that sanctions the binding of many for the benefit of a few (p. 148). Culture is not a way of life intervening upon and shaping social, economic, and political relations: "culture" is rather an alternative to "society," wherein govern-

22. *The Selected Writings of Ralph Waldo Emerson,* ed. Brooks Atkinson; foreword by Tremaine McDowell (New York: Random House, 1968), pp. 430–431. Further references will be to this edition, by page number in the text.

ments continue to underwrite relations of domination; culture for Emerson is simultaneously an affirmation of freedom and truth in a democratic intellectual world of equal opportunity and an implicit denial that actual collective life can be the ground of those values. At its worst, and by virtue of what Herbert Marcuse would call its affirmative inward turn, Emersonian "culture" becomes an implicit validation (via benign neglect) of the real social injustices rooted in real economic inequalities.

What now appears most dated in Emerson's American repugnance for our European social origins, where the dream of America was hatched, was perhaps for his audience the most thrilling and (we can say this with hindsight) the most duplicitous element in his writing. The clarion call for intellectual independence that he sounded on numerous occasions—"We have listened too long to the courtly muses of Europe"—was intended to urge his fellow Americans on to the cultural end of the adventure, political independence presumably having already been secured. But the overt message of "The American Scholar" and other essays which touch political themes directly is subverted time after time in Emerson's final bourgeois revenge against the history of economic privilege. The poet or scholar is the representative man who sums up the desire of history's dispossessed to come into possession—for possession is power and power is freedom. In taking revenge the Emersonian poet asserts on behalf of all the mute and inglorious Platos and Miltons the solidarity of unexchangeable values, of noble spirits and brilliant minds, for it is he who underwrites the proverb of American proverbs that it is not where you come from that matters but who you are: a natural ground of privilege. But the retreat to the interior enacted by Emerson's various metaphors against ownership in both feudal and capitalist systems of production carries the unhappy message of his metaphorics of property that cultural independence will not be the grace note of American history—in the citadel of subjectivity, where we contact the "sovereign agent," it will be the only independence we know.

But there is a complication. In spite of his obvious delight in trumping the card of capitalism—demonstrating that the poet, not Miller or Locke or Manning, is the real property owner—neither the poet nor any other isolable individual finally owns anything, not even himself. The primary fact of Emerson's transcendental economy (Henry Sr. was necessarily blind to this fact) is not owning but belonging, not possessing but being possessed. That to which we belong ("the only and sovereign agent") and that by which we are possessed is no individual. What Emerson called the "universal soul," "Reason," and the "Oversoul" he defined strategically with a perfection of vagueness as an "immensity not possessed and that cannot be possessed"—"we are its property." Whatever "it" is, whatever the word "immensity" signifies in his discourse, we can say that *it* is not quantifiable, that it cannot be economized as a "commodity." It neither buys nor sells; it controls no labor power. It is instead a condition of release from "possessive" selfhood and the commodified consciousness of liberal political vision. *It* is our possession by freedom, which Emerson (at his most hopeful) calls "the background of our being" (p. 263).

In the crucial definition of personal consciousness he offers in the first volume of *Principles of Psychology,* James chooses to ignore Emerson's rejection of all economic conceptions of selfhood: James finds (or thinks he finds) truly inalienable private property located at (and *as*) the core of selfhood. The price of James's anti-imperialism, his vision of human heterogeneity, may be the most radical of all possible alienation and disconnection, which he expresses as the first commandment of a capitalized psychology—thou shalt not steal individuality: "Each of these minds keeps its own thoughts to itself. There is no giving or bartering between them . . . Absolute insulation, irreducible pluralism, is the law. It seems as if the elementary psychic fact were not *thought* or *this thought* or *that thought* but *my thought,* every thought being *owned.* Neither contemporaneity nor proximity in space, nor similarity of quality or content are able to fuse thoughts together which are sundered by this barrier of belonging to different minds. The breaches between such thoughts are the most absolute breaches in nature . . . The worst a psychology can do is so to interpret the nature of these selves as to rob them of their worth."[23] Or, more emphatically still, in a statement that would have stunned his father: *"In its widest possible sense . . . a man's self is the sum total of all that he can call his,* not only his body and his psychic powers, but his clothes, and his house, his wife and his children, his ancestors and friends, his reputation and works, his lands and horses, and yacht and bank-account."[24] But all of the things that we think we "own," James says, in a lesson never learned by Thomas Sutpen, the archetypal American dreamer, are "transient external possessions" with the sole exception of the "innermost center within the circle," that "sanctuary within the citadel," the *"self of all the other selves,"* of which we can never be dispossessed: the "home," the "source," the "emanation" of "fiats of the will"—a feeling of an original spontaneity, of an active power without constraining ground that becomes the ground of our personal freedom to say yes and no, to open and shut the door, and a point of departure for James's radically pluralistic world. That feeling of original spontaneity can never be known: it becomes James's phenomenological postulate, instead, for the inviolability of self, or of a self that should be responded to as if it deserved to be inviolable.[25]

So Emerson's so-called resolute individualism, and its supposed benign or malevolent consequences, the fight over which lent to the James family some of its intellectual coherence, was a fight that Emerson himself could not have joined on the terms that William the philosopher laid out while introducing his father's essay to readers of the *Atlantic*. There was, William said (and in this he prefigures by several years brother Henry's memory), the *real* Emerson, who was "so squarely and simply himself"— this Emerson's "hottest side" was his nonconformist, even antinomian conviction of the unsurpassable value of the individual. Alongside this Emerson, William placed the transcendental idealist whose favored element was the "tasteless water of souls," an Emerson, William implied, suited to his father's socialist taste. In effect, William had set his father's essay up by creating

23. William James, *The Principles of Psychology* (New York: Dover Publications, 1950), I, 226.
24. Ibid., I, 291.
25. Ibid., I, 297–298; 299–305.

the conditions for a debunking readership, one which would not embrace the interpretation of Emerson that readers of Henry Sr. would find in the essay itself—an interpretation sharply at odds with the one William suggested in his headnote.[26]

Henry Sr. thought that he needed to rescue Emerson from his own ideas by giving his readers a picture of the impression that the actual man had made on his good friend and brave controversialist. This Emerson, the man James Sr. *saw*—not the Emerson he studied—had never in his life "felt the temptation *to bear false witness* against his neighbor, *to steal, to commit adultery,* or *to murder*"; he was an "unsexed woman, a veritable fruit of almighty power in the sphere of our *nature*"; a "literal divine presence in the house with me"; "like Christ," he was "somehow divinely begotten"—"unmistakeably virgin born," "treacherous to civilization," and an "impression of the great God Almighty."[27] Emerson and James Sr. become in this rewriting of their friendship the ironic polar coordinates of a text that James Sr. was writing all his life. The bodily presence of the contested authority himself was proof that "truth" lay on the side of James Sr. against Emerson and his sons. James Sr. "knew" Emerson—he perceived him—in a way that his sons could not "know" him, and in a way that Emerson could not "know" himself—James Sr. was the man, he was there. His main point, the one that set him irrevocably at odds with his sons, especially William, I can only put as an extreme paradox: Emerson the man, as opposed to Emerson the intellectual, *embodied* the absence, not the presence, of selfhood.[28]

William James's address at the Emerson centenary in Concord in 1903 is the climactic document for the history of the Emerson/James family romance—the major blow struck for an Emerson so "hot" in his "nonconformist persuasion" that the pathos of death itself appears overcome. James begins his address with a convention proper to his rhetorical occasion—Emerson is dead, but he is not dead because his "singularity" of self gave "a note so clear as to be victorious over the inevitable pity

26. Quoted in *The James Family*, pp. 431–432.
27. Ibid., pp. 435–436.
28. Ibid., pp. 437–438.

of . . . diminution and abridgement" which death works on the memories of those who witnessed our lives. What survives "the best of us," James says elegiacally—he is thinking now of his own literary survival—is the mere "phantom of an attitude," an "echo of a certain mode of thought." And maybe, if we are lucky, a "few pages of print" will survive to present the literary ghost of our living self. Not so for Emerson: his literary immortality, in the form of "influence over future generations," is assured.

In the body of his address, James moves to an exposition of his favorite Emerson, the author of "Self-Reliance," the voice who proclaimed the sovereignty of the singular individual. What makes the exposition more than interesting and beautifully phrased are the words that Emerson is made to speak on the subject of social reform. In response to one who would enlist him in the abolitionist movement, he is made to say, in illustration of his fidelity to his own vision of intellectual work: "I have quite other slaves to face than those Negroes, to wit, imprisoned thoughts far back in the brain of man, which have no watchman or lover or defender but me."[29] The Emerson that James took to the heart of his pragmatism was the Emerson who proclaimed the strict adherence to "private conscience," the "aboriginal reality" of the "present man," the derivative nature of institutions, and the irrelevance of the past man, who is "obliterate for present issues." Faith in and to oneself is the only authentic act, and it is an act that spreads itself, eventually, "from persons to things to times and places."[30] That is the substance of Emerson's radical political vision of the contagion of antinomian individualism, and also its severe limit: the heat of nonconformity may "spread itself," but it cannot be imposed, nor enforced, nor in any way legislated by groups, committees, or collectives of any kind.

What I think James knew is that for Emerson's self-reliant, autonomous individual all collective action is prohibited—even for the purpose of opposing imperialist policies that would obliterate the autonomy of different national, ethnic, or racial

29. Ibid., pp. 454–455.
30. Ibid., p. 457.

narratives. In other words, Emerson's transcendentalist commitment to a radical community of justice and dignity beyond all powers of oppression can have no material site for him—it is theoretical: Emerson's "active soul," an ideal instrument, working directly, if at all, from mind to mind, never works in, on, or through the mediations of actual social arrangement.[31] There can be no Emersonian practice. The faithful Emersonian, faced with James's political interests, in James's day, had to sit passively by while his country's leaders pursued their adventure in the Philippines, and the fake Emersonian radical—I refer to the current appropriation of democratic principles by the New Right—will in the name of democratic institutions actively undermine indigenous efforts to recapture stolen narratives in Nicaragua and El Salvador while working to shore up—the case of the Philippines is still exemplary—antidemocratic forces as long as they do not call themselves Marxist. The good Emersonian liberal of our day says that it would surely be arrogant, as well as contrary to our deepest principles, to try to force appreciation of human rights upon Marcos or Pinochet or Botha, as if the act of withdrawing economic and military support from these three was equivalent to imposing our ideals upon them.

In 1903, in the heat of James's anti-imperialist activity, Emersonian nonconformity was not quite enough —it lacked (my anachronism is the point) James's vigor, his muscular pragmatism—for its ultimate implication was political passivity, not political action. Any act of will attached to the organic action of antinomian selfhood is pure overlay, neither necessary nor appropriate: any act of would-be anti-imperialist will might become (ironically) a trace of the will of the imperialist that James and Emerson abhorred. But James's pragmatism was nothing if not a philosophy of will that would and did risk (without guarantee of moral purity) frightening appropriation of its tenets. If German culture and poststructuralist neo-Nietzscheans must be forced to face up to the Third Reich's reading of Nietzsche, then American culture—especially now, in the midst of our revival of the American pragmatists—must face Mussolini's love for William James. (Pointing to the fact that W. E. B. Du Bois, who took

31. Emerson, *Selected Writings*, p. 322.

his Ph.D. at Harvard in 1895, was also an enthusiast proves not that James was what he most assuredly was not—a Marxist—but that, like Emerson and Nietzsche, he was a man who might be and was variously "handled.") In his anti-imperialist mood James candidly transformed Emerson into his political ally: "He [Emerson] might easily have found himself saying of some present-day agitator against our Philippine conquest what he said of this or that reformer of his own time. He might have called him, as a private person, a tedious bore and canter." Then in the conclusion of his centenary address James imagines that Emerson "would infallibly have added" words to the effect that this same agitator against our Philippine conquest was nevertheless standing on universal truth. Emerson is made to speak—literally given speech by William James—so that he might "pace forth," beyond his personal death, on the side of the anti-imperialist movement.[32]

What ran deep in the James family and what was beyond argument altogether *there* in Emerson (it might be called the American instinct against the imperial social gesture), but which did not surface in William until late in his career, after he had been politicized, is a sense of American history and society as severely ruptured from its European origins and from European institutions synonymous with oppression: the Roman Catholic church, the army, the aristocracy, and the crown. James named these institutions as the true enemy of his philosophic method, which he sometimes associated with a Whitmanesque, unbuttoned, even anarchic notion of self-determination. So severe is the classic American consciousness of historical rupture that American history seems traumatized from the outset by what it seeks to flee. The American intellectual cut in the mold of Emerson is obsessively and suspiciously condemned to asserting his radical autonomy from an institutionalizing impulse to produce docile and conforming subjects—an impulse which very much resembles the rationalist craving for the refined and *confined* object (the object mastered and shorn of all peculiarity), an impulse that James darkly named an appetite of the mind—and he meant all minds, not just European ones.

32. Quoted in *The James Family*, p. 458.

Especially after 1900, James conceived of the role of the intellectual in specific American terms as one of guarding our freedom from those European institutionalizing impulses which might insidiously re-birth themselves here from the "passion of mastery" and in the form of "national destiny," a slogan which speaks for efforts to organize, first on native ground, in a "big" and "great" manner (James hated those words) against the "molecular forces that work from individual to individual," then *over there* in the form of bringing light to the uncivilized: "national destiny" as the will to impose our sense of national story—plant our order—on foreign soil.[33] It was the American intellectual's duty, James wrote in numerous letters to the *Boston Transcript* in protest against our imperialist policies, to expose the empty but murderously effective abstractions of the party of Roosevelt (like "responsibility" for the islands, "unfitness" of the Filipinos to govern themselves) and James was convinced that this could be done (and could continue to be done) only if intellectuals in America developed class-consciousness as intellectuals: a class with presumably no reason to align itself materially with special interests because it stood, or should stand, for ideal interests only—by which he meant the preservation of radical individual freedom. In 1985, however, even in the United States, this cannot but be characterized as an innocent view, but it is a view borne aloft in the morning freshness of the founding American myth—the democratic hope that with nothing resembling an aristocracy to encumber them, Americans would have less need to think of themselves as socially structured individuals: that in the new Eden we had the right to think of the individual as truly prior to society. But at the same time James saw that in such presumably fluid social circumstances we could have no equivalent to a permanent presence (like an aristocratic class) responsible for overseeing the integrity of the social process as a whole. (Who, anyway, could oversee the integrity of antinomianism?) He nominated intellectuals for that role because he thought that in a society without those entrenched institutions within which European intellectuals found themselves, the American intellectual could wield "no corporate

33. Ibid., pp. 624, 626, 633.

selfishness," and "no powers of corruption."[34] James under-rated, though he did not ignore, the corruptive power of capital in fluid democratic contexts—he did not imagine that capital could bind intellectuals; he could not imagine American intellectuals giving voice to the impulses of imperialism. At our point in American history it is easy to judge James harshly. But the self-conscious among us mockers will recognize that when we mock the failure of James's vision of the American intellectual we at the same time acknowledge (by our mockery) the failure of a social experiment that could not be called indecent, a failure commensurate with the failure of American hope, with the failure of ourselves. James himself recognized that we had always and already failed: his vision of intellectual work is a vision of struggle without end.

James's legacy for modern American literature is rich and difficult to specify, but a minimal account of his presence might consider some of the following: (1) Though there is no satisfactory way to explain the stunning diversity of modern American poetic projects, James's attack on "theory" helps us to understand why, as a critical generalization applicable to the poems of Frost, Stevens, Pound, Eliot, Williams, and Crane—to name only a few stellar figures—"modernism" is close to worthless. (2) On the positive side, James's insistent hope for a cultural and social diversity of human projects is as clear and eloquent a statement as we have of the sort of heterogeneous human environment that he wanted us politically to encourage, aid, and abet—precisely the sort of environment that might nourish an individuality so radical that it could produce, simultaneously, poetries as incommensurable as those of Frost and Eliot, or those of Pound and Stevens. (3) James's refusal to look back in either anger or delight, his exuberant vision of historical work as *present act* unencumbered by the anxieties of the backward look, is the equivalent in American philosophy of the characteristic modernist literary desire to make it new, to achieve a poetry of presence that would be at the same time

34. Ibid., pp. 633, 635.

a poetry of instinctual immediacy and vitality. But James's vision of historical presence shares the acute and also characteristic modernist awareness that all such desire to forget cannot be satisfied. (4) His urgent plea for the recognition of irreducible ideological plurality—the nontransferable and untranslatable character of any point of view, whether personal or social— speaks for the residual localism of a project like Frost's as well as for the project of Pound, which is beset by the sort of paranoia coincidental with the American tradition of the central crank (James is its noblest voice), in which distrust of the big organization is so strong that when these feelings are felt by Pound they tend to be expressed in a vision of history as conspiratorial *usura* which "lieth / between the young bride and her bridegroom." James's antitheoretical or antistructural (decentered) view of structure is precisely the sort of idea of structure which might be sympathetic with a world of distributed and diffused *eaches* which do not cohere and should not, must not be forced to cohere.

James's great gift to modern American literature was also his great challenge. His career as intellectual and writer says that writing and thinking undertaken without conscience, without concern for the social future of writing and thinking, was not writing and thinking worth undertaking. What has always made James's gift so difficult to accept, his legacy so different from Peirce's (who hated European institutions just as strongly, but who thought that science could find some "external permanency . . . upon which our thinking has no effect"[35] to replace those institutions) is that James offers nothing, definitely not science, as security for the American adventure, no escape from his most unsettling insight: that a rigorous philosophy of practice and consequences cannot in advance secure consequences without establishing precisely the sort of imperial authority—the structure that precedes experience and makes it cohere—which that philosophy is dedicated to undermining.

The key proposition of James's psychology—that the self is, or should be, inaccessibly private property—becomes after 1900 the motor principle of his anti-imperialism: each of us, he writes

35. C. S. Peirce, *Selected Writings,* p. 107.

in the essay "On a Certain Blindness in Human Beings," is
bound "to feel intensely the importance of his own duties and
the significance of the situations that call these forth. But this
feeling is in each of us a vital secret, for sympathy with which
we vainly look to others. The others are too much absorbed in
their own vital secrets to take an interest in ours. Hence the
stupidity and injustice of our opinions, so far as they deal with
the significance of alien lives."[36] Imperialist politics, whether in
its epistemological or political dimension (they are impossible
to separate), is not only unjust: it is also stupid. That is why,
James implies, the act of knowing must be accompanied by
critical reflection on the sometimes casual cruelty and oppressive
consequences of knowing. The elaborate but symptomatic difficulty in making sense of James is coming to see that his overt
commitment to the inalienable private property of selfhood, the
original feeling of spontaneous action, is not after all capitalist
because property under capitalism can be property only if it is
alienable—only if it can be bought, sold, stolen, and, when
necessary, appropriated. James's political turn taught him that
nothing was inalienable in the coercive world of imperialism.
James employs the language of private property in order to
describe the spiritual nature of persons and in an effort to turn
the discourse of capitalism against itself by making that discourse literal in just one instance: so as to preserve a human
space of freedom, however interiorized, from the vicissitudes
and coercions of the marketplace. James's anti-imperialism is
American anti-imperialism: his major effort is to combat the
hegemonic discourse of a capitalism rooted in a democratic
political context by appropriating the cornerstone economic
principle of capitalism to the advantage of a counterdiscourse
and a vision of human sanctity central not only to pragmatism
but also to the originating myth of American political history.
What James says in all but words is that if imperialism and
capitalism on their own are capable of destroying the self, then
in their unified American form they represent a world-historical
menace of unparalleled proportions. In the name of pragmatism
and the American dream James wanted to turn America against

36. Quoted in *The James Family*, p. 398.

the self-pollution of its foreign policy at the end of the nineteenth century; in such an act of self-criticism, he thought, we would subvert the economic and political postures that, by treating all human subjects as if they were objects, for all practical purposes convert us into objects who suffer degradations that nonhuman commodities cannot suffer. James's quasi-Cartesian postulate of an interior spontaneity is not ontological but thoroughly instrumental. It is his great heuristic principle, the energy of his criticism, and the basis of his anti-imperialism.

When James develops his political awarenesses, the private self of his *Principles of Psychology* is collectivized at least to the point of its national boundary: the isolated self becomes a political entity endowed with its own vital national secret and its indigenous story. So James's pluralism and his antinomianism become in his later writings more a pluralism of social narratives, an antinomianism of nations, cultures, and subcultures, and not so much of persons, though the antinomianism of persons remains his point of departure. Because in the United States we are something of an incoherent anthology of cultures, and of stories, rituals, and values organic to those cultures, the human costs of imperial stupidity and injustice, of imperialist imposition within our borders run very high—very high even where literary canonization does its work of homogenization and exclusion. The costs of an imperialism within are simultaneously social and aesthetic. The recent history of American literary scholarship is the history of the fabrication not only of "margins" (social and literary) but also of a "center" (social and literary). And that is the optimistic way of sizing up recent scholarship on American literature: at least so-called marginal cultures are beginning to get their due.

I doubt that James would have tolerated the discourse of "margins" and "center" because he would have recognized it as the mask of antidemocratic arrogance and intolerance of differences and peculiarities. For the radical pragmatist, there is no center: a key insight that enabled, simultaneously, James's committed radical pluralism and his comedic self-deflation. Jamesian anti-imperialist engagement on behalf of a world without a center and Jamesian self-deflation are symbiotic impulses: his ability to take others seriously and with respect rested on his ability not to take himself with solemnity or with too much respect. If he had to "live in a tub like Diogenes, he wouldn't mind at all if the hoops were loose and the staves let in the sun." He called himself a "happy-go-lucky anarchistic sort of creature," at home in the "loose universe" of pluralism which affects "your typical rationalists in much the same way as 'freedom of the press' might affect a veteran official in the Russian bureau of censorship; or as 'simplified spelling' might affect an elderly school mistress. It affects him as the swarm of protestant sects affects a papist onlooker." For rationalists and other imperialists James's "tramp and vagrant world" is a horror in comparison to which "home-rule for Ireland would be a millenium . . . We're no more fit for such a part than the Filipinos are 'fit for self-government.' "[37]

James is particularly invaluable for the contemporary scene in critical theory because he is capturable by no one of its orthodoxies and because he is a counterforce to the antitheoretical opportunism that is being promoted in his name by those in theory who are weary of theory and by those outside theory who have hated theory from the beginning. But if it is in the character of James's project not to issue in programs, not to be institutionalized without the most ludicrous contradiction of his intentions, then what really can contemporary theorists "do" with James? The answer, I think, is that they can do nothing. A "theory" and "criticism" of Jamesian spirit would necessarily be unfashionable. It could not become a machine for processing texts for advanced journals of critical inquiry. James is unteachable as a theorist because he has no system. And without system there can be no method, no theory, no criticism as we have known method, theory, and criticism. On the other hand, though there is no Jamesian program there is a complex Jamesian imperative which urges us to seek and to preserve radical difference, not in itself, but precisely at the dramatic point of its potential normalization. That is an imperative which historians of American literature of all generations should find congenial because it is a way of focusing the obsessive liberal vision of American literature at its extreme antinomian edge, where our

37. James, *Pragmatism,* pp. 124–125.

most powerful writers tend to live. For James it is the dangerous place of convergence of "subject" as individual instance, the singular voice, and "structure" as the potential imperial, even conspiratorial invasion and obliteration of individuality. Not, then, subject as variable expressive function of structure but subject as the antithesis of structure. Historians of American literature who have been socialized professionally in the ways of contemporary theory—contributors to the *New Cambridge History of American Literature* like myself are examples—will live with the Jamesian imperative only with difficulty. And perhaps the degree to which we permit the forces of our discomfort to play freely within us will be the degree to which the *New* Cambridge History will earn the right to call itself "new," the degree to which it will really be an expression of my generation's passions and not a re-play of the passions of our scholarly fathers.

A Critique of Pure Pluralism

> *Men may change their clothes, their politics, their wives, their religions, their philosophies, to a greater or lesser extent: they cannot change their grandfathers.*
>
> Horace Kallen

Reviewing the new (fifth) edition of James D. Hart's *Oxford Companion to American Literature,* Joe Weixlmann praises the editor's effort to expand the coverage of black authors, yet finds the volume's treatment of black, ethnic, female, and modern writers ultimately insufficient and wanting. Weixlmann concludes that "the old, venerable *Oxford Companion to American Literature,* despite its partial facelift, remains in its current incarnation, a product of such staid American and academic values as racism, sexism, traditionalism, and elitism."[1]

This identification of deplorable omissions with a scholar's bias is quite common in the current debates. Frequently an opposition is constructed between closeminded narrowness (sexism, racism, elitism) and the alternative of inclusive openness associated with what is often called "cultural pluralism." In his essay "Minority Literature in the Service of Cultural Pluralism," included in one of the several Modern Language Association readers on American ethnic literature which were published in the last decade, David Dorsey writes:

---

1. Joe Weixlmann, review of *Oxford Companion to American Literature,* *MELUS,* 11 (Spring 1984), 105.

Only from the diverse literatures can youth *feel* the meaning of the past . . . At present diversity is everywhere tolerated in theory, punished in practice, and nowhere justified or justifiable beyond an appeal to solipsism. But America has no choice. Only a genuinely pluralistic society can henceforth prosper here. It must be nurtured in our diverse hearts. And for that we need literature, which is the language of the heart.[2]

In this scholarly drama of diversity and pluralism versus traditionalism and prejudice there is emotion and prophecy just as there are heroes and villains. The editors of another MLA reader, *Ethnic Perspectives in American Literature* (1983), write:

Ethnic pluralism, once the anathema to those who espoused the melting-pot theory, has become a positive, stimulating force for many in our country . . . Transforming the national metaphors from "melting pot" to "mosaic" is not easy. Indeed, the pieces of that national mosaic have been cemented in place with much congealed blood and sweat. We must all continue to work at making the beauty of our multiethnicity shine through the dullness of racism that threatens to cloud it.[3]

Mosaics from the Heart

Perhaps only surpassed by the "melting pot," the "literary canon" may hold a record as a contemporary scapegoat. Sometimes angrily described as the typical fiction of a rather malicious white male imagination, the canon has been seen as a central source of evil in literary scholarship, in ways not so different from the manner in which nineteenth-century nativists condemned "popery." Attacks on exclusionary canons of the past and their presumably bigoted institutionalizers have often been accompanied by arguments in favor of the assumed democratic openness of uncanonized and apocryphal texts. This has tended to produce sectarian and fragmented histories of American lit-

2. David Dorsey, "Minority Literature in the Service of Cultural Pluralism," in *Minority Language and Literature: Retrospective and Perspective,* ed. Dexter Fisher (New York: Modern Language Association, 1977), p. 19.

3. Robert J. Di Pietro and Edward Ifkovic, eds., *Ethnic Perspectives in American Literature: Selected Essays on the European Contribution* (New York: Modern Language Association, 1983), pp. 1, 11.

eratures (in the plural) instead of American literary history. The "literary series" which are constructed in new American historical narratives are sometimes single-sex and single-ethnic-group series. In the absence of a pope, what are we to do about the problem of the canon in rewriting American literary history? Let me raise some questions here.

Is exclusionary canonization merely a matter of bad attitude or of prejudice? Are we likely to produce a more comprehensive literary history if we are dutifully penitent of our ethno-religious, regional, and sexual biases? The example of Thomas Wentworth Higginson suggests that this is not necessarily the case. Though Higginson, a Civil War colonel in the first Negro regiment, can hardly be described as insensitive toward blacks, he never mentions Frederick Douglass' *Narrative* or any other Afro-American text in his *Reader's History of American Literature* (1903).

Is lack of awareness the problem? Will we overcome our flaws and biases once we recognize them in other literary histories? Here the example of V. F. Calverton is discouraging: in *The Liberation of American Literature* (1932), Calverton includes a pretty strong antiexclusionary footnote:

In this connection it is important to remark that, despite this interest in the Negro by many Southern writers and despite the rise of many Negro writers, the hostility felt for the Negro is just as active to-day in the South as it was twenty years ago. This hostility is just as pronounced in many ways in literature as in life. *In the sixteen-volume library of Southern Literature, for example, not a single Negro writer's work is included.* While the biographical section gives mention to Frederick Douglass, Booker T. Washington, and W. E. D. Du Bois, it does not quote a single selection from their works. Paul Laurence Dunbar is not even mentioned in the entire sixteen volumes. Needless to add, dozens of Southern writers whose works are greatly inferior to those of Douglass, Washington, and Du Bois are included, with ample space provided for their ofttimes inferior selections. Equally revealing is the fact that Professor Fred L. Pattee in his recent volume, *American Literature since 1870,* does not even mention a single Negro writer, although he discusses hundreds of white writers, many of whose works are of no more than microscopical importance. Such promising Negro poets as Langston Hughes and Countee Cullen are not even mentioned in the index; Eddie Guest, on the other hand, is given two pages of discussion—and partial praise.[4]

Yet Calverton himself, aware though he was of the issue, never mentions Douglass (except in this footnote). Incidentally, despite his good anti-Southern intentions, Calverton adheres to an exoticist definition of Negro art which views actual Negro poets as unfortunately Westernized compromisers of some *real* Negro spirit that seems to exist only outside of bourgeois forms. Dunbar, he tells us, "was at his best when he wrote in the language of his people and not in the language of the poets."[5]

Is it a matter of defining literature? If only we can define literature broadly enough, will we be able to be more catholic in writing literary history? Yet another Douglass example tells us that this is not necessarily the case. Arthur Hobson Quinn's *History of American Literature* (1951), which emphasizes non-belles-lettres writing throughout the periods, contains a huge chapter on "Literature, Politics, and Slavery" that fails to mention Douglass.

I have used *The Narrative of Frederick Douglass* (1845) as an example because it is so conspicuously absent from past literary histories—it is mentioned neither in Barrett Wendell's *Literary History of America* (1905) nor in Robert Spiller's *Literary History of the United States* (1947)—and yet so unavoidable a text in a literary history of the 1980s. The case of its neglect illustrates that exclusionary canonization is not necessarily correlated to bias (in the manner in which Calverton correlated Southern racism and the *Library of Southern Literature* and Weixlmann ascribed racism and sexism to the *Oxford Companion*). My three literary historians (Higginson, Calverton, and Quinn) would have found fuel for their basic contentions in Douglass' work, yet it did not enter their notions of a "canon."

One further example may suggest that this case is not an exception. Granville Hicks's *The Great Tradition* (1935) ignores Abraham Cahan's *The Rise of David Levinsky* (the inclusion of

4. V. F. Calverton, *The Liberation of American Literature* (New York: Scribner's, 1932), p. 148.
5. Ibid., p. 143.

which would have strengthened Hicks's case), whereas the *Cambridge History of American Literature*—which appeared virtually at the same time as Cahan's novel (1917)—does devote a paragraph to the book. Ironically, this paragraph appears in a section on Yiddish writing, yet the contributor points out that the English-language *Levinsky* far surpasses all Yiddish-American prose publications taken together. The apocryphal text *Levinsky* thus is excluded when it would support the argument, and discussed when it undermines the rationale for a chapter.

Structuring or reconstructing an American literary canon is not necessarily a matter of good intentions or moral probity. Yet the contexts which are consciously or unconsciously accepted as guidelines for a massive history do influence our principles of inclusion (which are inevitably also principles of exclusion). In the past ten years the attacks on bigoted exclusionists—as we saw, prefigured by critics like Calverton—have encouraged the creation of new contexts according to previously excluded categories. The pluralistic demands are quite audible in discussions surrounding literary historiography. In a recent issue of *MELUS*, Marco A. Portales makes a plea to give "Space" to "other literary Traditions" (and not only to Anglo-American writers) in order to arrive at a new type of American literary history:

one that would detail the stories of writers who have not made it into the canon as the editors of the [*Literary History of the United States*] and their predecessors defined it, but who nevertheless are as American and the study of which would subtly serve not to continue divisions among our people, but to teach all of us to appreciate the rich cultural diversity that we *should* have been stressing since American Literature was brought into existence shortly before the turn of the century.[6]

It is Portales' declared (and laudable) intention to deprovincialize the teaching of American literature—but what is offered as the alternative is theoretically problematic. The proposal rests on the identification of assimilation with white Anglo-Saxon Protestant hegemony—which can thus be opposed in a wholesale fashion—and on the belief in "Traditions" which just continue because of the power of descent. The remedy "Space"

6. Marco A. Portales, "Literary History, a 'Usable Past,' and Space," *MELUS,* 11 (Spring 1984), 101.

is seen in what might appear a very American way; not a finite outer limit of, say, a selective 5,000-page history with certain minimal shares for different writers, but as a flexibly limitless and ultimately all-inclusive thing. Yet a literary history now could not be more inclusive than those of the past without being explicitly exclusive, too; and it is here that more theoretical statements have to be made to offset the unrealistic combination of pluralist faith and the idea of limitless space, which ethnic literature might traverse like Frederick Jackson Turner's frontier. Reference books will not just grow bigger and bigger in the near future, so we must think about the way limited space can be used to accommodate new trends and traditional expectations. Of course, writers should not be excluded by virtue of race, region, or gender; but at the same time, should the very same categories on which previous exclusivism was based really be used as organizing concepts? How, then, can literary histories become more responsive to the changes in canonization? How can they suit the needs of teachers of American literature and general readers?

The dominant assumption among serious scholars who study ethnic literary history seems to be that history can best be written by separating the groups that produced such literature in the United States. The published results of this "mosaic" procedure are the readers and compendiums made up of diverse essays on groups of ethnic writers who may have little in common except so-called ethnic roots while, at the same time, obvious and important literary and cultural connections are obfuscated. As James Dormon wrote in a recent review of such a mosaic collection of essays on ethnic theater, "there is little to tie the various essays together other than the shared theme 'ethnic American theater history,' as this topic might be construed by each individual author."[7] The contours of an ethnic literary history are beginning to emerge which views writers primarily as "members" of various ethnic and gender groups. James T. Farrell may thus be discussed as a pure Irish-American writer, without any hint that he got interested in writing ethnic literature after reading and meeting Abraham Cahan, and that his first

---

7. James H. Dormon, "The Varieties of American Ethnic Theater: A Review Essay," *Journal of American Ethnic History*, 4 (Spring 1985), 88.

stories were set in Polish-America—not to mention his interest in Russian and French writing or in Chicago sociology. Or, conversely, Carl Sandburg may be dismissed from the Scandinavian-American part of the mosaic for being "too American."

Taken exclusively, what is often called "the ethnic perspective"—which often means, in literary history, the emphasis of a writer's *descent*—all but annihilates polyethnic art movements, moments of individual and cultural interaction, and the pervasiveness of cultural syncretism in America. The widespread acceptance of the group-by-group approach has not only led to unhistorical accounts held together by static notions of rather abstractly and homogeneously conceived ethnic groups, but has also weakened the comparative and critical skills of increasingly timid interpreters who sometimes choose to speak with the authority of ethnic insiders rather than that of readers of texts. (Practicing cultural pluralism may easily manifest itself in ethnic relativism.)

Yet, if anything, ethnic literary history ought to *increase* our understanding of the cultural interplays and contacts among writers of different backgrounds, the ethnic innovations and cultural mergers that took place in America; and the results of the critical readings should not only leave room for, but actively invite, criticism and scrutiny by other readers ("outsiders" or "insiders") of the texts discussed. This can only be accomplished if the categorization of writers—and literary critics—as "members" of ethnic groups is understood to be a very partial, temporal, and insufficient characterization at best. Could not an openly transethnic procedure that aims for conceptual generalizations and historically be more daring, profitable, and conceptually illuminating than that of simply adding to the sections on "major writers" chapters on "the popular muse," "Negro voices," "the immigrant speaks," "generations of women," "mingling of tongues," and the rest of it?

Is it possible now to rewrite Quinn's chapter and include Douglass or do we need separate chapters for each ethnic group, to be written by "insiders"? Can we construct a chapter on intellectual life in the early twentieth century in which ideas entertained by Anglo-American, Irish-American, Jewish-American, and Afro-American figures can be discussed *together,* or do we have to separate men and women, immigrants and American-born authors? Is it possible to connect Alain Locke, who ended his introduction to *The New Negro* (1925) with the hope for "a spiritual Coming of Age"[8] with his college classmate Van Wyck Brooks, or are two heterogeneous ethnic experiences at work in them? These questions apply not only to the synchronic analysis of a period, but also to the construction of diachronic "descent lines." Do we have to believe in a filiation from Mark Twain to Ernest Hemingway, but not to Ralph Ellison (who is supposedly descended from James Weldon Johnson and Richard Wright)? Can Gertrude Stein be discussed with Richard Wright or only with white women expatriate German-Jewish writers? Is there a link from the autobiography of Benjamin Franklin to those of Frederick Douglass and Mary Antin, or must we see Douglass exclusively as a version of Olaudah Equiano and a precursor to Malcolm X? Is Zora Neale Hurston only Alice Walker's foremother? In general, is the question of influence, of who came first, more interesting than the investigation of the constellation in which ideas, styles, themes, and forms travel?

In order to pursue such questions I have set myself a double task. I shall review significant criticisms of the shortcomings of the concept of cultural pluralism in the hope that the arguments made by intellectual historians of the past decade may affect thinking about American literature today; and I shall attempt to suggest the complexities of polyethnic interaction among some of the intellectuals who were involved in developing the term "cultural pluralism." It is ironical that the story of the origins of cultural pluralism I shall tell could not have been told in the "pluralistic mosaic" format of group-by-group accounts of American cultural life: one protagonist would illustrate what the current fashion calls "the Jewish experience," another "the Black experience," a third "the white Anglo-Saxon Protestant experience." But the fact is that it was not any monoethnic "experience" that led to the emergence of the concept of cultural pluralism. It was the protagonists' troubled interaction with

8. Alain Locke, ed., *The New Negro* (1925; rpt. New York: Atheneum, 1969), p. 16.

each other. Pluralism had a fairly monistic origin in a university philosophy department in the first decade of this century; yet it is a notion whose very mobility challenges the concept's central tenet of the permanent power of ethnic boundaries.

Ku Klux Pluralism?

From its inception, the term pluralism has been used contrastively against racist ogres. When Horace Meyer Kallen, apparently for the first time in print, used "Cultural Pluralism" in his essay collection *Culture and Democracy in the United States* in 1924, he offered his capitalized phrase as the redemptive alternative to a forced concept of hierarchical homogeneity as envisioned by the Ku Klux Klan.

In manyness, variety, differentiation, lies the vitality of such oneness as they may compose. Cultural growth is founded upon Cultural Pluralism. Cultural Pluralism is possible only in a democratic society whose institutions encourage individuality in groups, in persons, in temperaments, whose program liberates these individualities and guides them into a fellowship of freedom and cooperation. The alternative before Americans is Kultur Klux Klan or Cultural Pluralism.[9]

In his opposition to racial myths and dreams of the Klan—which was newly revived after the success of *Birth of a Nation* (1916)— Kallen goes so far as to reject all concepts of American cultural cohesion as "Kultur Klux Klan," even nonracist and nonhierarchical ones such as the melting pot, the target of his most famous essay, "Democracy versus the Melting Pot." Kallen's antithetical spirit often manifested itself in such puns. In 1906 he disparaged "Cultur-Zionism";[10] and in 1930, invoking E. Boyd, he described Stuart Sherman as a "Ku Klux Kritic."[11] The printed phrase "cultural pluralism" was born in a literary polemic which equated all

9. Horace M. Kallen, *Culture and Democracy in the United States: Studies in the Group Psychology of the American Peoples* (New York: Boni and Liveright, 1924), p. 43. All further references to this work appear in the text, cited parenthetically as *C*.

10. Horace M. Kallen, "The Ethics of Zionism," *The Maccabaean*, 11 (August 1906), 70.

11. Horace M. Kallen, *Indecency and Seven Arts; and Other Adventures of a Pragmatist in Aesthetics* (New York: Liveright, 1930), p. 59.

forms of assimilation and acculturation with hard-core racism. This rhetorical strategy is still operative in the many attacks on the melting pot today, attacks which silently identify melting pot and Anglo-conformity and which delight in antitheses.

When it comes to defining cultural pluralism positively (and not merely contrastively against hierarchically conceived notions of oneness), Kallen is lyrically evasive. His invocations of "the outlines of a possible great and truly democratic commonwealth" are vague to the point of contentlessness, unpolitical, and sustained by faith in musically harmonious diversity. Speaking about his ideal commonwealth, Kallen sets the tone for our continuing confusions with cultural pluralism:

Its form would be that of the federal republic; its substance a democracy of nationalities, cooperating voluntarily and autonomously through common institutions in the enterprise of self-realization through the perfection of men according to their kind. The common language of the commonwealth, the language of its great tradition, would be English, but each nationality would have for its emotional and involuntary life its own peculiar dialect or speech, its own individual and inevitable esthetic and intellectual forms. The political and economic life of the commonwealth is a single unit and serves as the foundation and background for the realization of the distinctive individuality of each *natio* that composes it and of the pooling of these in a harmony above them all. Thus "American civilization" may come to mean the perfection of the cooperative harmonies of "European civilization"— the waste, the squalor and the distress of Europe being eliminated— a multiplicity in a unity, an orchestration of mankind.   (*C.* 124)

The buzz words that permeate today's ethnic discourse are all there, as a static notion of eternal groups—cast as pseudo-individuals—is made the basis of a lofty prophecy of an orchestrated American harmony. The abstract contrast with the squalor of Europe evokes little more than Walt Disney's International Village at Epcot Center with its permanent background music and country-of-origin waiters.[12]

12. As John Higham and Philip Gleason have pointed out, Kallen's vision of cultural pluralism is somewhat problematic. Higham called attention to the "chronic indistinctness of the pluralist idea in ethnic relations" (John Higham, *Send These to Me: Jews and Other Immigrants in Urban America* [New York: Atheneum, 1975], p. 196), and Gleason argued that cultural pluralism "has

Contrasted by Kallen against old-world hierarchies and squalor as well as monoethnic domination in America, cultural diversity itself appears as something redemptive in itself, an ideal to maintain and preserve, though the survival of the ingredients seems threatened in America. Kallen and his successors assume that while the whole concert of cultural pluralism is open-ended, the stable quality of each instrument must be preserved. Kallen's definition of cultural pluralism rests on quasi-eternal, static units, on the "distinctive individuality of each *natio*" (*nationes* are thereby removed from the history of their own emergence), on "ancestry," "homogeneity of heritage, mentality and interest," and mankind's "psycho-physical inheritance." Kallen writes: "In historic times so far as is known no new ethnic types have originated, and from what is known of breeding there comes no assurance that the old types will disappear in favor of the new" (*C.* 119).[13] In an earlier essay he had argued: "To preach assimilation is to preach the absurd and is an unworthy abasement, possibly only to the spiritually degenerate."[14] Kallen's polemically anti-assimilationist metaphors direct the pluralists' attention to unhistorical ethnic persistence rather than to historical change and to group survival rather than to group emergence (now termed ethnogenesis). Whereas the melting-pot image is eminently dynamic and accommodates the continuous processes of assimilation and ethnogenesis, both mosaic and orchestra are static.

At the root of cultural pluralism is a notion of the eternal power of descent, birth, *natio*, and race that Kallen shares with

---

always been more of a vision than a rigorous theory" (Philip Gleason, "American Identity and Americanization," in *Harvard Encyclopedia of American Ethnic Groups,* ed. Stephan Thernstrom, Ann Orlov, and Oscar Handlin [Cambridge, Mass.: Harvard University Press, 1980], p. 43).

13. One might characterize this position as creationist, and no Scopes-monkey trial in literary history has given evolutionists a foothold: mankind was seemingly created in a fairly finite and stable assortment of ethnic groups (a.k.a. races or stocks). American pluralism attempts to stabilize the existing groups into a state of symphonic bliss. Creationists, however, can hardly explain the emergence of American groups such as Southerners, Mormons, Appalachians, or Afro-Americans in historical times.

14. Kallen, "Ethics," p. 70.

his worst antagonist, the racist E. A. Ross, against whom he polemicizes, but with whom he also agrees, sometimes explicitly (*C.* 119).[15] Higham concluded that both the pluralist Kallen and the racist Ross "asserted that ethnic character was somehow rooted in the natural order."[16] Gleason fully explored the racist component in Kallen's cultural pluralism, and his conclusions deserve the serious attention of today's cultural pluralists:

Kallen's racialism was romantic in that he valued diversity as such and did not attempt to rank human groups as superior or inferior according to any absolute scale of racial merit. But he also resembled the romantics in attributing the distinctive characteristics of peoples to inborn racial qualities whose origin and nature were obscure . . . Kallen's racialism was also central to his conviction that ethnic nationalities would perpetuate themselves indefinitely . . . Kallen's whole handling of race was extremely ambiguous. He was certainly not a strict

15. It is also worth noting the case of nativist journalist Agnes Repplier (of Franco-German descent) who was troubled (as was Barrett Wendell) by Jewish immigrant Mary Antin's presumptuousness in taking "possession of Beacon Street" and calling the Pilgrim fathers "our forefathers." Repplier significantly associated immigrants with dirt and quotes Elizabeth Robins Pennell, who wrote that "if Philadelphia blossomed like the rose with Mary Antins, the city would be ill repaid for the degradation of her noble old streets, now transformed, into foul and filthy slums. Dirt is a valuable asset in the immigrant's hands" (Agnes Repplier, *Counter-Currents* [Boston: Houghton Mifflin, 1916], pp. 227–228; also see Mary Dearborn, *Pocahontas' Daughters: Gender and Ethnicity in American Culture* [New York: Oxford University Press, 1985], chapter 2). Repplier invoked none other than a slightly misquoted Kallen in order to support her nativism. "Mr. Horace Kallen," she writes approvingly, and some pages before the Philadelphia dirt sets in, "has put the case into a few clear conclusive words when he says, 'Only men who are alike in origin and spirit, and not abstractly, can be truly equal, and maintain that inward unanimity of action and outlook which makes a national life' " (Repplier, p. 203; compare with Kallen, *Culture,* p. 115). The culture critic Randolph Bourne, however, despite his dislike of assimilation, was more clearly aware of the political implications of the New Englanders' reaction to Mary Antin. "We have had to watch," Bourne writes in "Trans-National America" (1916), "hard-hearted old Brahmins virtuously indignant at the spectacle of the immigrant refusing to be melted, while they jeer at patriots like Mary Antin who write about 'our forefathers' " (Randolph S. Bourne, *War and the Intellectuals: Collected Essays, 1915–1919,* 2nd ed. [New York: Alfred A. Knopf, 1973], p. 107).

16. Higham, *Send These to Me,* p. 207.

biological racist like Madison Grant, but neither did he systematically distinguish between biological and cultural elements in the manner of Franz Boas . . . Kallen talked about "nationalities" as embodying this undifferentiated inheritance in such a way as to make it virtually impossible to determine which elements of an ethnic group's identity were genetically determined and which were culturally transmitted.

Kallen never clarified these issues, and those who came after him in the pluralist tradition apparently failed to recognize them . . . and certainly failed to address them. Therefore the crucial role of Kallen's ambiguous racialist assumptions still constitutes a major theoretical problem in the cultural pluralist interpretation of ethnicity and American identity.[17]

The current polemics in the name of cultural pluralism notwithstanding, Kallen's concept was not even a good theoretical basis for inclusiveness. One would expect that Kallen's system was not exactly hospitable to the many melting-pot Americans; and he did write in 1906: "We have to crush out the . . . chameleon and spiritual mongrel . . . For of all things, the realization of the race-self is the central thing."[18] Yet even within his racialist group-by-group approach there was sufficient ethnic exclusiveness to deserve mention. Kallen's pluralist orchestra did not have any room for Afro-Americans, among others.[19] It could play neither *Shuffle Along* nor *Rhapsody in Blue*. As Isaac Berkson's *Theories of Americanization* (1920) illustrates, the shortcomings of cultural pluralism certainly did not escape Kallen's contemporaries; Berkson perceptively remarked that Kallen's theory was "based on the assumption of

17. Gleason, "American Identity and Americanization," pp. 44–45.

18. Kallen, "Ethics," p. 71.

19. This criticism of Kallen's exclusivism was fully developed by Higham. "(T)here was a fatal elision when he wrote that America could become 'an orchestration of mankind' by perfecting 'the cooperative harmonies of European civilization.' Nothing in Kallen's writing gave away the magnitude of that elision. In the fullest statement of his argument there was only a single obscure footnote on the point. 'I do not discuss the influence of the negro,' Kallen confessed in fine print. 'This is at once too considerable and too recondite in its processes for casual mention. It requires separate analysis' [Kallen, *Culture*, p. 226]. The pluralist thesis from the outset was encapsulated in white ethnocentrism" (Higham, p. 208).

the ineradicable and central influence of race."[20] It is worth reconsidering the intellectual foundations on which even some current claims for the American literary mosaic are made. By accepting Kallen's anti-assimilationist bias which is so persuasively directed against the (equally anti-assimilationist) Ku Klux Klan, the new ethnic literary historians may inadvertently become well-intentioned practitioners of Pluralism Klux Klan.

Another Look at the Origins of Cultural Pluralism

The term cultural pluralism first appeared in print in 1924; but this was long after Horace Kallen started using it conversationally. The story of the origins of the coinage "cultural pluralism," in part unrecoverably lost and in part intriguingly suggestive, does little to detract from the theoretical criticism of the concept. However, it provides us with an exemplary tale of ideas criss-crossing not only ethnic lines, but originating from and traversing the color line at the height of racism.[21]

The son of Esther Rebecca and Jacob David Kallen (a rabbi of the German-speaking orthodox congregation Hevra ha-Moriah in Boston), Horace Kallen was born in Germany in 1882 and came to America at age five.[22] Kallen "felt close to his mother" but "was alienated from his father, whom he remembered as . . . proud, demanding, [and] domineering."[23] As a youngster, Kallen (like his contemporary, Mary Antin)[24] ex-

20. Isaac B. Berkson, *Theories of Americanization: A Critical Study with Special Reference to the Jewish Group* (New York: Teachers College, Columbia University, 1920), p. 81.

21. Parts of the story have been suggested by Gleason and Higham as well as by Barbara Solomon, Milton Konvitz, Moses Rischin (who views Kallen's role in a very favorable light), Sarah Schmidt, and Clara Crane; others are offered here for the first time.

22. Milton R. Konvitz, "Horace Meyer Kallen: Philosopher of the Hebraic-American Idea," *American Jewish Yearbook, 1974–75* (Philadelphia: Jewish Publication Society of America, 1974), p. 56.

23. Ibid., p. 56.

24. See Mary Antin, *The Promised Land* (Boston: Houghton Mifflin, 1912), pp. 225–232, and Mary Antin, *They Who Knock at Our Gates: A Complete Gospel of Immigration* (Boston: Houghton Mifflin, 1914), pp. 28–29, 98, and 142. Antin was born in Polotzk, in the Pale of Jewish Settlement, in 1881, and came to live in Boston at age thirteen.

plored the Boston sites of American history textbooks, Bunker
Hill and Tea Wharf, and later remembered the syncretistic overlay of Jewish and American lore in his mind.

In our household the suffering and slavery of Israel were commonplaces
of conversation; from Passover to Passover, freedom was an ideal
ceremonially reverenced, religiously aspired to. The textbook story of
the Declaration of Independence came upon me, nurtured upon the
deliverance from Egypt and the bondage in exile, like the clangor of
trumpets, like a sudden light. What a resounding battle cry of freedom!
And then, what an invincible march of Democracy to triumph over
every enemy—over the English king, over the American Indian, over
the uncivilized Mexican, over the American champions of slavery betraying American freedom, over everything, to the very day of the
history lesson![25]

When Kallen entered Harvard at eighteen he was a religious
renegade, thought of the Old Testament as a "narrow, bigoted"
book (*S*. 38), and was ready to absorb the teachings of Josiah
Royce, George Santayana, and, especially, William James and
Barrett Wendell—all of whom Kallen got to know well personally. One could sketch Kallen's interaction with all of these
teachers (he wrote poems about his philosophy professors), but
a brief consideration of (Anglo-American) Wendell and a cur-
sory reference to (Irish-American) James will suffice here.

Kallen remembered that Wendell emphasized "the role of the
Old Testament as a certain perspective, a certain way of life.
He showed how the Old Testament had affected the Puritan
mind, traced the role of the Hebraic tradition in the development of the American character" (*S*. 38). Kallen reluctantly
accepted the challenge of this approach.

I was an alienated intellectual being suddenly challenged in his alienation . . . And the challenge turned not on anything in the Hebraic
tradition at all [but] . . . on what Americanism came to mean to
me . . . in terms of the philosophical pluralism with which [William]
James was identified and . . . in terms of the interpretation of the
American tradition and the literary tradition of America by Barrett

25. Sarah L. Schmidt, "Horace Kallen and the Americanization of Zionism,"
Ph.D. diss., University of Maryland, 1973, p. 34. All further references to this
work appear in the text, cited parenthetically as *S*.

Wendell . . . The [Zionist] meanings came to me rather in terms of the American Idea than in terms of what I had learned of *Torah* [Jewish law] at home or in *Cheder* [Hebrew school]. (*S.* 40)

The result was that in 1902 Kallen became a Zionist at Harvard, "where a Yankee, named Barrett Wendell, re-Judaized" him (*S.* 36). Sarah Schmidt's excellent analysis of Kallen's Judaization stressed the compatibility between his Zionism and what Wendell (echoing Theodore Parker) called "the American idea." "To be a Zionist was to be a good American" (*S.* 39). Kallen's activities in the Menorah Society and as a self-styled Zionist permitted him to have it two ways, "to retain," or, perhaps more accurately, to reinvent, "his Jewish identity and to become, thereby, a better American" (*S.* v). Americanization and ethnicization went hand in hand as Kallen developed a modern ethnic identity that continued to remain at odds with his father's traditional faith. Kallen's transformation can be seen in the context of what Herbert Gans has termed "symbolic ethnicity" which goes along with assimilation: Kallen absorbed concepts from the surrounding culture (the American idea), but gave it an ethnic name (the Jewish idea). Kallen's own life story illustrates Higham's generalization that pluralism "has unconsciously relied on the assimilative process which it seemed to repudiate."[26]

If Kallen's new outlook was not traditionally Jewish, it also was not the result of a collective momentum. "Kallen's decision to become a Zionist was entirely a personal, abstract, one, not influenced by the Jewish community or by the fledgling American Zionist movement" (*S.* 39). The pervasive metaphors of individualism in Kallen's group thinking may point to this individual moment of his own ethnic rebirth, his personal ethnogenesis in an assimilative context. The orchestra image, too, recurs, when Kallen remembered the influence of William James's philosophical pluralism, which stressed

the reality of manyness, the refusal to accept the proposition that the many are appearance and only the one is reality. When I accepted this

26. Higham, *Send These to Me*, p. 198. Also see William Boelhower, *Through a Glass Darkly: Ethnic Semiosis in American Literature* (Venice: Edizioni Helvetia, 1984), p. 33.

idea I didn't have to think of it as an image that could be dissipated. I could think of it as a present perduring reality which, in my personal history, all my experiences joined and with which they orchestrated and made the me that I was becoming . . .

What it [James's pluralism] released me from was an attitude which shut out operational working of my past. It opened opportunities. Zionism became a replacement and reevaluation of Judaism which enabled me to respect it . . . which allowed me to see an ongoing pattern, a group personality, called Jew. (*S.* 40)

Through the intellectual contact with James and Wendell, Kallen underwent dramatic changes in ethnic outlook, yet began to formulate static and abstract notions of an "ongoing pattern," of ethnic persistence—imagining the individual as a collectivity and the collectivity as an individual.

Kallen's relationship to Wendell must have been complicated by Wendell's anxieties about the influx of immigrants who, like Mary Antin, made claims to a full American identity. Moreover, Wendell appears to have suffered from some physical revulsion caused by conviviality with blacks and Jews, a form of psychosomatic racism. Barbara Solomon called attention to Wendell's daughter's recollections.[27] Edith Wendell Osborne writes that her father, a "great believer in tradition," honored the annual recipient of the Jacob Wendell Scholarship (given out "for merit only") by "asking the scholar to dine at his house, inviting, amongst others, the President of Harvard to meet him." Wendell's daughter dwells on her father's fear "that eventually the scholar would be either an Ethiopian or a Hebrew, holding he would then permanently abandon the dinners." Yet she concludes with the comforting note that "up to the present they have all been Americans, and, with hardly an exception, gentlemen."[28] It is this narrow and exclusive definition of "Americans," of course, that we might expect to have startled Kallen. Wendell revealed at least some of his difficulties to Kallen; and the former student, far from taking the broader approach to Americanness, sounded just like his mentor when he criticized

27. Barbara Miller Solomon, *Ancestors and Immigrants: A Changing New England Tradition* (Chicago: University of Chicago Press, 1956), p. 173.

28. Edith Wendell Osborne, *Recollections of My Father Barrett Wendell* (privately printed, 1921), p. 17.

Antin for her American claims, describing her as "intermarried, 'assimilated' even in religion, and more excessively, self-consciously flatteringly American than the Americans" (*C.* 86). However, Kallen deflected the critique from nativist exclusion from the category "American" toward anti-assimilationism.

Kallen dedicated *Culture and Democracy* to the memory of Barrett Wendell with whom he had had an intensive exchange of letters up until Wendell's death. As Moses Rischin has recently shown in a thoroughly detailed and glowing account of Kallen's contribution to American pluralism, Kallen incorporated a Wendell letter into "Democracy versus the Melting Pot." This excerpt also makes clearer what Wendell feared about Antin: "Your Jewish race," he writes to Kallen in December of 1914, "is less lost than we, of old America. For all (its) sufferings . . . it has never lost its identity, its tradition, its existence. As for us, we are submerged beneath a conquest so complete that the very name of us means something not ourselves . . . I feel as I should think an Indian might feel, in the face of ourselves that were."[29] Kallen used the last sentence anonymously, ascribing it merely to "a great American man of letters, who has better than any one else I know of interpreted to the world the spirit of America as New England"(*C.* 93).

The pluralist plot begins to thicken in the years 1905–1908. Kallen who graduated in 1903 worked as a teaching fellow for Santayana and James in 1905–1907 and received a Sheldon fellowship to go to Oxford in 1907–1908, the same academic year during which William James delivered the Hibbert lectures at Oxford, later published under the title *A Pluralistic Universe.* The lectures were full of references that must have been meaningful to Kallen.[30] James used the image of the "federal repub-

29. Moses Rischin, "The Jews and Pluralism: Toward an American Freedom Symphony," in *Jewish Life in America: Historical Perspectives,* ed. Gladys Rosen (New York: Institute of Human Relations Press of the American Jewish Committee and KTAV, March 1980), p. 17.

30. William James drew out the ethnic and relativistic implications of pluralism in the essay "On a Certain Blindness in Human Beings" (1906)—which made a lasting impression on Robert Park when he was a student at Harvard (Robert E. Park, *Race and Culture: Essays in the Sociology of Contemporary Man* [New York and London: Free Press and Collier-Macmillan, 1964], pp. vi–vii). James read this piece occasionally to his students. Using the illustration

lic" which recurred in Kallen (*C.* 124);[31] significantly, James's
use takes the American political system as a philosophical model
for the universe: "The pluralistic world is thus more like a
federal republic than like an empire or a kingdom."[32] James
also posits a clear alternative between "pluralism" and "monism," and in a form that has persisted in the rhetoric of pluralism
since Kallen.

Is the many-ness-in-oneness that indubitably characterizes the world
we inhabit, a property only of the absolute whole of things, so that
you must postulate that one-enormous-whole indivisibly as the *prius* of
there being any many at all—in other words, start with the rationalistic
block-universe, entire, unmitigated, and complete?—or can the finite
elements have their own aboriginal forms of manyness-in-oneness, and
where they have no immediate oneness still be continued into one
another by intermediary terms—each one of these terms being one
with its next neighbors, and yet the total 'oneness' never getting absolutely complete?[33]

Meanwhile, the Philadelphia-born black intellectual Alain Locke,
who had taken Kallen's section in a Santayana class, graduated
from Harvard in 1907 and became the first (and, until 1962,
only) black Rhodes scholar at Oxford in the academic year of

---

of the difference between his negative perception of a North Carolina wood
clearing and the mountaineers' positive image of the same scene—not as denu-
dation of nature, but as a "paean of duty, struggle, and success"—James gen-
eralizes: "I had been blind to the peculiar ideality of their conditions as they
certainly would also have been to the ideality of mine, had they had a peep at
my strange indoor academic ways of life at Cambridge" (William James, *Talks
to Teachers on Psychology: and to Students on Some of Life's Ideals* [1906; rpt.
New York: Holt, 1910], p. 234). It should be noted, however, that Kallen was
critical of James in a letter written to Wendell shortly before James delivered
the Hibbert lectures: "Poor James! victim of a too excellent English style!"
(Horace M. Kallen, letter to Barrett Wendell, 11 March 1908, Wendell Papers,
Houghton Library, Harvard University).
    31. Also see Higham, *Send These to Me*, p. 206.
    32. William James, *A Pluralistic Universe* (Cambridge, Mass.: Harvard Uni-
versity Press, 1977), p. 145.
    33. Ibid., p. 147.

James's Hibbert lectures.[34] When Locke applied for the scholarship, Crane writes, he noted

sardonically that although Rhodes had acquired a huge fortune in Africa, no one of African descent had ever been awarded one of his scholarships. Physically small and prone to heart trouble, Locke met the athletic requirement for the Rhodes Scholarship by serving as coxswain on the Harvard crew; and his extracurricular activities in public speaking and music qualified him as an all-round student . . . In his personal interview with the committee, Locke stated that he wanted to go to Oxford not only to continue his studies in literature, but also because he wished to "see the race problem from the outside . . . to see it in perspective." Locke's "maturity of purpose" and brilliant college record resulted in his appointment.[35]

It was from Kallen's encounters with Locke that the idea of cultural pluralism germinated. As Kallen remembers:

It was in 1905 that I began to formulate the notion of cultural pluralism and I had to do that in connection with my teaching. I was assisting both Mr. James and Mr. Santayana at the time and I had a Negro student named Alain Locke, a very remarkable young man—very sensitive, very easily hurt—who insisted that he was a human being and that his color ought not to make any difference. And, of course, it was a mistaken insistence. It *had* to make a difference and it *had* to be accepted and respected and enjoyed for what it was.

Two years later when I went to Oxford on a fellowship he was there as a Rhodes scholar, and we had a race problem because the Rhodes scholars from the South were bastards. So they had a Thanksgiving dinner which I refused to attend because they refused to have Locke.

And he said, "I am a human being," just as I had said it earlier. What difference does the difference make? We are all alike Americans. And we had to argue out the question of how the differences made differences, and in arguing out those questions the formulae, then phrases, developed—"cultural pluralism," "the right to be different." (*S.* 49)

The remembered story of Kallen's coming to Locke's rescue has been retold several times as the myth of origins of "cultural

34. Clare Bloodgood Crane, "Alain Locke and the Negro Renaissance," Ph.D. diss., University of California, San Diego, 1971, p. 27.
35. Ibid., p. 27.

pluralism," and it was occasionally expanded to include Wendell's attempts to dissuade Kallen from making a public gesture for a black person (*S.* 49).[36] A closer look at the Wendell-Kallen correspondence, however, yields a much more complex situation. The "Locke affair"—that inspired Kallen to speak of "cultural pluralism"—begins with a letter from Kallen to Wendell, dated 22 October 1907, which, as far as I know, has not previously been cited:

Now I want to ask a favor of you. You will perhaps remember little Locke, the yellow boy who took . . . English 42. He is here as a Rhodes scholar; and some people have been in America officious and mean-spirited enough to draw "the color-line" for the benefit of Englishmen. The boy earned his scholarship in an open competition. He has said nothing to me himself. Others have deprecated his being here. But he is here, one of America's scholars, and a Harvard man. He finds himself suddenly shut out of things,—unhappy, and lonely and doesn't know how or why.[37]

Whether merely to placate Wendell (as Rischin suggested in a personal letter) or to express his own feelings, Kallen, the father of cultural pluralism, adds:

As you know, I have neither respect nor liking for his race—but individually they have to be taken, each on his own merits and value, and if ever a negro was worthy, this boy is. I have remembered your warning and have been silent on the matter, but I listened with great anger and I have said all that I could concerning what was commendable in him, and now I want you to write a word to Dyer and others, if you can, to help him right this wrong.[38]

Wendell answered on 3 November 1907 with a frank and detailed account of his race-repugnance.

As to Locke, I really feel regretfully unable to write as you would like me to. My own sentiments concerning negroes are such that I have always declined to meet the best of them—Booker Washington, a man whom I thoroughly respect,—at table. Had Locke won my father's scholarship, I should have given up my plan of an annual dinner at which the former Wendell scholars have, so far, come together here

36. Also see Rischin, "The Jews and Pluralism," p. 19.
37. Wendell Papers, Houghton Library, Harvard University.
38. Ibid.

to greet the new one. Professionally, I do my best to treat negroes with absolute courtesy. It would be disastrous to them, if they are gentlemen at heart, to expose them in private life to such sentiments of repugnance as mine, if we were brought into anything resembling personal relations.[39]

Wendell questioned Locke's legitimacy as a Rhodes scholar, for how could he be representative of what was "best in the state" that sent him?

At least for many years to come, no negro can take just this position anywhere in America. Before he can, the kind of American which unmixed nationhood has made me must be only a memory. It is sad, I admit—not least so to me for the reason that I am passing, perhaps of the past altogether.[40]

Wendell concluded with the following advice regarding Locke:

There is no reason, I think, why you should not invite some of your Oxford friends to meet him at tea; though to do so without intimation that he was coming might be inconsiderate. To make a 'cause' of the matter would be, at this juncture, deeply inexpedient.[41]

Wendell's term "repugnance"—a classic case of what another student of William James's, the sociologist Robert Park in 1928 termed "racial antipathy" in the essay "The Bases of Race Prejudice"[42]— is faithfully echoed by Kallen in his letter to Wendell of 12 November 1907:

As to Locke—you have phrased my own feeling toward the race, so well that I don't see that there is anything more to say. I have already done the thing you suggested. I have had him to tea—he has met a Rhodes scholar from Princeton,—an old pupil of mine,—Dyer, and the Diceys. One of my Princeton colleagues, Harper, whom you may have met, is here and has expressed spontaneously a wish to meet the boy. So he is to come to tea again tho' it is personally repugnant to me to eat with him. Shylock's disclaimer [*Merchant of Venice* I.iii.35ff.] expresses my feeling exactly; but then, Locke is a Harvard man and as such he has a definite claim on me. I think he is going to do us

39. Barrett Wendell to Horace Kallen, 3 November 1907, Horace M. Kallen Collection, American Jewish Archives, Cincinnati.
40. Ibid.
41. Ibid.
42. Park, *Race and Culture*, pp. 230–243.

credit. Already he has 'cox'd a boat to victory and won a silver cup.[43]

The birth of cultural pluralism was beset by ironies: a non-religious Jewish student was converted to Zionism by a Boston Brahmin professor who suffered from spells of repugnance brought about by race contact during dinners; the student denounces assimilation and endears himself to his professor by claiming the same feelings of repugnance toward a black fellow student whom, with the help of his professor, he yet wants to protect against racism; and he views the young black intellectual, perhaps tongue-in-cheek, not as a fellow-philosophy student, but as an athlete and credit to the university. It seems strange, indeed, that Kallen singled out the early contact with Locke as the stimulus for pluralism when his own letters at the time of the incident make Kallen such an unlikely ancestor for contemporary pluralists. Upper-case "Cultural Pluralism" emerged in a world which also contained lower-case "negroes."

Alain Locke, whose personal statements and letters might reveal another dimension of the story, or another story altogether, contributed some philosophical essays to collections edited by Kallen or dedicated to him in later years (essays that are curiously omitted in collections of Locke's works), and described his own conversion to cultural pluralism in a longer autobiographical statement published in 1935.

Verily paradox has followed me the rest of my days: at Harvard, clinging to the genteel tradition of Palmer, Royce and Münsterberg, yet attracted by the disillusion of Santayana and the radical protest of James: again in 1916 I returned to work under Royce but was destined to take my doctorate in Value Theory under Perry. At Oxford, once more intrigued by the twilight of aestheticism but dimly aware of the new realism of the Austrian philosophy of value; socially Anglophile, but because of race loyalty, strenuously anti-imperialist; universalist in religion, internationalist and pacifist in world-view, but forced by a sense of simple justice to approve of the militant counter-nationalisms of Zionism, Young Turkey, Young Egypt, Young India, and with reservations even Garveyism and current-day "Nippon over Asia." Finally a cultural cosmopolitan, but perforce an advocate of

43. Kallen, letter to Barrett Wendell, 12 November 1907, Wendell Papers.

cultural racialism as a defensive counter-move for the American Negro and accordingly more of a philosophical mid-wife to a generation of younger Negro poets, writers, artists than a professional philosopher.

Small wonder, then, with this psychograph, that I project my personal history into its inevitable rationalization as cultural pluralism and value relativism, with a not too orthodox reaction to the American way of life.[44]

Alain Locke, though he adopted Kallen's term here, saw the dynamic of "cultural racialism" as a counter-move for black intellectuals and interpreted it in a broad international context. In the introduction to his famous anthology *The New Negro* (1925), he called Harlem the "home of the Negro's 'Zionism.' "[45] Incidentally, Locke also once mentioned that he wrote a study entitled "Frederick Douglass; a Biography of Anti-Slavery" (1935).[46]

Beyond Pluralism

The point of this documentation was not to malign Horace Kallen—whose correspondence with Wendell deserves study beyond the uses that were made of it here[47]—but to ask new questions about some problems at the very source of cultural pluralism. Pluralism is not a redemptively transcendent category that removes its advocates from prejudice. Few champions of pluralism today share the racist sentiments expressed in the Wendell-Kallen correspondence, but Kallen's anti-assimilationist bias has remained pervasive in the many diatribes against melting pot and intermarriage. In the current cultural debates pluralism often implies purism.

The tradition of pluralism from 1924 to the present discussions of literary histories is, of course, characterized by several shifts and changes. Most notably, the terms pluralism and cultural pluralism came into high fashion in the period during and after

44. Alain Locke, "Values and Imperatives," in *American Philosophy Today and Tomorrow,* ed. Sidney Hook and Horace Kallen (New York: L. Furman, 1935), p. 312.

45. Locke, *New Negro,* p. 14.

46. Locke, "Values, " p. 312.

47. See, for example, M. A. DeWolfe Howe, *Barrett Wendell and His Letters* (Boston: Atlantic Monthly Press, 1924), pp. 183–184, and Kallen, letter to Barrett Wendell, 2 May 1908, Wendell Papers.

World War II, when the antithesis against totalitarianism made pluralism a desirable (though still largely undefined) concept. Though Kallen's influence has not been universally acknowledged, Kallen, too, participated in providing Cold War definitions of pluralism against totalitarianism. In the essay "Alain Locke and Cultural Pluralism" (1955), for example, Kallen writes:

There persists in the sciences of man and nature and in philosophies as they have developed in our country, a disposition to assert and somehow to establish the primacy of totalitarian unity at the beginning, and its supremacy in the consummation, of all existence. It is, of course, conceded that multitude and variety seem pervasive, always and everywhere. But it is denied that they are real. It is the One that is real, not the Many.[48]

Kallen thus substituted "totalitarian unity" for James's "monism" and instrumentalized the pluralist tradition for political purposes of the 1950s. As America was pitted against its "monolithic" adversaries, there was some ideological necessity to reconstruct the United States as the culture of the many. The current vogue for indeterminacy in interpretation (sometimes in combination with cultural relativism) may also originate in pluralist thought. Thus James argued that "pluralism involves indeterminism"; and even though he lectured that "if you say 'indetermination,' you are determining just *that*," he was only mocking Hegelian thinking in that passage.[49]

Albert Murray has very forcefully argued that the "mainstream is not white but mulatto,"[50] but literary pluralists of our time would like to construct a mosaic of ethnic stories that relies on the supposed permanence, individuality, and homogeneity of each ancestral tradition and has no space for the syncretistic nature of so much of American literary and cultural life. Ironically, while the pluralist argument is often phrased against a racist target, literary pluralists share their dislike of mixings and

48. Horace M. Kallen, "Alain Locke and Cultural Pluralism," *Journal of Philosophy*, 54 (February 1958), 119–120.

49. James, *A Pluralistic Universe*, pp. 5 and 48.

50. Albert Murray, *The Omni-Americans: New Perspectives on Black Experience and American Culture* (New York: Avon, 1970), p. 112.

"impurities" with the old nativists who, too, worked very hard at ignoring not only certain ethnic groups but also the polyethnic mixings in American culture.[51] Instead of accepting the possibility of a text's many mothers, pluralists often settle for the construction of one immutable grandfather. This bias in favor of purity and monoethnic myths of origins makes it far from unusual now for Americanists to publically profess the belief that only ethnic insiders are entitled to criticize literature from a given "ethnic tradition"; yet is this "biological insiderism"— advanced in the name of pluralistic diversity—not merely a timid approach that freezes ethnicity not only in the texts, but also in the interpreters themselves? Despite his claims for static ethnic persistence Kallen was ethnicized in a modern environment, as a result of reading and by an act of will rather than in the spirit of his own father. His ethnicity was a product of a transethnic experience of modernism, not of any tradition or "ethnic experience."

If we approach American literature, ethnic or mainstream, with an awareness of the dynamic nature of ethnogenesis,[52] we might arrive at an understanding of writing as more than a reflection of ethnically diverse "experiences." Instead, literature could become recognizable as a productive force that may Americanize *and* ethnicize readers, listeners, or other cultural participants. It is precisely this aspect that has often been emphasized by American writers who, from the Jewish American assimilationist Mary Antin to the black nationalist Malcolm X,[53]

51. The writer Jean Toomer is a good example here. He may have been excluded from older literary histories because he was black, but the new concern for Toomer as a black writer does injustice to Toomer's polyethnic ancestry and artistic interests. As Nellie McKay writes persuasively, Toomer "was convinced that in the melting pot of America, the people of this nation were evolving into a racial mixture that would make it not only inaccurate but impossible to select out strains of racial or ethnic heritage eventually" (Nellie Y. McKay, *Jean Toomer, Artist: A Study of His Literary Life and Work, 1894–1936* [Chapel Hill: University of North Carolina Press, 1984], p. 244).

52. See chapter 2 of my forthcoming *Beyond Ethnicity: Consent and Descent in American Culture* (New York: Oxford University Press, in press).

53. Antin, *Promised Land*, pp. xi–xii; and Malcolm X, *The Autobiography of Malcolm X* (New York: Grove Press, 1966), pp. 169–190, with the assistance of Alex Haley.

have emphasized the importance of reading in their ethnic conversion experiences.[54]

The additive approach that puts abstract group after group into a volume not only avoids generalizations and synthesis, but also cannot come to terms with American culture which abounds in ethnogenesis on the basis of transethnic contacts like the ones that were sketched here. Many other models of new transethnic approaches exist that focus on cultural interaction and ethnicization and avoid static and abstract uses of ethnic groups. Two recent books are of special interest in this respect as they illustrate these new approaches to American literature. In his excellent study *Through a Glass Darkly: Ethnic Semiosis in American Literature* (1984), William Boelhower, drawing on texts from Chief Joseph's (Heinmot Tooyalaket's) 1887 speech and Henry James's *The American Scene* to Maya Angelou's *I Know Why the Caged Bird Sings*, pursues new paths of ethnic inquiry in a semiotic context. Stressing semiosis as the production of ethnic

---

54. Even contemporary advocates of pluralism and proponents of the power of ethnicity sometimes go further than literary critics in recognizing cultural texts as a shaping force of supposedly "natural" group affiliations. Thus Andrew Greeley writes: "Subscriptions to any two of the following are sufficient to guarantee one membership at least on the margins of this ethnic group: *The New York Times, Commentary, Partisan Review, Saturday Review, The New York Review of Books, The Atlantic* (but not *Harper's*), *Dissent, The New Republic,* and *The Nation.* In case of doubt, a subscription to *The New York Review of Books* alone will suffice" (Andrew M. Greeley, "Intellectuals as an 'Ethnic Group,' " *New York Times Magazine,* 12 July 1970, p. 22). Greeley's not altogether facetious ethnic identification-by-subscription, ironically published in *The New York Times Magazine,* was echoed by Michael Novak, who, originally writing in the safety of *Harper's,* defines "ruling classes" parenthetically as "subscribers to the *New Yorker,* I suppose" (Michael Novak, *The Rise of the Unmeltable Ethnics: Politics and Culture in the Seventies* [New York: Macmillan, 1975], p. 68). Jules Chametzky observed that ethnic identity may not be "what you do or what you are but an image created by what you read or at least know about" (Jules Chametzky, "Styron's Sophie's Choice, Jews and Other Marginals, and the Mainstream," *Prospects,* 9 [1985], 435–436). Even Kallen's supposedly instinctual repugnance at interracial dinners may be seen as an extreme form of Shakespeare exegesis, since in his letter to Wendell he explicitly invokes Shylock's disclaimer: "I will buy with you, sell with you, talk with you, walk with you, and so following; but I will not eat with you, drink with you, nor pray with you" (*The Merchant of Venice* I.iii.35ff.).

signs,[55] Boelhower argues that "advocates of the multi-ethnic paradigm now often repeat the essentialist errors of their mono-cultural predecessors in attempting to trace out a blueprint of clear and distinct and ultimately reified ethnic categories" (*B.* 20). Instead, he directs our attention to the question: "Who can predict when the ethnic difference will surface and why?" (*B.* 31). Among Boelhower's many interesting conclusions is the following insight:

While there is a reasonably definable encyclopedic core to every ethnic culture, it is theoretically impossible to define its intensional limits. As long as there is an ethnic subject, any object can function as ethnic even in a non-ethnic context. (*B.* 105)

For Boelhower, "there is no parthenogenesis of ethnic codes. One ethnic novel or a particular encyclopedia does not account for the production of another." Therefore, "there is no unilat-eral aesthetic starting point for the multi-ethnic critic" (*B.* 35).

Similarly aiming for a transethnic perspective, Mary Dear-born has synthesized the fragmented approaches to ethnic and women's studies in her study, *Pocahontas' Daughters: Gender and Ethnicity in American Culture* (1985). Interpreting so-called ethnic and mainstream women writers from Frances Harper and Mary Antin to Gertrude Stein (another William James student) comparatively and against the background of literary criticism and ethnic theory, Dearborn suggests that strong similarities "exist between the male and female literary traditions." Viewing her own work as a contribution toward reconstructing the canon, Dearborn concludes that it is useful to look at ethnic women writers in an American context "to see the ways in which they try to rewrite, expand, revise, subvert that tradition and the ways in which they have been excluded from that canon."[56] A growing number of literary scholars are pursuing postpluralist, postethnic approaches in studying American literature. Eth-nogenesis, the emergence of ethnic groupings, sometimes with

55. Boelhower, *Through a Glass Darkly,* pp. 23, 83, 107. All further ref-erences to this work appear in the text, cited parenthetically as *B.*
56. Dearborn, Afterword.

the help of literary texts, is now being studied together with efforts at constructing myths of persistence. Ethnicity is being recognized as a dynamic phenomenon that needs theoretical and practical understanding—without the reified nativist and belligerently antithetical closures of the past.

Since the omission of Frederick Douglass' *Narrative* from American literary historiography was the point of departure here, the book may now serve as a concluding illustration for the process of ethnogenesis that transcends popular constructions of purism. There is an often-analyzed individual development which culminates in Douglass' creation of an American Christ-like *hero,* who undergoes a rebirth experience *despite* his enslavement; and there is a collective, and ethnic, aspect to Douglass' growing sense of selfhood as a living *man,* part of a living community of people who should not be slaves. The collective aspect is best grasped as the development of a sense of sacred peoplehood through a shared cultural activity. It is most clearly spelled out by Douglass when he describes the effects of the slaves' songs at the Great House Farm:

They would then sing most exultingly the following words:—

> "I am going away to the Great House Farm!
> O, yea! O, yea! O!"

This they would sing, as a chorus, to words which to many would seem unmeaning jargon, but which, nevertheless, were full of meaning to themselves . . . [These songs] told a tale of woe which was then altogether beyond my feeble comprehension; . . . they breathed the prayer and complaint of souls boiling over with the bitterest anguish. Every tone was a testimony against slavery, and a prayer to God for deliverance from chains . . . To those songs I trace my first glimmering conception of the dehumanizing character of slavery.[57]

As Douglass' account makes clear, the songs contribute to the process of ethnogenesis, of emerging peoplehood. Though the texts need contain no specific reference to freedom (many songs did) and though the songs need not be of "pure" African

---

57. Frederick Douglass, *Narrative of the Life of Frederick Douglass an American Slave, Written by Himself,* ed. Benjamin Quarles (1845; rpt. Cambridge, Mass.: Belknap Press of Harvard University Press, 1960), pp. 36–37.

origins (Lawrence Levine wrote about the "irrelevancy" of the question of origins "for an understanding of consciousness"),[58] the very act of collective singing is a revelation about the nature of things and a bonding process for the heterogeneous slaves who are united in a feeling of brotherhood through the ritual of singing. The sense of a dynamically emerging group identity is acquired, in a precise historical setting, and on the basis of words and music. Many other observers, among them ethnic outsiders like the literary historian and collector of spirituals Thomas Wentworth Higginson, noticed the centripetal force of "these peculiar but haunting slave songs."[59] Higginson's observation interested Alain Locke on whose materials Margaret Just Butcher's book *The Negro in American Culture* was based, which includes this reference. Butcher/Locke also stressed that Douglass "was far in advance of any narrowly racialist stand"[60]— including, we might add, that of many literary historians and pluralists. For the new literary histories that are in the making the time had come to follow Douglass' lead and to go beyond pure pluralism.

58. Lawrence W. Levine, *Black Culture and Black Consciousness: Afro-American Folk Thought from Slavery to Freedom* (New York: Oxford University Press, 1977), p. 24.

59. Margaret Just Butcher, *The Negro in American Culture: Based on Materials Left by Alain Locke,* 2nd ed. (New York: Knopf, 1973), p. 26. See also Levine, p. 29.

60. Butcher, p. 148.

ROBERT VON HALLBERG

American Poet-Critics since 1945

Imagine a time when a young poet looks to the critical essays published in journals with eagerness, excitement even. Critics would then genuinely influence the poems being written. Young poets would be learning their craft from the models also dominating the academic curriculum, and college students would perhaps not be mystified by the poems of their near-contemporaries—to say nothing of how their instructors would approach contemporary poetry. Critics would then lead the audience for poetry, and poets would be in an indirect relationship with their readers. This would be the sort of culture in which questions of whether literature counts for anything at all might seem implausible. It would also, of course, be one in which literary conventions, period styles, in short, orthodoxies would be easy to establish. Once orthodoxies were in place, one might well have good reason to expect the formation of an avant-garde to move against those conventions, for without established conventions, the last twenty-five years have shown, there can be no avant-garde. And in American literature the formation of an avant-garde is a sure sign of impending literary change, of movement in literary history; avant-gardes do well by us. In fact, the young poet was Robert Lowell, the time was 1937, and the critics were Allen Tate, T. S. Eliot, R. P. Blackmur, and

Yvor Winters. But that was a different literary world from the one poets know now.

The critics were all poet-critics, and this is my point. Along with Ezra Pound and John Crowe Ransom, they were the writers who for about twenty-five years explained what modernism had meant. They are all long gone, and their places have not been filled. Indeed their places have been lost, because the present literary culture has a radically different order from that of the prewar years. The greatest change has been the professionalization of literary studies as institutions of higher education have proliferated. In 1937 the Modern Language Association had 4,200 members and a budget of $23,000; at this writing there are 26,751 members and the expenses for 1983 were well over $3 million. In 1941, the distinguished Anglo-Saxonist and bibliographer A. G. Kennedy, then chairman of the Stanford English Department, told Yvor Winters that poetry and scholarship do not mix, and that Winters' publications had disgraced the department. Winters took this disagreement seriously and tried unsuccessfully to leave Stanford. Two decades later he would talk at the weekly Stanford department luncheons of Airedales and fruit trees. Once one of his colleagues said, "Yvor, you always talk about gardening and dogs, and never about literature." "That's because none of you knows anything about literature," he is said to have replied. The animosity between poets and academicians is felt on both sides of the divide, and it is nothing new, though lately it seems to have intensified.

The most influential critics of the postwar years have all been professors, not poets: M. H. Abrams, Northrop Frye, Wayne Booth, Harold Bloom, Hugh Kenner, and Raymond Williams. These critics have rather little to say to young poets about how poems should be written; poets learn their craft elsewhere. But the critics certainly have much to say to aspiring students about how literature should be criticized. There are conventions governing the writing of literary criticism as there were conventions governing the composition of verse in 1937. Now one can recognize period styles in literary criticism perhaps more easily than one can in poetry. If there are orthodoxies in place now on the poetry scene, they prevail over only one small camp; other camps are unmoved by each other's orthodoxies. There is little justification for speaking of an avant-garde in poetry now, and little expectation of one forming in the foreseeable future, exactly because the present literary culture is so diverse and amorphous. There is really nothing now for an avant-garde to attack, and thus little reason to expect marked change in the near future. The one label that is often used to identify the postwar literary culture expresses this absence of a center all too plainly: postmodern, we say, pathetically at a loss for definition.

Northrop Frye, among others, has said that criticism is an art. The conventions prevailing over this art indicate tacit agreement between readers and writers. Of course only weak writers are ruled by conventions, but aren't we professors mostly weak writers? How many of us really revise conventions, change the received ideas about what constitutes legitimate literary criticism? Most of us dance to old tunes, or to easily acceptable variations on the favorites. We are professors, after all, at least as loyal to the institutions that pay us as we realize. Aspiring doctoral candidates at, say, the University of Virginia observe the range of professional examples, and go and do largely likewise. We praise their inventiveness, and feel confirmed, I guess, by the mildness of their divergence from our examples. I don't want to sound entirely cynical about this process; poets as well as literary scholars learn from their craft by imitating mentors. Examples legitimate. Paradigms, we might say, to sound subtle on this score. What we mean are models; we all had them. They become especially powerful when a generation reaches consensus about the worthy models, and generations often do just that. Literary scholars of the last twenty-five years seem to have agreed that Abrams' *The Mirror and the Lamp*, Frye's *Anatomy of Criticism*, and Booth's *Rhetoric of Fiction*, to pick obvious examples, were the sort of books whose merits should be plain to us all, regardless of where our specialties lie.

This is not to say that Abrams, Frye, Booth, and others have imposed a set of conventions on a younger generation of scholars seeking legitimation, but rather that they have shown how nicely some procedures can pay off. One day some scholars will analyze their procedures from a distance greater than what I can now achieve. I don't even want to look closely at the methods that enabled their achievements, perhaps because I am old enough to still be under their spell. I want only to highlight how different they have been as models for young literary critics from the models of the 1940s and 1950s, and how much the range of professional literary criticism has narrowed lately.

Conventions are like roadsigns; they come at the outset of a long stretch. This is the way it is in poems too: metrical norms, for example, tend to be clearest in the first lines of a poem. For critics, those norms are set in the opening sentences of a preface or first chapter. Professors like to begin by saying what they have not achieved, lest they be attacked for patent failures. Northrop Frye spoke of his most ambitious and influential book as "a trial or incomplete attempt," nothing more than "suggestions" intended to be of some practical use.[1] Who can say that one has failed to deliver when one sets out so modestly?

But the modesty of professors is like the good intentions of the damned—not negligible, but not the last word either. Frye claims not to have succeeded, but to have indicated "the possibility of a synoptic view of the scope, theory, principles, and techniques of literary criticism." He identifies his "primary aim" and his "secondary aim." His book claims not to have done the

1. The following works, listed here in alphabetical order, are cited in the essay. M. H. Abrams, *The Mirror and the Lamp: Romantic Theory and the Critical Tradition* (New York: Oxford University Press, 1953); Matthew Arnold, *Culture and Anarchy,* ed. J. Dover Wilson (1869; rpt. Cambridge: Cambridge University Press, 1969); Arnold, "The Study of Poetry," in *Selected Poetry and Prose,* ed. Frederick L. Mulhauser (1880; rpt. New York: Holt, Rinehart & Winston, 1953); Robert Bly, *Talking All Morning* (Ann Arbor: University of Michigan Press, 1980); J. V. Cunningham, *The Collected Essays* (Chicago: Swallow Press, 1976); Northrop Frye, *The Anatomy of Criticism: Four Essays* (Princeton: Princeton University Press, 1957); Donald Hall, *Goatfoot, Milktongue, Twinbird: Interviews, Essays, and Notes on Poetry, 1970–1976* (Ann Arbor: University of Michigan Press, 1978); Robert Hass, *Twentieth-Century Pleasures: Prose on Poetry* (New York: Ecco Press, 1984); Randall Jarrell, *Poetry and the Age* (New York: Farrar, Straus & Giroux, 1953); Jarrell, *The Third Book of Criticism* (New York: Farrar, Straus & Giroux, 1965); Howard Nemerov, *Poetry and Fiction: Essays* (New Brunswick: Rutgers University Press, 1963); Robert Pinsky, *The Situation of Poetry: Contemporary Poetry and Its Traditions* (Princeton: Princeton University Press, 1976); Kenneth Rexroth, *Assays* (New York: New Directions, 1961); Karl Shapiro, *In Defense of Ignorance* (New York: Random House, 1960).

job adequately but to have attempted the Grand Thing, and to have known all along exactly where the book was aimed. One can sometimes sense a professor's pride just in the syntax, as in this passage from Abrams.

> To pose and answer aesthetic questions in terms of the relation of art to the artist, rather than to external nature, or to the audience, or to the internal requirements of the work itself, was the characteristic tendency of modern criticism up to a few decades ago, and it continues to be the propensity of a great many—perhaps the majority—of critics today. This point of view is very young measured against the twenty-five-hundred-year history of the Western theory of art, for its emergence as a comprehensive approach to art, shared by a large number of critics, dates back not much more than a century and a half.

One hears a desire to be exhaustive in the way Abrams' clauses accrue, enumerating alternatives, and the desire to be fair and accurate in the way numbers are tallied: tendencies should be characteristic, and a term like "a great many" must be nailed down a bit, to perhaps a majority. Abrams has a historian's concern for representativeness of evidence, because he wishes to generalize. From this viewpoint there was for twenty-five hundred years only one Western theory of art. The only challenge to this theory that counts for the scholar of literary history is a comprehensive theory shared by a large number of critics. (The subject here is not what a particular artist may have understood about his or her art.) To Abrams' demanding eye, a century and a half of consensus is a distinctly limited historical phenomenon, though Eliot and Pound might have died with smiles if they had thought that their writing would participate in such a consensus. Abrams takes in millennia on the one hand and a few decades on the other. He too was plainly out to do something grand.

There is no surprise in saying that poet-critics dance to different tunes. But during the last forty years some of the differences have often been extreme. Here are the opening sentences of an essay by Robert Hass:

> I told a friend I was going to try to write something about prosody and he said, "Oh great." The two-beat phrase is a very American form of terminal irony. A guy in a bar in Charlottesville turned to me once

and said, loudly but confidentially, "Ahmo find me a woman and fuck her twenty ways to Sunday." That's also a characteristic rhythm: ahmo FIND ME a WOman / and FUCK her TWENty WAYS till SUNday. Three beats and then a more emphatic four. A woman down the bar doubled the two-beat put-down. She said, "Good luck, asshole." Rhythms and rhythmic play make texture in our lives but they are hard to talk about and besides people don't like them to be talked about.

Among students of poetry, prosody is often wrongly spoken of as especially dry and pedantic. Hass begins with this sort of anecdote because he knows that the scholarly discussion of prosody is just what he wants to avoid, and his readers should know this at the outset. He begins outside of academia, at a bar near one of the most distinguished English departments, where he then worked. Vulgarity seems to be his point too. The power of rhythm in language can be coarse, brutal even; it does not depend upon literary history. Literary history depends upon organisms. And criticism does not depend upon universities. To a poet-critic instances do not need always to be representative of a larger class, so long as they are telling in themselves. Hass's criticism often proceeds by anecdote. He would rather be thought of as a narrator than an explainer. By beginning with this particular anecdote, he implies a measure of hostility against those conventions of academic criticism that lead to what we speak of as powerful explanations, for as literary art most academic criticism might be called many things before one got around to the word powerful.

When we speak of powerful explanations, we usually mean to refer to a compelling logic linking a series of propositions. Critics like Frye, Harold Bloom, Kenneth Burke, and a few others who have elaborated systems to support practical criticism, enjoy a special prestige among many literary scholars, especially younger ones—and the sharp distrust of most poet-critics. We like to speak of critical method, as though the best critics proceed according to rules of some sort. Karl Shapiro claimed that the "honest critic has no system and stands in no dread of contradicting himself," but Shapiro was admittedly anti-intellectual. Howard Nemerov, who has in fact been influenced by Burke, wrote of the objective of one of his own critical books, "Critical method. To try not to have one." We know well where this argument comes from, and where it leads, which is why it arouses our misgivings. Matthew Arnold took wicked glee in repeatedly conceding his limits to his critics:

An unpretending writer, without a philosophy based on interdependent, subordinate, and coherent principles, must not presume to indulge himself too much in generalities. He must keep close to the level ground of common fact, the only safe ground for understandings without a scientific equipment.

About twelve years later he complained that "Critics give themselves great labour to draw out what in the abstract constitutes the characters of a high quality of poetry. It is much better simply to have recourse to concrete examples." And the touchstones followed, consigning our hope of explanation to the mist of a seriousness that somehow transcends principles. Contemporary poet-critics have not taken Arnold's extreme position often. Indeed they have used what methodicalness they could muster as a means, if not of discovery, of argument. Randall Jarrell explained this procedure in 1952:

It is true that a critical method can help us neither to read nor to judge; still, it is sometimes useful in pointing out to the reader a few gross discrete reasons for thinking a good poem good—and it is invaluable, almost indispensable, in convincing a reader that a good poem is bad, or a bad one good. (The best critic who ever lived could not *prove* that the *Iliad* is better than *Trees;* the critic can only state his belief persuasively, and hope that the reader of the poem will agree.

Although we rarely read systematic criticism written by poet critics, they are in fact far more direct about stating their premises than academic critics. Poet-critics often say something, for instance, about what they think poetry is or does.

The poem, new or old, should be able to help us, if only to help us by delivering the relief that something has been understood, or even seen, well.   (Robert Pinsky)

There is a great difference between such a statement and a critical method, but poet-critics are forthright as well in speaking of the kind of criticism they wish to practice:

A work of art is the embodiment of an intention. To realize an intention in language is the function of the writer. To realize from language the intention of the author is the function of the reader or the critic, and his method is historical or philological interpretation.   (J. V. Cunningham)

By comparison with the explanations of method or first principles one reads in the works of academic critics, these statements are strikingly unmetaphorical and direct; there is nothing fancy here, above all no striving after novel formulation. If these critics are talking about life in general, as they often do, one can expect the same sort of directness: "Humaneness is the fine art of enjoying other people" (Kenneth Rexroth). They allow themselves the pleasure of putting grand things simply. And when defining life rather than just literature, they often do go after fresh conceptions and formulations.

It seems to me that we all live our lives in the light of primary acts of imagination, images or sets of images that get us up in the morning and move us about our days. I do not think anybody can live without one, for very long, without suffering intensely from deadness or futility . . . Images are powers: It seems to me quite possible that the arsenal of nuclear weapons exists, as Armageddon has always existed, to intensify life. It is what Rilke says, that the love of death as an other is the great temptation and failure of imagination.   (Robert Hass)

Literary criticism cannot tell us as much as speculation about life in general; it is a thoroughly limited affair, poet-critics tend to think. After writing at length about Whitman's merit, Jarrell wrote:

Critics have to spend half their time reiterating whatever ridiculously obvious things their age or the critics of their age have found it necessary to forget: they say despairingly, at parties, that Wordsworth is a great poet . . . There is something essentially ridiculous about critics, anyway: what is good is good without our saying so, and beneath all our majesty we know this.

Explanations of literature are at base rhetorical, aimed at the misunderstandings of a particular moment. In time the value of literary works becomes clear; the critic's job is useful only in the short run. He or she will ultimately not be needed, and should never really be believed anyway, since a critic speaks always for effect.

If someone has a good enough eye for an explanation he finally sees nothing inexplicable, and can begin every sentence with that phrase dearest to all who professionally understand: *It is no accident that . . .* We should love explanations well, but the truth better; and often the truth is that there *is* no explanation, that so far as we know it is an accident that . . . The motto of the city of Hamburg is: *Navigare necesse est, vivere non necesse.* A critic might say to himself: for me to know *what* the work of art is, is necessary; for me to explain *why* it is what it is, is not always necessary nor always possible.   (Jarrell)

We like to think that evaluative principles especially, but interpretative ones too, should be spelled out, and that particular judgments or claims should follow logically from those principles, though we know they often don't, which is one reason for speaking of "insights." Poet-critics characteristically begin with less lofty expectations: a phrase like "crisis of criticism" is more amusing to them than to professors. For poet-critics, criticism is an improvisatory art, unpredictable, full of inconsistencies, never better than approximate. "Criticism, in whatever fancy dress," Nemerov said, "remains an art of opinion, and though the opinion should be supported by evidence, even that relation is a questionable one."

What then counts as justification? Reading and a sense of fit between what a critic says and an experience of the text. A standard trope for poet-critics is to beg off of explanation in favor of a plea for a reading.

Nothing I say about these poems can make you see what they are like, or what the Frost that matters most is like; if you read them you will see.   (Jarrell)

We come to a point in these later books where [James] Wright's poetry is so compressed with self-reference, with recurrent meditation on these images and themes, that tracing them belongs to long reading and not the ten thumbs of criticism.   (Hass)

Jarrell wrote mostly appreciative criticism; he stops himself with a reminder of the impossibility of adequate explanation. But

Hass halts because it would be just tedious to go on with the sort of patient explication that scholar-critics often produce. Both writers agree, though, that a critic ought not to push too hard; one should defer to the act of reading, and it is rhetorically important not to be tardy with that deferral. Scholar-critics all too often press for conviction on the page.

When Jarrell in 1952 said that critics are rightly methodical only in order to be persuasive, he had a broad sense of the rhetoric of criticism: persuasion "covers everything from a sneer to statistics." "Vary a little, vary a little!" he said. Range is the issue: how rich are the stylistic resources of contemporary scholar-critics? Though they are their own overseers, they sometimes seem to mine only a single vein of lead. Their chief concern often is the establishment of their own authority and the maintenance of consistency and seriousness. When B. H. Haggin, the music critic, admitted that he had changed his mind about some of Stravinsky's work, Jarrell remarked: "This sort of admission of error, of change, makes us trust a critic as nothing else but omniscience could." You might say that it is relatively easy to admit to short-sightedness, once one has made the appropriate adjustment of vision. Yet the poet-critics sometimes just make a point of saying that they haven't quite mastered their subjects. "I don't entirely understand it [Marianne Moore's "Armour's Undermining Modesty"]," Jarrell wrote, "but what I understand I love, and what I don't understand I love almost better." And when Hass gets to the topic of sexual violence in Lowell's poems, he says simply, "I'm not sure how to talk about it." These are not critics in danger of taking themselves or their work too seriously. Cunningham gathered his essays together in one volume in 1976, and this is the sentence that introduces over thirty years of literary criticism: "There is less to be said about literature than has been said, and this book adds a little more." He would not have said the same about his poetry, or that of others, but criticism is a minor art.

Many recent poet-critics make an effort to seem thoroughly unmethodical, as I've suggested. The beginning of Hass's essay on prosody is the clearest example. Then there is Rexroth starting an essay on American racism: "Two documents on my desk."

No thesis statement there. These writers make their criticism seem circumstantial and personal. A critic begins with his or her own immediate situation—a cluttered desk, last night's reading—and proceeds by keeping close to one experience of reading, not to an argument or even a single train of thought. "It should be made clear, in a sort of parenthesis, that . . . " (Rexroth). "I should like now to seem to digress" (Cunningham). Between paragraphs these writers often shift gears quickly and without warning: to seem to move around unpredictably is quite alright for them. Jarrell, who seems to me the most gifted poet-critic of the last forty years, was frankly impressionistic and appreciative: "if you can't feel any of this, you *are* a Convention of Sociologists." The test for him—and frequently for other poet-critics—is feeling and belief, which is of course right for critics whose faith in argument, logic, and system is restrained. Part of what they gain here is a way of talking about those poems that are direct and explicit, or pathetic— Hardy and Whitman are instances. Scholar-critics have done rather poorly by their sorts of poems. Logic, method, consistency, coherence of argument are sometimes not helpful in describing accurately a power or quality of feeling.

To say that one type of critic has greater rhetorical range than another is a significant matter: an interpreter's job is often to tune critical prose as closely as possible to the qualities of a poem, a speech, or a narrative. By accepting the conventions of academic criticism, one can wind up agreeing in advance to represent certain texts only inadequately. Poet-critics, I think, are likelier than scholar critics to remember that criticism is an art. One of the corruptions that tempts most artists is specialization. A poet can learn to write one kind of poem—Merwin would be a perfect example—and spend his or her talent reaping the fruit of a single lesson, but ambitious writers often try to extend their command of the various kinds of literary art. Something similar can be seen in literary criticism.

Poet-critics try to vary their tone or rhetoric to suit a particular occasion. Rather than specializing, as professors routinely do, in earnestness and judiciousness, they often write so as to hold open their options at the poles opposite to earnestness, judiciousness, and civility. Speaking of academic taste in contemporary literature, Jarrell wrote:

Everybody has observed this in scholars, who feel that live authors, as such, are self-evidently inferior to dead ones; though a broadminded scholar will look like an X-ray machine at such a writer as Thomas Mann, and feel, relenting: "He's as good as dead."

Or Hass on the academic literary sensibility of the late 1960s:

Listening to lectures on literature and literary theory by a generation of professors in love with Henry James and Virginia Woolf, one of your friends had said he wanted to write a book called *Crude Materialism Reconsidered.*

And on the extreme seriousness of Lowell's early poems:

It is probably great writing in the sense that the state of mind couldn't be rendered more exactly. But I wondered about the state of mind and said a small prayer to the small gods—hilarity and carnality—that I could escape it.   (Hass)

In an essay on *The Clerk's Tale,* Cunningham provides an example of the Fiction of the Extreme Case: "There is that classic of the two homosexuals on a street corner. A blonde walks by, wind blowing against her dress, and one says to the other, 'Sometimes makes you wish you were a lesbian, doesn't it?' "

Set alongside of René Wellek, these writers just don't sound serious— and they are impolite. Moreover, these are representative passages (that is, I have a long list of jokes I'd love to quote). Nemerov said that in criticism he tries "to write all the dirty jokes and mean epigrams into the first draft, and then eliminate all but the irresistible ones in the fair copy." Humor and frivolity are some of the literary resources that poet-critics claim as legitimately their own. Bold exclamation ("There are things I love here"—Hass) is within bounds too. And even name-calling: Delmore Schwartz spoke of Johnson on "Lycidas" as "completely stupid"; and Rexroth called Whistler an "intellectual gigolo" and James a "provincial snob." They are often impatient critics. One of the conventions their examples enforce is to talk of literature with the same terms and concerns one has for the activities of one's friends and enemies. The connection between literary and ethical judgment is constantly in the background of this sort of criticism, and some of these writers, like Cunningham, push it forward regularly.

This separation between two kinds of criticism has led not merely to a parting in the rhetoric of contemporary literary criticism, but perhaps more important to a specializing in certain areas of inquiry. There are literary critical questions which poet-critics dwell on, but which academic critics mainly ignore. If these were arcane or trivial questions, there would be no cause for concern, but they are rather important. How many professors have asked about the role of poetry in contemporary American society? This has often been the most insistent question for poet-critics, for reasons that are plain. Likewise academics have indeed discussed the role of literary criticism in recent American society. Literature, or poetry at least, has lost the role it played, say, among educated people of Victorian England. Poetry is now looked after chiefly in universities. And just as an academic citizen need not be shy about ignorance of elementary particles, there is no reason to suppose that a properly educated member of a modern university knows anything about seventeenth-century English poetry—or about the poems of his or her contemporaries. Poetry is just one more specialty among others. And poets, as Jarrell observed, like scientists have celebrity status. Their conversations are taped, their lives remembered, their presences missed, but the poems are seldom read. In the last forty years one writer after another—Jarrell, Nemerov, Delmore Schwartz, Karl Shapiro—has set this charge down with irony or grief. The academics who read these writers have nodded knowingly and felt uplifted by an awareness of their superiority to those cretins who might misspell Jarrell. One consequence of this lament is worth pausing over now, though.

Barbara Herrnstein Smith has noticed how little attention literary scholars have devoted to the problem of evaluation in criticism. Frye has notoriously claimed that evaluation is not our business, and the history of recent literary scholarship indicates that he was preaching to the converted. Poet-critics, though, have never given up the task of evaluating poetry, sorting out and ranking, partly because the tradition of Samuel

Johnson, Matthew Arnold, Edgar Allan Poe, T. S. Eliot, Ezra Pound, and Yvor Winters sets that as the top item on the agenda, but also because poet-critics are by default the custodians of contemporary literature. With only a few exceptions, academic critics are content to keep their distance from the bulk of non-canonical writing that must finally be sorted out more or less intelligently. The evaluative criteria that poet-critics have used are especially involved with the sense that the role of poetry in contemporary culture has been badly eroded. In nineteenth-century England, poetry was expected to address the permanent concerns of us all—death (winter), new life (spring), love, the thrill of surprise. Poets were also expected to comment on the most notable current events. What has been lost is the interest that such poems met with then. Now poet-critics pay particular attention to those poems which meet these once traditional expectations. Poems offering wisdom of a recognizable sort are praised or condemned by critics who take into account the cost of poetry losing a powerful place in contemporary culture. Poems that plainly—and technique is the measure of plainness—take up where the modernists left off (poets like Charles Olson, Robert Creeley, Robert Duncan, and John Ashbery) are made to shoulder the burden of poetry being outside the mainstream of the culture. Some critics condemn James Merrill, Richard Wilbur, and John Hollander, say, for complicity with Babbitt; others have charged the avant-gardists with turning readers away from poetry. In the daily job of evaluating the great mass of contemporary writing, what one sees is a polarization of judgment motivated by dissatisfaction with how little poets have to say to the matters that are obviously central to American culture now. The line that has formed in evaluative criticism is not between good and better poets; that might be a refined distinction. Now we hear that poems are more or less authentic; the alternative is ethical: inauthentic poems are almost wicked. That this distinction is crude rhetorically as well as critically, goes without saying, I think—said one professor to another.

The writing of poetry has lately been discussed in terms of absolutes. When one poet can be praised as authentic, another can be dismissed as a fraud, and the categories of criticism are stiffly moralized. This is a direct consequence of the recent anxiety about the loss of an audience. "For whom does the poet write?" Jarrell's response: "For whom do you do good? Are you kind to your daughter because in the end someone will pay you for being [kind to her]?" Poetry, like virtue, he said, is its own reward. When poets become too concerned with their reception—as they nearly all are—they risk corruption.

Karl Shapiro has insisted on the duty of poets to address themselves to "the present *condition* of the audience," but the example of Auden has discredited the evaluative criterion of contemporaneity. Auden was extremely successful at using just those subjects that most engaged his intellectual contemporaries, so he acquired a largeish readership. However, his career never issued in a major work; it rather petered out all too slowly with a series of slight books. "The best of causes," Jarrell wrote, "ruins as quickly as the worst; and the road to Limbo is paved with writers who have done everything—I am being sympathetic, not satiric—for the very best reasons." Even so intelligible a poet as Nemerov has damned Shapiro's efforts to make poets speak directly to their audience: "many warriors of the simplistic party wanted poetry to be simple only in order that they might despise it without discomfort, and . . . since winning this victory they have sensibly gone home to read some more novels."

There have been other poet-critics, though—Baraka, Wendell Berry, Denise Levertov, Adrienne Rich, and Kenneth Rexroth—who rather than lament poetry's alleged loss of audience have used critical prose to advocate political objectives. All of these writers have presumed that poets, if not poems, have a legitimate role in the formation of ideology. The books and essays they have written on racism, strip-mining, nuclear disarmament, women's rights, and anarchism have been widely read, and influential in the public discussion of these topics. Some of these writers have occasionally been criticized for intervening in extraliterary affairs. However, the history of literary criticism in English is the history of poet-critics, and they have traditionally written about contemporary political as well as literary issues. In this century the two obvious examples are Eliot and Pound, both of whom incidentally were moved to write about political, social, and economic issues by their experiences in the London literary milieu. Books like *After Strange Gods* (1934), *The Idea of a Christian Society* (1939), *Notes Toward the Definition of Culture* (1948), *ABC of Economics* (1933), *Jefferson and/or Mussolini* (1935), and *Guide to Kulchur* (1938) set some standards for later poet-critics. First, Eliot and Pound successfully implicate literary and political judgment. Second, beyond making outrageous statements from time to time, they criticized not only reigning politicians but the complacencies of the literary sensibility as well. And, third, their cultural criticism was broadly synthetic; they attempted to form arguments that incorporated at once literary, political, historical, philosophical, social, and economic concerns.

Comparable works by recent poet-critics do not measure up entirely to these standards. It would take more space than I have to assess how finely literary and political judgments have been articulated to each other, but no one familiar with the easy way in which metrical forms are commonly associated with authoritarianism can doubt either the will of recent poet-critics to make such connections or the need for refinement in this matter. And although writing against racism, strip mining, nuclear weaponry, the systematic oppression of women, and the excesses of the state's authority does not broadly challenge the generally liberal predilections of the contemporary literary sensibility, these writers have often turned their pens against their readers. Denise Levertov, for instance, in criticizing the faint loyalties of American liberals, has argued that the sympathy of New York intellectuals for Russian dissidents is all too easy. And Adrienne Rich has claimed that the same skeptical scrutiny that liberals have brought to bear on the oppressiveness of class structure and of racism should be directed at what she calls the "institution of heterosexuality." Rexroth repeatedly said that a critic ought to be alert to the soft spots in the intellectual culture; highbrow movies, for example, are "our kind of corn, designed specifically to take in just our caste."

Where recent poet-critics most plainly fall short of the precedents set by Eliot and Pound is in regard to the scope of their prose. On the one hand, Cunningham, Nemerov, and Rexroth constantly validate their literary judgments by referring to ordinary experience. On the other, Charles Olson may be alone

among his contemporaries in recognizing that a poet-critic properly writes about more or less everything at once—poems, history, philosophy, geology. The most ambitious prose written by
recent poet-critics has been directed more at single issues, because there are audiences for such books. Although American
literary scholarship is big business, literary journalism is not.
When poet-critics write cultural criticism they are now com-
pelled by the market to address nonliterary political interest-
groups.

The severing of relations between poet-critics and academic
critics has brought the greater loss to the professors—or so I
see it. But then I myself am a professor, so my concern is rightly
with my own kind. Still, the loss has been by no means one-
sided. The conventions of academic criticism are, after all, mostly
those of intellectual discourse brought to bear on a particular
discipline. Poet-critics are not always helped by flying in the
face of these conventions, especially when they do so chiefly
out of willfulness. But willfulness has sometimes paid off. In
1945 Olson was unknown as a poet, known in Washington as a
political worker and administrator, and remembered around
Harvard as a promising young instructor who left abruptly; that
was when he wrote *Call Me Ishmael,* obviously a poet's book
on Melville. Pound helped him to publish it two years later,
and in 1950 he was ready to write "Projective Verse," an an-
tiacademic essay intended to turn around the writing of poetry
in America then. It took a decade but ultimately the essay had
its effect, less because its argument was compelling than because
its rhetoric was. Olson knew that to write as an academic advocate of free verse would affect no one writing poems in 1950.
He turned his back on academic prose and wrote as a poet-critic
in the line of Pound and Lawrence. Part of the price he paid
for his influence was an abiding temptation to achieve literary
success as a poet by indulging in what he knew to be loose
scholarship.

   In certain recent poet-critics one senses some bad faith, from
an intellectual point of view, with the entire project of literary
criticism. Poet-critics have certainly not stopped writing about

literature, but many of them have stopped trying to do so in ways that they would defend intellectually. The result is that as explanation some of what is written by poet-critics is simply embarrassing. Robert Bly, in a 1971 interview, attempted to explain American foreign policy of the Dulles years by employing what he takes as psychological terminology: "Some people apparently get trapped in one of the brains: a cold war militarist may be trapped in the reptile brain. It's no accident the peace was called the cold war because the hostility is basically an act of the reptile brain." Bly has been consistent in his anti-intellectual approach to literary criticism, and clear too about his debt to Lawrence the critic. No academic critic would admit to a wish to write a book "of unsupportable generalizations about things that interest us," and it seems to me that the professors have the advantage here. The explanations of literature put forward by Bly and others often seem, to an academic, decadent in that they purport to set our thinking in order without submitting to any discipline of thought whatsoever. That lack of discipline is accepted all too easily among poets. Donald Hall has expressed admiration for the way Bly

brings to the discussion of poetry all sorts of other disciplines, from brain research to anthropology. I don't care if he gets his facts wrong. He has, as he has been known to admit, a deficient sense of fact. He mistakes his sources, gets his facts wrong—and says exactly the right thing. Oh, the energy of his analogies! The intellectual *energy!* He's like a thousand horses stampeding.

Academics are notoriously wary of stampeding explanations, for just the reasons Hall acknowledges so blithely. Against this enthusiasm, there is something to be said for even the most pedestrian academic criticism: poets cannot afford to dispense with accuracy so easily without betraying the seriousness of their vocation.

There is some injustice, I know, in my citing a comment of Bly's from an interview. He should be judged as a critic principally by his essays—and his translations. Yet this is not so tricky a matter. Bly has published only one book of literary criticism, *Talking All Morning,* a collection of some essays and many interviews. And many of his contemporaries—Philip Levine, Robert Creeley, Ed Dorn—have similarly gathered their interviews into volumes, though earlier generations seem never to have thought of such a thing. The interview has evolved very recently as a genre of quasi-literary criticism. Every essayist knows that the most difficult part of writing expository prose is often weaving paragraphs together in a continuous, coherent argument. Interviews quickly do away with this burden on poet-critics: one can simply speak one's mind without regard for what adds up to an argument, or even a paragraph. Nor need one worry about citing evidence for a conclusion; one is after all being asked for opinions, remarks, not truth. Some, though not all, academic literary critics persist in the effort to write verifiably true statements about literature or literary history. In their eyes, Bly and others like him are not embarked upon the same project and do not deserve a hearing by students of literature. Although recent poets have published a great many interviews, very few would actually defend the worth of this particular form of commentary. It is common to read, as one does in Bly's book, sarcasm and disdain directed by the poets against their interviewers. And this too is a sign of bad faith.

I have talked freely of two separate kinds of critics writing two different kinds of commentary. That's not entirely accurate, from a scholarly point of view. Two of the poet-critics I've quoted, Cunningham and Pinsky, were in fact hired by my department in the same way that I was. And is John Hollander, whom I've not quoted, more a poet-critic or a Yale English professor? I don't care about the answer to this question; I take consolation in the question seeming somehow plausible. My real interest is not in sorting out scholars and poet-critics. The happier situation would be that they would be difficult to distinguish, that young literary scholars would be as likely to attend to the models of Pinsky, Hass, Jarrell, and Cunningham, as to those of Bloom, Paul de Man, and Geoffrey Hartman—that only personal choice and predisposition would be involved. As it stands, young scholars often think that one line of criticism is intellectually ambitious, in touch with philosophy, the most ambitious of intellectual disciplines, and the other is a reflection of how the contemporary literary culture has degenerated from some former glory. I think that poet-critics would now be timely models. They in fact have much to teach those who admire the various sorts of political and cultural criticism now in academic favor. There is a sense in which the work of Edward Said, Raymond Williams, and Terry Eagleton is more traditional in the eyes of literary history than what is routinely published in *PMLA*. And when contemporary leftist criticism is seen in this tradition, one understands how modest much of it is, for the problem of evaluation, which has been central to poet-critics, is as unexamined on the left as it is on the right of academic criticism.

ROBERT B. STEPTO

Distrust of the Reader
in Afro-American Narratives

> *"You know everything . . . A black mama birthed*
> *you, let you suck her titty, cleaned your dirty*
> *drawers, and you still look at us through paper*
> *and movie plots . . . 'Now this is the way it*
> *happened,' . . . I want you to* write *it on whatever*
> *part of your brain that ain't already covered with*
> *page print."*
>
> James Alan McPherson,
> *"The Story of a Scar"*

One does not have to read very far into the corpus of Afro-American letters to find countless examples of the exaltation of literacy and the written word. In Frederick Douglass' *Narrative* of 1845, he proclaims that learning his "A, B, C"—and over-hearing that, as a slave, he wasn't supposed to—was his "pathway from slavery to freedom." In Frances E. W. Harper's "Sketches of Southern Life" (1872), the persona of the "Aunt Chloe" poem, "Learning to Read," declares:

> So I got a pair of glasses,
>   And straight to work I went,
> And never stopped till I could read
>   The hymns and Testament.
>
> Then I got a little cabin,
>   A place to call my own—
> And I felt as independent
>   As a queen upon her throne.

Du Bois's *The Souls of Black Folk* (1903) offers many eloquent testimonials to literacy, including the famous passage that begins, "I sit with Shakespeare and he winces not." Richard Wright's *Black Boy* (1945) is essentially the chronicle of how, as a youth, the author/persona "burned to learn to read," partly so that he might leave the South for a full, literate life upon "undreamed-of shores of knowing." Such examples appear in every period; somewhere in the canon of nearly every Afro-American writer, literacy is extolled and the written word minted as the coin of freedom's realm.

I have argued that the Afro-American quest for freedom has been more precisely a quest for freedom *and* literacy—and that this dual quest has provided not just a subject but a narrative structure for much of the culture's written literature. There is a decided value to this argument: it enables discussion of the literature and culture alike in literary terms.[1] But my focus here is quite different, not opposed but broader and dialectical. What I will argue here is that Afro-American literature has developed as much because of the culture's distrust of literacy as because of its abiding faith in it.

Let me begin with two of literacy's most fervent advocates, Frederick Douglass and Richard Wright. In the years just after the publication of his great *Narrative,* Douglass encountered hostility from friend and foe alike, apparently because of his increasing skills as a speaker and writer. In his autobiography *My Bondage and My Freedom,* he tells us that friends urged that he confine his acts of literacy to the narrow straits of what they insisted was his story, while foes declared in so many words that his literacy in and of itself made them suspect that neither his story nor Douglass himself existed. It was in response to his foes, but possibly to his friends as well, that Douglass soon composed the *Narrative.* But recall: these annoying encounters with censorship of one form or another proved to be grist not for the *Narrative,* but for the autobiography still to come. While it was Douglass's audience's distrust of him that led to the *Narrative,* it was his increasing distrust of *them* that prompted *My*

---

1. I pursue this argument further in "Teaching Afro-American Literature: Survey or Tradition; or, The Reconstruction of Instruction" in Dexter Fisher and Robert B. Stepto, eds., *Afro-American Literature: The Reconstruction of Instruction* (New York: MLA, 1979), pp. 8–24, and in my *From Behind the Veil: A Study of Afro-American Narrative* (Urbana: University of Illinois Press, 1979).

Bondage as well as his newspapers, his novella, "The Heroic Slave," and his removal, in fine American form, to the "West."[2] In short, the illiteracy of the allegedly literate spurred Douglass the speaker to become also Douglass the writer and editor.

Richard Wright's career at times shows remarkable parallels to Douglass'. In what both men choose to recall of their early years in their autobiographies, the effort to gain literacy is a subject matched only by that of how each had to cloak or disavow his skills once even a measure of literacy was attained. The incidents they recall in this regard are often strikingly similar: at some point each had to find whites who were sufficiently unsuspecting to impart lessons or advice; each had to endure the distrust from and occasional betrayals by fellow blacks; each had to hide the few books they had. For each, youth was a time in which one had to learn how to perform, as it were, before unreliable audiences, white and black, especially if one aspired to a condition of literacy which, if realized and inadvertently displayed, would render those audiences all the more distrustful and hostile.

What Douglass and Wright learned as black youths in the South was just as useful to them once each gained a degree of freedom in the North. For all the obvious differences, personal and cultural, there are significant parallels between Wright's experiences among the American Communists and Douglass' among New England's abolitionists. The censoring of Wright by the Communists, for example, is unquestionably of a piece with the censorship to which the Garrisonians subjected Douglass. In both cases, sympathizers, men and women who strove to see through race to the individual and to champion that individual's right to free access to literacy, became confused about the distinction between employing and exploiting an individual as a race representative. And in both cases, they were also confused about whether access to literacy for that individual was to be for their purposes or those which the individual might construe. When one thinks of how Douglass' newspapers were soon blacklisted by the Garrisonians and of how Wright was barred from Communist May Day parades, it is not difficult to

2. For Douglass, the "West" was, in this instance, Rochester, New York.

see why Douglass removed to the West or why Wright expatriated to France. Friends found on "undreamed-of shores" had turned out to be the most distrustful sort of unfriendly natives.

Just as Douglass wrote his *Narrative* in response to his audience's distrust of him, so Wright composed *Uncle Tom's Children* (1938) and *Twelve Million Black Voices* (1941) partly to appease the distrust he encountered from blacks and whites alike once he came North. Similarly, Douglass' many writerly activities of the 1850s express *his* distrust of those who distrusted him, while Wright increasingly vented his own distrust of the American left, first in "Blueprint for Negro Literature" (1937), then in *Native Son* (1940), and finally in the whole of *American Hunger,* of which only the first section, *Black Boy,* was published in 1945. More specifically, *My Bondage and My Freedom* revises the *Narrative* in accord with Douglass' distrust of his audiences, much as the whole of *American Hunger* (that is, the original manuscript) revises *Black Boy.*[3]

For the most part, distrust of the American reader prompted Douglass and Wright to write, and affected the choices they made regarding what they would write about. Distrust motivated them to improve their writing skills and to venture into new areas of inquiry and writerly performance, including those which were designated by custom, ideology, and an implicit racism as the provinces of others. (In *American Hunger,* for example, Wright asks, "Didn't Lenin read bourgeois books?" and a "comrade" replies, "But you're not Lenin.") Once we consider distrust of the American reader and of American acts of reading to be a primary and pervasive motivation for Afro-American writing, we are equipped to read the autobiographies of Douglass, Wright, and many other writers in fresh and useful ways. This distrust is not merely a subject or theme of certain autobiographies. Nor is it something that exists in some festering

3. Regarding the latter revision, it must be noted that while Wright composed both portions of his autobiography in the 1940s, many readers were not aware of both until the second, "American Hunger," saw print in 1977. While we can speculate about the whys and wherefores of this curious publishing history, one result of it seems clear: Wright's most explicit statement of distrust of the audiences which initially supported him was virtually suppressed for thirty years; intentionally or not, the act of reading Wright was manipulated.

form within the writer, or within his or her act of writing as distinct from the resulting texts. While distrust prompts some Afro-American writers to write about almost anything and everything, it has led others to write about distrust itself—to create and refine what I call a discourse of distrust. In short, a study of distrust in Afro-American writing can (and should) lead to new perceptions of the various strains and historical contours within Afro-American literature as a whole.

In the following section I offer a few of my thoughts in this regard, principally by choosing to see the distinction between distrusting writers who write and those who write about their distrust as being more precisely that between storywriters and (writing) storytellers. Part of what allows this last distinction is the requisite presence, and frequently active role, of the distrusting American reader—thinly guised as an unreliable story listener—in storytelling texts. With this in view, I then raise questions about the adequacies of the "social models" for reader-response literary analysis, especially since they do not seem to be, in Du Bois's terms, "frank and fair" about the American "race rituals" which invariably affect American acts of reading. In the concluding section, I describe the narrative strategies of several storytelling texts, mostly contemporary ones, to provide thereby a morphology of the Afro-American storytelling narrative.

The Afro-American discourse of distrust assumes many narrative forms and infiltrates many literary genres. My focus here is not on the autobiographical or confessional modes of this literature (for example, the Douglass and Wright autobiographies), or on literary essays such as Ralph Ellison's "The World and the Jug"—which is justly famous in part because it so eloquently expresses Ellison's distrust of Irving Howe as a reader of modern black fiction. Nor will I turn to poems such as Gwendolyn Brooks's "Negro Hero" or Michael Harper's "Nightmare Begins Responsibility," even though both poems are major texts largely because they portray how a "distrusting [black] self" may cope with that self as well as with those "audiences" which "read" him or her, often cavalierly or distrustingly. My concern is instead with fiction, and with coming to some understanding

of why some Afro-American storywriters and novelists distrust
the term "fiction," and choose to see themselves as storytellers
instead of storywriters, even though they can hardly surmount
the fact that they *are* writing, and that simulations of storytelling
performances in written art are, no matter how artful, simulations and little more. In the texts of these writers, distrust is
not so much a subject as a basis for specific narrative plottings
and rhetorical strategies. Moreover, the texts are fully "about"
the communicative prospects of Afro-Americans writing for
American readers, black and white, given the race rituals which
color reading and/or listening. If we can understand these prospects, we can have a surer sense of how American culture is
developing and in what direction.

The effort to draw a distinction between storytelling and
storywriting in a written Afro-American literature is by no means
unique on my part. Authors and critics alike have engaged in
this task for years. Novelist Gayl Jones, for example, remarks
in a 1975 interview,

> . . . for me fiction and storytelling are different. I say I'm a fiction
> writer if I'm asked, but I really think of myself as a storyteller. When
> I say 'fiction,' it evokes a lot of different kinds of abstractions, but
> when I say 'storyteller,' it always has its human connections . . . There
> is always that kind of relationship between a storyteller and a hearer—
> the seeing of each other. The hearer has to see/hear the storyteller,
> but the storyteller has to see/hear the hearer, which the written tradition
> doesn't usually acknowledge.[4]

What Jones attempts to describe here is a mode, if not exactly
a genre, in written narrative which accommodates the performative aesthetic of oral storytelling by fashioning characters
(voices) who pose as tellers and hearers and occasion thereby
certain types of narrative structuring. In acknowledging and
discussing this mode, several Afro-Americanist scholars have
produced a useful intrinsic criticism of storytelling within texts.
I think here of John F. Callahan's essays on the "spoken in the

4. Michael S. Harper, "Gayl Jones: An Interview," in Michael S. Harper
and Robert B. Stepto, eds., *Chant of Saints: A Gathering of Afro-American
Literature, Art, and Scholarship* (Urbana: University of Illinois Press, 1979),
pp. 355, 374–375.

written word," Robert O'Meally's discussions of the written
"preacherly" voice, and of the recent studies which strive to
make distinctions between black speech and literary dialect.[5]

However, I believe that Jones is making another point as
well, one which both complicates our notion of written storytelling and challenges us to discuss the texts in ways which are
not exclusively intrinsic. Jones suggests that storytelling narratives not only present voices as tellers and hearers but also
coerce authors and readers (or, if you will, texts and readers)
into teller-hearer relationships. In other words, storytelling narratives create "interpretive communities"[6] in which authors,
texts, and readers collectively assert that telling and hearing
may be occasioned by written tales, and that the distinctions
between telling and writing on the one hand, and hearing and
reading on the other, are far more profound than they are
usually determined to be in those interpretive groupings constituted by other types of fictive narrative.

The role of the reader is the key issue here, and not just
because examinations of the reader require new, less intrinsic
approaches to storytelling texts. I would submit that the reader
in the storytelling paradigm is what makes that model different.
Many models accommodate rather easily the idea of an author
or text "telling" a story, but only the storytelling paradigm posits
that the reader, in "constituting" himself through engaging the
text, becomes a hearer, with all that that implies in terms of
how one may sustain through reading the *responsibilities* of
listenership as they are defined in purely performative contexts.

5. John F. Callahan, "Image-Making: Tradition and the Two Versions of
the Autobiography of Miss Jane Pittman," *Chicago Review*, 29 (Autumn 1977),
45–62, and two as yet unpublished essays, "Storytelling Narrative and the
Rhetorical Tradition in Afro-American Letters" and "The Spoken in the Writ-
ten Word: Narrative Form and Afro-American Personality in the Tales of Joel
Chandler Harris and Charles Chesnutt"; Myron Simon, "Dunbar and Dialect
Poetry," in Jay Martin, ed., *A Singer in the Dawn: Reinterpretations of Paul
Laurence Dunbar* (New York: Dodd, Mead, 1975), pp. 114–134; Houston A.
Baker, Jr., *The Journey Back: Issues in Black Literature and Criticism* (Chicago:
University of Chicago Press, 1980), pp. 1–52, passim. This list is hardly inclusive
and is only meant to be suggestive.

6. The phrase is Stanley Fish's; see his *Is There a Text in This Class?* (Cambridge, Mass.: Harvard University Press, 1980), passim, but esp. pp. 171–173.

In reading experiences occasioned by storytelling texts, the reader may be an "implied," "informed," or "competent" figure, as Wolfgang Iser, Stanley Fish, and Jonathan Culler have declared the engaged readers of most written traditions to be.[7] But within the storytelling interpretive community, implication (especially insofar as it embraces complicity), knowledge, and competency are all measured according to a different scale. That scale measures hearing, not reading, the distinction being most apparent when the acts of authoring that hearing and reading spawn are compared.

To speak of the authoring a reader performs is to refer as well to the risks assumed when a reader is invited to partake in either type of communicative event. The written traditions that encourage fiction-making incite competitive authoring; readers of these writerly texts author competing texts both when they attempt to articulate what the prompting text means (or what its author intends) and when they go the other, "deconstructionist route" and playfully mime the prompting text's apparent deviousness or meaninglessness. In either case, the risk undertaken is that the prompting text will be rightfully or wrongfully superseded by one of its competing offspring—as countenanced, of course, by the jury of "informed" authors engendered by text. Glory and probable canonization come either through angst or anxiety. In the first scenario, the reader is in varying degrees defeated as an author but left with the consolation of knowing that the competing text he can imagine (but not yet or perhaps ever fully render) has at least a pedagogic or scholarly value. In the second scenario, the reader is characteristically triumphant as an author, which is to say that the prompting text has entered the firmament precisely because its authorship has been not so much passed along as conquered. In either case, the prompting text "lives" because its authorship has been contested.

7. Wolfgang Iser, *The Implied Reader* (Baltimore: Johns Hopkins University Press, 1974); Stanley E. Fish, *Self-Consuming Artifacts* (Berkeley: University of California Press, 1972); Jonathan Culler, *Structuralist Poetics* (Ithaca: Cornell University Press, 1975). Appropriate selections from these studies conveniently appear in Jane P. Tompkins, ed., *Reader-Response Criticism* (Baltimore: Johns Hopkins University Press, 1980).

Competition of a kind occurs in storytelling, but most of the communicative impulses within that tradition discourage competition of the order found in most written traditions, and risk is defined in new terms. While fictionmaking and its kindred activities incite competitive authoring, storytelling invites comparable authoring; the "hearer" within the storytelling model is encouraged to compose what are essentially authenticating texts for the prompting story narrative.[8] What this means in part is that competition within the model is largely a matter of hearers vying with hearers as authenticators, and not one of readers attempting to create through their "reading" a stronger text than that which initiated their interpretive community. The risks that written storytelling undertakes are thus at least twofold: one is that the reader will become a hearer but not manage an authenticating response; the other is that the reader will *remain a reader* and not only belittle or reject storytelling's particular "keen disturbance,"[9] but also issue confrontational responses which sustain altogether different definitions of literature, of literacy, and of appropriate reader response. The threat to most texts in the written tradition is that readers will cause them to swerve; the threat to a storytelling text is that readers will hasten its death.

While the risks to written storytelling are just this high, the rewards are equally great, especially in terms of the opportunities provided for authors and texts alike to be an advancing force within various literary traditions *and* a subversive factor within them as well. Subversion is probably most apparent in storytelling's persistent efforts to sustain the tenets of a performative aesthetic in an artistic medium ostensibly hostile to that aesthetic. Consider, for example, how subversive it is for storytelling to pursue various explicitly didactic strategies ("Now this is the way it happened, . . . I want you to *write* it on whatever part of your brain that ain't already covered with page

8. See my discussion of authenticating narratives in *From Behind the Veil*, pp. 5, 26–31.
9. Iser's phrase; see Wolfgang Iser, "Indeterminancy and the Reader's Response," in J. H. Miller, ed., *Aspects of Narrative* (New York: Columbia University Press, 1971), p. 2.

print.") in an era in which most critics proclaim that "true art ignores the audience"[10] and most writers write accordingly. Subversion is also apparent in the previously discussed notion that the competent reader must become a competent *hearer* who eventually tells authenticating stories, especially since it is obviously "bad form" for any author or text to insist upon that degree of "submission" as an element of reading well. However, the most subversive, and hence most interesting, claim that storytelling makes is that, contrary to what most modern critics and even some writers tell us, it is the reader—not the author or text and certainly not the storyteller in the text—who is unreliable.

Most theories of creative reading and/or authoring offer episodes in which a devious or elusive text is grappled, if not altogether subdued, by a comparably ingenious reader. All such assaults are rationalized as a necessary, creative activity: it is the reader's lot to control or "reauthor" a text, which, by its taunting deviousness or playfulness—its *unreliability*—has actually invited the reader's aggression. Storytelling seeks to turn this model inside out. In Afro-American storytelling texts especially, rhetoric and narrative strategy combine time and again to declare that the principal unreliable factor in the storytelling paradigm is the reader (white American readers, obviously, but blacks as well), and that acts of creative communication are fully initiated not when the text is assaulted but when the reader gets "told"—or "told off"—in such a way that he or she finally begins to *hear*. It is usually in this way that most written tales express their distrust not just of readers but of official literate culture in general.[11] It is also in this way that they sustain the

10. Wayne C. Booth discusses this "truism" in *The Rhetoric of Fiction* (Chicago: University of Chicago Press, 1961), esp. in chap. 4, pp. 89–116.

11. The "Americanness" of this Afro-American activity should be apparent. Mark Twain—to cite the most obvious example—also fashioned written tales expressing distrust of the reader and of the definitions of literacy represented by that reader. Indeed, it is fair to argue that some twentieth-century Afro-American writers (Sterling Brown and Ralph Ellison in particular) are in their storytelling as much American as Afro-American precisely because of their reading of Twain. But let us not lose sight of when this activity is distinctly

instructional nature of performed storytelling in a cultural context which devalues didactic art.

Wayne Booth has written, "Much of our scholarly and critical work of the highest seriousness has . . . employed . . . [a] dialectical opposition between artful showing and inartistic, merely rhetorical, telling."[12] It should not be surprising, then, to find that in American literary studies, the biographies of Mark Twain are generally superior to the critical studies of his works, that the many fine examinations of Faulkner and Ellison usually minimize their subversive activities as storytellers, and that within the realm of Afro-American letters alone, the studies of storywriters (for example, Wright and Baldwin) are both more voluminous and more thoughtful than those of storytellers (Gaines, McPherson, and Jones).[13] And so we must ask how literary history may be reconstituted to accommodate the storytelling strain in its own right.

The challenge occurs on two fronts: the intrinsic analysis of what is most minimally conceived to be the text, and the extrinsic analysis of what might be termed the text seen "large," that is, the text performing itself as well as its subversive activities. In the first case, the scholar of written literatures must consider the extent to which current *oral* literature theories illuminate the inner workings of a written text. These theories are primarily structuralist and thereby immune (for the most part) to the seductions of ferreting out intrinsic meaning or intention. It also occurs because most of the theories proceed from assumptions regarding the contextual origins of oral stories (and storytelling) which yield a critical language that usefully examines written tales as well.[14] What oral literature scholars mean in their use

---

"Afro-American" as well: while both traditions may pit teller against hearer in terms of country versus city, South versus North, West versus East, commonsense versus booksense, and New World versus the Old, it is mainly, and perhaps exclusively, in Afro-American letters that this match may be fully played out across the ubiquitous net of America's color line.

12. Booth, *The Rhetoric of Fiction,* p. 27.

13. The obvious exception is the rush of good work on Zora Neale Hurston.

14. Part of my point here is that new concepts for the scholar of written literatures, such as Harold Scheub's theory of the expansible image, advance one's discussion of the written tale. See Scheub, "The Technique of the Ex-

of familiar terms such as "theme" and "repetition" is often different from what scholars of written literatures mean, and those differences encourage fresh approaches to written literatures. To argue, for example, as Albert Lord did some twenty years ago, that a theme is not so much a "central or dominating idea" but a repeated incident or description—a "narrative building block"—is to confront most literary scholars with a new idea of thematic criticism.[15] Similarly, Harold Scheub's notion that narrative repetition finds its form in "expansible and patterned and parallel image-sets" usefully takes one beyond conventional considerations of the reiterated word or phrase or of the reworded idea.[16] Generally, what the oral literature scholars provide are methods and terms for critical discourse on the large units of narrative structure—the "macro-units," if you will—which most readily identify tales as the distilled products of various artistic impulses both collected and controlled. Since even the written Afro-American tale is similarly multigeneric in intention and often in result, it is also open to "macronic" analysis.

Regarding the extrinsic analysis of written storytelling, I should acknowledge at once that what I have just described as an intrinsic method could equally be seen as extrinsic. Oral literature scholars always assume that narratives are performed art forms and accordingly view the written texts of narratives as necessary but altogether limited approximations of complex events. When David Buchan directs our attention to the stanzaic units in Scottish ballads rather than to the stanzas themselves, he does so because the clustering of stanzas into larger structural units has a far greater bearing on the production and reception of ballads than that of the stanza itself.[17] Buchan is aware of the solitary

pansible Image in Xhosa Ntsomi-Performances," *Research in African Literatures*, 1, 2 (1970), 119–146.

15. Albert Lord, "Umbundu: A Comparative Analysis," in Merlin Ennis, ed., *Umbundu: Folktales from Angola* (Boston: Beacon Press, 1962), p. xvi.

16. Scheub discusses narrative repetition at length in "Oral Narrative Process and the Use of Models," in Alan Dundes, ed., *Varia Folklorica* (Mouton, 1978), pp. 71–89. Also useful is his "Performance of Oral Narrative," in William R. Bascom, ed., *Frontiers of Folklore* (1977), pp. 54–78.

17. David Buchan, *The Ballad and the Folk* (London: Routledge and Kegan Paul, 1972), pp. 87–104.

stanza's autonomy and authority on the printed page; yet he submits not to that authority but to that of stanzas-in-performance and fashions his narrative analysis accordingly. In sum, his intrinsic analysis is distinctly extrinsic.

Nonetheless, I find it useful to distinguish between discussions of narrative structure and those of reader or listener response, and to refer to these respectively as intrinsic and extrinsic critical discourse. Written tales present at least two challenges to most reader-response theories. One is offered by the framed tale readily found in both nineteenth- and twentieth-century Afro-American writing. Framed tales by their nature invent storylisteners within their narratives and storyreaders, through their acts of reading, may be transformed into storylisteners. In tale after tale, considerable artistic energy is brought to the task of persuading the reader to constitute himself as a listener, the key issue affecting that activity being whether the reader is to pursue such self-transformations in accord with or at variance with the model of the listener found within the narrative itself. In other words, the competent reader of framed tales always must decide just how much he will or can submit to the model of listening which almost always is the dominating meta-plot of the tale. He must decide as well to what extent a refusal to submit endangers his or her competency.

What this suggests is that framed tales seem to require two kinds of "reader-response" analysis, one of teller-listener relations within the narrative, another of those relations incorporating the "outside" reader. Moreover, a full extrinsic study of a framed tale does not declare as supreme the latter analysis, as most reader-response theories aggressively do, but attempts to fashion an accommodation of both analyses. The challenge is to manage such accommodations.

Beyond this lies the specific challenge presented by the Afro-American framed tale in particular. In its depictions within narratives of demonstrably white or black listeners, and in its presumption that most of its readers are white (and specifically, white Americans), the Afro-American framed tale confronts interracial and intraracial rituals of behavior while fashioning various models of readership. While these features invariably distinguish the Afro-American framed tale from other framed tales, they do not remove these tales from the mainstream of the Afro-American written story. Tales that aren't framed are much like those that are, especially since the narrating voices within them are normally those of whites or blacks who have undergone listenership and who are now attempting storytelling at a level comparable to that which first engaged their attention. Once we acknowledge as well that nonframed Afro-American tales also assume a white readership, we may say that, in their narrative intentions and recognition of communicative prospects, both types of written tales are far more candid than the reader-response literary critics have been about how acts of listening and reading may be complicated by race.

The second kind of challenge that written storytelling presents to reader-response theories is therefore obvious: to what extent are the psychological, intersubjective, and even the social models of reader-response analysis articulate about the communicative situations black authors in the Americas have confronted for two hundred years? While something useful may be gleaned from all three models, the social models of Stanley Fish (in his most recent phase) and Steven Mailloux are the most useful, even though they are relatively underdeveloped for these purposes.[18]

Fish advances a sophisticated concept of the "authority" invested in interpretive communities by acts of reading, which is useful, for example, in suggesting how written tales manage authority in simulated performative communities. On the other hand, he seems rather naive about interpretive arbitration within those bodies comprising readership on a large scale. Mailloux criticizes Fish's notion of interpretive communities for referring only to "one aspect (though a most important one) of historical communities—shared constitutive conventions for making sense of reality" (p. 137). He argues that "More often, however, historical communities are made up of several conflicting in-

18. I refer to Fish's "most recent phase" because I distinguish as others do between his concept of the early 1970s of the informed reader and his more recent idea of the interpretive community. See again the essays collected in *Is There a Text in This Class?* Regarding Mailloux, see his *Interpretive Conventions: The Reader in the Study of American Fiction* (Ithaca: Cornell University Press, 1982), pp. 126–139; further references are by page number in the text.

terpretive communities," (p. 137), from which I infer that Mailloux envisions America as being made up of many historical *and* interpretive communities often contending with each other over the prime issues of which conventions are shared and which render the world real.

However, one must ask—as Afro-Americanists always must of Americanists—which working definition of community underlies Mailloux's assertion? I say "working" because quite often the bone of contention between Afro-Americanists and Americanists is less a matter of pure definition than one of how terms are put to use. For example, it is difficult to find fault with Mailloux's claim that "common ties remain the most relevant general criteria for defining community," or with what he understands "common ties" to be: "shared traditions, imposed or agreed upon behavior patterns, and common ways of making sense—that is, as traditional, regulative, and constitutive conventions" (p. 137). However, where these thoughts lead Mailloux is, I think, a curious matter, especially in light of his posture as a revisionist literary historian.

After usefully citing Jessie Bernard's definition of communities as " 'clubs' whose conventions constitute a kind of boundary-maintenance device," Mailloux then argues that

the historical communities that fill the category of 'literature' can be whole societies, but more often they are societal groups based on economic organization (for example, the network of authors, publishers, periodical editors, and book reviewers), social rank (for instance, intelligentsia and governing classes), or institutional and professional position (such as English professor).   (pp. 137–138)

What is exposed here is the bare outline of an all too familiar story: intentionally or not, another Americanist is shying away from confronting the role that race has played in America in creating communities (black *and* white) veritably bristling with traditional, regulative, and constitutive conventions. Should Mailloux argue that racial societal groups in America are not as pertinent or substantial as those based upon economic organization, social rank, or professional position, he would be sadly mistaken. Should he contend instead that America's racial societal groups have not "filled" the category of American literature, he would be more mistaken still. In either case, Mailloux offers no guidance on this considerable issue. Just as his new readings of Hawthorne, Melville, and Crane are illuminating but in no way reflective of the *many* historical and interpretive communities in nineteenth-century America, his social model for what might be called the American act of reading is insufficiently social.

It is quite possible that the most useful, amending model—useful especially in terms of comprehending the abiding link in America between race and readership—is to be found in rough form within the aggregate literature of the Afro-American written tale. We must therefore attempt to extract and formalize the social mode of reading collectively authored by Afro-American writers as various as Frederick Douglass, Charles Chesnutt, Jean Toomer, Zora Neale Hurston, Ralph Ellison, Ernest Gaines, Toni Morrison, Gayl Jones, James Alan McPherson, Alice Walker, and David Bradley. In doing so, we should be less concerned with offering a chronology or even a history of Afro-American literature based upon those authors than with suggesting how the "basic" written tale has been modified over time, usually in an effort to accommodate the changing subtleties of America's race rituals, so that appropriately revised models of competent readership can be advanced.

The basic written tale is fundamentally a framed tale in which either the framed or framing narrative depicts a black storyteller's white listener socially and morally maturing into competency. In thus presenting a very particular reader in the text, the basic written tale squarely addresses the issue of its probable audience while raising an issue for some or most of its readers regarding the extent to which they can or will identify with the text's "reader" while pursuing (if not always completing) their own act of reading. Where matters develop beyond this is the subject of the next section.

Let me begin by noting that while there are many white storytellers throughout the Afro-American written canon, they are always novices—freshly elevated to the rank of teller by virtue of their newly acquired competency as listeners—and never master storytellers. Many black storytellers, especially in modern and contemporary narratives, also are novices, but a few (Charles Chesnutt's Uncle Julius, Ernest Gaines's Miss Jane Pittman, David Bradley's Old Jack Hawley) are master storytellers, custodians of the prompting tales. They seem to pass from knowing to possessing the tales (as a curator "possesses" a fine painting) as they share them. We may thus recognize several tale types which are created by the presence or absence in narratives of master tellers, novice tellers, and unreliable listeners in varying combinations, and by the positioning of these figures as primary or ancillary tellers or listeners in narratives as wholes. The accompanying chart will be of assistance here.

Type A stories are the basic tales in the written storytelling tradition. By "basic" I do not mean that they are primitive or unsophisticated, or that they are numerically dominant within the canon. Rather, these are the stories in which (a) the primary narrators are black master storytellers, (b) tales of a didactic nature are told to conspicuously incompetent listeners, largely out of distrust of them, (c) the listeners are fully present as characters or voices and not as "implied" personages, (d) the tales within the stories are autobiographical only insofar as they partake of episodes from the master teller's personal history, and (e) the framed-tale structure of the narrative as a whole is fully intact and seemingly inviolate.

Type A and A′ stories differ in terms of the race of the listener—and hence in terms of the stated or implied performative context in which the master teller's tale is told. The story types also differ as to the frequency with which they are composed as discrete written stories. While a number of type A stories appear in the canon as full-fledged narratives—such as James Alan McPherson's "Problems of Art"—they emerge more often as the tales within the type B story cited in the chart. In contrast, type A′ stories frequently are discrete stories. McPherson's "Solo Song: For Doc" and "The Story of a Scar" enhance this category, as does Zora Neale Hurston's *Their Eyes Were Watching God.*

Type B tales are told by novice storytellers who have just recently achieved competency as listeners. This fact is important for it explains why the tale offered is basically an account of

Storytellers and Tales in Afro-American Framed Tales

Type A: basic story	*Type A': basic story with black listener*
Master teller—white listener Tale, usually with veiled instructions for listener	Master teller—black listener Tale, usually with veiled instructions for listener
Type B: basic novice story	*Type B': basic novice story with black novices*
White novice teller—readers Tale = basic story A	Black novice teller—readers Tale = basic story A'
Type C: novice story II	*Type C': novice story II with black novice*
White novice teller—readers Tale = framing narrative of basic story A	Black novice teller—readers Tale = framing narrative of basic story A'
Type D: novice story III	*Type D': novice story III with black novice*
White novice teller—readers Tale = type C tale varied without master teller	Black novice teller—readers Tale = type C tale varied without master teller

the storytelling event which occasioned the novice teller's competency, and why the master teller *and* his or her tale fully dominate that account. In other words, the novice teller is seemingly still too close to the moment when competency was achieved, and too overwhelmed by the teller, tale, and other features of that moment, to author a story which is anything other than a strict account of that moment.

The characteristics of Type B (and B') stories are therefore as follows: (a) although the story's primary narrator is a novice teller (white or black), the black master teller is fully present

as the teller of the story's tale; (b) although the novice teller
may tell the tale of his or her previous incompetency to listeners
situated within the tale's frame, direct address to the "listener"
outside the story (the "outside" reader) is both possible and
likely; (c) although the predominating autobiographical statement is still that offered by the master teller in the tale, the
novice teller's self-history also has a place, sometimes a significant one, in the story as a whole; (d) although the story is
normally a framed tale, with this type we begin to see improvisations upon that structure, especially in those instances where
the story is repeated and otherwise developed for the needs and
purposes of novellas and novels.

Two points must be stressed here, both involving story features which the basic novice's story initiates. One is that the
novice teller's story is essentially autobiographical, the other is
that his or her act of composing the narrative whole is a form
of what I have described before as comparable storytelling.
What makes the basic novice's story "basic" is that both of these
features are pursued at an elementary level. Invariably, a single
episode passes for autobiography, and repetition of the master
teller's tale—albeit with some record of how the teller, when a
listener, thwarted and/or abetted a given performance of the
tale—passes for comparable telling. Once we see that these
resolutions to the two most basic impulses within the novice's
story are the obvious resolutions, we can also see why at least
two more types of novice stories have developed. There is room
in the form for a larger measure of the novice teller's autobiography and room as well for acts of comparable telling which
exclude the master teller and do not repeat any of his or her
specific tales. This is not to say that type B stories are unre-
markable; Douglass' sole fiction, "The Heroic Slave," and Charles
Chesnutt's Uncle Julius stories are type B stories, and the type
B' category includes such estimable texts as Ernest Gaines's *The
Autobiography of Miss Jane Pittman,* Hurston's *Mules and Men,*
McPherson's "The Story of a Dead Man," and Gayl Jones's
Corregidora. However, these stories offer but one solution to
how one may create a written art out of the storytelling event
most accurately simulated in story types A and A'.

I have devised story type C chiefly to acknowledge that for

some novice tellers the event (or events) of storytelling which initiated their transformation from listeners to tellers may be appropriately recognized and recounted without full reference to the tale the master teller told at that time. The tale is thus incidental to the event in some accounts; in others, no one tale stands out as central to the former listener's epiphanic experience. In the type C story, the master teller is nonetheless on the scene, though full versions of his or her story are not. This means that his or her presence in the type C story is often more figurative than literal.

These economies in the rendering of master teller and master tale alike are usually to some major purpose. In Chesnutt's "The Dumb Witness," reducing the role Julius (the master teller) and his tale play leaves a space which John (the novice teller) fills with fragments of the tale he himself has collected. On the other hand, in the "Kabnis" section of Jean Toomer's *Cane,* the great effect of Father John (the master teller) saying so little so cryptically is that the novice/persona can be that much more autobiographical in his account of the advent of his competency. In either case, the larger role the novice plays in telling every aspect of the story leads to certain manipulations or dismantlings of the basic framed-tale structure. "The Dumb Witness" is a framed tale, but the fact that John's voice dominates both the frame and the tale means that, in this particular Julius story, we cannot distinguish between the frame and the tale in terms of what Alan Dundes and other folklorists would call linguistic textures. Toomer's "Kabnis" modifies the storytelling story in precisely the opposite way. While the encounter with Father John is framed, and while differing vernaculars or textures are employed to distinguish his voice from that of the novice (and from those of the other figures assembled), there quite simply is no tale of any expected sort residing within either the frame or the language presumably created for tale telling.

These developments suggest that a new concept of comparable authoring emerges in the type C story. The manipulation of the framed-tale structure, diminution of the master tale, and virtual transformation of the master teller from voice to trope all seem to constitute acts of authorial competition; but I would contend that each of these activities is pursued in an effort to create a story that authenticates the essentials or essences of storytelling instead of the details of any one story or story event. The framed-tale structure is manipulated so that the novice teller may confirm in a fresh way that *telling grows out of listening*. Both acts are nearly simultaneously initiated by the acquisition of competency. Such confirmations may be possible in story types A and B, but because they are far better managed in structures which do not segregate acts of telling from those of listening to the degree commonly found in rigidly executed framed tales. Moreover, the cost of reducing or deleting the master tale is willingly paid if the result is a self-portrait of the novice teller that persuades us that something more has been accomplished on the order of cultural integration (or reintegration) than that of tale memorization.

This feature yields our best clue as to why the master teller appears more as trope than voice. Something has to embody the historical and/or interpretive community of which the novice teller is now presumably a part, and of which he or she now tells stories. That "something" is commonly the master teller who, in one sense, began the whole business. If the pursuit of these activities in a type C story fashions a narrative which authenticates the communal context from which master teller and tale alike emerge, and which authenticates as well the essential oneness of context, teller, and tale, then it is a good and comparable story within the tradition. If any of this is mismanaged, the aesthetics of storytelling counsel us to receive the novice teller not as a promising competitive author, but as one who is still at base an unreliable listener. This is one of the several points at which the aesthetics of storytelling also urge us to subvert our usual critical habits, for the disapproval with which we are to greet the erring novice is also to be freely bestowed upon his or her author.

Much of the description just offered for the type C story holds for the type D story as well. However, the type D story attempts comparable storytelling without the outward presence of a master teller in a narrative. What this generally means is that the historical and/or interpretive community embodied by the master teller is configured in different but comparable terms. "Comparable" is a key word here. This is not just because we are discussing modes of comparable storytelling; it is essential to see that in these stories configurations such as family, kin, menfolk, womenfolk, the neighborhood, the black belt, the South, the ghetto, our people, and home (among others) occupy much the same space in the story that a master teller solely occupies in a type C tale. Indeed, one might say that they are identical to the master teller as signs for the same referent. However, this does not mean that master tellers are altogether absent from these stories. In many instances, it is impossible to evoke fully a given family, neighborhood, or "club" without acknowledging the storytellers who are unquestionably presences in the group. In other words, these storytellers no longer stand for the group as a whole, nor do they function as intermediaries between the group and the novice. When and if they appear in type D stories as tropes, what they configure is not so much a community as one or more of that body's shared conventions. Moreover, insofar as mediation between a community and "outsiders" occurs, it is pursued in varying degrees of explicitness by the novice teller. Central to all such mediations, especially in the type D story, is the manner in which the novice first forges, then wields, and then at strategic moments forsakes *his* distrust of outsiders. In this respect above all others, his act of mediation is yet another aspect of an attempt to manage comparable authorship.

Much of this comes clear when one thinks of the luminous figures of the South—and especially of the palpable presence of Georgia—in Toomer's *Cane*. Zora Neale Hurston's all-black town of Eatonville also is a communal context for storytelling, as are the black enclaves in Toni Morrison's novels and the Louisiana plantations in the fiction of Ernest Gaines. Each of these communities offers an unusually rich display of nearly archetypal characters, including a fair number of estimable raconteurs. And yet each of these communities looms larger than any one master teller or tale, and indeed subsumes teller and tale alike while becoming in every sense the major presence in a type D story.

I am well aware, of course, that certain texts do not neatly fall into one of my four categories, or mischievously blur them. As is often the case, there is something to be learned from such exceptions to the rule. Most of these "problem" texts are very new—some written yesterday, as it were. Many of them are long narratives—novellas or novels. Many can be usefully described as long narratives which in some measure are long precisely because they *combine* the story types just described. The texts include such acclaimed titles as Toni Morrison's *Song of Solomon* (1977), James Alan McPherson's "Elbow Room" (1977), David Bradley's *The Chaneysville Incident* (1981), and Alice Walker's *The Color Purple* (1982). The combinations achieved are various and at times stunningly comprehensive. The Bradley novel, for example, traces the career of a young historian who, after forsaking his stacks of note cards (his totems of official literacy), is transformed into an increasingly reliable listener and then into a better and better storyteller. In this fashion, the novel combines key aspects of the B', C', and D' story types as it unfolds, only to become, rather remarkably, a type A basic written tale at its closure.

Stories of this sort figure in this discussion partly because they challenge my categories, but mostly because they confirm, in their storytelling *about* storytelling, that storytelling has developed its own store of artistic conventions. They are "artistic" conventions, not strictly "literary" ones, chiefly because they have their origins in both oral and written artmaking—for example, in both the oral and written versions of Frederick Douglass' story of the slave revolt hero, Madison Washington. When our contemporary writers employ these conventions, they acknowledge that a particular tradition in Afro-American writing exists, and, knowingly or not, they place themselves within it. In this way, the tradition endures, and necessarily complicates, in rich and complex ways, our thinking about the points of congruence between Afro-American and other Western literatures.

WENDY STEINER

Collage or Miracle:
Historicism in a Deconstructed World

> *This is a universal law: a living thing can only be*
> *healthy, strong, and productive within a certain*
> *horizon; if it is incapable of drawing one round*
> *itself, or too selfish to lose its own view in another's,*
> *it will come to an untimely end.*
>
> *Friedrich Nietzsche*

Paul de Man has taught us that the modernist impulse is paradoxical: at once the breaking free of history through the assertion of a fresh start and the inauguration of history through
the initiation of an historical origin.[1] Postmodernism under these
circumstances is all the more problematic. For it marks a presumed end point to modernism and a new beginning, though
no one has clearly differentiated the modernism gone by from
the postmodernism that has replaced it. It is instructive, then,
to look at an exemplar of each period: perhaps the most famous
high modernist text in English, T. S. Eliot's *Waste Land,* and
the fresh start that Thomas Pynchon makes of it in *The Crying
of Lot 49.*[2]

This pairing is especially revealing because the two works
share so much. Indeed, I think that *The Crying of Lot 49* is a
wholesale rewriting of *The Waste Land* for the purpose of re-

1. Paul de Man, "Literary History and Literary Modernity," *Blindness and
Insight* (New Haven: Yale University Press, 1979), pp. 142–65.
2. T. S. Eliot, *The Waste Land, Collected Poems, 1909–1962* (London: Faber
and Faber, 1963; New York: Harcourt Brace Jovanovich, 1966); Thomas Pynchon, *The Crying of Lot 49* (New York: Bantam, 1966). All quotations are to
these editions and are identified by page number in the text.

323

opening the issues that that poem raised and recasting them in
the postmodernist context. Both works focus on the problem
of how solipsism and interpretive indeterminacy flatten historical consciousness.[3] When the objectivity of knowledge and the
dependability of interpretation are in doubt, the past becomes
utterly elusive, unknowable in its own terms and thus purely
subject to the present. How then can we distinguish history from
fiction; how can we read beyond our time into another? To put
it into words unavailable in Eliot's day, what is historicism in a
deconstructed world?

   This is a problem posed in art well before the time of Derrida
and de Man. Beckett's Lucky in *Waiting for Godot* notes that
the human mind has shrunk at a constant rate each year since
the time of Bishop Berkeley, according to the careful records
of the Acacacacademy of Anthropopopometry. As positivism
declined, historians have worried more and more over the
status of their knowledge, Hayden White representing perhaps
an extreme reaction. Twentieth-century scholarship initially responded to this problem by avoiding it, by bracketing off history from system. Structuralism, the New Criticism, and
phenomenology all perform this act of exclusion. But the un-
satisfactoriness of imagining a present unaffected by past and
future is now generally recognized. Marxism kept this criticism alive throughout the century; more recently Foucault and
others have insisted on the utter dependence of concepts on
their historical contexts. And yet Foucault does not acknowledge the embedding of his own discourse in such a context and
the possible idiosyncrasy of his or any individual's construal of
the past.

   If one does assume that systems can be understood only in
their historical circumstances and that that understanding is historically conditioned, how can one see such construals as share-
able, as reasonably probable (never mind true), that is, *as*
knowledge? In breaking down the presence of the present and
the pastness of the past, deconstructivism is trapped in a double

---

3. Michael Wood, for example, speaks of *The Crying of Lot 49*, like *V*, as
an "attempt to situate Americans in history" ("The Apprenticeship of Thomas
Pynchon," *New York Times Book Review* [April 15, 1984], pp. 1, 28).

bind: knowledge unconditioned by historical considerations is incomplete, but historical knowledge is not knowledge, at least not in the sense that Socrates meant when he contrasted it to belief. Paul de Man implies a wholly new notion of historical knowledge when he states that "to become good literary historians, we must remember that what we usually call literary history has little or nothing to do with literature and that what we call literary interpretation—provided only that it is good interpretation—is in fact literary history."[4]

The two texts before us represent two stages of literary thinking about these dilemmas, Eliot's contemporary with the move to separate text from history, and Pynchon's with the move to relate the two. The images and structures that they use to convey these concerns are surprisingly similar. In particular, both make complicated references to "Narcissus"—Ovid's self-absorbed youth as well as a Saint Narcissus. This early bishop of Jerusalem miraculously lit his Easter lamp with water when oil was lacking and hid himself in the desert until he "reappeared as one risen from the dead, and resumed his office at the entreaty of the people."[5] The mythic Narcissus is a symbol of modernist solipsism and isolation; the Narcissus of sacred legend introduces the possibility of revelation, miracle, and rebirth.

But the conjunction of opposites in this name is handled very differently by Eliot and Pynchon. Eliot wrote a poem entitled "The Death of Saint Narcissus" whose opening lines, slightly altered, became part of the final version of *The Waste Land.* "Come in under the shadow of this red rock" (l. 26) is the temptation to comfort in the wasteland, the "heap of broken images, where the sun beats, / And the dead tree gives no shelter, the cricket no relief, / And the dry stone no sound of water" (ll. 22–24). What one finds under the red rock, however, is mortality: "fear in a handful of dust" (l. 30). And what is under the rock in "The Death of Saint Narcissus" is the dead body of the saint himself.

The poem tells us how he got there:

4. De Man, "Literary History and Literary Modernity," p. 165.

5. S. Baring-Gould, *Lives of the Saints,* October, part 2 (Edinburgh: John Grant, 1914), p. 702.

He walked once between the sea and the high cliffs
Where the wind made him aware of his legs smoothly passing
  each other
And of his arms crossed over his breast.
When he walked over the meadows
He was stifled and soothed by his own rhythm.
By the river
His eyes were aware of the pointed corners of his eyes
And his hands aware of the tips of his fingers.
Struck down by such knowledge
He could not live mens' ways, but became a dancer before God.
If he walked in city streets
He seemed to tread on faces, convulsive thighs and knees.
So he came out to live under the rock.[6]

A composite of ascetic and narcissist, the saint ends up a corpse
holding his own dark shadow in his mouth. This final transfigu-
ration is just one more of the broken promises in the wasteland.

In Pynchon's *Crying of Lot 49* the quest for knowledge begins
likewise as self-concern. The heroine Oedipa Maas, whose ini-
tials spell the mantra "Om," drives to a town called San Narciso
and stays in a motel called the Echo Courts. While there she
attends a performance of a revenge tragedy which opens with
the good duke fatally kissing the poisoned feet of a statue of
Saint Narcissus. Self-exploration is perilous (and ludicrous, too),
but Pynchon implies that it is better to take this trip than to
stay at home. For only so can one encounter the possibility of
miracle. As Pynchon's narrator puts it, linking Saint Narcissus's
miracle with more secular wonders, "The saint whose water can
light lamps, the clairvoyant whose lapse in recall is the breath
of God, the true paranoid for whom all is organized in spheres
joyful or threatening about the central pulse of himself, the
dreamer whose puns probe ancient fetid shafts and tunnels of
truth all act in the same special relevance to the word, or whatever it is the word is there, buffering, to protect us from. The
act of metaphor then was a thrust at truth and a lie, depending

---

6. Lines 10–20, from *The Waste Land: A Facsimile and Transcript of the
Original Drafts by T. S. Eliot,* ed. Valerie Eliot (London: Faber and Faber,
and New York: Harcourt Brace Jovanovich, 1971); reprinted by permission of
Mrs. Valerie Eliot and the publishers.

where you were: inside, safe, or outside, lost" (p. 95). Narcissus is one of those radiant or deceptive metaphors that abound in Pynchon's text: the promise of relationality and knowledge or the threat of solipsism and tautology.

The radical relativism of knowledge is a central theme of the literary romance as a whole, its maidens locked in towers serving as ready symbols of the self-enclosed solipsist who must be released into a world of others. The myth of Narcissus directly conjoins solipsism and love, as do Eliot and Pynchon, the failure of intersubjectivity and the failure of interpretive authority becoming one and the same dilemma. In Part V of *The Waste Land,* we find the locked prison of the self and the caution that the key turns once in the lock and once only. Moreover, the central consciousness of the poem, Tiresias, is the very figure in Ovid who predicts Narcissus's fate. In *The Metamorphoses,* the story of Tiresias contains the embedded narrative of Narcissus and Echo; *The Waste Land*'s Tiresias likewise witnesses the debased coupling of the typist and the young man carbuncular. And when we recall Sophocles's Tiresias exclaiming, "Alas, how terrible is wisdom when / it brings no profit to the man that's wise!"[7] we see another linkage between failed or impotent knowledge and the theme of narcissism. The very structure of *The Waste Land* indicates the relativism of knowledge. Through juxtaposition and repetition, the poem dramatizes the power of context to alter meaning, reducing great art to "withered stumps of time."

With the past hopelessly diminished by modern habits of seeing, history is not a continuous narrative with imaginative shape and predictive connection to the present, but merely "a heap of broken images," fragments that do not cohere: "I can connect / Nothing with nothing," as one of the Thames daughters puts it. The Notes to *The Waste Land* are obvious symbols of the blight of interpretive relativity, themselves non-artistic fragments that while purporting to interpret and explain the poem often confuse, mislead, or mock the earnest attempt to discover what the author meant through his explanations. And for the

7. Sophocles, *Oedipus the King,* tr. David Grene, in *Sophocles,* vol. 1, ed. David Grene and Richard Lattimore (Chicago: University of Chicago Press, 1954), p. 23, ll. 316–17.

uninitiated, *The Waste Land* poem itself serves as a potent image
of the decay of interpretive wholeness and artistic transcendence.

The Crying of Lot 49 runs over precisely this ground. At the
beginning of the novel, Oedipa Maas remembers a time when
she saw herself as Rapunzel locked in a tower, waiting for a
knight to release her. The tragedy of solipsism is thus shifted,
temporarily, to the latency of the romance innocent. When her
lover, Pierce Inverarity, finally does release her, they go off to
Mexico, where Oedipa sees a painting of maidens locked within
a tower embroidering a tapestry that flows out the window and
fills the world outside, becoming that world. Oedipa then re-
alizes that the ground "she stood on had only been woven together a couple thousand miles away in her own tower, was
only by accident known as Mexico, and so Pierce had taken her
away from nothing, there'd been no escape" (pp. 10–11). And
what she had been trying to escape, we are told, is the unknowable force that locked her in the tower in the first place
and gave the tower the shape it has.

There is hardly a more explicit image of the solipsistic dilemma to be found in literature: the paradox that all knowledge
is limited to the self, but that that self cannot be known as
another, objectively, accurately, historically. Even after Oedipa
has been drawn through the extraordinary discoveries of
the novel, she is left absolutely ignorant of the tower's source.
As she puts it to herself, "Either you have stumbled . . . onto
a secret richness and concealed intensity of dream . . . Or you
are hallucinating it. Or a plot has been mounted against you . . . so
labyrinthine that it must have meaning beyond just a practical
joke. Or you are fantasying some such plot, in which case you
are a nut, Oedipa, out of your skull" (p. 128). No interpretation
is grounded, and all quests for knowledge threaten to become
like Oedipa's first view of the philatelist Gengis Cohen "framed
in a long succession or train of doorways, room after room
receding in the general direction of Santa Monica, all soaked
in rain-light" (p. 68).

The failure in both texts of any determinate construal of meaning
leads to the problem of history. *The Waste Land* in particular
contains a number of traditional historical plots that all are
shown to fail as ways of understanding. From Jesse Weston and

Sir James Frazer comes the notion of the vegetative cycle, the eternal return of the seasons that appears in historiography in Vico and Yeats (if one can call Yeats a historian). Eliot's response is the famous image of April cruelly raising the thought of past and future—"memory and desire"—in a world that is spiritually dead.

Pynchon makes this image of empty return the occasion for one of his typical ironic-poignant moments. Gengis Cohen, the same figure seen in the infinitely receding doorways of interpretation, pours Oedipa some wine made from dandelions that grew in a cemetery which has, since their picking, been bulldozed to make way for the East San Narciso Freeway. " 'It's clearer now,' " Cohen tells Oedipa. " 'A few months ago it got quite cloudy. You see, in spring, when the dandelions begin to bloom again, the wine goes through a fermentation. As if they remembered' " (p. 72). The anecdote is another testimony to the fact that "April is the cruellest month . . . mixing / Memory and desire." But Oedipa thinks sentimentally that the wine clouds up not because it remembers the obliterated past, but because the past still lives in it, "in a land where you could somehow walk, and not need the East San Narciso Freeway, and bones still could rest in peace, nourishing ghosts of dandelions, no one to plow them up. As if the dead really do persist, even in a bottle of wine." *The Waste Land* is much less hopeful on this score. "That corpse you planted last year in your garden, / Has it begun to sprout? Will it bloom this year? / Or has the sudden frost disturbed its bed? / Oh keep the Dog far hence, that's friend to men, / Or with his nails he'll dig it up again!" (ll. 71–75). In the bulldozer-dog and scores of other images, *The Crying of Lot 49* recapitulates the failure of the natural cycle that Eliot dramatized in *The Waste Land*. The mythic plot of eternal renewal no longer functions as a way of finding meaning.

From *The Tempest* and Ovid comes another historical plot, that of metamorphosis: the shift from one order of being to an entirely different one. The key example in *The Waste Land* is the passage from *The Tempest* where Ariel informs Ferdinand that his drowned father has been transformed into a thing of beauty: "Those are pearls that were his eyes." The magical change of the corpse into a precious gem is the kind of redemption art promises to life, and a pattern that in historiography implies revolutionary change, recuperation of loss, or justice as the moving force of history. But the plot of metamorphosis is stymied in both texts.

Even the trustworthiness of the historical document comes into question. Eliot borrows Ovid's story of Philomela, who weaves a tapestry of her rape that speaks as eloquently as direct testimony and leads to retribution. But in Eliot, Philomela's tapestry fails to say anything to us. Past history and culture are an abundance of such testimony that amount to nothing more than "withered stumps of time." In Pynchon too, evidence is either mute or says too much. Oedipa turns out to be an arch-empiricist, whose college training gave her nothing if not sound research skills. Here she follows in the path of her namesake, Paul Maas, who provided a handbook to classical philology in his *Textkritik*. In the course of investigating *The Courier's Tragedy*, Oedipa carries out a full-fledged bibliography project, in which textual variants proliferate and manuscripts abound. It becomes impossible for her ever to decide what the authoritative text of the play in fact is, and the evidence that she amasses can point to radically different hypotheses depending on which interpretive strategies she employs. Eyewitness reports, artistic texts, and historical documents are alike indeterminate indicators of "how things really are," and the historian's situation thereby becomes directly analogous to that of the skeptical literary interpreter.

In Part V of *The Waste Land* a condensed history of the world is presented, with the rapid-fire fall of the great centers of civilization: "What is the city over the mountains / Cracks and reforms and bursts in the violet air / Falling towers / Jerusalem Athens Alexandria / Vienna London / Unreal" (ll. 371–376). And Pynchon in turn digs up the obscure history of European and American mail delivery systems and their sinister underground rivals. In fact, an astonishing amount of *The Crying of Lot 49* is based on historical facts, but the integration of all this perfectly factual material in the amazing adventures of Oedipa Maas makes history seem like fantasy.

Eliot even implants a lesson in historical and textual interpretation in *The Waste Land* in the allusion to the journey to Emmaus (Luke 24) in Book V, ll. 359–365. In the biblical passage, the resurrected Christ explains to his grieving disciples that they could have anticipated the crucifixion if they had only read the Old Testament properly. They should have understood Moses and the prophets as types of Christ and hence prophesies of His fate. Typological interpretation in the secular sphere would be hermeneutic "presentism," the unabashed reading of the past through the eyes of the present. Divine authority guarantees the truth to be gained from this procedure in the religious context, but failing that authority, the modern typologist is left in a historical vacuum, unable to know whether the projection of present into past is anything more than the embroidery of the tower-bound maidens. And certainly, in *The Crying of Lot 49* the question is how to avoid the conclusion that the self is the type of everything.

Solipsism, indeterminacy of knowledge, and the failure of these various historical plots and strategies lead to the fragmented knowledge of *The Waste Land.* With its encyclopedic range and mania for allusion, it ends up presenting the past not as a continuous narrative but as an atemporal simultaneity, a collage. And yet, standard as this view of *The Waste Land* is, the concept of a given history as an atemporal collage is not exactly what Eliot advocates in his essay "Tradition and the Individual Talent." His famous description of the history of culture as a "simultaneous order," "a living whole of the poetry that has ever been written,"[8] does present history as a configuration. However, this ideal order is altered by the appearance of every new work and every new poet. The history of culture is the history of the concretizations of culture in the minds of artists and critics. It is, in effect the history of definitive interpretations.[9] By compressing the past into an aesthetic pattern, art generates history, engaging the reader in the interplay of collage simultaneity and the historical disjunctions of its elements.

According to Eliot, artists and critics were not to construct

8. "Tradition and the Individual Talent," *Selected Essays, 1917–1932* (New York: Harcourt, Brace, and London: Faber and Faber, 1932), pp. 4, 7.

9. This is a kind of reader response model based on a Nietzschean "monumental history"—the past understood as a record of the interpretations of great minds. See Nietzsche, *The Use and Abuse of History,* trans. Adrian Collins, 2d ed. (New York: Liberal Arts Press, 1957), pp. 12–17.

this vision of tradition idiosyncratically. Instead they were to exercise "a continual self-sacrifice, a continual extinction of personality,"[10] so that the resulting art or criticism comes to resemble a science. "No poet, no artist of any art, has his complete meaning alone. His significance, his appreciation, is the appreciation of his relation to the dead poets and artists. You cannot value him alone."[11] *The Waste Land*'s lessons of giving, sympathy and control are apparently not only advice about how to deal with people or transcend the senses, but a vital and presumably learnable hermeneutic strategy for producing determinate readings of texts.

But how, we might ask, *is* this strategy learned? Certainly other models of simultaneous synthesis produced in this century did not promise such an easy transition into historical knowledge. Indeed, the early twentieth century, a period rich in atemporal models,[12] tended to present these models as inherently incompatible with history. Saussure offered one of the most influential, with his splitting of linguistics into diachronic and synchronic sciences. Like Eliot's notion of culture as a configuration that is utterly changed by the introduction of even a single new element, Saussure presents language as a system of pure values determined by the momentary arrangement of their terms. Since this system at any given moment is the reality of language for a speaker, to understand that speaker the linguist must take a synchronic approach. "The opposition between [synchrony and diachrony] . . . is absolute and allows no compromise."[13]

10. Eliot, "Tradition and the Individual Talent," p. 7.

11. Ibid., p. 4.

12. At this time, according to Maurice Mandelbaum, historicism as a notion—the "radically temporalistic view of the world"—was being formulated by thinkers like Mannheim as a reaction to the atemporal knowledge of medieval Christianity and empiricism. See "Historicism," *Encyclopedia of Philosophy,* vol. 4, ed. Paul Edwards (New York: Collier and Macmillan, 1967), p. 23.

13. Ferdinand de Saussure, *Course in General Linguistics,* trans. Wade Baskin (New York: McGraw-Hill, 1966), p. 83. "The linguist who wishes to understand a state must discard all knowledge of everything that produced it and ignore diachrony. He can enter the mind of speakers only by completely suppressing the past. The intervention of history can only falsify his judgment. It would be absurd to attempt to sketch a panorama of the Alps by viewing them simultaneously from several peaks of the Jura; a panorama must be made from a single vantage point"(pp. 81–82).

Wimsatt and Beardsley produce a similar argument in their famous article on the intentional fallacy. They picture the poem as a linguistic fact whose meaning is not determined by either the poet who produced it or the critic who interprets it. "For all the objects of our manifold experience, for every unity, there is an action of the mind which cuts off roots, melts away context—or indeed we should never have objects or ideas or anything to talk about."[14] As with Saussure, knowledge depends on our ability to decontextualize and dehistoricize objects and ideas. And because the intensity of organization in poetry encourages this synchronic mode of perception, several New Critics valued poetry as the archetypal carrier of knowledge.[15]

Thus, Saussure dealt with the problem of solipsism by actually privileging it, by claiming that ahistorical, synchronic knowledge was the only possible and proper knowledge of the speaking subject. Wimsatt and Beardsley overcame solipsism by making the poem a linguistic fact, knowable as an object of present knowledge. But Eliot, wanting a synchronic system that provided accurate, even scientific, knowledge of what was diachronic, still needed to account for the poet's or critic's ability to supersede his own horizons.

The key to historical awareness lies in Eliot's use of allusion.[16]

14. William K. Wimsatt and Monroe Beardsley, "The Intentional Fallacy," in *Critical Theory since Plato,* ed. Hazard Adams (New York: Harcourt Brace Jovanovich, 1971), p. 1019.

15. For a summary of these notions, see my "Case for Unclear Thinking: The New Critics versus Charles Morris," *Critical Inquiry,* 6 (Winter 1979), 259.

16. Anachronisms and obsolete or passé survivals were used similarly against Saussure's absolute divorce of synchrony and diachrony by Roman Jakobson and Jurij Tynjanov in "Problems in the Study of Literature and Language," trans. Herbert Eagle, in *Readings in Russian Poetics: Formalist and Structuralist Views,* ed. L. Matejka and K. Pomorska (Cambridge, Mass.: M.I.T. Press, 1971): "Pure synchronism now proves to be an illusion: every synchronic system has its past and its future as inescapable structural elements of the system: *(a)* archaism as a fact of style; the linguistic and literary background recognized as the rejected old-fashioned style; *(b)* the tendency in language and literature recognized as innovation in the system. The opposition between synchrony and diachrony was an opposition between the concept of system and the concept of evolution; thus it loses its importance in principle as soon as we recognize that every system necessarily exists as an evolution, whereas, on the other hand, evolution is inescapably of a systemic nature . . . The concept of a synchronic

This trope posed a special problem for Wimsatt and Beardsley, who spent more than a quarter of "The Intentional Fallacy" discussing it. "The frequency and depth of literary allusion in the poetry of Eliot and others," they wrote, "has driven so many in pursuit of full meanings to the *Golden Bough* and the Elizabethan drama that it has become a kind of commonplace to suppose that we do not know what a poet means unless we have traced him in his reading—a supposition redolent with intentional implications."[17] Wimsatt and Beardsley suggest a number of ways around this supposition, all of which minimize the historical valence of allusions, making them either purely formal structures (the meaning comes through even if you do not know the source), ahistorical fictions (Eliot might as easily have made them up himself), or reflexes of the poem as a whole (neither Eliot nor anything outside the poem should be consulted about their meaning). Eliot's *"historical sense,"* the hallmark of the mature critic or artist, could not survive under these circumstances, for the knowledge potential of allusions would be limited to what was already present and knowable in the poem itself. (It is perhaps unnecessary to point out how little of *The Waste Land* is not allusive, that is, "present and knowable in itself.")

Without the historical sense, the centrifugal otherness of allusions, we are locked within the wasteland solipsism that the poem deplores. I believe that *The Waste Land* is actually a kind of hermeneutic training manual for avoiding the very mode of reading that Wimsatt and Beardsley were so anxious to promote. This training would be specifically to read everything that Eliot had read, or at least everything that he alluded to in his poem. One would do so not to become a pale version of Eliot, but to become a historical reader.

If we take even the first step in carrying out this program the

---

literary system does not coincide with the naively envisaged concept of a chronological epoch, since the former embraces not only works of art which are close to each other in time but also works which are drawn into the orbit of the system from foreign literatures or previous epochs" (pp. 79–80). See also Peter Steiner, *Russian Formalism: A Metapoetics* (Ithaca, N.Y.: Cornell University Press, 1984), pp. 108–111, 218–220.

17. Wimsatt and Beardsley, "The Intentional Fallacy," p. 1020.

results can be quite surprising. Eliot's Notes to *The Waste Land* open with an acknowledgment of his debt to Jesse Weston's *From Ritual to Romance*. "Indeed, so deeply am I indebted, Miss Weston's book will elucidate the difficulties of the poem much better than my notes can do; and I recommend it . . . to any who think such elucidation of the poem worth the trouble." This statement has led critics to vegetation rituals, tarot lore, and medieval romances. But what critics have not discussed in Weston is the project of her study itself, what Hayden White would term the "metahistorical" content of Weston's history.[18]

Weston opens with two epigraphs which are direct clues to Eliot's antisolipsistic historicism. The first is from Bacon: "The spirit must be extended from its small measure to the breadth of Mystery, and not Mystery constricted to the narrowness of the spirit."[19] Bacon is urging just the opposite of the New Critical or solipsistic position—that the mind of the scientist change to accommodate what must be grasped, and not that nature be reduced to a preexistent understanding of things.

The second epigraph is by F. M. Cornford. "Many literary critics seem to think that a hypothesis about obscure and remote questions of history can be refuted by a simple demand for the production of more evidence than in fact exists.—But the true test of an hypothesis, if it cannot be shewn to conflict with known truths, is the number of facts that it correlates, and explains."[20] Historical hypotheses should be valued not for their invulner-

18. See Hayden White, *Metahistory: The Historical Imagination in Nine-teenth-Century Europe* (Baltimore: Johns Hopkins University Press, 1973).

19. *From Ritual to Romance* (Gloucester, Mass.: Peter Smith, 1983), p. v, my translation; other quotations to this edition are identified by page numbers in the text.

20. Ibid. Hayden White's explanation of the "poetic" nature of historians and philosophers of history such as Michelet and Hegel sounds like an echo of Cornford's words: "Their status as possible models of historical representation or conceptualization does not depend upon the nature of the 'data' they used to support their generalizations or the theories they invoked to explain them; it depends rather upon the consistency, coherence, and illuminative power of their respective visions of the historical field. This is why they cannot be 're-futed,' or their generalizations 'disconfirmed,' either by appeal to new data that might be turned up in subsequent research or by the elaboration of a new theory for interpreting the sets of events that comprise their objects of representation and analysis," *Metahistory*, p. 4.

ability to refutation, but for their coverage, for their reach, for the sheer quantity of the past that they put in order. For Weston the issues of coverage and ordering were crucial, since the facts she was concerned with, the Grail legends, were numerous, fragmented, and seemingly inconsistent. Despite a series of studies on the subject, no solution had managed to remedy what Weston called the "ensemble problem." "The main difficulty of our research lies in the fact that the Grail legend consists of a congeries of widely differing elements—elements which at first sight appear hopelessly incongruous, if not completely contradictory, yet at the same time are present to an extent, and in a form, which no honest critic can afford to ignore" (p. 2).

I would submit that Weston presents her historical task as the ordering of an Eliotian "heap of broken images." The literary past that she has received—Grail romances—makes no sense in its current state, just as European culture is a puzzling chaos in the wasteland world. Some historical context is missing that would account for the mysterious stories that remain, and that context for Weston is ancient ritual. Once the starting point of ritual is established, the transformations leading to romance can be located and a story chain forged. Weston, by constantly enlarging the range of facts in her research, finally constructs a seamless history that turns the fragments and contradictions into a smooth and complete story.

Weston actually was discovering two stories: one the Ur-narrative that underlay all its corrupt descendents, and the other the historical passage from Ur-narrative to corrupt remains. The coincidence of these two stories, the literary and the historical, is a fascinating element of Weston's book, for reconstructing the literary story involved reconstructing history itself and realizing that what appeared to be merely the literary plot of romance was in fact a disguised historical sequence of events. The Ur-story of romance, Weston came to believe, was itself a piece of history.

Briefly, the Grail romances begin with a land laid waste by drought or war and a king who is ill or impotent. The knight-hero must set off on a quest to restore the land's fertility and the king's health by achieving a vision of the Holy Grail in a Perilous Chapel and asking a question concerning its nature. In many Grail romances, the knight fails to ask the question and the land remains infertile. Weston traces the wasteland and wounded king motifs to vegetative rites prevalent throughout the ancient world. Every year the passage from winter drought to spring flood was assured by the ritual replacement of the old sick king by a new vital one. When merchants and others transmitted these rituals to Britain, they were forced underground. The hiding of the rites was then incorporated into the Ur-narrative, symbolized as a physical or spiritual drought which could be cured only by the coming of a new initiate. The Grail romance records the visit of a wandering knight to a hidden temple in which he passes the lower initiation rite but fails a higher one.

But the analogy does not stop with religious history and the plot of romance. Though Weston does not draw it, there is another obvious analogy: that between the historian herself, who must unify a senseless mass of literary elements by seeking the Ur-narrative and asking the question of its nature, and the questing knight who must redeem the wasteland by seeking the Grail and asking about its nature. The historian is a quester. Indeed, she invests the successful outcome of her scholarly search with many of the emotional and spiritual values that surround the romance quest. She speaks with pride of discovering the "golden chain which connects Ancient Ritual with Medieval Romance" (p. 174), and describes the Grail literature as the "restatement of an ancient and august Ritual in terms of imperishable Romance" (p. 209). The discovery of this golden chain makes a meaningless world meaningful, and justifies the thirty-year quest that it involved, a quest that necessitated the expansion of Weston's mind to the breadth of Baconian Mysteries and the forging of an all-inclusive solution.

If we apply this historicist analogy to Eliot's poem, a further possibility arises. Since the historical scholar is, like the questing knight, trying to redeem the wasteland or understand the mystery by asking the question of its nature, the reader, faced with the "heap of broken images" in *The Waste Land* is in exactly the same situation. The reader's task is encoded in the poem. To redeem this verbal wasteland is to turn the poem from a mass of unfamiliar allusions into a coherent, unified vision of art, that is, a vision of artistic history. The question one asks the text is what it means, and one finds the answers by following up the allusions and discovering what they might mean in terms of the text. To fail to ask the question is to leave the poem the enigma that it inevitably is at first; to ask the question is to recreate oneself by expanding into the amplitude that the poem encompasses. *The Waste Land* is a poem geared to educate its reader by making him or her capable of reading it at all. And thus immanent interpretation is precisely what must be superseded, because full meaning enters the text for Eliot only when history does, and the modern wasteland is redeemed only when people again read literature, value the tradition, and themselves create the syntheses that actively remake the past into a historical present.

Accordingly, the reader is urged to stop being passive, to create the text rather than to let its chaos dominate or dull him. All the failed historical plots of renewal, metamorphosis, return, revenge, transcendence, and typological repetition require an actor, a hero, a knight-questioner who actively educates him- or herself.

Proof of this claim is the lack of fit between the standard romance quest and the structure of *The Waste Land*'s plot. Everyone knows that *The Waste Land* leaves everything suspended. The "damp gust bringing rain" never arrives within the poem, and Eliot stops his story in a Babel of unresolved, often non-English, climaxes interrupted by an English-speaking narrator who explains: "These fragments I have shored against my ruins." The narrator presents these scraps of the past as support for the ruin of the present. But a voice then answers him, Hieronymo's from Kyd's *Spanish Tragedy,* as if defying the narrator's complacency who would merely keep the ruin standing by propping it with the blighted treasures of the past. "Why then Ile fit you," says Hieronymo, as he does to his son's murderers in the play. The play that Hieronymo arranges is his own composition and is carried on in four foreign languages, very much like *The Waste Land* passage immediately before Hieronymo's words. Through the play, the Tower of Babel is symbolically felled, the Whore of Babylon is destroyed, and justice replaces what appears to be societal madness. However, an analogue for this play is *not* contained in *The Waste Land.* It is merely promised there when the poem comes to its rather abrupt end. If the play never appears in Eliot's poem, though its presence is heralded there, it must take place, if at all, outside the poem, in the education of the reader and in the allusive history that the poem calls up. By no means do we know that the play will ever be enacted. That is up to us. But the quest plot and all its allusive analogues thrust the action of the poem outside it into the realm of the reader's extra-artistic life. Eliot's disjunctive plots project the struggle for meaning and its resolution into life, where all expansions beyond the solipsistic self into the unity outside it must go on.

I am aware that this is not likely to be a popular reading of *The Waste Land.* In Eloise Knapp Hay's recent *T. S. Eliot's Negative Way* we learn that "*The Waste Land* . . . can now be read simply as it was written, as a poem of radical doubt and negation, urging that every human desire be stilled except the desire for self-surrender, for restraint, and for peace . . . [W]e should lay to rest the persistent error of reading *The Waste Land* as a poem in which five motifs predominate: the nightmare journey, the Chapel, the Quester, the Grail Legend, and the Fisher King . . . if . . . 'the plan and a good deal of the incidental symbolism of the poem were suggested by Miss Jesse L. Weston's book on the Grail legend,' the plan can only have been to question, and even to propose a life without hope for, a quest, or Chapel, or Grail in the modern waste land. . . . Nowhere in the poem can one find convincing allusions to *any* existence in another world."[21]

The poem can certainly sustain such a reading, but it is an immanent wasteland reading consistent with interpretive solipsism and ahistoricism. *The Waste Land's* allusions do point to an "existence in another world," that of history, past art, and the reader's future, but unfortunately not a world that the poem can itself image.

---

21. Eloise Knapp Hay, *T. S. Eliot's Negative Way* (Cambridge, Mass.: Harvard University Press, 1982), pp. 48–49.

Pynchon picks up the problem of interpretive relativism at this
point. He symbolizes the self-enclosure of radical solipsism in
a fairytale version of Bradley's tower prison. But unlike Eliot,
he models the reader *in* his fiction by having a single protagonist.
This heroine, Oedipa Maas, not only sees what we see, but her
job is to interpret it in the best detective story tradition. If *The
Waste Land* has only callous automatons or helpless watchers
like Tiresias, *The Crying of Lot 49* documents the transformation of one such automaton, Oedipa, into a watcher who
chooses and keeps choosing to act. And whereas Eliot all but
excludes the tragic Oedipus,[22] Pynchon puts Oedipus back at
the center of a story of self-discovery, feminizing him in keeping
with the switch from tragedy to romance that Eliot's allusions
have proposed. Self-knowledge will not destroy one, as in the
classical frame of Sophocles, nor will it exist only as a peda-
gogical dream of the future, as in *The Waste Land*. Instead, by
burning away the stereotypes of popular romance, Oedipa will
embark on a quest, and redefine its structure so that knowledge,
or rather knowing, is again a value.

Oedipa's last name, Maas, is Spanish for "more." She acquires it from her husband, Mucho Maas, "much more," who
as a former used car dealer belonged to the National Auto-
mobile Dealers' Association, NADA, or "nothing." The NADA
sign waving in the car lot all day was a source of considerable
depression to Mucho, as was the used car lot itself. Its description lies in a direct tradition from Eliot's "heap of broken images" to Fitzgerald's junkyard in *The Great Gatsby*. "The endless
rituals of trade-in, week after week, never got as far as violence
or blood, and so were too plausible for the impressionable Mucho
to take for long . . . he could . . . never accept the way each
owner, each shadow, filed in only to exchange a dented, mal-
functioning version of himself for another, just as futureless,
automotive projection of somebody else's life" (p. 3). The endless exchanges and trade-ins produce no resolutions, no solu-

22. The pathetic cry, "O City city" in l. 259 of *The Waste Land* is a disembodied echo of Oedipus' words in l. 629 of *Oedipus the King*.

tions, no metamorphoses. The lot is mere arbitrary substitution, and Mucho wants more, much more.

The word "lot" is early connected to "fate," Mucho taking on a job as a disk jockey spinning the top 200 as "a buffer between him and that lot. He had believed too much in the lot" (p. 6). And in the title of the book, the word "lot" comes up again as the section or lot of Pierce Inverarity's stamp collection up for auction. The crying of lot 49 is the auctioning off of it, and at the same time it is the cry of the hopeless shadows at the car lot going through their ritual trade-ins, and the cry of the stamps that hold a world of meaning within them, it turns out, if only one is sensitized enough to find this out. The kind of fate, destiny, and oracle available at the beginning of Pynchon's book is that of *The Waste Land*'s Sibyl, locked in her death-in-life, or even the doom pronounced by Oedipus' oracles that he will kill his father and marry his mother. Mucho thinks of the commerce between used car buyers and sellers as "Endless, convoluted incest" (p. 3).

Oedipa herself, temporarily roused by the romance of Pierce Inverarity with his limitless capitalist interests (a key word in the text linking epistemology with economics and axiology), marries Mucho and settles into a routine of fondue and suburban Tupperware parties as an escape from the insights she had gained from the painting in Mexico. But within a year of her marriage she is called upon to become the executrix of Pierce Inverarity's will. She remembers a crazy telephone call at 3:00 A.M. the year before, when Pierce put on a series of voices, from a Gestapo officer's to Lamont Cranston's, in a kind of parody of the Babel that initiates the climax in *The Spanish Tragedy* and *The Waste Land*. Oedipa's psychiatrist, Dr. Hilarius,[23] also calls in the middle of the night, sounding like Pierce's imitation of a Gestapo officer, but Hilarius actually seems to have been one— or at least a Nazi medical researcher. Like Pierce, Hilarius wants Oedipa's involvement in his interests, an LSD experiment to discover "the bridge inward," *die Brücke* as he calls it. As the

23. Weston mentions a "feast called Hilario, a mystery which discloses the way of our salvation from Hades" (p. 155), but perhaps this is too far-fetched an allusion.

German name suggests, the bridge inward is related to Expressionism, an artistic program for the solipsistic quest which Oedipa has been fearfully avoiding. And at Dr. Hilarius's imperative "We want you" (p. 7), she imagines "the well-known portrait of Uncle that appears in front of all our post offices."

The central associative circuit of the book is here established. Oedipa hears the call of her old lover, a P.I. who wishes her to pierce into "verarity" or into "*in*verarity" as the case may be, in order for her to become the trixy female executor of a will and testament.[24] Pierce calls on her to act out a witnessing, to take on interests, to extend herself into him. She is also ordered to the bridge inward—pure self-concern, abdication of control and responsibility, and nightmare possibilities like Nazism. And then too, she hears the call of the American Republic in the figure of Uncle Sam, whose voice is the sound of legal, democratic, and normative communication through the U.S. Postal Service.

Spurred on by her lawyer, who is perennially engaged in writing a brief for the legal profession versus Perry Mason, Oedipa becomes interested in what she might find out by executing the will. She leaves the safely anaesthesized world of Kinneret among the Pines, and heads for Pierce's domicile, San Narciso. Pierce is a dweller in narcissism, by implication, whose voracious capitalist interests have involved him in virtually every shady aspect of American life—the Mafia, war-profiteering, cancer-producing cigarette filter-making, land speculation, and especially an underground communication system rivaling the U.S. Mail called W.A.S.T.E. Its letters are posted in garbage cans below freeway overpasses, and delivered in nightspots frequented by splinter groups of every political and social stripe.

Ocdipa journeys to San Narciso, stays at the Echo Courts Motel, and has an affair with her coexecutor, Metzger, whose name means butcher or slaughterer. Metzger, as a figure of both love and death, manages to confuse all oppositions, particularly

24. Part of *The Crying of Lot 49* was published as "The World (This One), the Flesh (Mrs. Oedipa Maas), and the Testament of Pierce Inverarity," *Esquire* (December 1965), pp. 170–173, 296–303. The possibility that the book is the testimony/testament of Pierce, that is, his eyewitness account as well as the enactment of his will, is worth keeping in mind.

that between fiction and reality—the ultimate solipsistic dilemma. He is a child-actor turned lawyer, the beauty of whose situation, he says, "lies . . . in this extended capacity for convolution. A lawyer in a courtroom, in front of any jury, becomes an actor, right? Raymond Burr is an actor, impersonating a lawyer, who in front of a jury becomes an actor. Me, I'm a former actor who became a lawyer. They've done the pilot film of a TV series, in fact, based loosely on my career, starring my friend Manni Di Presso, a one-time lawyer who quit his firm to become an actor. Who in this pilot plays me, an actor become a lawyer reverting periodically to being an actor. The film is in an air-conditioned vault at one of the Hollywood studios, light can't fatigue it, it can be repeated endlessly" (p. 20). What Metzger supplies Oedipa, then, is a version of the same knowledge she received earlier in Mexico—the endless repetition of solipsistic art and its tie with death.

Nevertheless, this awareness is a step beyond the deadness of Oedipa's life in Kinneret. "If one object . . . were to bring to an end her encapsulation in her tower" (p. 28), then it was the infidelity with Metzger. And from the time of the trip to San Narciso and the infidelity with Metzger, "Things then did not delay in turning curious" (p. 28), a glancing allusion to Alice in Wonderland's "curiouser and curiouser" and the double sense of the word "curious" as "peculiar" and hence "creating curiosity or interest." Oedipa becomes an Alice, a Pandora, one of a long line of intuitive, prying heroines. She is immediately struck at this point by the feeling that "revelation [is] in progress all around her." Her first view of San Narciso from above on the highway shows the city as a printed circuit containing "a hieroglyphic sense of concealed meaning, of an intent to communicate" (p. 13). She recognizes the same pattern in a map of Pierce's housing development, Fangoso Lagoons, in the fate lines on her hand that Metzger kisses, and in the crazy path of the hairspray can careening endlessly through her bathroom in the Echo Court Motel. Everything is pregnant with meaning, and Oedipa, thus sensitized, takes on the role of interpreter and researcher. Inspired by the director Driblette, whose eyes are just such hieroglyphs as the town and Fangoso Lagoons, and whose imagination gives flesh to the mere words of *The*

Courier's Tragedy, Oedipa decides to become "the dark machine in the center of the planetarium, to bring the estate into pulsing stelliferous Meaning" (p. 58). "Shall I project a world?" she asks (p. 59).

The world that she discovers or projects is a clarification of those oppositions that Metzger and boredom confuse. It is a world, in fact, of binary oppositions. Whereas before, everything in her life was a dull sameness, Oedipa's research reveals an endless train of contrasts. Perhaps the most important is that of collective versus individual. The Yoyodyne Corporation, an electronics firm owned by Pierce, is run by gray-suited administrators who force their inventors to sign away the patent rights to their own inventions. The legal bureaucracy of the U.S. Postal Service is opposed by the underground W.A.S.T.E. system; the official monopoly of the European Thurn and Taxis mail system is countered by the shadowy, disinherited Tristero system; the Pony Express is attacked by the American remains of Tristero masquerading as Indians; the gray flannel Gennaro (generic man) takes over after the struggle between Niccolo and the usurpers in the parodic revenge play, *The Courier's Tragedy.* Mucho Maas ends his long lonely fight against NADA by taking the bridge inward and becoming what a friend describes as "less himself and more generic" (p. 104). This generalization of character resembles the decay of personality in *The Waste Land,* where, as Eliot's note states, "Just as the one-eyed merchant, seller of currants, melts into the Phoenician Sailor, and the latter is not wholly distinct from Ferdinand Prince of Naples, so all the women are one woman, and the two sexes meet in Tiresias" (p. 70).

The ultimate reason for the Tristero and every other underground in the book is the individual's need to struggle against the generic, and so the ultimate underground is Inamorati Anonymous, a group communicating through W.A.S.T.E. that is dedicated to keeping its members from the worst addiction, love. It is a society of isolates. This ridiculous paradox in the binary pairs is precisely the point. A communication system meant to inspire isolation is as much a contradiction as a republic formed to foster the individual. As Oedipa toward the end of the book is drawn lovingly and pityingly toward all those in

America sharing Tristero's exile, she imagines distributing Pierce Inverarity's estate among them, and then being disqualified as an executrix and hounded into joining Tristero itself, "waiting for a symmetry of choices to break down, to go skew. She had heard all about excluded middles; they were bad shit, to be avoided; and how had it ever happened here, with the chances once so good for diversity? For it was now like walking among matrices of a great digital computer, the zeroes and ones twinned above, hanging like balanced mobiles right and left, ahead, thick, maybe endless. Behind the hieroglyphic streets there would either be a transcendent meaning, or only the earth. . . . Either Oedipa in the orbiting ecstasy of a true paranoia, or a real Tristero. For there either was some Tristero beyond the appearance of the legacy America, or there was just America and if there was just America then it seemed the only way she could continue and manage to be at all relevant to it, was as an alien, unfurrowed, assumed full circle into some paranoia" (pp. 136–137). It was America that Pierce Inverarity had bequeathed Oedipa; she even finds herself pregnant with America at one point. But this country can be had, created, known only by lurching back and forth in belief between the terms of its binary oppositions.

Pynchon's insistence on the peculiarly American quality of this situation is worth noting. The ninety-one-year-old Mr. Thoth relates the story told him by his ninety-one-year-old grandfather of the slaughter of a company of Pony Express agents—early postal workers of the republic—by a band of men disguised as Indians. The reference to the Boston Tea Party seems unavoidable here, but so is the realization that that band of underground rebels became the patriots of the republic and ultimately the official establishment of that republic. The history of America can be written as a sequence of struggles between oppressive officialdom and freedom-seeking undergrounds, with the underground winning and turning into the next oppressor. Pynchon is serving up a Hegelian dialectics as American history, but a dialectics that destroys the identity of the individual in the antithesis. The individual caught in the matrices of the digital computer is the pawn of history, controlled by either the conservative efforts of the establishment or the mechanically reactive rebellion of the underground, with no future to look forward to but switching roles. As investigator and interpreter of this "machine of history," Oedipa needs a way to stand outside it or to move freely between the poles.

What Oedipa needs is an America different from the one "coded in Inverarity's testament" (p. 135), one that permits excluded middles so that both p and $\sim p$, both self and other, can be experienced at once. And the closest scheme to that is the information theory miracle proposed by Stanley Koteks's Nefastis Machine. Here the random distribution of speeding molecules can produce energy or information without work-input if an intelligence—Maxwell's Demon and a sensitive— can sort the faster from the slower molecules. The imbalance in heat can then be used to drive a piston. In the process, information is produced about the location of the molecules, so that where the initial disorder or entropy decreases, information increases. In information theory, an analogous relation exists between entropy and information. The coincidence of the thermodynamic and information theory notions serves as one of the miraculous convergences that creates belief. If one can imagine knowing anything in the relativistic world that Pynchon depicts, it is those structural unities created by puns that link what appear to be unrelated realms.

The notion of information itself involves a convergence of opposites. For it is not simply the opposite pole of entropy. The total absence of entropy is not information, but redundancy, and there is no information when there is either complete ran- domness or complete order. Information is some magical in- termediate state between the two poles. Thus, Oedipa's search for information oscillates between her construal of Pierce In- verarity's legacy as a chaos that must be ordered and her sus- picion that it is an overdetermined plot, redundant, repetitive, and ultimately deathlike.

Oedipa is facing, in effect, the same existentialist dilemma as *The Waste Land* presents, with reality either a hopeless jum- ble—"a heap of broken images," a garbage dump, a waste- land—or a deadening sameness—the routine of tea eternally at 4:00, all people reduced to types, the inevitability of death constantly before one. The self-consciousness that the Sibyl or

Tiresias or Madame Sosostris or any of the other wise observers has—like Sisyphus' self-consciousness—ultimately changes nothing. And thus characters are caught between the contrary feelings of exhaustion and boredom—exhaustion from the taxing chaos of a life without meaning, boredom from its utter redundancy. In *The Crying of Lot 49,* these emotions are encoded in Oedipa, who begins bored and deadened in Kinneret and becomes utterly exhausted in her experience in the night world of San Francisco. The reader tends to mimic these polarized emotions in encountering the tiresome quantities of information that all add up to the same thing, and at the same time the sheer interpretive depth and range of this short book with its deadpan and often silly comedy. Like blends of Mucho and Hilarius, we shift from boredom to exhaustion, from bathos to hilarity; the book's mingling of deeply serious and funny elements is a stylistic analogue for the plight of its characters and readers.

The middle state of information is imaged in the novel as a miracle, an interpenetration of worlds that produces information because it leaves both worlds intact. Inverarity's stamps carried this promise, "thousands of little colored windows into deep vistas of space and time," and his violation of Oedipa's tower was a similar attempt at miracle. If Oedipa had managed to communicate with the Demon in the Nefastis Machine, she too would have worked a miracle. As she fails to move the piston in it, she thinks, "Why worry, she worried; Nefastis is a nut, forget it, a sincere nut. The true sensitive is the one that can share in the man's hallucinations, that's all. How wonderful they might be to share" (pp. 78–79). The miracle is to splice two minds together, to understand another while maintaining the otherness of that other. This situation is a version of the surrealist image of the intersection of wildly disparate worlds. Oedipa's old anarchist acquaintance, Jesús Arrabal, describes this idea, his name itself a merger of two versions of the word made flesh—Christ and the surrealist playwright Arrabal. He had met Inverarity and Oedipa during their ill-fated trip to Mexico, when Inverarity had "played the rich, obnoxious gringo so perfectly that Oedipa had seen gooseflesh come up along the anarchist's forearms" (p. 88). Arrabal calls Pierce Inverarity a miracle: "You know what a miracle is. Not what Bakunin said. But another world's intrusion into this one. Most of the time we coexist peacefully, but when we do touch there's cataclysm. . . . Like your friend. He is too exactly and without flaw the thing we fight. In Mexico the privilegiado is always, to a finite percentage, redeemed—one of the people. Unmiraculous. But your friend, unless he's joking, is as terrifying to me as a Virgin appearing to an Indian" (pp. 88–89).

The text contains another miracle, when Oedipa is pulled onto a dancefloor of deafmutes, all performing different dances but never colliding, as if the different rhythms in their heads were all part of a single score. This is an anarchist miracle, the text explains, a case of perfect intersubjective harmony rather than violent intrusion. The coincidence of the formulas for entropy in thermodynamics and information theory is another miracle, as is the parallel case of DT and dt in delirium tremens and the "vanishingly small instant in which change had to be confronted at last for what it was . . . where velocity dwelled in the projectile though the projectile be frozen in midflight, where death dwelled in the cell though the cell be looked in on at its most quick . . . there was that high magic to low puns . . . DT's must give access to dt's of spectra beyond the known sun" (pp. 95–96). This image of time's dynamic locked in the instantaneity of the moment is the historical miracle itself, the possibility of grasping in a text or phenomenon what is temporal, unfolding, or of seeing through the eyes of the present what is alien to them in the past.

The opposition between order and chaos, redundancy and entropy, thus becomes analogous to that between synchrony and diachrony. History can enter system only through miracle, in the form of a pun, a word inhabiting two worlds. Like Eliot's allusions, puns are multitemporal pivots. But whereas Eliot's allusions take on power by their presence in aesthetic structures, what we have termed collages, in Pynchon the pun is the occasion of religious experience—the miracle. This shift from aesthetic to religious metaphor—from collage to miracle—is significant. It suggests a role for art much more powerful than that of historical instruction or aesthetic pleasure, as in Eliot. The work becomes revelation, a mode that Eliot could evoke only as debased allusions in *The Waste Land*. Art becomes, paradoxically, a record of presence, like the trace of two worlds in the verbal pun or the stuttered "t-t-t-t-t" of *The Courier's Tragedy*, "the shortest line of iambic pentameter" in literature. Rather than a totalizing context like the collage, the miracle erupts through context to reveal a truth that transcends time.

Oedipa cradles in her arms the sailor who occasions the dt/DT miracle for her, and loves him, if ever so briefly. It is an instant of miraculous empathy, as Oedipa holds him like a Madonna with child or the Madonna of a pietà—mothering and mourning the child, America, doomed to an underground existence. Out of that love, information momentarily emerges: he tells her where to find the W.A.S.T.E. box below the freeway overpass.

But the novel's miracles are as ambiguous as any other information in it, and certainly rarer. Oedipa fails to communicate with the Demon in the Nefastis Machine, she does not realize the wonder of Pierce Inverarity while she knows him, and the deafmute dance leaves her depressed and exhausted. If any permanent information transfer does take place in the book, it is the communication to Oedipa of America as Pierce apparently saw it. For after making a host of discoveries in order to execute his will, she had "a new compassion for the cul-de-sac he'd tried to find a way out of, for the enigma his efforts had created. Though he had never talked business with her, she had known it to be a fraction of him that couldn't come out even . . . ; her love, such as it had been, remaining incommensurate with his need to possess, to alter the land, to bring new skylines, personal antagonisms, growth rates into being. 'Keep it bouncing,' he'd told her once, 'that's all the secret, keep it bouncing.' He must have known, writing the will, facing the spectre, how the bouncing would stop" (p. 134).

Oedipa learns the terms of the game from Pierce Inverarity, and learns that it is a game that is to be played for the sake of playing—to keep the ball bouncing. Thus, at the end, she sets out once again to follow out a clue "with the courage you find you have when there is nothing more to lose" (p. 137). She discovers that the mysterious "book bidder" for lot 49 has decided to appear in person at the auction, and so she goes there to find out who he is and hence whether Tristero actually exists.

Oedipa enters a room where all the bidders are identically dressed in black and have cruel faces "trying each to conceal his thoughts" (pp. 137–138). She sits in back, seeing rows of identical napes, with the auctioneer hovering like a puppet-master before them. The doors lock, blocking out the sun, and the auctioneer spreads out his arms like a strange priest or a descending angel. Oedipa sits back to hear the crying and the book comes to an end.

As in *The Waste Land,* we are left with a suspended closure. And yet, unlike that poem, this work does not propel us outside it for a resolution of meaning. Oedipa certainly will not solve the mystery at the auction, since the mystery is not solvable. Rather, she is keeping the ball bouncing, a tremendously heroic and at the same time comic act. The death symbolism in the ending (and throughout) could be taken literally, of course, but it seems more consistent to treat it as a clarification of the quest's end. The only conclusion to Oedipa's quest, as to Pierce Inverarity's, will be death. To go on looking, to go on taking an interest in the reality of America is always to court knowledge of its underside, its darkness, its danger, and to know what existentialism posits, that all knowledge ends in death. Oedipa sits by quite sanguinely as the death symbols proliferate. Her real focus by this time is on the bouncing ball, the interests, the meanings that her clues will allow her to entertain. Though no meaning can ever be verified outside the solipsistic frame of the verifier, the attempt at verification and the involvement in that attempt are all we have. And they are what keep Oedipa going, rather than retreating once more into fondue and Tupperware parties.

This is quite different from Eliot's view. Eliot's history involved the recovery of determinate knowledge, a sense of culture that only the right immersion in past culture could create. Though the achievement of this historical understanding is pushed out of the text into the interpretive acts of the reader, the aim is a final state of rest when the reader will have learned the past well enough to have grasped the present of the poem, and hence will have been recreated as a historical reader. But for Pynchon the quest is not to be imagined as a determinate beginning-middle-end structure, but a continuity of ever enlarging hypothesis and data, punctuated by miracle. Oedipa's world is expanding, though the possibility of final meaning is as elusive as ever. Should that meaning ever come, the system would have lost the power to produce information; that would be death.

Pynchon takes a solution to solipsism that is only partially available in *The Waste Land*—through the allusion to Weston and through the ideas in "Tradition and the Individual Talent." This solution is another sort of miracle that Marxists bank on, the possibility that a change in quantity eventually creates a change in quality. An interpreter whose data base is constantly expanding and giving rise to new hypotheses will be a constantly changing interpreter. Historicism in a deconstructed world then becomes a heroic casting of solipsistic nets to catch a self greater and more varied than the self that seeks them. It is a miracle indeed, and it is imaged in *The Crying of Lot 49*, which gathers Eliot and Sophocles and Lewis Carroll and revenge tragedy and thermodynamics and the U.S. Postal Service into the compass of its interpretive net, and recasts us in the process.[25]

25. I presented a version of this essay at the NEH Colloquium on the New Humanities held at Wayne State University, March 1984. My thanks go to Professor Piotr Michalowski for pointing out the reference to Paul Maas's *Textkritik* (*Textual Criticism*, trans. Barbara Flower [Oxford: Oxford University Press, 1958]), and to all my students who have shared an enthusiasm for Pynchon's remarkable book.

Contributors

MORRIS DICKSTEIN
Queens College, City University of New York

ROBERT A. FERGUSON
University of Chicago

PHILIP FISHER
Brandeis University

SANDRA M. GILBERT
Princeton University

FRANK LENTRICCHIA
Duke University

WALTER BENN MICHAELS
University of California, Berkeley

BARBARA PACKER
University of California, Los Angeles

WERNER SOLLORS
Harvard University

WENDY STEINER
University of Pennsylvania

ROBERT B. STEPTO
Yale University

ERIC J. SUNDQUIST
University of California, Berkeley

ROBERT VON HALLBERG
University of Chicago